CRISIS MANAGEMENT IN THE
NEW STRATEGY LANDSCAPE

CRISIS MANAGEMENT IN THE
NEW STRATEGY LANDSCAPE

WILLIAM "RICK" CRANDALL | JOHN A. PARNELL | JOHN E. SPILLAN

University of North Carolina, Pembroke

Los Angeles | London | New Delhi
Singapore | Washington DC

For information:

SAGE Publications, Inc.
2455 Teller Road
Thousand Oaks,
   California 91320
E-mail: order@sagepub.com

SAGE Publications India Pvt. Ltd.
B 1/I 1 Mohan Cooperative
   Industrial Area
Mathura Road, New Delhi 110 044
India

SAGE Publications Ltd.
1 Oliver's Yard
55 City Road
London EC1Y 1SP
United Kingdom

SAGE Publications
   Asia-Pacific Pte. Ltd.
33 Pekin Street #02-01
Far East Square
Singapore 048763

Printed in the United States of America.

Library of Congress Cataloging-in-Publication Data

Crandall, William 1956–
Crisis management in the new strategy landscape / William Crandall, John A. Parnell, John E. Spillan.
      p. cm.
Includes bibliographical references and index.
ISBN 978-1-4129-5413-6 (pbk. : acid-free paper)
   1. Crisis management. I. Parnell, John A. (John Alan), 1964- II. Spillan, John E. III. Title.

HD49.C73 2009
658.4'056—dc22   2008049626

This book is printed on acid-free paper.

09   10   11   12   13   10   9   8   7   6   5   4   3   2   1

Acquisitions Editor:	Lisa Shaw
Associate Editor:	Deya Saoud
Editorial Assistant:	MaryAnn Vail
Production Editor:	Brittany Bauhaus
Copy Editor:	Kris Bergstad
Typesetter:	C&M Digitals (P) Ltd.
Proofreader:	Jenifer Kooiman
Indexer:	Holly Day
Cover Designer:	Candice Harman
Marketing Manager:	Jennifer Reed Banando

Brief Contents

Detailed Contents

Preface

Ever since my graduate school years, I have been fascinated with the area of crisis management. In the late 1980s, the field was just emerging and we had witnessed a trio of great calamities: the 1984 Bhopal, India, gas leak that killed thousands; the 1986 radiation accident at Chernobyl that killed thousands more; and in the same year, the tragic loss of the Space Shuttle *Challenger,* an unmistakable fireball in the sky that took the lives of seven American astronauts. Then, in 1989, while we were catching our breath, Exxon's supertanker, the *Exxon Valdez,* hit a reef off the coast of Alaska. The result was one of the most geographically dispersed oil spills ever and a front-page example of crisis management gone astray. There were containment booms in the dock that could not be mobilized because that particular boat was under repair. There was the CEO, Lawrence Rawl, who, although meaning well, did not travel to the disaster site to address the situation directly. Oil spilled everywhere, creating a monstrous slick that sucked life out of the environment. The ship's captain had consumed too many drinks and had illegally put the tanker under the leadership of a junior officer. The rest is history; the importance of crisis management was clear.

While developing this fascination in the field of crisis management, I met John Parnell. John was a prolific writer with a passion for strategic management. Our discussions prompted the idea for a book that would address the field of crisis management within a strategic context. Our other colleague, Jack Spillan, shared our growing interest in the field of crisis management and was a logical choice for collaborating on this book.

Our diverse research backgrounds—human resources management, strategy, and marketing—influenced our growing interest in the field and our eventual decision to write the book. Collectively, we have lectured in a number of countries, including China, the United Kingdom, Egypt, Mexico, Peru, Guatemala, Chile, Bolivia, and Poland. We learned that crisis management approaches differed markedly across borders and we began to consider the pros and cons of myriad perspectives on the field.

We were convinced that crisis management should not be just a response to an unfortunate event; it needed to be a management mindset practiced within a proactive strategic framework. After a number of long discussions, the framework for the book finally emerged. Crisis management is a process, not a reactive event that comes up only occasionally. The four stages we propose should be incorporated into the strategic management process of the organization.

There are many others whose research influenced this project. You will find their names in the reference sections of this book. We are indebted to them for documenting their interest in crisis management and making this much-needed field a growing discipline. I remember reading Larry Barton's first book on crisis management, *Crisis in Organizations,* and thinking, I want to make this my research field too. As I read more on the topic, a number of other writers seemed to be major contributors to this growing area of management. Ian Mitroff was an early contributor to the field, and is still writing today. Others were frequent contributors to the growth of this field, including Stephen Fink, Thierry Pauchant, Christopher Roux-Dufort, Paul Shrivastava, Denis Smith, and Karl Weick. Robert Hartley's manner of writing case studies of catastrophic events is the best I have ever seen. He concludes each case with practical lessons learned, an obvious need for students and practitioners as well as impatient researchers like the three of us. "Reframing Crisis Management," by Christine Pearson and Judith Clair, appeared in a 1998 issue of *Academy of Management Review.* This article not only influenced the prevailing perspective on crisis management as a field, but also helped advance the field. Academically, crisis management was getting noticed, and it was now a respectable and growing research field.

In recent years, there have been a number of new major contributors to the field. Timothy Coombs has written extensively on the communication aspects of crisis management. He has also advocated crisis management as a necessary component for all organizations, referring to it as the DNA of the organization. Other names continue to surface in the literature on a regular basis, including Dominic Elliott, Sarah Kovoor-Misra, Christopher Lajtha, Timothy Sellnow, Matthew Seeger, Robert Ulmer, and again Ian Mitroff. You will find many more mentioned in the reference section at the end of each chapter. To these authors, we are grateful for what you have done to advance this growing field.

On behalf of John Parnell and John Spillan, I would also like to take this moment to thank Deya Saoud, Associate Editor at SAGE Publications, for her excellent guidance and patience with us while we produced this manuscript. For your hard work and dedication to this craft we call writing, we are indeed very grateful. I would also like to thank the following reviewers for their valuable critiques of earlier versions of the manuscript: Julie A. Davis, *College of Charleston;* Linda M. Dunn-Jensen, *Indiana University;* Gary Ford, *Webster University;* Barbara S. Gainey, *Kennesaw State University;* Naim Kapucu, *University of Central Florida;* Simon Moore, *Bentley College;* Anne H. Reilly, *Loyola University Chicago;* Irv Schenkler, *New York University;* Stephen Sloan, *University of Central Florida.*

I would also like to acknowledge and thank our production editor, Brittany Bauhaus, for her work on making sure the final copy of the book looked right. In addition, I would like to thank my daughter, Renee Phile, for her final edit of the manuscript. Daddy loves you dearly.

We would be remiss if we did not thank our wives, Susan, Denise, and Martha, who patiently put up with our obsession for researching and writing, which, translated, meant many hours in front of our computers. To you three we are most grateful, and appreciate your love and patience with us.

—*William "Rick" Crandall*, PhD

CHAPTER 1

A Framework for Crisis Management

Visualizing Crisis Management

Visualize the term *crisis management* and a number of images may pop into your head. Consider these possibilities:

- Maybe you thought immediately of extremely catastrophic events that occurred during the first half of the decade, such as the September 11, 2001, terrorist attack on the World Trade Center in New York City and on the Pentagon in Washington, D.C.; the Southeast Asia tsunami in December 2004; or the onslaught of Hurricane Katrina on New Orleans in August 2005.
- Maybe the second half of the decade with its catastrophic natural disasters popped into your mind. In 2008, two major events occurred closely together, both in terms of time and geography: the May 2 cyclone that struck Myanmar (Burma), and the May 12 earthquake that caused mass damage and casualties in the Peoples Republic of China.
- Perhaps you envisioned a team of managers, trying to work their way through a product recall. Indeed, product recalls are significant crisis events that can destroy brand loyalty, perhaps forever.
- You might have visualized a crisis management team meeting in a mobile trailer, a block away from their burning factory, where total production capacity has now been reduced to a heap of ashes. For this team, the hard part of getting the company back online is just beginning.

One item you may not have considered was the conceptual framework that is currently growing in this specialized field of management. A framework functions as a map that helps us see how the different parts of a discipline are related to each other.

(Continued)

1

(Continued)

This book offers a framework to help you understand the field of crisis management and how you can better prepare for crisis events that may occur in your organization.

The onset of crises in organizations is a common occurrence in our contemporary environment. The authors have noted a number of crisis events while preparing this book. Consider these two related examples from the mining industry, each with vastly different outcomes:

- During the month of August 2007, six miners were trapped and later presumed to have died in the Crandall (no relationship to the author of this book) Canyon Mine in Utah. Search and recovery efforts at the mine also resulted in the deaths of three rescuers (Torres, 2007).
- During the first week of October 2007, 3,200 miners became trapped in a South African gold mine after an electric cable broke that powered the lift that moved workers to and from the mine. Fortunately, all of the miners were eventually rescued in good health.

These two examples illustrate "sensational" types of crises; indeed, mention the term *crisis* and many think about unprecedented events that result in catastrophic damage and mass casualties. However, not all crises fall into this category. The problem with associating only catastrophic events with a crisis is that they sound so dramatic that most organizational leaders may assume an "it can't happen to us" mentality. But then, consider these crises that are more widespread, yet less dramatic:

- A drought across the southeast United States during the summer of 2007 threatened the drinking water supply in Atlanta, Georgia.
- A number of pet food manufacturers were affected by contaminated wheat gluten, an input for making their product that has been linked to the deaths of at least 15 animals.
- Toy maker Mattel recalled a number of toys after reports that many were coated with lead paint. The toys had been manufactured in China on a contract with Mattel (Parnell, 2007).

As these examples illustrate, not every organizational crisis is dramatic, but crises can have far-reaching impacts if not managed properly.

Setting the Context

Unfortunate events will occur in the life of most organizations. In this book, we refer to these events as crises. There are two broad approaches to the managing of these events: (1) Try to keep them from reoccurring, and (2) mitigate or soften the impact of the crisis when it does occur. Crisis management is the discipline that addresses these two approaches.

This book is about crisis management. It is a field of growing interest because many managers realize they are not immune to those sudden, unexpected events that can put an organization into a tailspin, and sometimes even out of business.

This book is written for students of crisis management. As present or future leaders in your organizations, the key issue you will face is not if a crisis will occur, but when, and what type. As a result, an understanding of crisis management is an essential part of your toolkit for organizational and professional success.

Developing a Framework for Studying Crisis Management

A starting point for understanding crisis management is to look at it in terms of a framework. Frameworks are ways of grouping or organizing what we see in organizational life. This book is about a framework, a way of visualizing crisis management through the lens of a particular viewpoint. Our perspective is built on the work of a number of crisis management researchers who have gone before us. However, we add a new dimension to our framework. That dimension is the existence of the internal and external landscapes that engulf the organization and the crisis events that surround it. In the next section, we begin the foundation of this framework by building on the work of past contributors to the field of crisis management.

Crisis Definition

The definition of a crisis must be established before a suitable framework can be developed. Numerous definitions have been offered, and most synthesize previous definitions to some extent. Pearson and Clair (1998) offered one of the first of the comprehensive definitions:

> An organizational crisis is a low-probability, high-impact event that threatens the viability of the organization and is characterized by ambiguity of cause, effect, and means of resolution, as well as by a belief that decisions must be made swiftly. (p. 60)

The following implications of this definition should be highlighted:

- A crisis is a low-probability event. This characteristic makes the planning for a crisis even more troublesome. Events that are not perceived to be imminent are hard to plan for. In addition, it is often difficult for management to find the motivation to plan for such an event. The notion is, "Why plan for something bad if it may not occur?" (Spillan & Crandall, 2002). Many managers have asked that same question, until they got hit with a big crisis.
- A crisis can have a high-damage impact. Because of this reality, it should be remembered that a crisis can devastate an organization, drive it into the ground, kill it, or, at best, leave it reeling.
- The reference to ambiguity means that the causes and effects of the crisis might be unknown, at least initially. Causes are often attributed to some type of negligence, and the media can be an attacker in its quest to single out the one culprit that caused the crisis to occur in the first place. Unfortunately, as we will see throughout this book, crises can

OPENING QUESTION

What factors should Mattel have considered w/ China? Loss?

Negligent failure to plan

QUESTION: WHAT ARE CONTRIBUTING FACTORS WHEN MAKING A BUSINESS DECISION? PROFIT & LOSS?

have multiple interrelated factors that can lead to a trigger event that initiates the crisis.

- The ambiguity in this definition also implies that the means of resolving the crisis are often debatable. In other words, several viable options may be available for the crisis management team to use in its goal of mitigating the crisis.
- Certain aspects of managing a crisis may require swift decision making. The failure to act decisively during the acute stage of the crisis can often intensify the ordeal.

A more recent definition by Timothy Coombs (2007) states:

A crisis is the perception of an unpredictable event that threatens important expectancies of stakeholders and can seriously impact an organization's performance and generate negative outcomes. (pp. 2–3)

This definition emphasizes perception. A crisis is generally perceived to be a threat by the organization's stakeholders. Stakeholders are various groups that have an interest in the organization. For example, employees, customers, and the community in which the organization resides are considered stakeholders. Coombs infers that not all stakeholders will perceive that a crisis is actually occurring. A product defect that is detected by consumers, but not the company, is an example of the incongruity that can take place. Nonetheless, a crisis has occurred, because the perceptions of at least one group of stakeholders have been impacted in a negative manner by the event. Recognizing this distinction is important because there are occasions when management has gone into denial, proclaiming that no crisis has occurred (or could ever occur, for that matter), when in fact one has transpired (Sheaffer & Mano-Negrin, 2003). Textbooks are full of examples of this type of denial, such as General Motors' (GM) denial that anything was wrong with their Corvair automobile (Nader, 1965). In this early-1960s example of a corporate crisis, consumers and the media claimed that the Corvair automobile was subject to instability when going into a turn. Indeed, several accidents involving fatalities had occurred as a result of this structural problem. GM maintained that the problem of instability was caused by driver error, not a defect in the car. This denial that a crisis even existed resulted in a huge public image problem for GM.

This book follows the crisis definition guidelines offered above. We will build on the definition guidelines offered by Pearson and Clair in 1998 (which is the most frequently cited in the crisis management literature), but we will also include the perspective offered by Coombs. To paraphrase Pearson, Clair, and Coombs, we offer the following definition to serve as our reference point throughout the book:

A crisis is an event that has a low probability of occurring, but should it occur, can have a vastly negative impact on the organization. The causes of the crisis, as well as the means to resolve it, may not be readily clear; nonetheless, its resolution should be approached as quickly as possible. Finally, the crisis impact may not be initially obvious to all of the relevant stakeholders of the organization.

Strategic Orientation

In many instances, crisis events in organizations are addressed with a short-term, reactive perspective. When a crisis occurs, select individuals in an organization—perhaps those on an established crisis management team—convene to minimize the damage and present a positive image to the public. Any preparations for dealing with such crises often focus on effective communications and public relations. In contrast, organizations constantly face strategic challenges. They must adapt to their changing business environments and modify their strategies to survive and remain competitive. In doing so, their leaders tend to adopt a long-term, proactive, and analytical perspective on strategic planning.

Between the extremes of traditional organizational crises and strategic challenges are important obstacles to organizational success that are not always easy to classify. At times, distinguishing between a crisis and a strategic challenge may be difficult. Consider these potential scenarios, all of which are based on a number of actual events that have occurred over the last several years:

- A supplier in another country produces a product that turns out to be defective. The result is that the product is assembled as a component into a domestic product, which causes the final product to fail, and in the process, kills three people. Is this a crisis or a strategic challenge? The answer is both. It is a crisis because there has now been a loss of life due to a defective product. It is a strategic challenge because the supplier was selected for its ability to offer a low cost for the product.

- A labor union stages a mass boycott of certain products that are manufactured overseas. The message from the protest is that these products have caused the loss of domestic jobs. The boycott causes some revenue loss for the companies that manufacture and retail these products. In a few cases, vandalism occurs on store properties that offer the products. Is this a crisis or a strategic challenge? Again, it is both. It is a crisis because of the sudden and unexpected loss of revenue for the companies involved. Furthermore, the damage and public apathy is of concern because it requires swift and effective decision making to ease the problem. It is a strategic challenge because the products are made overseas for cost reasons.

- A major pharmaceutical company begins a program for expansion that involves venturing into product lines that are cutting edge, and aimed at addressing health needs for baby boomers, a market that is seen as a major revenue source in the years to come. Several new drugs are approved and introduced to the market. After a few years, however, one of the drugs is linked to a deadly heart disease. Pressure to withdraw the drug is put firmly on the pharmaceutical company. Is this a crisis or a strategic challenge? Once again, it is both. It is a crisis because media attention is questioning the credibility of the drug and, indirectly, the credibility of the company. A major repercussion could result from this event, and swift and decisive decisions are required. On the other hand, it is a strategic challenge because the drug was in the firm's long-term arsenal of products that would be popular and viable over the next 20 years.

- A major corporation establishes a compensation plan for its management staff that rewards them on the basis of performance. As hoped, performance indicators begin to look good in certain areas of the company, despite the fact that the local economy has been faltering lately. For seven fiscal quarters, two managers in particular are awarded bonuses based on meeting their performance indices established under the compensation plan. Unfortunately, it is discovered later that both managers have "cooking the books." Both been eventually fired, and the company is fined. During the ordeal, the company receives much negative press because of the "unethical acts of its managers." Is this a crisis, or a strategic challenge? Of course, this answer is both. The crisis aspect was manifested by showing the company in a negative light, and resulted in both reputational and financial damage. This dilemma also has roots as a strategic challenge. The decision to set up a bonus plan based on performance was, in itself, not a bad decision. Indeed, most managers in both service and manufacturing industries are compensated, in part, by performance. But some plans are set up in such a way that they can invite unethical decisions on the part of management.

Because of their link with strategic challenges, planning for crises should be a part of the strategic management process. While traditional crisis management approaches put this function as a separate planning process, crisis planning should not exist in a vacuum, but should intertwine with strategic planning. This theme is developed throughout the book.

Previous Crisis Management Frameworks: Classifications of Crises

There are different types of crisis management frameworks. Some of the earlier ones looked at types of crises. In their work on presenting corporate policy during a crisis, Marcus and Goodman (1991) identified three types of crises: accidents, product safety and health incidents, and scandals. Pearson and Mitroff's (1993) framework identified seven crisis families: economic attacks, environmental accidents, occupational health diseases, psycho events (e.g., terrorism, sabotage, product tampering), damage to reputation, informational attacks, and breaks (e.g., recalls, product defects, computer breakdowns). In a similar crisis family arrangement, Myers (1993) offered a framework of crises consisting of natural disasters (floods, hurricanes, etc.), environmental events (aircraft accidents, contamination events, explosions), and incited incidents (arson, sabotage, vandalism). Crandall, McCartney, and Ziemnowicz (1999) used a five-family crises framework in their study of internal auditors. Specifically, they identified crises in terms of operational problems, negative publicity events, fraudulent crises, natural disasters, and legal issues.

Coombs (2006) offered the most recent framework and classified crises as follows:

- Attacks on organizations: computer hacking or tampering, rumors, product tampering, workplace violence, and terrorism. The common theme running through these crises is that the attacks originate from outside the organization. However, that is not to say that all attacks are externally generated. Certainly a disgruntled employee can cause an attack as well, particularly in relation to workplace violence episodes.

- When things go bad: defective products caused by company error, loss of key personnel, industrial accidents, transportation problems, and stakeholder challenges (when an outside group accuses the company of wrongdoing). Often, these types of crises arise because of operational problems in the company.
- When the organization misbehaves: not addressing known risks, improper job performance that leads to an accident, legal and regulatory violations. The common theme running through these crises is an ethical breach of some type. Ask for recent examples ENRON/WORLDCOM/AIG?

Coombs's framework is noteworthy because it takes into account many of the more recent crisis events that have occurred since the attacks of September 11. Crisis classification need not be complicated to be useful, as Coombs's classification illustrates.

Another framework is worth mentioning, especially in light of the 2007 Virginia Tech massacre incident, when a student, Seung-Hui Cho, went on a shooting rampage, killing 32 people. Prior to this incident, Mitroff, Diamond, and Alpaslan (2006) had completed their own categories of crises that could occur on an American college or university campus. Their framework consisted of criminal activities, informational crises (identity theft, fraud, confidentiality problems), building safety issues, athletic scandals, public health problems (such as a disease outbreak or food safety problem), unethical behavior/misconduct (plagiarism, record tampering, or fraud), financial crises, natural disasters, legal/labor disputes, and reputation problems. While such a framework may seem like just a list, it is important to remember that crises tend to reside in families or categories.

Using a framework for classifying crisis events into families is a useful way to organize the phenomena we see. Mitroff (1989) was one of the first crisis management researchers to point out that while it is impossible to prepare for every type of crisis that might happen to an organization, preparing for a few families of crises is feasible. In this book, we present a framework of crisis families that take into account the internal and external landscapes of the organization's environment. But first, we need to acknowledge that crisis events also occur in stages.

Previous Crisis Management Frameworks: Stages of Crises

Frameworks have also been developed that account for the various stages of a crisis. The more familiar frameworks emerged in the 1990s and generally followed a three- or four-stage approach to analyzing the life of a crisis. Crisis researchers knew that analyzing the stages of a crisis helped account for a more holistic approach to understanding the crisis phenomenon. A crisis was more than just an event. It was a life cycle phenomenon that had a birth, an acute stage—the crisis—and an aftermath. Table 1.1 provides an overview of the various frameworks that will be discussed next.

Three-Stage Frameworks

The most basic framework is the simple three-stage approach that follows a precrisis, crisis, and postcrisis format. Smith (1990) offered a three-stage format

TABLE 1.1 Frameworks for Crisis Management

3-Stage Framework: General	3-Stage Framework: Smith, 1990	3-Stage Framework: Richardson, 1994	4-Stage Framework: Myers, 1993	4-Stage Framework: Fink, 1996	5-Stage Framework: Pearson & Mitroff, 1993	This Book: Crandall, Parnell, & Spillan, 2009
Before the Crisis	Crisis of management	Precrisis/disaster phase	Normal operations	Prodromal crisis stage	Signal detection *RARE*	Landscape survey
					Preparation/ Prevention	Strategic planning
During the Crisis	Operational crisis	Crisis impact/ rescue phase	Emergency response	Acute crisis stage	Containment/ Damage limitation	Crisis management
			Interim Processing	Chronic crisis stage		
After the Crisis	Crisis of legitimation	Recovery/demise phase	Restoration	Crisis resolution stage	Recovery	Organizational learning
					Learning	

consisting of a precrisis period, the crisis of management; a crisis period, the operational crisis; and a postcrisis stage, the crisis of legitimation. The crisis of management stage held that the actions of organizational leaders, plus a culture that does not put a premium on preparedness, can lead to a climate where all that is needed is a trigger event to start the crisis. Once the crisis is under way, Smith maintains that the organization manages the crisis as best it can during the operational crisis stage. This stage is characterized by building a supportive climate among the key players involved in the crisis. Unfortunately, the crisis of legitimation stage may be characterized by scapegoating on the part of a number of parties, including the organization itself, as well as the government and the media. Smith is correct when he identifies the human need to appear legitimate in the eyes of the public after a crisis occurs.

Richardson (1994) offered a three-step framework similar to the one proposed by Smith. The precrisis/disaster phase focuses on prevention by addressing the threats that can cause a crisis. The crisis impact/rescue stage is the occurrence of the actual crisis. During this period, management should work at mitigating the crisis and offering support to those affected by it. The recovery/demise stage involves restoring stakeholder confidence in the organization.

Four-Stage Frameworks

By adding an additional stage, these frameworks are meant to offer more precision in examining the crisis progression. Myers (1993) offered a four-stage approach that begins with the normal operations stage, a time when prevention practices are established. In this stage, operations are normal, but preparations are made to address an event should one occur. The second stage, emergency response, involves the first hours immediately following the onset of the crisis. Interim processing, the third stage, represents an intermediate phase where temporary procedures are set up until normal operations can resume. Restoration, the final stage, focuses on the transition back to normal operations.

Fink (1996) also offered a four-stage framework beginning with the prodromal stage. This stage occurs before the full-blown crisis, and is laced with warning signs that a crisis may be imminent. In this stage, it is possible to prevent the crisis if the warning signs are heeded. The acute crisis stage follows next and is evidenced by the sudden onset of the event. This stage is where the crisis is most noticeable by outsiders to the organization. The chronic crisis stage is less dramatic in appearance, but is still significant since the organization is attempting to mop up the lingering damages from the episode. The final stage is the resolution stage, where the organization is returning to its precrisis existence.

Five-Stage Framework

Unlike the previous four-stage frameworks, Pearson and Mitroff's (1993) five-stage framework provides an even more comprehensive approach to understanding the stages of a crisis. These stages include:

- Signal detection: The occurrence of a crisis always begins with some forms of warning. Signal detection is the stage that advances those warnings.

Not true

"Bolts-out-of-the-blue"
- *Lone gunman*
- *Well planned attack*

The missing element is gaming out potential events, not just detecting.

Becoming adept at signal detection is a mindset, as well as a skill, that organizations need to embrace.

- Preparation/prevention: This stage involves the formation of crisis management teams and plans for attacking those crises that may occur. Crisis management is approached in a systematic and ongoing manner to the point where it is almost a science. The goal is to prevent as many crises as possible and effectively manage those that do occur.
- Containment/damage limitation: This stage is where the actual management of the crisis occurs. The intent is to contain the crisis to the greatest extent possible, and to mitigate the event so that organizational and stakeholder damage is kept to a minimum.
- Recovery: In this stage, attempts are made to resume activities to as close to normal as feasible. The recovery will often proceed in stages as well. Short-term recovery aims to get the system back on line so a minimal acceptable level of service is achieved. Long-term recovery follows as operational activities are restored to their precrisis level. In some cases, improvements are made in the recovery process that bring the level of operations up to a higher level than before the crisis. An example would be a company that experiences a fire in its production facilities. After the fire, the new facility that is built is usually better equipped with new machinery and technology than what existed in the old facility.
- Learning: This stage involves activities of reflection where lessons are learned from the crisis. The emphasis is not on searching for scapegoats and displacing the blame onto other parties, a response often encouraged in a litigious society. Instead, maximum attention is focused on improving current operational problems and preventing future ones.

A Framework for Crisis Management

Table 1.1 presents another framework for crisis management—the one we have adopted in this book. With this framework, we draw from the work of previous crisis management researchers and add another dimension to the analysis, the existence of the internal and external landscapes that engulf and surround the organization. The internal landscape lies within the organization. It consists of the employees, as well as the organizational culture of the organization. It is the human side of the company that displays the strengths and weaknesses of the organization.

The external landscape resides outside of the organization. It consists of all stakeholders who have some vested interest in the organization, but are not directly part of it. These include government regulatory agencies, consumer groups, industry associations, and the media. It also consists of groups that are not necessarily stakeholders but can still have a huge impact on the operations of the company. These may include terrorist groups, or a jealous spouse of an employee who works in the organization. The external environment can also include vague types of forces, such as the weather and other natural disasters, as well as a downturn in the economy.

TABLE 1.2 A Framework for Crisis Management				
	Landscape Survey	**Strategic Planning**	**Crisis Management**	**Organizational Learning**
The Internal Landscape	☐ Identify the organization's weaknesses ☐ Determine the enthusiasm for crisis management ☐ Overview the organizational culture ☐ Assess the ethical environment ☐ Evaluate company safety policies	☐ Form the crisis management team ☐ Develop worst-case scenarios ☐ Formulate crisis management plan ☐ Conduct mock disasters and training **Crisis**	☐ Return the organization to an operational status ☐ Manage the primary stakeholders	☐ Evaluate the success and failure outcomes of the crisis management process ☐ Strive for organizational learning ☐ Strive for organizational renewal
The External Landscape	☐ Determine the degree of industry vulnerability ☐ Determine the degree of political stability ☐ Assess the organization in relation to globalization implications ☐ Assess the technological implications	☐ Consider existing government regulations ☐ Consider current industry standards ☐ Develop working relationships with the media	☐ Manage reactions of external stakeholders ○ Negative media coverage ○ Public outcry ○ Web-based criticism and company hate Web sites ○ Impending government regulations	☐ Reap the benefits of industry renewal ☐ Be ready for new government regulations ☐ Be aware of new stakeholder outlooks

The progression of stages of a crisis follows a four-phase model. Table 1.2 illustrates this framework in the form of a two-by-four matrix. There is the landscape survey, followed by strategic planning, then crisis management, and finally the organizational learning stage. Of course, these stages can overlap to some degree. Each stage is overviewed next.

Landscape Survey

The crisis manager's work begins with the landscape survey, shown on the far left side of the figure. The top half of the landscape survey looks at processes that management needs to evaluate (i.e., inside the internal landscape). Identifying weaknesses that exist within the organization is one such process. Such weaknesses indicate where the company may be vulnerable to a crisis attack. Enthusiasm for crisis management planning is another key element to gauge. Some organizations are highly prepared for crisis events, whereas others are more complacent (Pearson & Mitroff, 1993). The degree of enthusiasm for crisis management is also a function of the organization's culture (Stead & Smallman, 1999), its ethical environment, and the diligence with which the company enforces its safety policies.

The bottom half of the landscape survey focuses on events occurring outside of the organization, the external landscape. The industry vulnerability is at the forefront of the types of crises a specific organization encounters. For example, companies in the chemical industry are concerned about chemical leaks. Food manufacturers focus on crises pertaining to disease problems such as an *E. coli* outbreak. Within the hotel and lodging industry, the physical safety of guests is a major vulnerability in terms of a potential crisis.

For companies operating across international borders, the degree of political stability of the host country is important to consider. Another key factor is the general attitude of the host country toward the home country of the multinational corporation (MNC). Any heightened tensions that may exist between these two groups can lay the groundwork for a potential crisis. Globalization implications must also be evaluated. Much globalization seems to progress at the expense of a major stakeholder. For example, manufacturing operations that leave the home country for cheaper labor in another country usually leave a wake of unemployed workers back in the home country. Such moves do not sit well with local stakeholders such as labor unions. LOWER QUALITY?

The technological ramifications of the industry must also be considered as part of the external landscape. For some industries, technology can lay the groundwork for a crisis. In the aerospace industry, the smooth functioning of all technological systems is essential for the safety of those in space, as well as the successful accomplishing of the mission. In other industries, technology is important but not necessarily life threatening—yet can still be the source of a major crisis. Retail chains rely on information technology to communicate and manage back and forth with their field units. A malfunction in such a system will create a crisis, but not one that is physically harmful to employees or customers.

Strategic Planning

The strategic planning phase focuses on preventing crises when possible, and planning how to mitigate their effects when prevention is not possible. Within the internal landscape of the organization, crisis planning begins with forming the crisis management team. The team acts as the body that prevents or manages crisis events. One of the tasks of the team is to periodically assess potential crises that may happen to the organization. For example, school districts for all grade levels, as well as colleges and universities, should plan regularly for a dysfunctional student who may become violent on school property. Another potential crisis involves the quick evacuation of a building, such as in the event of a fire.

Crisis management teams also formulate plans that lay out general guidelines for managing a crisis (Coombs, 2006). Such guidelines include who should address the media, where to locate key contact information for stakeholders such as employees and customers, and procedures for managing specific crises that are unique to the organization. In other words, these guidelines address the organization's potential crises. During the strategic planning stage, some teams will conduct mock disasters in order to test the organization's crisis management response.

A survey of the external landscape looks at what is going on in the industry to prevent and manage crisis events. Existing government regulations in many industries are designed to prevent a crisis from occurring. Examples of these types of agencies abound. The Federal Aviation Administration (FAA) and the Transportation Security Administration (TSA) work to ensure safety in the air travel industries. Almost all industries impose additional standards through associations that exist for that particular industry.

The strategic planning process will also focus efforts on developing effective working relationships with the media in the community. It is important that these relationships be established before a crisis occurs, so that if one does occur, the company spokesperson(s) will be familiar with those individuals from the media. In actual practice, most larger organizations have public relations personnel who work with the media on a regular basis.

Crisis Management

The crisis management stage addresses the acute phase of the crisis. From the organizational (internal landscape) perspective, efforts are focused on containing the crisis and resuming operations as quickly as possible. Up to this point, we have discussed stakeholders in a broad sense, without regard to the varying effects they may experience from the crisis. In actuality, there are primary and secondary stakeholders of the organization. Primary stakeholders typically include the owners, employees, customers, local communities, and suppliers (Wheeler & Sillanpää, 1997). Secondary stakeholders include any other groups that have some type of interest in the organization. For example, People for the Ethical Treatment of Animals (PETA) has an interest in companies that use animals for laboratory research. A crisis can result when such a group takes an activist stand against a company that uses animals for this purpose.

Organizational Learning

After the crisis ends, the organization must take time to learn from what has occurred. One of the keys to learning the most from a crisis is not to wait too long after the event has occurred. If too much time elapses before reflection and evaluation occur, management may reach a stage termed "forgetfulness" (Kovoor-Misra & Nathan, 2000). In this stage, the organization has returned to normal operations, and the motivation to evaluate and learn from the crisis wanes.

At a minimum, management must evaluate how the crisis was handled and what changes need to be made in the crisis management plan. Pearson and Clair (1998) suggested that such an evaluation can be examined in terms of degrees of success and failure. For example, an organization may succeed in resuming operations in a timely manner, but fail at protecting its reputation. Instead of learning from a crisis, some organizations do not seem to heed the lessons from the event, and as a result, repeat the same mistakes when similar incidents occur in the future. On the other hand, an organization that is successful at learning will change its policies and procedures when necessary and apply that new knowledge to future crisis events.

In the external landscape, industry regulators often reevaluate and renew their procedures after a crisis. Certainly the airline industry has changed dramatically in terms of safety regulations after America's worst terrorist incident on September 11, 2001. Government regulations are often implemented after a crisis, usually to increase the safety of stakeholders in the affected industry. Stakeholders external to the organization may also change their outlooks after a crisis. At a minimum, such stakeholders will be more aware and compassionate toward an organization that has experienced a crisis. The Virginia Tech massacre generated a wave of sympathy and solidarity among many citizens throughout the country, and even worldwide. At the same time, some parties were also critical of the university, questioning whether certain measures could have been taken to prevent or mitigate the crisis.

Development of the Book

This book is organized around the crisis management framework introduced above. The layout of the book is in six sections.

Section One: Introduction to the Book

Chapter 1. A Framework for Crisis Management

The present chapter outlines the framework that will be presented in the book. Figure 1.1 overviews the progression of the remaining chapters.

Section Two: Landscape Survey

Chapter 2. The Crisis Management Landscape

This chapter begins our survey of the strategic landscape that breeds many of the crises facing organizations. The focus is on six of the broader trends that are common across most cultures and business environments.

Chapter 3. Sources of Organizational Crises

In this chapter, we explore the sources of crises from several perspectives. First, an analysis of the external environment is presented from the political–legal, economic, social, and technological perspectives. The external environment is important to analyze because many crisis events emerge from the volatility of these four sectors of the environment. Crises are also viewed from the organizational life cycle perspective because different stages of the life cycle have their own unique vulnerabilities to a crisis.

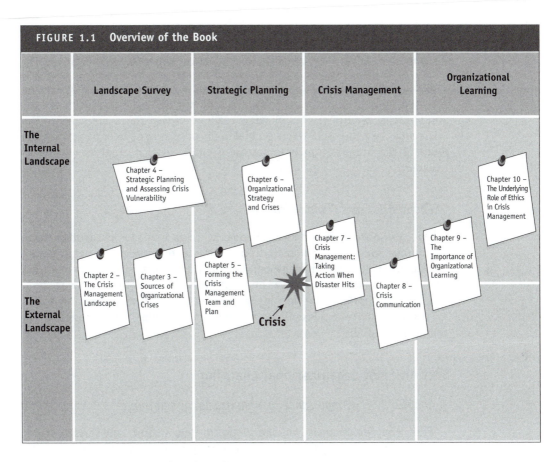

FIGURE 1.1   Overview of the Book

Section Three: Strategic Planning

Chapter 4. Strategic Planning and Assessing Crisis Vulnerability

In this chapter, we outline the strategic planning process and its link to crisis anticipation and prevention. The second part of the chapter focuses on crisis vulnerability, the anticipation of unique events that may occur at a specific organization.

Chapter 5. Forming the Crisis Management Team and Plan

The essence of crisis planning is forming the crisis management team and then the crisis plan. In this chapter, guidelines are provided for both tasks. The chapter offers advice on how crisis management training efforts should proceed.

Chapter 6. Organizational Strategy and Crises

This chapter concludes the discussion on strategic planning by turning the reader's attention to the various levels of business and corporate strategy. We also emphasize the importance of control mechanisms in the planning process.

Section Four: Crisis Management

Chapter 7. Crisis Management: Taking Action When Disaster Hits

Managing the crisis when it hits is the topic of Chapters 7 and 8. While the first two phases of our framework are proactive (i.e., the landscape survey and strategic planning), this phase is reactive in that the acute stage of the crisis must be addressed. Decision making proceeds at a faster pace since the focus of the organization is to restore operations to normal as quickly as feasible.

Chapter 8. Crisis Communication

One of the most important challenges of crisis management is to manage communication effectively both from within and outside the organization. Indeed, the area of crisis management originally concentrated on communication with outside stakeholders. In fact, much of the early days of crisis management was more appropriately considered "damage control" procedures with the media. This chapter returns to this tradition and updates the reader on the latest trends in crisis communication.

Section Five: Organizational Learning

Chapter 9. The Importance of Organizational Learning

This chapter focuses on the need to learn from the crisis event. Organizational learning does not come naturally, however, as the push to get the organization back to normal often supersedes the need for reflection on preventing future crises. This chapter concludes by examining factors that can impede learning, as well as how to build a learning organization.

Chapter 10. The Underlying Role of Ethics in Crisis Management

This chapter examines how executive misbehavior is a major force behind many crises that occur in organizations today. Much of the discussion focuses on why these ethical blunders come about and what can be done to prevent them.

Section Six: An Alternative Paradigm and Emerging Trends

Chapter 11. Chaos Theory: An Alternative Paradigm in the Study of Organizational Crises

A number of researchers have noted that crisis events are complex phenomena and should be studied using analyses that acknowledge this complexity. Chaos theory offers one such viewpoint. This chapter draws on the concepts of chaos theory as an alternative perspective to studying crisis events.

Chapter 12. Emerging Trends in Crisis Management

This chapter takes a look into the future of crisis management. Emerging trends are identified in each of the four areas of the framework: landscape survey, strategic planning, crisis management, and organizational learning.

Summary

The field of crisis management is growing in scope and sophistication. This book acknowledges such changes by recognizing that crisis management should be a part of the strategic management process. Drawing on the work of others in the field, we employ a crisis management framework that utilizes a two-by-four matrix that recognizes four phases of the crisis management process. In addition, we add the importance of acknowledging the internal and external landscapes that exist within each phase. Such a framework is important because it guides us through the process of crisis management in a systematic manner that is both reactive and proactive. By reactive, we mean responding to the crisis event effectively with a minimal amount of damage. By proactive, we mean planning for such events before they occur, and learning from these events after they have transpired.

Questions for Discussion

1. Why do you think crisis researchers put so much emphasis on classifying crisis events according to different categories?

2. Why is it important to understand a crisis in terms of its different stages?

3. Discuss a recent crisis event that occurred where you work. Discuss the different stages of the crisis in terms of:
   • Landscape survey—what events were going on inside and outside of your organization that contributed to the formation of that crisis?
   • Strategic management—what plans designed to address the occurrence of this particular event were already in place at your organization? What mechanisms existed outside of the organization (such as industry controls or government regulations) that were designed to prevent the occurrence of this event?
   • Crisis management—how did your organization respond to the crisis? Were any outside agencies or stakeholders involved in helping your organization manage the crisis?
   • Organizational learning—what lessons did your organization learn from experiencing this crisis? Were there any changes in agencies or other stakeholders that will lead to their doing things differently in the future should a similar crisis recur?

Chapter Exercise

As a class, determine the following:

- What events could happen to the class that would constitute a crisis? (*Write these on the board and then seek a consensus as a class on what the top five crisis events would be. Then focus on these as you go to the next step below.*)
- What crisis plans are available that could address each of these five potential crises? Distinguish between resources that are available inside the classroom and those that exist outside of the classroom.

[Handwritten note: HAVE students turn to this case. REVIEW it AS A class, AND tell them to select 2 A cases tonight AND EMAIL ME the cases BEFORE Next class]

MINI CASE

PET FOOD CRISIS

During the spring of 2007, a widespread crisis erupted within the pet food industry. Many dog and cat owners noticed their pets were getting sick and some even died. The common thread that was eventually found was melamine, a chemical that shows up as protein when chemical tests are conducted on the food item. Melamine was added to wheat gluten and rice concentrate that had been imported from China. The gluten and concentrate are ingredients that are added to pet food (Malanga, 2007).

The crisis eventually resulted in a widespread recall of pet foods. More than 100 U.S. pet food companies recalled their products, including Procter & Gamble's company, Iams. As it turned out, Iams was hurt the most by the crisis; its sales plummeted nearly 17% (Neff, 2007a). Other brands affected included Del Monte's Jerky Treats, Gravy Train Beef Sticks, and Pounce Meaty Morsels. Wal-Mart's Ol' Roy and Supervalu's Happy Trails brands were also recalled (McTaggart, 2007).

But within this crisis was another crisis. Criticism was emerging from, of all places, a crisis management consultant who claimed the pet food companies waited too long to issue a recall. Mike Paul, a crisis communications consultant, stated: "In any crisis, the first 24 to 48 hours are most important, and there's an expectation that in the first 24 hours a lot can and should be done" (Neff, 2007b, p. 29). Mr. Paul's concern centered on the fact that consumers first reported a problem around February 20. Recalls, however, were not under way until March 16. The lapse of time may have caused more pets to die from the ill-fated food.

The actual number of deaths has not been determined, and may never be. The problem is that many pets all over the country were reported sick, but not all of them died. Inevitably, some pets would have died anyway of other causes, so tracing these deaths back to the tainted pet food is difficult. For the record, Menu Foods, a pet food manufacturer, reported that 15 cats and 1 dog had died from eating the food (Neff, 2007b).

Sources

Malanga, S. (2007, May 9). Pet plaintiffs. *Wall Street Journal,* A16.

McTaggart, J. (2007). Pet food crisis rocks industry. *Progressive Grocer, 86*(5), 10–12.

Neff, J. (2007a, May 14). In the wake of pet-food crisis, Iams sales plummet nearly 17%. *Advertising Age, 78*(20), 3–91.

Neff, J. (2007b, March 26). Pet-food industry too slow: Crisis-PR gurus. *Advertising Age, 78*(13), 29.

References

Coombs, W. (2006). *Code red in the boardroom: Crisis management as organizational DNA.* Westport, CT: Praeger.

Coombs, W. (2007). *Ongoing crisis communication: Planning, managing, and responding* (2nd ed.). Thousand Oaks, CA: Sage.

Crandall, W. R., McCartney, M., & Ziemnowicz, C. (1999). Internal auditors and their perceptions of crisis events. *Internal Auditor, 14*(1), 11–17.

Fink, S. (1996). *Crisis management: Planning for the inevitable.* New York: American Management Association.

Kovoor-Misra, S., & Nathan, M. (2000, Fall). Timing is everything: The optimal time to learn from crises. *Review of Business,* pp. 31–36.

Malanga, S. (2007, May 9). Pet plaintiffs. *Wall Street Journal,* p. A16.

Marcus, A., & Goodman, R. (1991). Victims and shareholders: The dilemmas of presenting corporate policy during a crisis. *Academy of Management Journal, 34*(2), 281–305.

McTaggart, J. (2007). Pet food crisis rocks industry. *Progressive Grocer, 86*(5), 10–12.

Mitroff, I. (1989, October). Programming for crisis control. *Security Management,* pp. 75–79.

Mitroff, I., Diamond, M., & Alpaslan, C. (2006). How prepared are America's colleges and universities for major crises? *Change, 38*(1), 60–67.

Myers, K. (1993). *Total contingency planning for disasters: Managing risk . . . minimizing loss . . . ensuring business continuity.* New York: John Wiley.

Nader, R. (1965). *Unsafe at any speed.* New York: Grossman.

Neff, J. (2007a, May 14). In the wake of pet-food crisis, Iams sales plummet nearly 17%. *Advertising Age, 78*(20), 3–91.

Neff, J. (2007b, March 26). Pet-food industry too slow: Crisis-PR gurus. *Advertising Age, 78*(13), 29.

Parnell, J. (2007, September 10). Importing problems with Chinese goods. *News & Observer,* p. 11A.

Pearson, C., & Clair, J. (1998). Reframing crisis management. *Academy of Management Review, 23*(1), 59–76.

Pearson, C., & Mitroff, I. (1993). From crisis prone to crisis prepared: A framework for crisis management. *Academy of Management Executive, 7*(1), 48–59.

Richardson, B. (1994). Socio-technical disasters: Profile and prevalence. *Disaster Prevention & Management, 3*(4), 41–69.

Sheaffer, Z., & Mano-Negrin, R. (2003). Executives' orientations as indicators of crisis management policies and practices. *Journal of Management Studies, 40*(2), 573–606.

Smith, D. (1990). Beyond contingency planning: Towards a model of crisis management. *Industrial Crisis Quarterly, 4*(4), 263–275.

Spillan, J., & Crandall, W. R. (2002). Crisis planning in the nonprofit sector: Should we plan for something bad if it may not occur? *Southern Business Review, 27*(2), 18–29.

Stead, E., & Smallman, C. (1999). Understanding business failure: Learning and un-learning lessons from industrial crises. *Journal of Contingencies and Crisis Management, 7*(1), 1–18.

Torres, K. (2007). Mine tragedy in Utah. *Occupational Hazards, 69*(9), 15.

Wheeler, D., & Sillanpää, M. (1997). *The stakeholder corporation: A blueprint for maximizing stakeholder value.* London: Pittman Publishing.

CHAPTER 2

The Crisis Management Landscape

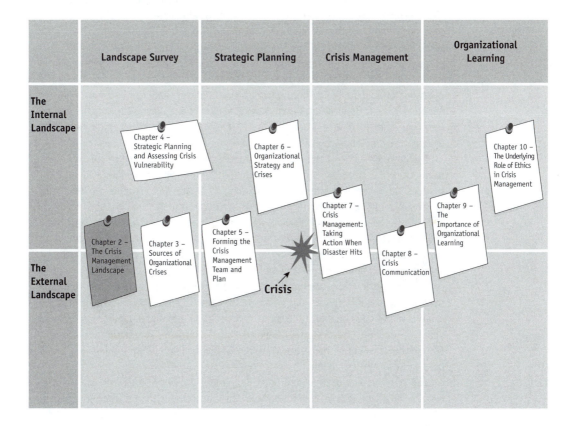

	Landscape Survey	Strategic Planning	Crisis Management	Organizational Learning
The Internal Landscape	Chapter 4 – Strategic Planning and Assessing Crisis Vulnerability	Chapter 6 – Organizational Strategy and Crises	Chapter 7 – Crisis Management: Taking Action When Disaster Hits	Chapter 9 – The Importance of Organizational Learning / Chapter 10 – The Underlying Role of Ethics in Crisis Management
The External Landscape	Chapter 2 – The Crisis Management Landscape / Chapter 3 – Sources of Organizational Crises	Chapter 5 – Forming the Crisis Management Team and Plan / **Crisis**	Chapter 8 – Crisis Communication	

The SK-II Crisis

Although its success in the western part of the world has been outstanding, Procter & Gamble (P&G) has been plagued with a number of problems in the People's Republic of China. In May 2005, P&G negotiated a US$24,000 settlement following a 20-day investigation after a consumer spent 840 yuan (US$100) on P&G's De-Wrinkle Essence, an SK-II product. The product advertisement claimed the treatment would work to help eliminate 47% of deep lines and wrinkles after 1 month of usage (Crandall, Parnell, Xihui, & Long, 2007). According to Lu Ping, the victim in this suit, the product caused only a painful allergic reaction. P&G's assertions were based on a study involving 200 Japanese women a claim that the Nanchang Commercial and Industrial Bureau in Jiangxi suggested lacked proof ("P&G Accepts Fine," 2005).

In June 2005, the Zhejiang Provincial Industrial and Commercial Administration (ZPICA)—a local advertising standards agency in China—ordered P&G to remove an advertisement for its Pantene V shampoo. The ad claimed that the product made hair ten times more resilient than normal, an assertion ZPICA contested. ZPICA also challenged advertisements for three other P&G products—Safeguard soap, Crest toothpaste, and Head and Shoulders shampoo—although formal action was only taken for Pantene V (Liu, 2005).

For a year, the stormy relationship between P&G and Chinese regulators appeared to have subsided, until the unfortunate SK-II incident. The SK-II product line is a brand of cosmetics sold by P&G. These products are made in Japan and sold to stores in Australia, China, Hong Kong, Japan, Korea, Malaysia, Singapore, Taiwan, the United Kingdom, and the United States. In the United States, the product line is available through the high-end retailer Saks.

The current SK-II crisis began on September 14, 2006, when quality authorities in south China's Guangdong province detected chromium and neodymium in an SK-II product. These metals can cause skin irritation and disease and therefore are banned in all cosmetics in China and many other parts of the world.

P&G's initial public response was one of denial, stating that it was working with the local Chinese authorities to verify the validity of the findings. After the number of allegedly contaminated SK-II products increased to nine, the company reluctantly agreed to offer refunds to consumers (Crandall et al., 2007). To be eligible, however, consumers had to return the product to the store of purchase with no less than one third of the product remaining, complete and sign a form acknowledging that the product was of good quality, and wait several weeks for a refund to be processed (Guan, 2006). Meanwhile, China's General Administration of Quality Supervision warned that SK-II products would be banned from import if the contamination problem continued (Xinhua News Agency, 2006).

The crisis took a dramatic turn on September 21 when hundreds of Shanghai women sought refunds at P&G's specified locations. Tempers flared when the women were told that their refunds would take 3 weeks to process. The next day, P&G announced that it would suspend its refund operations due to security concerns and discontinue selling the Japanese-made line of SK-II products in China, at least temporarily.

Cultural

Regulatory

'Blood-in-the-WATER'

Later that same day, a group of angry consumers kicked down the front door of P&G's Shanghai office. Media calls to P&G officials in Guangzhou and Shanghai were not returned. The company's China Web site was reportedly hacked that weekend. In a frenzied response, some of the local retailers began offering immediate cash refunds to customers after P&G suspended its refund program ("Consumers Angry," 2006).

Product impurities, negative publicity, unexpected natural disasters, or a fire that destroys a production facility are examples of crises to which no organization is immune. All of these are unexpected events that can produce serious negative repercussions. Any organization can be confronted with and should be prepared for a "what-if scenario," what we commonly call a crisis. As stated in Chapter 1, a crisis is an event that has a low probability of occurring but, should it occur, can have a vastly negative impact on the organization.

One of the most prominent examples of a crisis in recent history is the terrorist attacks on September 11, 2001, on New York City's World Trade Center buildings and the Pentagon in Washington, D.C. However, such terrorism events represent only one form of crisis events. Other types of crises include fires, natural disasters, industrial accidents, workplace violence, extortion, boycotts, and bribery. A more recent area of crises relates to "information age" activities, including computer system sabotage, copyright infringement, and counterfeiting, as well as political unrest such as urban riots (Miller, 2001; Pearson & Mitroff, 1993). The effects of crises on an organization can vary widely around the world and can be especially traumatic in emerging nations where recovery can be more difficult and costly (Parnell, Crandall, & Menefee, 1997).

This chapter begins our study of crisis events by examining the crisis management landscape. Important trends are identified that are occurring on a widespread basis throughout the global environment. In our discussion, we will overview and link these trends to crisis management.

The Crisis Management Landscape

Six scenarios in the crisis management landscape trending from less to more controllable are identified in Figure 2.1. Those listed on the left side of the figure identify scenarios that are less subject to strategic planning on the part of the organization. As they progress toward the right side of the figure, they become more capable of being influenced by strategic planning initiatives. They also shift upward as they move from left to right, indicating that the internal environment becomes an increasingly stronger factor in the origin of these crises events. Our discussion will begin with the occurrence of unusual weather patterns and the multiple disaster problem, and then proceeds in order to the right of the figure, ending with a discussion on the movement toward globalization and outsourcing.

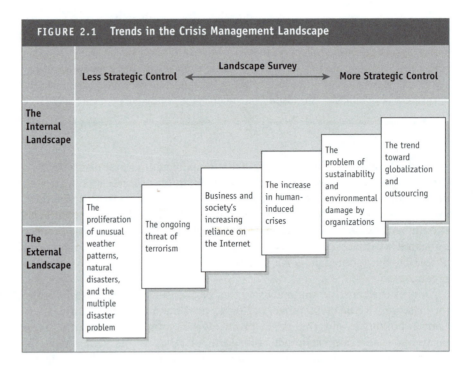

FIGURE 2.1   Trends in the Crisis Management Landscape

The Proliferation of Unusual Weather Patterns, Natural Disasters, and the Multiple Disaster Problem

Severe weather and natural disasters are part of organizational life. Although weather-related crises are not preventable, their effects can be mitigated to some degree. Preparation for an oncoming storm can reduce injuries and fatalities. Seismic construction codes can be updated to better support buildings during an earthquake. Moving an organization to a less hazardous location is also possible in some circumstances. After Hurricane Katrina, a number of businesses, including the Hancock Bank of Gulfport, Mississippi, moved their headquarters farther inland to escape future potential flooding (Mitchell, 2008).

The frequency of natural disasters is often a function of geography. Earthquakes, for example, occur near fault zones. In the United States, active fault zones exist in California and along the New Madrid seismic zone, an area that encompasses southeastern Missouri, northeastern Arkansas, and western Tennessee. We also know that unusual weather patterns such as typhoons and cyclones, as well as tsunamis, can be especially particularly devastating in developing countries. In these areas, fatalities can be especially high. The Bay of Bengal (India), for example, has been hit by two deadly cyclones, one in 1970 resulting in approximately 500,000 fatalities and another one in 1991, involving 139,000 deaths (Davis, 2001).

From an economic point of view, disasters are billion-dollar events that can have major economic and political impacts (Green, 2004). The Hurricane Katrina disaster of 2005 had a devastating effect on organizations in the New Orleans and Gulf of Mexico region. Grocery chain Winn-Dixie, for example, contemplated closing down its operations in the area, where it operates about

125 stores. Sometimes, though, a crisis produces an opportunity. Because Winn-Dixie was in Chapter 11 bankruptcy, the firm had an option to exit with fewer repercussions than other grocers would face, because bankruptcy protection makes it easier to cancel costly store leases. But its CEO, Peter Lynch, saw the situation as an opportunity to use the millions of dollars the company would receive in insurance payments to rebuild the stores to be brighter and better stocked. Instead of departing the ravaged region, Winn-Dixie decided to bank on a strong rebound in the region (Adamy, 2005).

Weather and natural disasters sometimes are coupled with a human-induced crisis to create "packages of disasters" (Green, 2004, p. 61). Developing countries are especially vulnerable to these types of crises, with the result usually involving a large number of fatalities. For example, a civil war may be followed by a famine, or a natural disaster may be followed by a flood of refugees as people must leave their ravished homes. The wars in Mozambique illustrate how an already damaged country fared very poorly when hit with heavy rains and flooding in 2000 (Green, 2004). Developed countries such as the United States have not seen such high rates of casualties from these multiple disasters, although Hurricane Katrina was an example of a package of crises with many fatalities. In this example, the hurricane was followed by the breakdown of law and order, and by general government incompetence in responding to the needs of victims in a timely manner.

The multiple disaster problem raises a concern for crisis planning in the new landscape: What happens when society in general seems to break down, albeit temporarily, during a major disaster? Are firms prepared to ride out the storm, without government intervention, if necessary? These are not easy questions to address, but if history proves correct, such events will continue to be part of the crisis management landscape.

The Ongoing Threat of Terrorism

Terrorism has always been a threat to entities throughout the world. Historically, terrorist acts were motivated by political ideals rather than religious ones (Pedahzur, Eubank, & Weinberg, 2002). Within the past 2 decades, though, terrorism has changed on at least three fronts. First, the number of victims per attack has increased. Suicide bombers in particular are able to move into crowded areas before detonating their explosives, thus increasing the number of casualties tremendously. Second, religious idealists are behind the majority of the attacks (Perliger, Pedahzur, & Zalmanovitch, 2005). Finally, the targets of terrorist attacks are extending around the globe, not just in troubled areas such as the Middle East. In the United States, for example, the 1993 bombing of the World Trade Center signaled that terrorism with Middle Eastern ties had struck close to home. But then the 1995 bombing of the Alfred P. Murrah Federal Building in Oklahoma City destroyed the long-held notion that terrorism originates only from abroad, as this event was carried out by an American citizen. The innocence of the United States had been violated. Then, there was September 11, reinforcing the continued threat of terrorism from abroad.

One of the tactics of the new terrorism is to strike in urban areas. Such targets are desirable because they represent the financial, political, and cultural center of the state (Perliger et al., 2005). Thus, striking an urban target inflicts a psychological as well as a physical blow to the local area. Urban areas are also desirable for terrorists because of the higher number of casualties that can be inflicted. Because of the high concentration of businesses and government offices in urban areas, crisis management plans that include terrorist contingencies are desirable.

Managers and employees who were not previously convinced of the serious nature of terrorism changed their views after the attacks of September 11, 2001. In one day, the need for organizations to anticipate, prepare for, and respond to these potential events was made clear (Greenberg, Clair, & Maclean, 2002). For some businesses, the attack resulted not only in the tragic loss of a substantial number of employees, but also a loss of key facilities and data (Greenberg, 2002). Many organizations decimated by this attack never reopened. The companies that were located in the World Trade Center's Twin Towers were affected directly. Thousands of other businesses were affected indirectly, however. Supply chains were interrupted, key information networks were destroyed, clients were lost, and business travel, at least in the short run, was seriously curtailed.

Preparing for terrorist attacks is not an easy task for either the small business owner or the large corporate management team. Indeed, most organizations depend on the government to provide most of the protection from terrorist attacks. Formally declaring terrorism as a national problem, the U.S. government created the first Department of Homeland Security. Because terrorism will not disappear in the near future, crisis management teams need to prepare for this threat that may not only remain, but could intensify in the years to come.

Business and Society's Increasing Reliance on the Internet

Like most business functions and activities, crisis management efforts cannot escape the substantial effects of the Internet's proliferation. The Internet has provided a new channel of distribution, a more efficient means of gathering and disseminating strategic information, and a new way of communicating with customers. It has also provided a means to create havoc in a business through hacking and other illegal means of exploiting the easy and rapid flow of information. Vulnerable users can easily be victimized, resulting in huge losses in time, capital, and opportunities.

The Internet has several characteristics that can create a crisis-prone environment. One that may not be readily apparent is the movement toward information symmetry. Information symmetry exists when all parties to a transaction share the same information concerning that transaction (Parnell, 2008). Simply stated, greater information symmetry means that the public knows more about an organization and its processes. Consequently, information that could foster a crisis is in the hands of customers, members of the media, and other stakeholders. It creates a vulnerable portal from which a crisis can easily erupt.

Negative information about organizations can readily circulate on the Internet. Consumers can discuss their negative experiences with products and services on discussion forums or in chat rooms. Private individuals and groups have established Web sites dedicated to disseminating negative information about major firms. Two examples of many are www.allstateinsurancesucks.com and www.walmartwatch.com. Blogs (i.e., Web logs), can contain negative statements about an organization. In March 2007, Home Depot was the target of an onslaught of negative publicity when MSN Money columnist Scott Burns stated that the company was an abuser of the customer's time. The comment section to MSN was soon filled with similar stories from customers who were tired of the skimpy service they were receiving due to cutbacks in store staff. In just a few hours, there were more than 10,000 angry e-mails and another 4,000 posts blasting the company for its poor service (Conlin, 2007).

The Internet can also intensify a crisis, because the filters that are traditionally associated with print journalism do not exist in cyberspace (Bernstein, 2006). Magazines, journals, and newspapers have some degree of oversight over the material that is printed in their venues. Opinions, whims, and downright anger can be expressed on the Internet, however, and in real time. As a result, organizations are urged to monitor the Web regularly to stay abreast of public sentiment (Hasely, 2004). Some companies such as Southwest Airlines and Dell even have specialists who not only monitor bloggers and social networks, but respond to these outlets as needed (Conlin, 2007).

Another aspect of the Internet that contributes to a crisis-prone environment is the existence of a highly motivated hacker community (Koyoor-Misra & Misra, 2007). Several types of hacking can occur. A denial-of-service attack causes the organization's Web site either to slow down or to stop functioning altogether. Such an attack can lead to a sizable loss of revenue, similar to shutting down the store for the duration of the attack. Hacking can also occur in the form of security breaches, where customer database information is stolen. Such hacking can then lead to identity theft, a crisis that can lead to monumental problems for both the company and its customers.

The Increase in Human-Induced Crises

Since 1994, the Institute for Crisis Management has been tracking the types of crises that strike organizations. In the consulting firm's 2007 annual report, 52% of all reported crises originated with management while 29% were caused by employees (Institute for Crisis Management, 2008). Certainly corporate scandals, mismanagement, and other forms of white-collar crime contribute to the high percentage of management-induced crises. What is disturbing about these findings is that the majority of these crises need not occur in the first place. Unlike externally induced crises such as hurricanes or natural disasters, human-induced crises are often a function of examples set by top management (Carroll & Buchholtz, 2003; Hartley, 1993). When lower-level employees are not sure how to react in a certain situation, they look to their leaders for guidance. Depending on the ethics of their leaders, ethical problems can arise, leading to the spread of crises throughout the organization. Because this area of crisis management is complex, a separate chapter of this book is devoted to the ethical implications of organizational crises.

Human-induced crises also include various forms of workplace misbehavior. Griffin and Lopez (2005, p. 988) coined the term *bad behavior* to refer to those behaviors that are potentially injurious to the organization and/or its members.

They have further classified bad behavior into four categories: deviance, aggression, antisocial behavior, and violence. *Workplace deviance* is behavior that violates the accepted norms of the organization. Organizational deviance is composed of actions taken against the company and includes leaving early, wasting resources, stealing, and sabotaging equipment. Interpersonal deviance is directed toward another individual in the workplace and can include verbal abuse, gossiping, and sexual harassment (Diefendorff & Mehta, 2007). *Workplace aggression* is assertive and threatening behavior that is directed toward a person or an object. It is nonphysical in nature. An example would be a terminated worker who threatens his supervisor. If those threats were to become physical in nature, then the behavior would be a form of *workplace violence,* which is characterized by a direct physical assault on an individual (O'Leary-Kelly, Griffin, & Glew, 1996). *Antisocial behavior* is a set of behaviors that can produce physical, economic, psychological, or emotional harm (Robinson & O'Leary, 1998). This behavior is manifested when an employee is not sociable with others and/or is hostile and disruptive to the regular norms of the organization (Griffin & Lopez, 2005).

Of the behaviors described by Griffin and Lopez, it is workplace violence that generates the most attention in the field of crisis management. In the past 10 years, there has been an abundance of new research on workplace violence. A personality profile of a potential killer in the workplace has been identified, new security procedures have been enacted in organizations, and better screening devices are in place to identify applicants who may be prone to violence. Nevertheless, workplace violence continues to be a problem in the crisis management landscape, as a number of such events have occurred across the nation.

[handwritten margin note: Not true, there is no profile of a potential killer]

In addition to unethical decisions and the "bad behaviors" described above, human-induced crises also include operator errors, which are a major contributor to industrial accidents. Errors of this kind can be caused when the work environment is both complex and "tightly coupled." Charles Perrow (1999) claimed that this type of scenario can lead to a normal accident. Tight coupling can be understood by considering the interdependence that exists between departments, units, teams, and other groups within an organization. The higher the interdependence (i.e., the more the departments depend on each other in order to function), the more tightly the departments are coupled. If the departments can exist within the organization but are not highly interdependent, then they are loosely coupled. For example, in a restaurant, the service staff and the cooking staff are tightly coupled because one cannot adequately function without the other. If the chef and several cooks were suddenly to become ill, a major crisis would ensue and the restaurant might have to close, albeit temporarily. On the other hand, the relationship between the cooks and the cleaning staff of dishwashers is more loosely coupled. The restaurant can survive if there is a shortage of dishwashers, even if the cooks have to take over this function temporarily.

The above example considered the notion of interdependence within an organization. However, the concept of coupling also involves entities outside of the organization. Consider that some of the organization's suppliers are more tightly coupled with the company than others. Tightly coupled suppliers must be available to make regular deliveries with the full order and in a timely fashion if the business is to perform well. In our restaurant example, the food suppliers are tightly coupled to the restaurant. In contrast, suppliers of paper and cleaning goods, although important, are more loosely coupled. A crisis can develop when an entity that is tightly coupled, either within the organization or outside of it, is temporarily incapacitated. The other groups aligned with that unit are now also part of the crisis. For example, in a just in time (JIT) work system, if a major supplier cannot make the delivery, the assembly line will shut down since there is very little slack built into the system. If the delay continues, the company may have to close as well. This is not a hypothetical example, but one that plays itself out every time there is a major disruption in a supply chain. Natural disasters, civil unrest, wars, and inclement weather can initiate a crisis of this sort since these events have the ability to disrupt supply chains.

Perrow's original contributions to normal accident theory were aimed at addressing technologies that create both complexity and tight coupling to the user who must operate these technologies. In such a situation, a user error can create a major crisis. User errors of this sort are inevitable in certain facilities such as chemical plants and nuclear power plants (Choo, 2008). The most notable example was the March 28, 1979, near-meltdown of a reactor at the Three Mile Island nuclear power facility outside of Harrisburg, Pennsylvania (Hopkins, 2001). In this incident, plant operators were at a loss to explain both what had happened to cause the accident and what to do about it (Barton, 2001). The plant met the conditions that Perrow had outlined; it was complex, and tightly coupled. The sheer complexity of the facility made it difficult to identify actions needed to remedy the problem. The plant was tightly coupled in that changes in one subsystem would impact the rest of the system as well. In fact, one of the initial means used by operators to control the rising temperature in the reactor core was to shut down high-pressure cooling pumps (Hopkins, 2001). Ironically, leaving pressure pumps on would have alleviated the problem, a tight coupling phenomenon. Although this example has its roots in technology, it is also a case study on how human error can intensify a crisis.

Previous to Perrow's normal accident theory, Turner (1978) posited that human-induced crises were caused by what he labeled as sloppy management. Whereas Perrow blamed human error (referring to the operators of the technology) on technological factors, Turner maintained that human operating error was caused by poor management of these operators and the systems in which they operated. One of the characteristics of sloppy management is the failure to heed warnings from previous problems (Hopkins, 2001). In other words, managers are presented with warning signs, but they fail to act upon them, which ultimately leads to a crisis. The September 11 terrorist attack on the World Trade Center in New York City has been framed in this light (The 9/11 Commission, 2004). Sloppy management has also been linked with groupthink, a phenomenon in which poor decisions are made by groups because of a desire to appear united and cohesive (Janis, 1982). In fact, failing to heed warnings can actually be a by-product of groupthink because nobody in the group wants to be viewed as an alarmist.

Choo's (2008) recent work adds to the body of knowledge on sloppy management by offering three explanations as to why warnings are not heeded by management: epistemic blind spots, risk denial, and structural impediments. An epistemic blind spot occurs when warnings are not acted on because the information does not fit any existing frame of reference. Put another way, information is selectively interpreted to fit what we think is true. For example,

Enron's board did heed the warnings that were surfacing about how the company was setting up its assets and holdings on its financial statements. The board's perception, instead, was that this type of disclosure was just a normal part of doing business (Choo, 2008).

Unlike blind spots, where the warning is completely missed, risk denial is a mindset that acknowledges that there is a warning present, but the norms and culture of the organization dictate that a response to that warning is not necessary. This is one of the most perplexing of all matters related to crisis management since so many of the crises that we study could have been avoided if the correct decision maker(s) had acted on the warning. A common theme that seems to run through the minds of many managers is the "it can't happen to us" mentality. Thus, management thinks their organization is invulnerable and crises happen only to other companies.

The third item, structural impediments, prevents management from acting on warnings because there are structural imperfections within the organization. Unlike risk denial, where the warnings are acknowledged but not considered important, structural impediments hinder warnings from being addressed, even when management believes they are legitimate warnings. Choo (2008) cites the example of a 5-year-old boy who was admitted to a hospital for elective neurosurgery. Despite the surgery going well, the boy developed complications and seizures. Unfortunately, there was a structural impediment in this case: there was no main physician in charge of the boy's care. The patient care was set up with a research physician, a neurological resident, a neurosurgeon, and an attending physician at the hospital, but nobody had ownership of the case (Snook & Connor, 2005). Eventually, the boy's condition worsened to the point where he stopped breathing. In this example, everyone agreed that the warnings were serious, but the structure of the situation meant that nobody was really in charge: a prescription for a crisis.

SEE ALSO The Checklist MANIFESTO

The Problem of Sustainability and Environmental Damage by Organizations

Two separate but related issues make up this trend. Sustainability seeks economic growth while ensuring natural resources are available for the next generation of users (Stead & Stead, 2004). Sustainability is a trend that is to be encouraged in the business environment. On the other hand, environmental damage due to an accident or deliberate exploitation is not to be encouraged. While this may appear obvious, the reality of how many companies operate, particularly in developing countries, seems to contradict what should be clear: do not destroy the environment needlessly.

Companies that cause damage to the environment will encounter a public relations nightmare. The *Exxon Valdez* oil disaster illustrates this classic point vividly. In 1989, the *Exxon Valdez* tanker hit a reef in Alaska's Prince William Sound, spilling approximately 10.5 million gallons of oil. Although there was no loss of human life, the loss of animal and bird life was extensive, and the negative press was daunting. The company's untested crisis management plan made the assumption that a spill could be contained in 5 hours. Unfortunately, due to bureaucratic and weather delays, efforts to contain the spill were not implemented for 2 days (Hartley, 1993). The onslaught of media coverage was brutal, putting Exxon in a negative light throughout the world. Some may think that environmental crises occur in large manufacturing companies or those that process oil. Service industries, which typically are not perceived to be as prone to environmental crises, are also under scrutiny. Fast food giant McDonald's found itself in the middle of an environmental quagmire in the early 1990s. The problem was that excessive packaging of menu items was bulky and a potential landfill problem. Fortunately, the company met voluntarily with members of the Environmental Defense Fund (EDF) over a period of a year to discuss what could be done (Sethi & Steidlmeier, 1997). The result was a major revamping of packaging practices that not only reduced the Styrofoam used, but also placed McDonald's in a favorable light among environmentalists. What could have been a potential public relations crisis was instead handled proactively by the company, with a cost savings to the firm as an added benefit (Sethi & Steidlmeier, 1997).

On a more positive note, sustainable development has been a popular buzzword within business and government entities since the early 1990s. Proceeding with economic growth while maintaining the integrity and resources of the environment is necessary for the well-being of local societies at the micro level and humankind in general at the macro level. Two scenarios exist involving crises and sustainable development (Crandall & Mensah, 2008). First, a sudden environmental crisis can impair the sustainability of certain resources in the long term. For example, a crisis event such as an oil spill can negatively influence the long-term survivability of the seafood industry in the affected area. This is an example of an event that is both sudden and unexpected. In the second scenario, the events occur slowly in a more organized fashion. For example, the steady growth of a firm (and on a larger scale, a society) can gradually deplete renewable resources faster than they are being replenished. It is these slower types of economic growth that are of special importance in sustainability. Water, air, and land are noticeable resources that have been used negatively—depleted or contaminated—by various businesses, industries, and even societies.

Sustainable development will become even more newsworthy in the future as continued attention is focused on the depletion of renewable resources. Companies and even countries that are perceived to be detractors to sustainable development will find themselves viewed in a negative light, which can lead to an array of public relations crises. One country in particular that has seen its share of negative press is the People's Republic of China, where two concerns have been repeatedly voiced concerning environmental practices. First, its pollution is crossing its borders into Japan, Korea, and Taiwan in the form of acid rain. Second, China's inability to enforce basic environmental regulations has resulted in lower production costs for Chinese manufacturers when compared to competitors in other countries. The result is that it puts millions of people out of work and depresses wages in other countries (Navarro, 2007).

Concern for the environment remains a strong priority in the crisis management landscape. Companies must not only work to prevent environmental damage, but they should also portray to the public their efforts to be champions of sustainable development. Even today, McDonald's provides leaflets in their restaurants (on recycled paper) that outline what they are doing to use environmental resources wisely. In addition, municipalities, states, and entire countries will need to do their share to protect the environment and ensure resources are available for those in the future. Indeed, the cost of needlessly damaging the environment while not promoting sustainability will create a twofold crisis. In the short run, a public relations crisis will result in which external stakeholders will view the offending entity negatively. In the long run, there is a deeper problem: damage to the environment and the cavalier attitude that resources exist only for the whims and consumption of the current generation.

The Trend Toward Globalization and Outsourcing

Globalization refers to the development of economic interdependence among nations. Its existence is undeniable, although debates abound concerning the extent to which its effects are positive or negative. Globalization has created an environment in which crisis events are more likely to occur.

The past 2 decades in India and China illustrate the fact that increased globalization and global outsourcing result in a more complex business environment and can create opportunities for crisis events in organizations. As Western firms rely more heavily on their Asian counterparts, for example, they can be directly affected by political or cultural unrest abroad. In addition, a number of American firms—including retail giant Wal-Mart—have been fighting crisis events of their own, such as negative publicity and boycotts resulting from their ties to countries where "cheap labor" is more prevalent. Wal-Mart critic Arindrajit Dube suggests that Wal-Mart's relatively low wages emanating from its promotion of outsourcing result in an annual wage loss in the retail sector of almost $5 billion. Hollywood's Robert Greenwald even produced a movie about the giant retailer—*WAL-MART: The High Cost of Low Price*—chronicling the plight of an Ohio-based hardware store when Wal-Mart moved to town (York, 2005). The net effect of this sentiment against Wal-Mart is unclear, and not all press has been negative. As Jason Furman of New York University notes, Wal-Mart's economic benefits cannot be ignored, as the retailer saves its customers an estimated $200 billion or more on food and other items every year (Mallaby, 2005).

There is also evidence to suggest that globalization may contribute to organizational and even domestic industry crises in the long term. The growing Chinese automotive market will inevitably lead to crises and upheaval in the U.S. auto industry, and perhaps in those in Britain, Germany, and Japan as well. The concern is the availability of low-cost labor in China coupled with the growing demand for motor vehicles in that country. Leading global automakers have ventured into China and entered into partnerships with one or more Chinese automakers. The Chinese counterparts benefit from the experienced automakers' knowledge, while the automakers can take advantage of the lowered labor costs. But outside of China, labor unrest, particularly from unions, questions the long-term benefits these relationships can bring. For U.S. automakers, the prognosis is not good. Declining sales and union dissatisfaction are setting the stage for a major change in how the industry will look in the years to come.

As the opening vignette illustrates, large, well-known companies may be at a unique risk for a publicity crisis when they expand globally. In the case of P&G and its SK-II cosmetic line, some have suggested that this particular crisis might stem from deep-seated animosity between China and Japan. There is a contingent of Chinese consumers who are hesitant to purchase P&G products because the firm employs Taiwanese model Lin Zhiling as the SK-II brand spokesperson. Zhiling's father once campaigned for Chen Shuibian in his bid to become Taiwan's president. Because Shuibian is an ardent supporter of independence for the province, many Mainland Chinese consumers have linked P&G to the Taiwanese independence movement through its affiliation with Zhiling (Crandall et al., 2007). P&G officials, however, have stated that it holds no political position on the matter. Nonetheless, in August 2005 a group of "netizens" (i.e., citizens utilizing the Internet) sought to secure 400,000 signatures on a petition opposing Lin Zhiling and P&G products. This group has committed to a boycott of all P&G products as well as those produced by manufacturing facilities her father owns in China ("Chinese Fanatics Urge Boycott," 2005).

Both Pepsi and Coca-Cola found themselves in the midst of an international crisis in India. In 2003, The New Delhi Center for Science and Environment published a report asserting that local samples of Pepsi and Coke products contained pesticide residues at 30 times the acceptable limits in Europe. India's parliament stopped serving the beverages, and Indian nationalist activists in Allahabad smashed bottles and vandalized the property of a Coke distributor. Daily sales dropped by about one third in less than 2 weeks, further curtailing efforts by the soft drink giants to spawn consumption of a product in a country where the average resident consumes less than one soft drink per month. The soft drink giants responded by questioning the methodology and credentials of the group's laboratory (Slater, 2003).

Outsourcing

A business phenomenon associated with globalization that has become popular during the past 2 decades is *global outsourcing*. This term refers to contracting out a firm's non-core, non-revenue–producing activities to organizations in other nations primarily to reduce costs. Many consumers and activists have become increasingly disturbed about job losses that occur when a firm moves a production facility abroad or a retailer stocks its shelves with imported products (Ansberry & Aeppel, 2003). A number of American firms have closed production facilities in the United States and opened new ones in Mexico, China, India, and other countries where labor costs are substantially lower (Dean, 2004; Luhnow, 2004; Millman, 2004; Morse, 2004). In 2003, China and Mexico accounted for almost one quarter of imported apparel in the United States, followed by Honduras, Bangladesh, and El Salvador. Analysts also suggest that differences in wages could spark increased global outsourcing in a broad array of professional and technical fields, such as architecture, medical transcribing, and accounting (Buckman, 2004; Maher, 2004). These changes suggest that a greater prevalence of crisis events may proliferate throughout the world.

Global outsourcing can increase the likelihood of crisis events in an organization for two key reasons. First, when an organization chooses to allow business functions to be completed by other organizations, it inevitably loses some control over these functions. In addition, when outsourcing involves partner firms across borders, the organization must contend with the political, legal, and other international influences associated with its partners. Union Carbide's Bhopal, India disaster was one of the first crisis events to illustrate what can happen when partners in other countries do not maintain the same standards as the home company. In 1984, gas leaked from a methyl isocyanate (MIC) tank at a Union Carbide plant in Bhopal, initially killing more than 2,500 people and injuring another 300,000. The plant was jointly owned and operated by parties in India and in the United States (49.1% was owned by the Indian stakeholders, the rest by Union Carbide in the U.S.). Inadequate safety practices, equipment failures, and careless operating procedures contributed to the disaster, which was caused when water accidentally entered Tank 610, which held the deadly gas (Hartley, 1993).

Herein lies the heart of the dilemma—outsourcing relinquishes control of the production of a product or the providing of a service. That in itself is not necessarily a bad thing—in fact, it is a good thing beneficial when the outsourcer has expertise in the field and is better equipped to perform a particular task. But one of the dilemmas of any outsourcing relationship is the potential gap between the expected quality and the quality that is actually provided. When cultural differences between partners create different expectations of quality, this gap becomes problematic. Clarifying specifications in purchasing contracts can reduce, but not always eliminate, this problem of quality. There are other issues that may not be covered in an outsourcing relationship, such as how well the outsourced facility is maintained in terms of cleanliness and equipment functioning abilities. In other words, purchasing contracts usually look at the final product, but not necessarily the functional capabilities of the plant that produces those products.

The accident at Bhopal remains the poster child for how a push for globalization and outsourcing can lead to a devastating crisis. Safety standards were not being met in the manufacturing of the deadly MIC gas. Control of these standards and equipment maintenance at the plant were in the hands of the Indian owners, under an elaborate arrangement called Union Carbide (India) Limited (Sethi & Steidlmeier, 1997). One might liken this situation to giving a toddler a loaded gun. As business ethicist Robert Hartley (1993) states: "A laissez-faire decentralization is not appropriate in underdeveloped countries when safety and environmental degradation are at stake" (p. 156).

A second reason why globalization can lead to crises lies in the social opposition to outsourcing, which can harm public sentiment and weaken customer loyalty for firms directly or indirectly involved. Retailing icon Wal-Mart is often the brunt of criticism from politicians, activists, and union leaders. Detractors, for example, contend that Wal-Mart's aggressive negotiating tactics ultimately decimate American manufacturers and send American jobs overseas (Fishman, 2006). Some critics charge that the mega-retailer seeks to destroy small businesses in the communities in which it operates (Edid, 2005; Quinn, 2000). Others, however, cite positive influences, noting such factors as job creation and the benefits of low prices (Etter, 2005; York, 2005).

Outsourcing has led to a substantial number of U.S. jobs going overseas. Consider the case of India. General Electric's (GE) Jack Welch was instrumental in one of the earliest partnerships with the populous Asian nation. Welch first met with the Indian government in 1989, and GE formed a joint venture to develop and market medical equipment with Wipro Ltd. in 1990. By the mid-1990s, much of GE's software development and maintenance activities had been shifted to Indian companies. GE Capital Services (GECIS) established the first international call center in India in 1999. GE sold 60% of GECIS for $500 million in 2004, freeing it to compete against IBM, Accenture, and Indian firms. In 2005, India received more than $17 billion from foreign corporations seeking to outsource a variety of jobs (Solomon & Kranhold, 2005). The outsourcing of legal jobs from the United States—especially to India—has also risen in recent years and was expected to hit 30,000 jobs abroad by 2008. The argument for such outsourcing is simple—reduced operational costs. According to one analyst, the cost of developing a particular legal database for contracts might be about $60,000 in the United States, but only about $5,000 in India (Bellman & Koppel, 2005).

The outsourcing debate illustrates how strategic decision making can later lead to an organizational crisis. On one hand, the pressure to lower costs is overwhelming. Global competition has forced many businesses to look for ways to cut costs, and global outsourcing is one such option. But there is a dark side to this decision that can backfire on the organization—negative publicity. Entire books have been written on the subject and emotions often run high since outsourcing does lead to a loss of jobs, at least in the short run. Television commentator Lou Dobbs has charged that corporate greed is behind the job losses since it is the company that purposely chooses to outsource jobs overseas (Dobbs, 2004). While it is convenient and simplistic to invoke the "corporate greed" argument, ultimately the reality of why jobs are lost is typically more complex. In the long run, companies must acknowledge that consumer demand is what generates revenues, and consumers want low prices. While it may sound noble and patriotic to retain jobs in a certain country (the U.S., for example), the reality is that the jobs will not exist if the company cannot survive in the long run. To survive in the long run, cost cutting must occur because consumers demand low prices; this results in strategic decisions in favor of global outsourcing. The reality then, is that whether we like it or not, global outsourcing is a trend that is utilized to ensure long-term company survival.

The effects of outsourcing have been mixed. When implemented properly, outsourcing can cut costs, improve performance, and refocus the business back to its core functions. Many outsourcing efforts fail, however, due to unforeseen hidden costs, loss of control of the outsourced activity, or simply outsourcing activities that should not be outsourced (Barthelemy, 2003). For example, Cincinnati's Standard Textile experienced a number of problems when it opened its first factory in northern China in 2005. The heating did not work for 2 weeks, causing more than an inconvenience for workers whose jobs were to separate thousands of fine cotton threads. Custom-made parts ordered from Chinese suppliers did not meet specifications and, initially, Chinese authorities hiked electricity charges for the plant by 18% (Fong, 2005).

The outsourcing debate is complex and can intensify when companies outsource business activities that are politically sensitive or involve safety concerns. In 2005, for example, JetBlue flew a number of its Airbus A320 jets to El Salvador for maintenance. In the same year, about half of U.S. carrier heavy-overhaul work was performed outside of the United States (Carey & Frangos, 2005). As emerging nations develop, however, their firms may find it useful to outsource certain activities to more developed nations. In 2004, for example, Indian telephone giant Bharti Tele-Ventures outsourced hundreds of millions of dollars of work to Western firms. Most of Bharti's information technology services, including billing and internal e-mail systems, were contracted to IBM (Buckman, 2005).

Some firms have attempted to avoid the publicity crises associated with the outsourcing controversy. In the auto industry, Chrysler, Ford, and General Motors are under some restrictions in their efforts to outsource globally due to union contracts. As a result, the automakers have responded by putting pressure on their suppliers to outsource (Shirouzu, 2004). In addition, a number of firms have become more sensitive to the public disapproval that outsourcing can bring to their companies. An interesting case occurred in 2004, when e-Loan announced that customers would be given a choice to have their loan applications processed in Delhi, India, or Dallas, Texas. Although Dallas was considered the more patriotic choice for American consumers, it would also take 2 days longer than selecting the Delhi option (Drucker & Brown, 2004). Hence, the outsourcing debate remains a key consideration for consumers and organizations alike, and its potential for creating publicity-oriented crises should not be underestimated.

Summary

This chapter examined six major trends in the crisis management landscape, each of which contributes to the proliferation of crisis events that organizations must face. Within each trend is a tradeoff between strategic control and influence from the external environment. Management has the most strategic influence in its decisions to move toward globalization and outsourcing. The least amount of control can be seen in addressing weather and natural disaster–related crises. Understanding these trends is useful as we look at where crises events originate, the topic of the next chapter.

Questions for Discussion

1. What types of crises have weather events caused in the area where you live in? How well did local government officials respond to these events?

2. This chapter discussed a phenomenon called "multiple disasters." What are some examples of this type of crisis?

3. How far should companies go in preparing for acts of terrorism?

4. How has the rise of the Internet influenced crisis management over the past decade?

5. What types of human-induced crises have occurred where you work?

6. What environmental damage is being caused by corporations today?

7. What is sustainable development? What is its association with crisis events?

8. How has globalization contributed to the increase of crisis events?

9. How has global outsourcing influenced crisis management?

Chapter Exercise

Organizations rely more heavily on the Internet today than ever before. For some, the Internet is the most prominent means of communicating, obtaining information, and even transacting business. Form a team of three to five students and select a well-known "e-tailer" such as Amazon.com, Lands' End, or eBay. Visit the firm's Web site. What would happen if the organization you selected encountered a server crash that halted all of their Internet traffic for 24 hours? What actions would your team recommend to prepare the organization for such a crisis?

MINI CASE

THE BLACKBERRY OUTAGE

Research In Motion (RIM) designs, manufactures, and markets wireless solutions for the worldwide mobile communications market. The BlackBerry is RIM's most famous product. The Blackberry provides handheld, wireless access to e-mail and the Web, as well as telephone capabilities and an organizer function. There are about 8 million BlackBerry subscribers worldwide. In the United States, RIM's BlackBerry is a leader in the more than $15 billion mobile data service market. BlackBerry users purchase the product and pay access fees for one simple reason, to stay connected whenever they want and wherever they go.

BlackBerry connectivity was compromised in 2007, however. On Tuesday, April 17, e-mail service for North American and overseas roaming customers was disabled from shortly after 8 p.m. through the following morning. During this time, users were unable to check or send e-mail.

News of the outage traveled rapidly, especially through the financial community. Following the outage, RIM stock dropped about 2% on premarket trading. Early Wednesday some customers were calling for financial compensation similar to what online auctioneer eBay had paid when it faced extensive service outages in 1999. Interestingly, investors shrugged off the outage and RIM's stock closing price actually rose by 2.4% by the end of the day.

RIM's first definitive statement on the situation came on Thursday, April 19, when company officials blamed the problem on a noncritical software upgrade that had not been properly tested. RIM cofounder Mike Lazaridis later identified the cause of the outage as internal, citing the fact that RIM had endured 2 years of hypergrowth without experiencing an outage. By April 19, then, the crisis was under control.

In the end, RIM emerged relatively unscathed for three reasons. First, the outage was the first in 2 years. BlackBerry users seemed willing to accept an occasional brief outage as long as problems were not frequent. In effect, the 2 years of service without an outage could be categorized as consumer goodwill. Simply stated, RIM had won the loyalty of its customer base.

(Continued)

(Continued)

Second, the problem was resolved promptly and without any loss of data. When e-mail service is halted for any period of time, a tremendous amount of e-mail can accumulate in the system. Restoring complete service to all users simultaneously could have created a more serious problem. Instead, access was restored in an orderly fashion that ended the crisis without additional problems.

Finally, although one might consider RIM's initial response to have been delayed, it was professional and accurate. There was no reason for current and prospective customers to be concerned that the RIM staff was not highly trained and professional or that future outages might follow.

Sources

Branscombe, M. (2007, June 14). Q&A: RIM co-founder Mike Lazaridis. Retrieved October 28, 2008, from www.itpro.co.uk/features/115382/qa-rim-cofounder-mike-lazaridis.html

Lipton, J. (2007, April 18). Little outrage over BlackBerry outage [Electronic version]. *Forbes.com.*

Vascellaro, J. E., & Sharma, A. (2007, April 20). BlackBerry users stew in wake of outage. *Wall Street Journal,* p. B4.

References

Adamy, J. (2005, October 3). The aisles of optimism. *Wall Street Journal,* pp. B1, B6.

Ansberry, C., & Aeppel, T. (2003, October 6). Surviving the onslaught. *Wall Street Journal,* pp. B1, B6.

Barthelemy, J. (2003). The seven deadly sins of outsourcing. *Academy of Management Executive, 17*(2), 87–98.

Barton, L. (2001). *Crisis in organizations II.* Cincinnati, OH: South-Western.

Bellman, E., & Koppel, N. (2005, September 28). More U.S. legal work moves to India's low-cost lawyers. *Wall Street Journal,* pp. B1, B2.

Bernstein, J. (2006). Who are those bloggers and why are they saying those terrible things? *Associations Now, 2*(11), 58–61.

Branscombe, M. (2007, June 14). Q&A: RIM co-founder Mike Lazaridis. Retrieved June 15, 2007, from http://www.itpro.co.uk/features/115382/qa-rim-cofounder-mike-lazaridis.html

Buckman, R. (2004, March 22). Apparel's loose thread. *Wall Street Journal,* pp. B1, B8.

Buckman, R. (2005, January 18). Outsourcing with a twist. *Wall Street Journal,* pp. B1, B4.

Carey, S., & Frangos, A. (2005, January 21). Airlines facing cost pressure, outsource crucial safety tasks. *Wall Street Journal,* pp. A1, A5.

Carroll, A., & Buchholtz, A. (2003). *Business & society: Ethics and stakeholder management* (5th ed.). Cincinnati, OH: Thompson South-Western.

Chinese fanatics urge boycott over Lin's green parents. (2005). *Taipei Times.* Retrieved October 28, 2008, from http://www.taipeitimes.com/News/front/archives/2005/08/11/2003267233

Choo, C. (2008). Organizational disasters: Why they happen and how they may be prevented. *Management Decision, 46*(1), 32–45.

Conlin, M. (2007, April 16). Web attack. *Business Week,* pp. 54–56.

Consumers angry as SK-II pulled from shelves. (2006). *China Daily.* Retrieved September 28, 2006, from http://www.chinadaily.com.cn/china/2006-09/23/content_695363.htm

Crandall, W. R., & Mensah, E. C. (2008). Crisis management and sustainable development: A framework and proposed research agenda. *International Journal of Sustainable Strategic Management, 1*(1), 16–34.

Crandall, W. R., Parnell, J. A., Xihui, P., & Long, Z. (2007). When crisis management goes abroad: The demise of SK-II in China. *Journal of International Business Research and Practice, 1*(1), 38–49.

Davis, M. (2001). *Late Victorian holocausts: El Nino famines and making of the third world.* London: Verso.

Dean, J. (2004, February 17). Long a low-tech power, China sets its sight on chip making. *Wall Street Journal,* pp. A1, A16.

Diefendorff, J., & Mehta, K. (2007). The relations of motivational traits with workplace deviance. *Journal of Applied Psychology, 92*(4), 967–977.

Dobbs, L. (2004). *Exporting America: Why corporate greed is shipping American jobs overseas.* New York: Time Warner.

Drucker, J., & Brown, K. (2004, March 9). Latest wrinkle in jobs fight: Letting customers choose where their work is done. *Wall Street Journal,* pp. B1, B3.

Edid, M. (2005). *The good, the bad, and Wal-Mart.* Ithaca, NY: Cornell University Institute of Workplace Studies.

Etter, L. (2005, December 3–4). Gauging the Wal-Mart effect. *Wall Street Journal,* p. A9.

Fishman, C. (2006). *The Wal-Mart effect: How the world's most powerful company really works—and how it's transforming the American economy.* New York: Penguin.

Fong, M. (2005, April 11). Woven in China. *Wall Street Journal,* pp. B1, B4.

Green, W., III. (2004, Fall). The future of disasters: Interesting trends for interesting times. *Futures Research Quarterly,* pp. 59–68.

Greenberg, D., Clair, J., & Maclean, T. (2002). Teaching through traumatic events: Uncovering the choices of management educators as they respond to September 11th. *Academy of Management Learning & Education Journal, 1*(1), 38–54.

Greenberg, J. (2002). September 11, 2002: A CEO's story. *Harvard Business Review, 80*(10), 58–64.

Griffin, R., & Lopez, Y. (2005). "Bad behavior" in organizations: A review and typology for future research. *Journal of Management, 31*(6), 988–1005.

Guan, X. (2006, September 18). Refunds offered on harmful cosmetics. Retrieved September 28, 2006, from the *China Daily* Web site: http://www.chinadaily.com.cn/china/2006-09/18/content_691155.htm

Hartley, R. (1993). *Business ethics: Violations of the public trust.* New York: John Wiley.

Hasely, K. (2004, November 22–29). Twenty years after Bhopal: What you need to know about managing today's crises. *Chemical Market Reporter,* pp. 21–22.

Hopkins, A. (2001). Was Three Mile Island a "normal accident"? *Journal of Contingencies and Crisis Management, 9*(2), 65–72.

Institute for Crisis Management. (2008). *Annual ICM crisis report: News coverage of business crises during 2007.* Retrieved October 28, 2008, from http://www.crisisexperts.com/2007CR.pdf

Janis, I. (1982). *Groupthink: Psychological studies of policy decisions and fiascoes.* Boston: Houghton Mifflin.

Kovoor-Misra, S., & Misra, M. (2007). Understanding and managing crises in an "online world." In C. Pearson, C. Roux-Dufort, & J. Clair (Eds.), *International handbook of organizational crisis management* (pp. 85–103). Thousand Oaks, CA: Sage.

Lipton, J. (2007, April 18). Little outrage over BlackBerry outage [Electronic version]. *Forbes.com.*

Liu, W. (2005, June 29). P&G again faces false ad claims. Retrieved September 28, 2006, from http://www.chinadaily.com.cn/english/doc/2005-06/29/content_455372.htm

Luhnow, D. (2004, March 5). As jobs move East, plants in Mexico retool to compete. *Wall Street Journal,* pp. A1, A8.

Maher, K. (2004, March 23). Next on the outsourcing list. *Wall Street Journal,* pp. B1, B8.

Mallaby, S. (2005, November 29). Wal-Mart: A progressive dream company, really. *Fayetteville Observer,* p. 11A.

Miller, A. (2001). The Los Angeles riots: A study in crisis paralysis. *Journal of Contingencies and Crisis Management, 9*(4), 189–199.

Millman, J. (2004, March 3). Blueprint for outsourcing. *Wall Street Journal,* pp. B1, B4.

Mitchell, R. (2008, March 31). Disaster survivors. *Computerworld,* pp. 26–27.

Morse, D. (2004, February 20). In North Carolina, furniture makers try to stay alive. *Wall Street Journal,* pp. A1, A6.

Navarro, P. (2007). *The coming China wars: Where they will be fought, how they can be won.* Upper Saddle River, NJ: Financial Times.

The 9/11 Commission. (2004). *The 9/11 Commission report: Final report of the National Commission on Terrorist Attacks Upon the United States.* Washington, DC: Government Printing Office.

O'Leary-Kelly, A., Griffin, R., & Glew, D. (1996). Organization-motivated aggression: A research framework. *Academy of Management Review, 21*(1), 225–253.

P&G accepts fine for "bogus" advertising. (2005, April 11). *China Daily.* Retrieved September 28, 2006, from http://www.chinadaily.com.cn/english/doc/2005-04/11/content_432925.htm

Parnell, J. (2008). *Strategic management: Theory and practice* (3rd ed.). Cincinnati, OH: Atomic Dog Publishing.

Parnell, J., Crandall, W., & Menefee, M. (1997). Management perceptions of organizational crises: A cross-cultural study of Egyptian managers. *Journal of the Academy of Strategic and Organizational Leadership, 1*(1), 8–19.

Pearson, C., & Mitroff, I. (1993). From crisis prone to crisis prepared: A framework for crisis management. *Academy of Management Executive, 7*(1), 48–59.

Pedahzur, A., Eubank, W., & Weinberg, L. (2002). The war on terrorism and the decline of terrorist group formation: A research note. *Terrorism and Political Violence, 14*(3), 141–147.

Perliger, A., Pedahzur, A., & Zalmanovitch, Y. (2005). The defensive dimension of the battle against terrorism: An analysis of management of terror incidents in Jerusalem. *Journal of Contingencies and Crisis Management, 13*(2), 79–91.

Perrow, C. (1999). *Normal accidents: Living with high risk technologies.* Princeton, NJ: Princeton University Press.

Quinn, B. (2000). *How Wal-Mart is destroying America.* Berkeley, CA: Ten Speed Press.

Robinson, S., & O'Leary-Kelly, A. (1998). Monkey see, monkey do: The influence of work groups on the antisocial behavior of employees. *Academy of Management Journal, 41*(6), 658–672.

Sethi, S., & Steidlmeier, P. (1997). *Up against the wall: Case in business and society* (6th ed.). Upper Saddle River, NJ: Prentice Hall.

Shirouzu, N. (2004, June 10). Big three's outsourcing plan: Make parts suppliers do it. *Wall Street Journal,* pp. A1, A6.

Slater, J. (2003, August 15). Coke, Pepsi fight product-contamination charges in India. *Wall Street Journal,* pp. B1, B4.

Snook, S., & Connor, J. (2005). The price of progress: Structurally induced inaction. In W. H. Starbuck & M. Farjoun (Eds.), *Organization at the limit* (pp. 178–201). Oxford, UK: Blackwell.

Solomon, J., & Kranhold, K. (2005, March 23). In India's outsourcing boom, GE played a starring role. *Wall Street Journal,* pp. A1, A12.

Stead, W. E., & Stead, J. G. (2004). *Sustainable strategic management.* Armonk, NY: ME Sharpe.

Turner, B. (1978). *Man-made disasters.* London: Wykeham.

Vascellaro, J. E., & Sharma, A. (2007, April 20). BlackBerry users stew in wake of outage. *Wall Street Journal,* p. B4.

Xinhua News Agency. (2006, September 21). Japanese cosmetics cause concern in China. Retrieved September 28, 2006, from http://www1.china.org.cn/english/2006/Sep/181859.htm

York, B. (2005, November 23). Panic in a small town. *National Review* (on-line). Retrieved October 28, 2008, from http://commonsensepoliticalthought.com/?p = 85

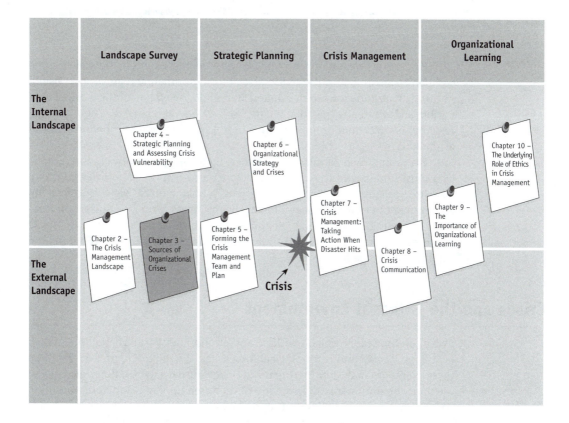

CHAPTER 3

Sources of Organizational Crises

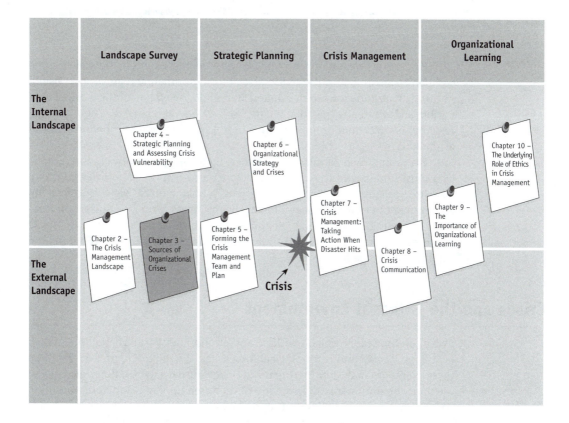

Royal Caribbean

Royal Caribbean is a successful cruise line based in Miami, Florida. It is also an environmentally conscious company, but this was not always the case. In the early 1990s, the cruise line was dumping oil sludge, dry cleaning fluids, and photochemicals into the waters of New York harbor, the Port of Miami, the Caribbean, and the Alaskan Inside Passage (Thorne, Ferrell, & Ferrell, 2003). To hide this dirty deed, ship engineers falsified records and set up pipes that bypassed the onboard pollution control equipment ("Trash Overboard," 1999).

While all of this was happening below the ship, crew members on the decks wore badges with the slogan "Save the Waves," an environmentally motivating gesture. The U.S. Coast Guard saw a different side, though: a 7-mile-long trail of oil in the Atlantic. In addition, court documents revealed that the oil-discharge records on some of the ships were called the "Eventyrbok," Norwegian for "fairy-tale book" ("What the Brochures Don't Tell You," 1998). Amazingly, the company even fought the charges of environmental crime by claiming the United States had no jurisdiction over a Liberian-registered company (Barton, 2001, 2007).

Crisis events emanate from many sources. As this example illustrates, some companies resort to illegal activities to avoid environmental regulations. Despite its arrogant attitude toward the United States and the waters of the world, Royal Caribbean eventually pleaded guilty to 22 federal charges. Their penalty resulted in a $27 million dollar fine and 5 years' corporate probation (Thorne et al., 2003).

Crisis events such as this have sources; they are not merely random events. One must understand these sources before steps can be taken to avoid them. Likewise, practitioners and management scholars often view the external environment in terms of general forces that originate from four areas: political–legal, economic, social, and technological. These four areas are not only consistent in strategic analysis, but also lay the groundwork for examining the external landscape for crises.

Crises and the External Environment

Every organization exists within a complex network of political–legal, economic, social, and technological forces, as depicted in Figure 3.1. Together, these elements make up the organization's external environment, also called the macroenvironment. Shifts in any of these realms can lead to crises.

It is important to distinguish among external environmental shifts—trends that organizations should factor into their strategic activity—and crisis events that are spawned by external factors. Recall that a crisis is an event that has a low probability of occurring, but should it occur, can have a vastly negative impact on the organization. Most would agree that a new law prohibiting the sale of a firm's products would create a substantial disruption and thereby

FIGURE 3.1 Crises and the External Landscape

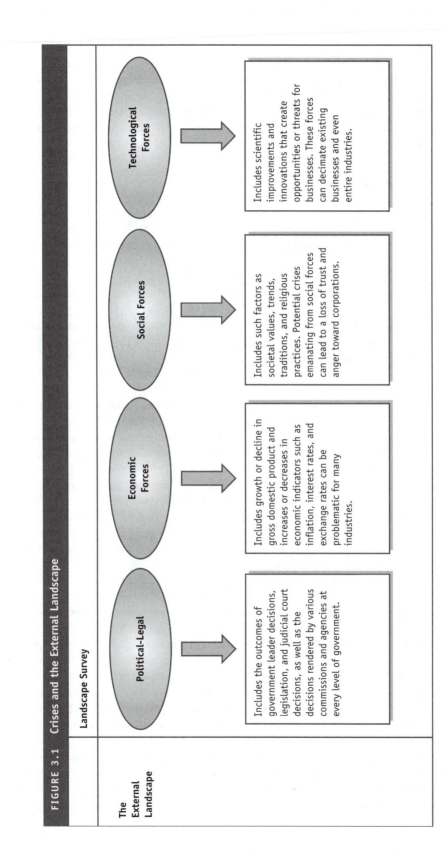

Landscape Survey

The External Landscape

Political-Legal

Includes the outcomes of government leader decisions, legislation, and judicial court decisions, as well as the decisions rendered by various commissions and agencies at every level of government.

Economic Forces

Includes growth or decline in gross domestic product and increases or decreases in economic indicators such as inflation, interest rates, and exchange rates can be problematic for many industries.

Social Forces

Includes such factors as societal values, trends, traditions, and religious practices. Potential crises emanating from social forces can lead to a loss of trust and anger toward corporations.

Technological Forces

Includes scientific improvements and innovations that create opportunities or threats for businesses. These forces can decimate existing businesses and even entire industries.

constitute a crisis. In contrast, a new law requiring that a firm list its ingredients on the package in two languages instead of one would probably not create a substantial disruption and, hence, would not be considered a crisis. While not every external threat faced by an organization should be called a "crisis," many organizations frequently face actual and potential crisis events without recognizing the serious nature of the situation. The examples discussed in the following sections illustrate this reality.

Political–Legal Forces

Political–legal forces include the outcomes of government leader decisions, the impacts of existing and new legislation, and judicial court decisions, as well as the decisions rendered by various commissions and agencies at all levels of government. As with the other forces, political–legal factors sometimes affect different firms in the same industry in different ways.

The terrorist attacks of September 11 were followed by a number of political decisions on the part of the United States that both created crises and opportunities. Following the sharp decline in air travel in the United States, airlines on the verge of bankruptcy campaigned for and received $15 billion in government support in 2002 and an additional $2.9 billion in 2003 (Sevastopulo, 2003). The subsequent war in Iraq created a number of crises for organizations, especially those with tight global ties. For example, during the early part of the military conflict, when Allied forces were marching toward Baghdad, many firms modified their advertising campaigns, fearing that their television promotions might be considered insensitive if aired alongside breaking coverage of the war. This move was intended to avoid a potential public relations crisis. At the same time, other firms viewed the war as an opportunity for revenue growth and began planning for Iraq's future needs in the areas of cell phones, refrigerators, and automobiles. After Saddam Hussein's regime was ousted in mid-2003, American firms began to compete vigorously for lucrative reconstruction contracts. Overall, the war has created crises for some firms while offering opportunities for others (Cummins, 2003; King, 2003; Trachtenberg & Steinberg, 2003).

Organizations are often affected by legislation and other political events specific to their line of business. For example, changing legislation that concerns food safety and health can lead to organizational crises. Consider the appearance of variant Creuztfeldt-Jakob disease (vCJD), or as it is better known as, mad-cow disease. The disease is a rare malady of the brain passed through tainted meat. When it began to show up in the United Kingdom in 1996, most of Europe responded by banning the import of British beef. Firms in the industry were not able to defend themselves effectively, and financial losses were staggering (Higgins, 2001). Although measures were imple- mented to stop the spread of the disease, they seemed to be damaging to those stakeholders in the beef and food-related industries. For example, the economic impact in Canada has been around $10 billion in lost trade and compensation, despite the fact that very little is actually known about the disease (Fortier, 2008). As an example, in 2003, a single cow in northern Alberta was found to have the disease. But what resulted was the widespread closing of the borders, with thousands of cattle slaughtered and sales of Canadian beef falling to crisis levels, from $1.10 per pound to 30 cents (Fortier, 2008). While the disease itself is a crisis, the reaction to it created a secondary crisis.

Most societies have laws and regulations that affect business operations. Table 3.1 summarizes some of the major legislation in the United States over the past century. Most of these laws were created in reaction to an industry or organizational crisis that already existed. It was as if public outcry led to a call for the government to do something about the perceived problem in society (Hartley, 1993). For example, the passage of the Foreign Corrupt Practices Act was in response to the infamous Lockheed bribery case. In this incident, Lockheed paid $12.5 million in bribes and other commissions to secure a sale of $430 million in commercial aircraft to All-Nippon Airways in Japan (Carroll & Buchholtz, 2003). At the time, the president of Lockheed argued that paying bribes was an accepted way of doing business in Japan.

TABLE 3.1 Examples of United States Legislation and the Crises That Led to Its Enactment		
Legislation	*Purpose*	*Crises That Led to Its Enactment*
Occupational Safety and Health Act (1970)	Requires employers to provide a hazard-free working environment	A response to a number of workplace safety issues that had occurred in the previous decades.
Foreign Corrupt Practices Act (1978)	Outlaws direct payoffs and bribes of foreign governments or business officials	A response to the early 1970s Lockheed bribery incident, in which the company paid bribes to secure contracts to sell aircraft to All-Nippon Airways, a Japanese airline.
Oil Pollution Act (1990)	Mandates that oil storage facilities and vessels provide a detailed plan of how they will respond to a large oil spill	A response to the 1989 *Exxon Valdez* oil spill in Prince William Sound, off the coast of Alaska.
Aviation and Transportation Security Act (2001)	Created the Transportation Security Administration to help ensure the safety of the nation's air travel system	A response to the terrorist attacks on the World Trade Center on September 11, 2001.
Sarbanes-Oxley Act (2002)	Makes businesses more accountable by requiring them to adhere to higher standards of financial disclosure	A response to a number of corporate scandals involving inappropriate bookkeeping, including the most famous one, the Enron Corporation.
CAN SPAM Act (2003)	The Controlling the Assault of Non-Solicited Pornography and Marketing Act prescribes regulations for e-mail spammers	A response to the proliferation of unwanted e-mail that has glutted cyberspace.

Even court rulings can spark a crisis. In 2006, a U.S. federal court ruled that cigarette manufacturers cannot use the adjectives "light" or "low tar" to describe their products. This ruling not only required firms to rename some of their products, but it also required them to reposition those products and hope that smokers did not assume that other aspects of the cigarettes had been changed as well. Hence, familiar brands like Altria's Marlboro Lights and Reynolds American's Camel Lights had to be changed to accommodate the ruling (O'Connell, 2006).

The global and cross-cultural nature of regulations can lead to crises. Internet search firms Yahoo! and Google must negotiate Chinese regulations to be successful in that country. The Chinese government attempts to control the use of the Internet to maintain social stability, thereby imposing strict censorship and security laws. This represents a distinct challenge for the search engines, whose purpose is to enable users to access the full spectrum of information available, not just what some governments would prefer users to see (Dean & Delaney, 2005).

Economic Forces

Economic forces can be a source of crises for organizations. Growth or decline in gross domestic product (GDP) and shifts in economic indicators such as inflation, interest rates, and exchange rates can be problematic for many companies. Other factors such as hikes in energy prices and health care costs can also create challenges for firms in many industries. Indeed, such a crisis was faced by automobile manufacturers like Ford and General Motors when gasoline prices spiked in 2008. When predictable, changes in economic forces are usually manageable. When abrupt, however, they can lead to crisis.

Although many shifts in economic forces can create crises that permeate an industry, some firms may be better situated to withstand them than others. When oil prices spiked in 2005, for example, firms in oil-intensive industries such as airlines and carmakers began to experience severe cost pressures (Michaels & Trottman, 2005). These hikes in fuel prices did not have the same effect on all airlines, although specific effects are difficult to determine because of other, simultaneous environmental and competitive changes in the industry. Weak players like Delta seemed to have been hit the hardest, while budget carriers like Southwest and Ryanair experienced mild gains. This advantage occurred because fuel represents a lower percentage of operating costs on short-haul flights such as those championed by budget carriers, and such increases can be spread over more customers when occupancy rates are higher (Michaels & Trottman, 2005).

Fuel economy standards can require that producers develop new vehicles or modify existing ones so that average fuel economy goals are met. This can be a costly venture. When the Bush administration proposed that the smallest trucks reach 28.4 miles per gallon and the largest trucks reach 21.4 miles per gallon by 2011, it estimated that the industry would spend $6.3 billion over 4 years to comply, adding $275 to the price tag of a large truck by 2011 (Meckler & Lundegaard, 2005). Hence, the new regulation—a political–legal force—had the potential to create a crisis for automobile manufacturers.

When oil prices spiked in 2008, however, firms in the automobile industry faced a different kind of crisis, one sparked by an economic factor. Expectations that gasoline prices would remain high over the long term affect demand for automobiles, as consumers shift from sport utility vehicles (SUVs), large cars, and trucks to smaller, more fuel-efficient alternatives. Hence, the cost of complying with the regulations was no longer a consideration because producers were required to radically alter both their research and development and their production priorities to address these new demand patterns. Ford and General Motors acknowledged this reality early in 2008, while start-up firms around the world began the race to develop vehicles that consume less fuel or eschew gasoline altogether (Stewart, 2008; Taylor, 2008). As a result, what began as a potential crisis with political–legal origins was transformed into a more substantial crisis with an economic impetus.

Unfortunately, the automobile industry crisis spilled over into other related industries as well. U.S. automobile parts suppliers were forced to realign their workforces and production schedules to meet the overall decline and the shift toward more fuel-efficient vehicles. In addition, suppliers typically must absorb lower margins when their customers experience a downturn in sales (Bennett, 2008).

With health care costs increasing an average of 15% annually in the United States, controlling them has been a major concern for many American firms in a variety of industries. The fact that the health care problem in the United States is frequently referred to as a "crisis" attests to the degree to which firms are affected. Union Pacific, for example, has stopped hiring smokers in states where it is legal to do so. Publisher Gannett began adding $50 to monthly health care premiums of smokers who do not participate in a smoking cessation program. Health care costs at General Motors (GM) approached $6 billion in 2005, prompting the giant automaker to consider asking its hourly employees to pay more of their own expenses, a move that always meets stiff resistance when union contract negotiations begin. Like many other firms, GM has broadened its efforts to encourage healthy living by discouraging unhealthy habits and adding fitness centers at some of its production facilities (Hawkins, 2005).

The problem that many companies face is how to offer health care benefits while simultaneously containing health-related costs. Sometimes, just suggesting a solution can be controversial, particularly for large firms like Wal-Mart. This issue created a public relations crisis in late 2005 when a draft of an internal Wal-Mart memo proposed to the Board that the retailer cut costs by discouraging "unhealthy" people from applying for jobs. The memo proposed adding physical activity to all jobs—such as requiring cashiers to collect shopping carts—so that those not able to perform the tasks would be less likely to apply. The problem with this approach is that it is not legal. Andrew Stern, president of the Service Employees International Union, summed it up well: "When you add physical requirements to jobs that don't need them, you begin to weed out a whole pool of people such as the elderly, the obese, people with preexisting medical conditions. I think this memo steps over the line of what's legal" (Zimmerman, Matthews, & Hudson, 2005).

Current human resource law, particularly the Americans With Disabilities Act, seems to support this assertion, since job descriptions, required by most employers, must list the essential functions needed to perform the particular job in question. What made the internal memo all the more noticeable was the fact that it was from Wal-Mart, which by its size and prominence makes it a lightning rod for criticism (Wojcik, 2005). Nonetheless, these examples of attempts to contain health care costs illustrate how the distinction between a crisis and a strategic challenge can be blurred, a point mentioned in Chapter 1.

Sometimes a disaster can trigger an economic force that creates a two-stage crisis. Hurricane Katrina in 2005 was such an event. After the onslaught of the storm on the Gulf Coast region of the United States, damage to the already constrained oil-producing facilities knocked out 20% of their production capacity (Birger, 2005). The result was the second prong of the crisis, a rise in retail gas prices. Another two-stage crisis occurred with the *Exxon Valdez* oil spill in 1989. Although this disaster is remembered more for its environmental impact, the greatest economic impact was on the area's seafood industry (Gold & Bravin, 2008; Hartley, 1993). Wars can have similar effects, often devastating a local economy during the ordeal.

This discussion of economic forces should also include a reference to the banking crisis that emerged in mid-2008. This crisis resulted in the collapse of a number of financial institutions, including Lehman Brothers. Banks such as Washington Mutual and Wachovia were distressed and acquired by healthier banks. Declines in the U.S. stock market sent shock waves throughout the world (Schwarzman, 2008). From a crisis management perspective, this series of events is especially noteworthy for two reasons. First, it is important to understand what caused the crisis and to learn from it. A number of contributing factors have been suggested, including unworkable government policy, poor oversight of Fannie Mae and Freddie Mac, ethical shortcomings among some bank executives, and poor management of personal finances. At the organizational level, firms must take steps to lower their vulnerabilities to similar crises that may occur in the future. Minimizing their reliance on the business and consumer credit markets, for example, is one way firms can palliate the effects of future banking crises.

Second, when a financial crisis strikes, firms must be ready to take swift and responsible action to avoid becoming a casualty. Should employees be laid off to reduce costs? Should production lines be scaled back? Many retailers announced plans to reduce their inventories and limit new hiring prior to the 2008 holiday season. U.S. carmakers scrambled to restructure as demand for autos waned and the availability of consumer credit became uncertain. These incidences represent difficult decisions in uncertain times because each firm seeks to survive in the event of a prolonged recession, but thrive if the economy rebounds more quickly. Top managers must consider financial, political, economic, and social trends when charting a response. This text provides the framework for thinking about severe crises such as these, including prevention, response, and organizational learning.

Social Forces

Social forces can trigger a number of crises. Social forces include such factors as societal values, trends, traditions, and religious practices. Societal values are beliefs that citizens tend to hold in high esteem. In the United States, major values include individual freedom, fairness, free markets, concern for the environment, embracing diversity, and equality of opportunity. Potential crises emanating from social forces can lead to a loss of trust and anger toward corporations, and to various forms of social disapproval including boycotts, negative Web sites, and bad publicity. Interestingly, when negative publicity results, rumors may circulate, thus increasing the intensity of the crisis. Procter & Gamble discovered this when a rumor circulated in the early 1980s that its company logo was a satanic symbol and its CEO was a devil worshipper, a claim the CEO allegedly made on the Merv Griffin television show (Cato, 1982). What followed was the distribution of literature urging consumers to boycott Procter & Gamble. Although the rumor was unfounded, the company expended legal resources in efforts to stop those who were spreading the literature, mostly in the form of photocopied flyers. Interestingly enough, devil rumors seem to surface from time to time. In the early 1990s, another such rumor surfaced, this time claiming that the popular toys, Cabbage Patch Dolls, were actually possessed by the devil (Steele, Smith, & McBroom, 1999).

One of the more visible social trends in the United States is the movement away from racial discrimination, including efforts by companies to provide equal access to all customers, regardless of race. The Denny's discrimination case is an example of how an incident of racism on the part of a large company can result in a strong public backlash. The incident began in 1993 when a waitress at an Annapolis, Maryland, restaurant purportedly refused to serve six African American Secret Service agents (Chin et al., 1993). The result was a major media frenzy that eventually became a key story on the *CBS Evening News*.

The appearance of racism, even if not intended, can result in serious public scrutiny. Cracker Barrel, the family-oriented restaurant chain based in Lebanon, Tennessee, found itself in a crisis when Rose Rock, mother of comedian Chris Rock, visited the Murrells Inlet Cracker Barrel (near Myrtle Beach, South Carolina) on May 16, 2006. Ms. Rock and her daughter waited for 30 minutes without service while white customers were served (Fuller, 2006). The incident eventually led to a news conference, held in the parking lot of the restaurant, which included Al Sharpton and officials from the restaurant's headquarters. The official statement made by Cracker Barrel was that the incident was a service issue, not a racial issue. Apparently, Rock and her daughter had been seated but not assigned a server (Fuller, 2006).

Social forces can result in a crisis for firms in one industry and an opportunity for those in another. For example, the health and fitness trend that emerged in the 1990s has spawned growth in a number of industries including fitness equipment, sport drinks, and low-fat foods. However, this same trend has hurt a number of businesses in less health-friendly industries such as tobacco, alcohol, and fast food. The fast food industry, and particularly McDonald's, has been the target of much criticism concerning the health qualities of their menu offerings (Copeland, 2005). High fat content and large servings are common in this industry.

Sometimes social factors appear to be in conflict with each other. During the past several years, many fast food restaurants have been "supersizing" their meal combinations by adding extra fries and larger drinks, while at the same time expanding alternatives for items such as grilled chicken sandwiches and salads (Ellison & Steinberg, 2003). In 2004, Coca-Cola and PepsiCo began to emphasize smaller cans and bottles (McKay, 2004), while McDonald's introduced low-carb menu items (Leung, 2004). Sometimes a company will appear to buck the social trend and offer products that seem counter to society's higher-road wishes. With the introduction and reported success of products like Hardee's Monster Thickburger with 107 fat grams and 1,418 calories, the extent to which many American consumers consider health factors when purchasing fast food is not always clear (Gray, 2005). In this instance, what one firm considers to be a potential crisis might be seen as a business opportunity by another.

The beer industry has been in a public relations crisis of sorts for several decades, as it is constantly hounded by charges of contributing to poor health, alcoholism, and drunk driving. Coors Brewing Company experienced an ironic crisis in the summer of 2006 when Vice Chairman Pete Coors was arrested for drunken driving (Cardona, 2006). Recognizing the controversial nature of the industry, many beer companies now promote responsible drinking in their advertisements. Some have even advocated the health benefits of beer. In late 2005, Anheuser-Busch teamed up with noted Harvard epidemiologist Meir Stampfer to tout the potential medical benefits of beer consumption. Stampfer cites a number of studies suggesting that moderate consumption of alcohol may reduce the risk of heart attack, diabetes, and other ailments (Hellier & Ellison, 2005).

A major social force in many parts of the world is the heightened concern for the environment. Although many stakeholders agree that the problem needs to be addressed, there is much disagreement on how to solve it. An issue that seems to draw the most attention is the problem (or perceived problem, depending on your viewpoint) of global warming. Some scientists argue that burning fossil fuels such as gasoline, natural gas, oil, and coal increases the amount of carbon dioxide and methane in the atmosphere, which in turn leads to the warming of the atmosphere (Thorne et al., 2003). The long-term result is that the polar ice caps will melt, causing flooding of some populated areas of the world. Another concern is that weather patterns may be altered. In the future crisis management landscape, public policy will be increasingly focused on this environmental issue. Policymakers and corporate executives who fail to address this problem will find themselves the subjects of continuous public relations crises.

Technological Forces

Technological forces include scientific improvements and innovations that create both opportunities and threats for businesses. The rate of technological change varies considerably from one industry to another and can affect a firm's operations as well as its products and services. Firms have used advances in technology such as computers, satellites, and fiber optics to perform their traditional tasks at lower costs and higher levels of customer satisfaction.

Technological forces not only create opportunities for firms, but they can also be a source of crises. These forces can decimate existing businesses and even entire industries by shifting demand from one product to another. Examples of such changes include the shifts from vacuum tubes to transistors, from steam locomotives to diesel and electric engines, from fountain pens to ballpoints, from propeller airplanes to jets, and from typewriters to computers (Wright, Kroll, & Parnell, 1998).

History is full of examples of those who have shunned technology. For some, technology itself was the crisis. The Luddites, for example, carried out violent attacks on technology in the early 1800s by smashing machines in industrial settings. However, the attacks, which originated in England during the Industrial Revolution, were actually more of a social protest against falling wages, unemployment, and rising food prices (Malcolm, 1970; Wren, 1987). In such an environment, the threat that machines would displace jobs seemed realistic. Unfortunately for the Luddites, their actions went too far, even to the point of burning down the houses of machine inventors John Kay and James Hargreaves (Wren, 1987).

A modern-day American group that shuns most technology, particularly electricity, is the Amish. Their rationale is that traditional Amish culture and social customs may be diluted (Berry, 1977). It can be argued that the Amish represent "the truest geniuses of technology, for they understand the necessity of limiting it, and they know how to limit it" (p. 212). It is not that the Amish oppose technology per se, but rather, they argue that it must be used only when it adds to the goodness of the people and the community (Rheingold, 1999; Schultze, 2002). The Amish, then, have reasoned that technology does carry consequences. Therefore, technological changes must be carefully evaluated when adopting a lifestyle.

From a crisis management perspective, the implications of such suspicions of technology are worth noting. Though not to the degree of the Luddites and the Amish, many groups today fear technology. They work in our organizations and their resistance can spawn a crisis. Consider these common examples (all of which have been encountered by the authors of this book) seen in various forms throughout a number of organizations today:

• A supervisor in a department creates problems for the IT department when new software is introduced to replace the existing one. The result is poor morale in the resisting department, and a headache of implementation for the IT department. The situation reaches a crisis when the department supervisor and the IT manager get in a shouting match in the company cafeteria.

• A group of teachers in a public school district refuse to access their e-mail from their school-issued computers placed in the classrooms. This older group of teachers lacks technical savvy and still feels that "the old ways are the best ways," a veiled reference to their resistance to learning how to use a personal computer. As a result, the school district must send e-mails to all teachers and print hard copies for those who resist the change. Two minicrises are present in this situation. One, the printing of hard copies and the subsequent unnecessary use of paper is a needless waste of resources. Two, the very group of people responsible for teaching our children and inspiring a love of learning are resistant to learning new things themselves.

• A senior accounting instructor in a small 4-year college refuses to use spreadsheets as part of his instruction. The reason he gives is that "accounting is at the tip of the pencil," an obvious reference to the thinking skills required of every accountant. The real reason, however, is that this instructor does not know how to use spreadsheets himself, despite the fact that their usage has become mainstream in the field. This particular instructor had been resisting technology for years, and when he announces his retirement, the department finally advances into the 21st century in terms of the delivery of its accounting instruction.

- A supply chain manager who has kept up to date in his knowledge of the field is resisted by the company finance director when he proposes changes in how the company can place orders with its suppliers. The changes involve upgrading to electronic interfacing, already a common practice in many organizations. Each time the proposals are made, the finance director blatantly states that it costs too much. Again, two crises are present. One, the company misses out on a chance to make a much-needed upgrade to its purchasing function. Second, the supply chain manager seriously considers leaving his present employer for work in a more progressively run organization.

Resistance to changes in technology remains prevalent. In the above examples, the overlap between strategic challenges and crisis events is evident. What begins as a strategic challenge ends up as a mild to moderate crisis, because of some form of resistance to technology.

The advent of the Internet has created both opportunities and potential crises for government agencies. On the one hand, local governments can utilize the Internet to collect fees, disseminate information, and even provide some limited services to citizens. These types of arrangements emanate from strategic planning that, in the case of the government, seeks to serve a wider number of citizens at the least cost possible. On the other hand, governments are charged with securing large amounts of data and protecting it from thieves. Indeed, the Internet has opened a new arena of organizational crises created by hackers, disgruntled consumers and employees, and others. Criminals throughout the world can extort thousands of dollars from organizations fearful of a Web crash. So-called cyber-blackmailers may have the ability to disrupt or even halt Internet activity associated with certain sites (Bryan-Low, 2005).

Crises and the Industry Life Cycle

Industries develop and evolve over time. Competitors within an industry change constantly, and as a result, the nature and structure of the industry can also change as it matures and its markets are redefined. An industry's developmental stage influences the nature of competition and potential profitability among competitors (Hofer, 1975; Miles, Snow, & Sharfman, 1993). Likewise, the stage of the industry life cycle can serve as a breeding ground for certain type of crises. In theory, each industry passes through five distinct phases of an industry life cycle: introduction, growth, shakeout, maturity, and decline.

Introduction

In a young industry, demand for the industry's outputs is low while product and/or service awareness is still developing. Most purchasers are first-time buyers and tend to be relatively affluent, risk tolerant, and innovative. Technology is a key concern because firms are seeking ways to improve their production and distribution efficiencies. Crisis situations can develop with a new firm whose viability is linked to a developing technology or innovative product design that may be particularly vulnerable to imitation and even copyright infringement.

The untested domain of a new industry can also create a potential crisis. Certainly the area of transportation can attest to this. As commercial air travel grew during the 1940s and 1950s, a string of aviation accidents also occurred. Most of these accidents were caused by pilot error, some by weather conditions, and some by the design of the aircraft. Two aircraft in particular that had their share of fatal crashes during these early years were the British-made de Havilland Comet and U.S.-built Lockheed Electra. Both of these suffered from structural defects in their earlier models.

Growth

The second industry stage, growth, is characterized by rising customer demand. Technological issues are addressed so that higher production can take place. The industry grows rapidly until market demand approaches saturation. Fewer first-time buyers remain, and most purchases tend to be upgrades or replacements. Many competitors are profitable, but they may be cash poor since available funds are heavily invested in new facilities or technologies.

Some, such as the cruise ship industry, have been around for quite some time but are entering a surge of growth as baby boomers and their families seek out vacation retreats. At present, existing ships are being renovated and newer, larger vessels are joining the fleets of many of the cruise lines. But with more people hitting the seas, there is also a greater potential for accidents and crises. There have been several high-profile cruise ship fires in recent years, most notably the 2006 Carnival Cruise incident involving the *Star Princess,* a ship carrying 3,813 passengers and crew when it caught fire while bound for Jamaica. Two people suffered significant smoke inhalation, and one person died of a heart attack ("Fire Breaks Out Aboard Cruise Ship," 2006). Although this event happened to only one ship, it is an industry-wide threat, not just a company one, because there is a fire potential on any cruise ship (Coombs, 2007).

Another incident common to the entire industry is that of missing passengers who apparently fall overboard. In 2004 and 2005, for example, a total of 13 passengers disappeared from cruise ships (Martinez, 2005). Inevitably, such events can result in wrongful death lawsuits. Royal Caribbean, referenced in the opening vignette, faced this crisis in December 2005 when passenger George Smith disappeared on his honeymoon while in the Mediterranean. His parents filed a wrongful death lawsuit claiming Royal Caribbean, the world's second largest cruise ship company, did not take sufficient action to prevent his disappearance (Martinez, 2005).

Shakeout

As growth slows, the industry may enter a "shakeout," a point when industry growth is no longer rapid enough to support the increasing number of competitors. Competitive crises become common, as firms take advantage of economies of scale. As a result, some of the industry's weaker competitors may not survive.

A shakeout of a particular business may occur faster if a marginally performing firm is also hit with a crisis. Such was the case with the Mexican restaurant chain Chi-Chi's when it was struck with an outbreak of hepatitis A in September 2003. The sudden crisis sickened more than 660 people and caused three deaths. To make matters worse, the chain was already in Chapter 11 bankruptcy when the illnesses hit (Veil, Liu, Erickson, & Sellnow, 2005). Unfortunately, the impact of the crisis was enough to put the company out of business permanently.

Maturity

Industry maturity occurs when the market demand for the industry's outputs is completely saturated. Virtually all purchases are upgrades or replacements, and industry growth may be slow if it is growing at all. Industry standards for quality and service have been established, and customer expectations tend to be more consistent than in previous stages. When an industry reaches maturity, its remaining firms tend to be large and are more likely to become targets of interest groups, trade unions, and the like.

Because industry leaders are larger companies, they are also targets for criticism from various stakeholders. A large company may be charged with some type of misdeed it has allegedly committed, while smaller companies in the same industry go unnoticed. The Nestlé company was targeted for a massive boycott in the 1970s for marketing infant formula to third world countries. Other companies that took the same marketing strategy were not targeted. Union Carbide was targeted by the newly created Environmental Protection Agency in 1970 not only for its large size, but for the extent of its pollution in the Ohio Valley area in West Virginia. Fast forward to today, and one can see industry leaders like Wal-Mart, Starbucks, PepsiCo, Inc., and Coca-Cola under the gun for various alleged misdeeds. As mentioned in Chapter 2, blogs and hate Web sites seem to attack big business incessantly.

Decline

Sales decrease if and when an industry approaches the final stage; decline. This trend often begins when consumers turn to more convenient, safer, or higher-quality offerings from firms in substitute industries. Some firms may divest their business units in this stage, whereas others may seek to "reinvent themselves" and pursue a new wave of growth associated with a similar product or service. Some companies may become weaker and more prone to crises. The tobacco industry is one that has seen its share of crises, including product sales declines in the United States (although not in all parts of the world), as well as aggressive antismoking campaigns and lawsuits.

Crises and the Organizational Life Cycle

While the sources of many crisis events can be linked to factors common to firms in a given industry, many others are a function of an organization's unique attributes and business processes. Organization-specific factors may be linked to a firm's stage in the organizational life cycle, the most common description of which is a five-stage model based on the work of several researchers (Lester & Parnell, 2006; Lester, Parnell, & Carraher, 2003; Miller & Friesen, 1984). The following discussion looks at the relationship of the life cycle in terms of being a source of different crisis events.

Stage One: Existence

Stage one, also known as the existence or entrepreneurial stage (Quinn & Cameron, 1983), marks the beginning of an organization's development (Churchill & Lewis, 1983). The focus is on identifying a sufficient number of customers who will desire the firm's products or services. Decision making and ownership are in the hands of one or only a few individuals.

Most firms in this stage are small; however, many young organizations are launched with a significant amount of venture capital and may be quite large (Starbuck, 2003). The existence stage is characterized by long hours and diverse responsibilities on the part of employees. Because sufficient resources are not always available to hire staff specialists, employees may have to share responsibilities and even perform duties they might not be very familiar with.

Sources of crises for organizations in the existence stage are often associated with resources and specialization. A new firm may lack the resources to protect itself from acts such as copyright infringement and may not be able to hire the specialists necessary to perform critical functions. Because employees often perform multiple roles, the potential for mental errors and/or physical accidents may also be greater during this stage.

As an example, Film Recovery Systems, Inc., experienced a crisis early in its history. The company was formed in late 1979 with the purpose of extracting silver from used film. Two years later, however, an employee died from what was later determined to be acute cyanide poisoning. The medical examiner ruled that the victim died from breathing cyanide fumes at the Film Recovery Systems facility (Sethi & Steidlmeier, 1997). After several court cases, three company officials were sentenced for involuntary manslaughter. Eventually, the firm went bankrupt.

Stage Two: Survival

Stage two, survival, is characterized by firm growth (Adizes, 1979). Formalization of structure (Quinn & Cameron, 1983) and establishing distinctive competencies—special abilities that distinguish a firm from its competitors (Miller & Friesen, 1984)—are sought during this stage. Firms in this stage are trying to generate enough cash flow to survive (Churchill & Lewis, 1983).

The growth of the company is often due to a unique differentiating feature that makes it attractive to consumers. Odwalla, Inc., a 25-year-old company that makes fruit juices, is an example of a firm that was in the growth stage when a major crisis hit. The company had enjoyed success based on marketing its juices as fresh, with as little processing as possible. In October 1996 an *E. coli* outbreak in its unpasteurized apple juice product contributed to the death of a 16-month-old girl and caused 61 other children to become ill (Lawrence, 1999). Prior to the crisis, Odwalla made its juices without preservatives or any artificial ingredients. In addition, the juices were not pasteurized because the process changed the flavor as well as depleted important vitamins and enzymes. This differentiating factor led to the company's success and, ultimately, to a major crisis as well. Odwalla survived the crisis, but in the process switched to the flash pasteurization of its juice in order to prevent another *E. coli* outbreak (Lawrence, 1999).

Stage Three: Success

Organizations in the success stage have passed the survival test, growing to a point where top management focuses on planning and strategy, leaving daily operations to middle managers and unit managers. Formalization and bureaucracy are the norm in the success stage as can be seen through specific written job descriptions, the adoption of official policies and procedures, standardization of work, a clear division of labor, and hierarchical reporting relationships (Quinn & Cameron, 1983).

When an organization becomes successful, it may become the target of various forms of extortion attempts. Wendy's, the successful hamburger chain based in Dublin, Ohio, faced an unusual crisis in March 2005 when a San Jose, California customer, Ann Ayala, allegedly found a finger in her chili. Law enforcement officials quickly got involved and, as expected, attempted to identify the fingerprint on the finger. The finger was also officially autopsied and it was determined it had not actually been cooked in the chili. This clue led investigators to believe that the finger incident was actually a case of product tampering. It was later discovered that Mrs. Ayala and her husband planted the finger in the chili in an attempt to collect monetary damages from the company. Nonetheless, Wendy's lost millions of dollars in sales in the Northern California market during the ordeal (Coombs, 2006).

Extortion attempts also target successful companies via the Internet. Such online extortionists have made threats against big-name companies, including Microsoft and Google. Although these firms have been able to successfully fight off such attacks, not all companies have been as fortunate. A credit-card processing company, 2Checkout, received an online extortion threat that it promptly rebuffed. It was later hit with a denial-of-service attack that put the company offline for more than a week (Fogarty, 2005).

Stage Four: Renewal

The renewing organization displays a desire to re-create a leaner organization that can respond more quickly and effectively to environmental changes (Miller & Friesen, 1984). In effect, the renewal stage can be viewed as one in which a firm seeks to regain control over how it responds to crisis-creating shifts in its environment. Firms in the renewal stage are trying to recapture a spirit of collaboration and teamwork that fosters innovation and creativity.

In an effort to renew itself, an organization may take radical steps to boost its market share. The sport entertainment genre of professional wrestling is one that has enjoyed success, downturns in popularity, and more recently, a resurgence of interest. In an effort to renew itself, elaborate stunts have been part of the shows. Unfortunately, on May 23, 1999, pro wrestler Owen Hart fell 78 feet to his death in a stunt that went awry (Margolies, 2003). The resulting lawsuits and bad publicity were setbacks for World Wrestling Entertainment (WWE), the promoters of the event.

Stage Five: Decline

Firms may exit the life cycle at any stage by dying or simply by going out of business. The decline stage embodies an internal environment characterized by politics and power (Mintzberg, 1984) as organization members become more concerned with personal goals rather than organizational goals. For some organizations, the inability to meet the external demands of a former organizational stage leads them to a period of decline where they experience lack of profit and loss of market share. Control and decision making have a tendency to return to a handful of people, as desire for the power and influence of earlier stages erodes the viability of the organization.

In general, all firms in the decline stage are experiencing a crisis of some sort. Whether it is a struggle against stiff competition or an internal battle for control of the organization, the resolution of this crisis inevitably determines the survival or failure for the organization. The organizational life cycle is summarized in Figure 3.2.

Summary

Crisis events emanate from many sources and can be triggered by forces in a firm's macroenvironment, including political–legal, economic, social, and technological forces. Political–legal forces include such factors as the outcomes of elections, legislation, and judicial court decisions, as well as the decisions rendered by various commissions and governmental agencies. Economic forces include growth or decline in gross domestic product, and increases or decreases in economic indicators such as inflation, interest rates, and exchange rates. Social forces include such factors as societal values, trends, traditions, and religious practices. Technological forces include scientific improvements and innovations that create opportunities or threats for businesses. Each of these forces can create crises for organizations.

Industries develop and evolve over time. Because competitors within an industry change constantly, the nature and structure of the industry can also change as it matures and its markets are redefined. The sources of crisis events can be linked to an organization's position within the industry life cycle or its own developmental cycle.

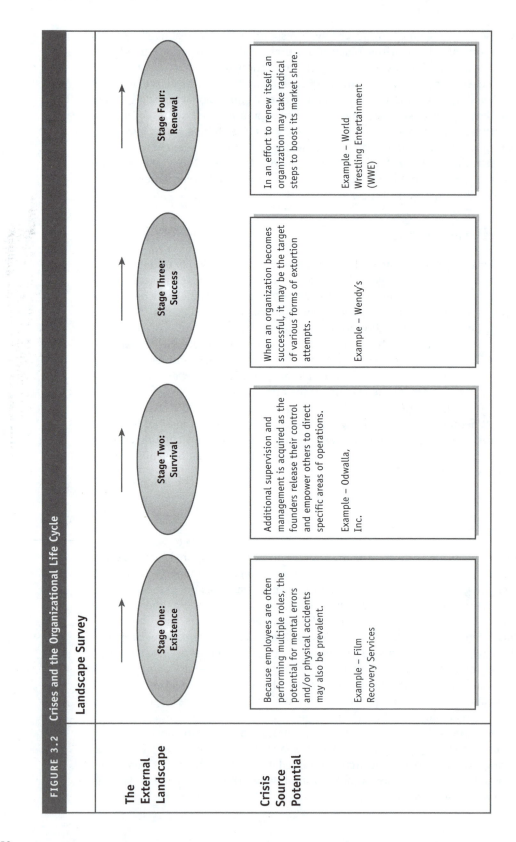

FIGURE 3.2   Crises and the Organizational Life Cycle

Landscape Survey

The External Landscape

Stage One: Existence

Stage Two: Survival

Stage Three: Success

Stage Four: Renewal

Crisis Source Potential

Because employees are often performing multiple roles, the potential for mental errors and/or physical accidents may also be prevalent.

Example – Film Recovery Services

Additional supervision and management is acquired as the founders release their control and empower others to direct specific areas of operations.

Example – Odwalla, Inc.

When an organization becomes successful, it may be the target of various forms of extortion attempts.

Example – Wendy's

In an effort to renew itself, an organization may take radical steps to boost its market share.

Example – World Wrestling Entertainment (WWE)

Questions for Discussion

1. Identify political trends in your local area that have contributed or could contribute to a crisis for an organization or industry.

2. How are political and economic events related in terms of creating a crisis?

3. What crisis events are talked about the most on the blogs and Internet sites that you visit?

4. What examples of resistance to technology have you seen where you work? Have you seen resistance at your school? If so, do you think it is a crisis or a strategic issue at this point?

5. What life cycle stage is the organization you work for in? Because of its stage, do you think a crisis could be inevitable in the future?

6. How can the stage in the *industry* life cycle affect crises in individual organizations?

7. What industries are most vulnerable to a crisis in the near future?

Chapter Exercise

CBS and MSNBC faced a publicity crisis in 2007 when radio talk show host Don Imus made disparaging and racially insensitive comments about members of the Rutgers University women's basketball team. CBS initially suspended Imus from its radio program for 2 weeks, and MSNBC followed shortly thereafter by canceling its television simulcast of the program after firms began to pull their advertisements from the show and consumers threatened boycotts of other firms and the networks. Several days later, CBS fired Imus from the radio show, marking an end to the crisis (Steinberg, Barnes, & Steel, 2007).

Crises born of publicity problems can be especially challenging when society places conflicting demands on an organization. CBS and MSNBC were faced with conflicting expectations in responding to this crisis. Many Americans expect networks to defend free speech even if it is unpopular. Although Imus's comments were viewed as insulting, he offered an apology for them. Others disagree, arguing that Imus crossed the line of racial insensitivity and that networks must take action to ensure that discourse on the airwaves meets a basic level of decency. If you were in charge of MSNBC, how would you have responded to the crisis, and why?

MINI CASE

THE PERRIGO RECALL

Based in Michigan, Perrigo is one of the largest manufacturers of store-brand, over-the-counter pharmaceuticals in the United States. The company makes more than 1,000 different products, including vitamins, pain relievers, and cold and flu remedies. Most of its products are privately

(Continued)

(Continued)

labeled for retailers, although Perrigo produces some products under the Good Sense brand name. The company produces private label products for major supermarkets and drugstore chains including Wal-Mart, Target, CVS, Walgreen, and Safeway.

In November 2006, Perrigo discovered that some of its acetaminophen tablets were contaminated with metal fragments and recalled about 11 million bottles of its generic pain reliever sold through more than 100 stores over the previous 3 years. Company officials discovered the metal fragments during quality-control checks and traced the problem to a third-party supplier. Perrigo officials and the U.S. Food and Drug Administration (FDA) emphasized that no injuries had been reported and that the likelihood of serious injury from ingesting a contaminated tablet was remote.

The financial toll on the company was not insubstantial, but not as great as it could have been. The estimated cost of the recall was about $3 million, not including indirect costs. Perrigo shares declined about 5% immediately following the recall announcement.

It is interesting to compare and contrast the recall to one of the most famous in U.S. history. A quarter century earlier, in 1982, Johnson & Johnson's (J&J) Tylenol Extra Strength pain reliever was laced with deadly cyanide. Seven people in West Chicago died from the tainted Tylenol capsules, but there were no serious injuries associated with the Perrigo tablets.

An interesting point of comparison between the J&J and Perrigo cases is the issue of branding. Because J&J's Tylenol brand was directly associated with the problem, J&J was faced with a major public relations crisis (Hartley, 1993; Mitroff & Anagnos, 2000). On the other hand, Perrigo's tablets were privately labeled so customers did not associate quality problems with the manufacturer per se. Although one might suspect that the private label distinction limits Perrigo's downside from the crisis, the opposite may be true. Another way of looking at the crisis is that Perrigo's recall affected over 100 private brands, all of which were out of Perrigo's direct control. In other words, Perrigo experienced more than 100 small crises instead of one major one.

The source of the crises is also an issue. In both instances, the contamination occurred outside of the company production facilities. Whereas Perrigo's problem occurred at a third-party supplier *before* production and packaging at a Perrigo facility, J&J's contamination occurred *after* the capsules had left production facilities. Both companies shared in the responsibility and were proactive in instituting recalls.

In the end, Perrigo weathered the storm. The initial decline in share price was erased within 2 months, and shares 6 months after the crisis were about 15% higher than the day of the recall. Perrigo's assertiveness and responsiveness seemed to pay off, regardless of the fact that the crisis originated from an outside source.

Sources

Childs, D. (2007, November 9). Manufacturer recalls millions of bottles of acetaminophen. Retrieved November 10, 2008, from http://abcnews.go.com/Health/story?id=2641539&page=1

Hartley, R. (1993). *Business ethics: Violations of the public trust.* New York: John Wiley.

McGinley, L. (2007, March 25). Buying store-brand drugs. *Wall Street Journal,* p. B1.

Mitroff, I., & Anagnos, G. (2000). Crisis in crisis management. *Corporate Counsel, 8*(2), 58–61.

References

Adizes, I. (1979). Organizational passages: Diagnosing and treating life cycle problems. *Organizational Dynamics, 8*(1), 3–24.

Barton, L. (2001). *Crisis in organizations II.* Cincinnati, OH: South-Western College Publishing.

Barton, L. (2007). *Crisis leadership now: A real-world guide to preparing for threats, disaster, sabotage, and scandal.* Boston: Harvard Business School Press.

Bennett, J. (2008, June 23). Auto-parts firms face trouble as carmakers retool production. *Wall Street Journal,* p. B3.

Berry, W. (1977). *The unsettling of America: Culture and agriculture.* San Francisco: Sierra Club Books.

Birger, J. (2005, October 3). The truth about oil. *Fortune, 152*(6), 22–26.

Bryan-Low, C. (2005, May 5). Tech-savvy blackmailers hone a new form of extortion. *Wall Street Journal,* pp. B1, B3.

Cardona, F. (2006, July 14). Pete Coors apologizes in drunk driving case. Retrieved October 28, 2006, from http://www.denverpost.com/ci_4046846

Carroll, A., & Buchholtz, A. (2003). *Business & society: Ethics and stakeholder management.* Mason, OH: Thomson South-Western.

Cato, F. (1982). Proctor & Gamble and the devil. *Public Relations Quarterly, 27*(3), 16–21.

Childs, D. (2007, November 9). Manufacturer recalls millions of bottles of acetaminophen. Retrieved November 10, 2008, from http://abcnews.go.com/Health/story?id = 2641539&page = 1

Chin, T., Naidu, S., Ringel, J., Snipes, W., Bienvenu, S., & DeSilva, J. (1993). Denny's: Communicating amidst a discrimination case. *Business Communication Quarterly, 61*(1), 180–197.

Churchill, N., & Lewis, V. (1983). The five stages of small business growth. *Harvard Business Review, 61*(3), 30–50.

Coombs, W. (2006). *Code red in the boardroom: Crisis management as organizational DNA.* Westport, CT: Praeger.

Coombs, W. (2007). Ongoing crisis communication: Planning, managing, and responding (2nd ed.). Thousand Oaks, CA: Sage.

Copeland, M. (2005). Ronald gets back in shape. *Business 2.0, 6*(1), 46–47.

Cummins, C. (2003, March 24). Business mobilizes for Iraq. *Wall Street Journal,* pp. B1, B3.

Dean, J., & Delaney, K. (2005, December 16). As Google pushes into China, it faces clashes with censors. *Wall Street Journal,* pp. A1, A12.

Ellison, S., & Steinberg, B. (2003, June 20). To eat, or not to eat. *Wall Street Journal,* pp. B1, B4.

Fire breaks out aboard cruise ship; one dead. (2006, March 23). Retrieved August 11, 2008, from http://www.cnn.com/2006/US/03/23/ship.fire/index.html

Fogarty, K. (2005). Your money or your network. *Baseline.* Retrieved November 8, 2008, from http://www.baselinemag.com/c/a/Projects-Security/Your-Money-Or-Your-Network/1/

Fortier, J. (2008). U of O research examines risks of mad cow disease. *Ottawa Business Journal, 13*(33), 14.

Fuller, K. (2006, October 19). Restaurant: Poor service wasn't bias: Rock speaks to media on Cracker Barrel incident. *The Sun News* (Myrtle Beach, SC). Retrieved October 28, 2006, from Ebscohost database.

Gold, R., & Bravin, J. (2008, June 26). Exxon oil-spill damages slashed by Supreme Court. *Wall Street Journal,* p. A1.

Gray, S. (2005, January 27). For the health-unconscious, era of mammoth burger is here. *Wall Street Journal,* pp. B1, B3.

Hartley, R. (1993). *Business ethics: Violations of the public trust.* New York: John Wiley.

Hawkins, L., Jr. (2005, April 7). As GM battles surging costs, workers' health becomes an issue. *Wall Street Journal,* pp. A1, A11.

Hellier, K., & Ellison, S. (2005, December 9). Anheuser wants world to know beer is healthy. *Wall Street Journal,* pp. B1, B4.

Higgins, A. (2001, March 12). It's a mad, mad, mad-cow world. *Wall Street Journal,* pp. A13–A14.

Hofer, C. (1975). Toward a contingency theory of business strategy. *Academy of Management Journal, 18*(4), 784–810.

King, N., Jr. (2003, April 11). The race to rebuild Iraq. *Wall Street Journal,* pp. B1, B3.

Lawrence, A. (1999). Odwalla, Inc., and the E. coli outbreak (A), (B), (C). *Case Research Journal, 19*(1).

Lester, D., & Parnell, J. (2006). *Organizational theory.* Cincinnati, OH: Atomic Dog Publishing.

Lester, D. L., Parnell, J. A., & Carraher, S. (2003). Organizational life cycle: A five-stage empirical scale. *International Journal of Organizational Analysis, 11,* 339–354.

Leung, S. (2004, January 28). McDonald's makeover. *Wall Street Journal,* pp. B1, B10.

Malcolm, T. (1970). *The Luddites: Machine breaking in Regency England.* Hamden, CT: Archer Books.

Margolies, D. (2003, October 1). Companies settle lawsuit stemming from wrestler's death. *The Kansas City Star.* Retrieved November 8, 2008, from http://0-search.ebscohost.com.un020.coast .uncwil.edu/login.aspx?direct = true&db = nfh& AN = 2W64180472763&site = ehost-live

Martinez, A. (2005, December 10). RCL incident adds to safety debate. *The Miami Herald Online.* Retrieved November 8, 2008, from http:// 0web.ebscohost.com.un020.coast.uncwil.edu/ ehost/detail?vid = 6&hid = 13&sid = 191eda50- 830a-4af7-98cb-0397839231ad % 40SRCSM1 &bdata = JnNpdGU9ZWhvc3QtbGl2ZQ % 3d % 3 d#db = nfh&AN = 2W62W6369592817

McGinley, L. (2007, March 25). Buying store-brand drugs. *Wall Street Journal,* p. B1.

McKay, B. (2004, January 27). Downsize this! *Wall Street Journal,* pp. B1, B5.

Meckler, L., & Lundegaard, K. (2005, August 24). New fuel-economy rules help the biggest truck makers. *Wall Street Journal,* pp. B1, B2.

Michaels, D., & Trottman, M. (2005, September 7). Fuel may propel airline shakeout. *Wall Street Journal,* pp. C1, C5.

Miles, G., Snow, C., & Sharfman, M. (1993). Industry variety and performance. *Strategic Management Journal, 14*(3), 163–177.

Miller, D., & Friesen, P. H. (1984). *Organizations: A quantum view.* Englewood Cliffs, NJ: Prentice Hall.

Mintzberg, H. (1984). Power and organization life cycles. *Academy of Management Review, 9*(2), 207–224.

Mitroff, I., & Anagnos, G. (2000). Crisis in crisis management. *Corporate Counsel, 8*(2), 58–61.

O'Connell, W. (2006, August 21). From the ashes of defeat. *Wall Street Journal,* pp. B1, B4.

Quinn, R., & Cameron, K. (1983). Organizational life cycles and shifting criteria of effectiveness: Some preliminary evidence. *Management Science, 29*(1), 33–41.

Rheingold, H. (1999). Look who's talking: The Amish are famous for shunning technology, but their secret love affair with the cell phone is causing an uproar. *Wired,* Retrieved November 8, 2008, from http://www.wired.com/wired/archive/7.01/ amish.html

Schultze, Q. (2002). *Habits of the high-tech heart: Living virtuously in the information age.* Grand Rapids, MI: Baker Academic.

Schwarzman, S. (2008, November 4). Some lessons of the financial crisis. *Wall Street Journal.* Retrieved November 7, 2008, from http://online.wsj.com/ article/SB122576100620095567.html

Sethi, S., & Steidlmeier, P. (1997). *Up against the corporate wall: Case in business and society* (6th ed.). Upper Saddle River, NJ: Prentice Hall.

Sevastopulo, D. (2003, October 2). US airlines are on life support. *Financial Times, 2,* p. 15.

Starbuck, W. H. (2003). The origins of organization theory. In H. Tsoukas & C. Knudsen (Eds.), *The handbook of organization theory: Meta- theoretical perspectives* (pp. 143–182). Oxford, UK: Oxford University Press.

Steele, T., Smith, S., & McBroom, W. (1999). Consumer rumors and corporate communications: Rumor etiology, background, and potential devastating consequences. *Journal of Marketing Management, 9*(2), 95–106.

Steinberg, B., Barnes, B., & Steel, E. (2007, April 12). Facing ad defection, NBC takes Don Imus Show off TV. *Wall Street Journal,* p. B1.

Stewart, J. B. (2008, May 28). Auto makers can find opportunity in $4 gasoline. *Wall Street Journal,* p. D3.

Taylor, E. (2008, May 6). Start-ups race to produce "green" cars. *Wall Street Journal,* p. B1.

Thorne, D., Ferrell, O., & Ferrell, L. (2003). *Business and society: A strategic approach to corporate citizenship.* New York: Houghton Mifflin.

Trachtenberg, J., & Steinberg, B. (2003, March 20). Plan B for marketers. *Wall Street Journal,* pp. B1, B3.

Trash overboard. (1999, September 18). *The Economist, 352*(8137), 33.

Veil, S., Liu, M., Erickson, S., & Sellnow, T. (2005). Too hot to handle: Competency constrains character in Chi-Chi's green onion crisis. *Public Relations Quarterly, 50*(4), 19–22.

What the brochures don't tell you. (1998, November). *Consumer Reports, 63*(11), 8.

Wojcik, J. (2005). Wal-Mart cost strategy sparks healthy debate. *Business Insurance, 39*(44), 24–25.

Wren, D. (1987). *The evolution of management thought* (3rd ed.). New York: John Wiley.

Wright, P., Kroll, M., & Parnell, J. (1998). *Strategic management: Concepts.* Upper Saddle River, NJ: Prentice Hall.

Zimmerman, A., Matthews, R., & Hudson, K. (2005, October 27). Can employers alter hiring practices to cut health costs? *Wall Street Journal,* pp. B1, B4.

CHAPTER 4

Strategic Planning and Assessing Crisis Vulnerability

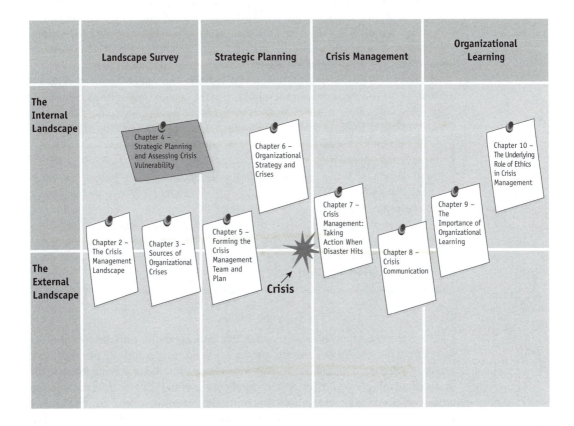

	Landscape Survey	Strategic Planning	Crisis Management	Organizational Learning
The Internal Landscape	Chapter 4 – Strategic Planning and Assessing Crisis Vulnerability	Chapter 6 – Organizational Strategy and Crises	Chapter 7 – Crisis Management: Taking Action When Disaster Hits	Chapter 10 – The Underlying Role of Ethics in Crisis Management
				Chapter 9 – The Importance of Organizational Learning
The External Landscape	Chapter 2 – The Crisis Management Landscape Chapter 3 – Sources of Organizational Crises	Chapter 5 – Forming the Crisis Management Team and Plan **Crisis**	Chapter 8 – Crisis Communication	

Source Perrier

Imagine you are a water tester for a local municipal government and your job involves checking samples of water from various locations throughout the city. Now imagine that to help you do your job, you use small amounts of purified water to dilute the samples you are testing. One day, you have a sample that shows traces of benzene, a substance that should not be in the water supply. You immediately suspect the water sample is contaminated. Yet, after several other inspections, you notice that the same substance is appearing in all of your samples, a situation that has never occurred before. Something is amiss, and you are not sure how to proceed. Then it occurs to you—the problem is not with the samples of water, but with the "ultra-pure" water that you use to dilute your samples. Something is wrong with *that* water. Such was the beginning of the Perrier water crisis.

Source Perrier, the French company that bottles Perrier water in the familiar green bottles, faced a significant crisis in February 1990 when traces of benzene were found in its water. Ironically, the contamination was discovered by government officials in North Carolina who used the bottled water as a diluting agent in lab experiments. Finding the source of the problem was a bit of a challenge, however. Two days after the initial detection, Source Perrier announced that a careless worker had used cleaner laced with benzene on a bottling line. However, a different cause was later revealed: Carbon dioxide filters that were used in the bottling process had not been changed (Brookes, 1990). Unfortunately, the discovery of the real problem led to another concern for Source Perrier: These gas filters were used to eliminate benzene in the carbon dioxide that was added to the spring water. Thus, carbon dioxide was used to add an artificial boost of bubbles to a product that was inappropriately labeled "naturally sparkling" ("Perrier Relabeled," 1990).

This disclosure forced the company to admit that its product was not what it claimed—natural sparkling water. Later, Source Perrier was required by the U.S. Food and Drug Administration (FDA) to relabel its U.S.-bound bottles "natural mineral water." In the interim, 72 million bottles of Perrier were recalled in the United States (Miller & Gleizes, 1990).

This example illustrates the fact that a crisis usually originates from a distinct, identifiable source. In this case, the internal environment of the company was fostering a deceptive advertising secret, one that eventually led to not just one, but two, separate yet related crises.

Effective crisis management requires that managers not only understand the sources of crisis events, but also the strategies needed to identify and plan for these events. A crisis event rarely occurs "out of the blue." Instead, it usually follows one or more warning signs. A set of less significant events typically interact before a crisis can occur, a combination of actions that eventually lead to the "trigger event" that causes the actual crisis (Shrivastava, 1995; Smith, 1990). Recall that in 1984, gas leaked from a methyl isocyanate tank at a Union Carbide plant in Bhopal, India, initially killing more than 2,500 people and injuring another 300,000. The trigger event for this crisis was the entry of water into a storage tank that subsequently caused the unit's temperature and tank pressure to rise. The resulting pressure increase forced the dangerous gas, methyl isocyanate (MIC) to escape into the atmosphere. The gas drifted into a populated neighborhood near the plant, thus increasing the number of victims. Numerous preconditions contributed to the origin of the accident. These included shutting down a refrigeration system designed to keep the gas cool, failing to reset the tank temperature alarm, neglecting to fix a nonfunctioning gas scrubber, and not performing the maintenance and repair on an inoperative flame tower designed to burn off toxic gases (Hartley, 1993). Each of these four systems was designed to help alert plant workers and contain the toxic effects of a gas leak. Each of them was inoperable the day of the accident.

In the evolution of a crisis, the warning signs may not be identified until it is too late, either because decision makers are not aware of them or because they do not recognize them as serious threats. Sometimes executives are simply in denial. Some assert that a crisis cannot happen to them or that the probability of it occurring is so low that it does not warrant spending the time and resources required to prevent it (Nathan, 2000; Pearson & Mitroff, 1993; Spillan & Crandall, 2004). Many who feel this way erroneously reason that insurance coverage is sufficient to cover any losses in the event of a crisis.

Identifying the warning signs is not always easy, however. Indeed, the popular press is usually replete with "warnings" about various catastrophes, many of which never seem to materialize. If all such warnings were heeded, much human activity would simply grind to a halt. Discerning actual warnings from the imposters is a difficult task, one that requires organization and industry experience, as well as sound judgment. All of this underscores the importance of crisis identification, the practice of scanning the environment and identifying those threats that could happen to the organization.

Indeed, many crises not only offer warning signs, but emerge gradually, giving decision makers sufficient time to address the problem in its early stages before it becomes a crisis. Again, managers often avoid taking action in a timely manner, choosing instead to believe that a problem will go away on its own or that the problem will not escalate.

Consider the following scenario, versions of which are common to many industries. An automobile manufacturer receives a single report of an engine fire in one of its vehicles following an accident. Such an incident can be viewed as a warning sign of a potential crisis, although it is certainly too early to tell at this point. While a company investigation of the cause of the fire is warranted, it is also appropriate not to overreact by assigning a cause until enough research has been done. After all, the details surrounding the accident are not yet clear. Later, however, there are additional reports of similar engine fires. An astute manager would not see this as a mere coincidence or the likely *end* of the engine fire problem, but as the potential *beginning* of an engine fire crisis. It would behoove the car producer to take action at that time, such as convening its top engineers to speculate on possible oversights in the vehicle design, contacting dealers about possible recalls or modifications, and the like. As this example illustrates, management should consider the possibility that initial events that might not be serious enough to classify as a crisis could precede other events that could ultimately lead to one.

Heeding the warning signs of a potential crisis is the outcome of the risk identification process. The process of risk identification, as well as the appropriate response to prevent future crises, is an important part of a total crisis prevention program. This chapter focuses on crisis prevention and how to adopt a strategic approach to this function of the overall crisis management program.

A Strategic Approach to Crisis Prevention

Crisis prevention requires a *strategic* mindset or perspective (Pauchant & Mitroff, 1992; Preble, 1997; Smith, 1992). Therefore, understanding effective crisis prevention requires that we first understand the four key distinctions of a strategic orientation perspective. First, it is based on a systematic, comprehensive analysis of internal attributes and of factors external to the organization. Being systematic is important because it ensures that potential crises are not overlooked. Thus, we must look both inside and outside the organization as we determine the risk factors that must be confronted. Second, a strategic orientation is long term and future oriented—usually several years to a decade—but built on knowledge about the past and present. Third, it is distinctively opportunistic, always seeking to take advantage of favorable situations and avoid pitfalls that may occur either inside or outside the organization. Finally, it involves choices. While win-win strategic decisions are often possible, most involve some degree of tradeoff between alternatives, at least in the short run. Because preparing for every conceivable crisis can be costly, priorities must be established. For example, resources must be spent to ensure safety in the workplace. The expenditure of resources, however, does take money directly off the bottom line. Because this approach is strategic, the expenditure may actually ensure the overall well-being of the firm in the long run. Therefore, some expenditures should not be viewed solely as cost items, but as investments in the future longevity of the company.

Because of these distinctions, the overall crisis management program, including its subset, crisis prevention, must include the top executive and members of his or her management team. The chief executive is the individual ultimately accountable for the organization's strategic management, as well as any crises that involve the organization. Except in the smallest companies, he or she relies on a *team* of top-level executives, all of whom play instrumental roles in the strategic management of the firm (Carpenter, 2002; Das & Teng, 1999).

Strategic decisions designed to head off crises are made within the context of the strategic management process, which can be summarized in five steps (Parnell, 2008):

1. *External analysis.* Analyze the opportunities and threats or constraints that exist in the organization's macroenvironment, including industry and external forces.

2. *Internal analysis.* Analyze the organization's strengths and weaknesses in its internal environment; reassess the organization's mission and its goals as necessary.

3. *Strategy formulation.* Formulate strategies that build and sustain competitive advantage by matching the organization's strengths and weaknesses with the environment's opportunities and threats.

4. *Strategy execution.* Implement the strategies that have been developed.

5. *Strategic control.* Engage in strategic control activities when the strategies are not producing the desired outcomes.

Crisis prevention is an important consideration in each step, in different ways. In the first step, strategic managers become familiar with the sources of crises that exist in the firm's external environment, and more specifically, with the actions that might be taken to minimize the likelihood that a crisis will occur. The threat of online viruses and other denial-of-service attacks, for example, may suggest that the firm invest in upgrading firewall and virus protection measures so that its Web site is not taken offline by hackers (Robb, 2005).

Government regulations, formed in response to a previous crisis, are part of the external environment. Following a salmonella outbreak and subsequent recalls of tomatoes in 2008, the U.S. Food and Drug Administration strengthened inspection and other measures to reduce the likelihood of a similar crisis in the future. Initially, the agency focused on tomatoes as the culprit. Later, various types of peppers were also part of the investigation (O'Rourke, 2008). Food-related firms from growers to producers to restaurants should consider how this crisis evolved and what strategic changes might be appropriate (Zhang, 2008).

The second step focuses on vulnerabilities within the organization that may result in a crisis event. A poorly trained workforce, for example, could lead to a workplace accident. Likewise, dubious advertising claims vis-à-vis one's competitors could result in litigation. Aging equipment is another area of weakness.

Chalk's Ocean Airways, a small air carrier based in Miami, Florida, experienced an equipment failure in 2005 when one of its planes crashed into the shipping channel next to the Port of Miami. The company was a novelty in the area because it flew vintage seaplanes to the Bahamas, a feature that made it popular with local Bahamians who found the arrangement convenient when returning to their homes. The plane that crashed shortly after takeoff was a Grumman G-73T Mallard, built in 1947. All 18 passengers and both pilots died when the plane plunged into the water when the right wing separated from the fuselage shortly after taking off from the shipping channel. The National Transportation Safety Board (NTSB) determined the cause of the crash to be faulty maintenance and a lack of oversight in regard to flying older aircraft. "This accident tragically illustrates a gap in the safety net with regard to older airplanes," said Mark Rosenker, NTSB Chairman. "The signs of structural problems were there—but not addressed. And to ignore continuing problems is to court disaster" (Vines, 2007, p. 14). This example illustrates how older and faulty equipment can lead to a crisis. Unfortunately, the event led to the demise of what was once the nation's oldest airline, founded in 1919. After the crash, the Federal Aviation Administration (FAA) grounded all Grumman G-73Ts because metal cracks were being found in the wings of the airplanes (Lebovich, 2007). The company eventually folded when the Department of Transportation revoked its certification, thus ending one of the nation's most colorful airlines.

The third and fourth steps concern the development and execution of the firm's strategies at various levels. Indeed, some strategies are more prone to

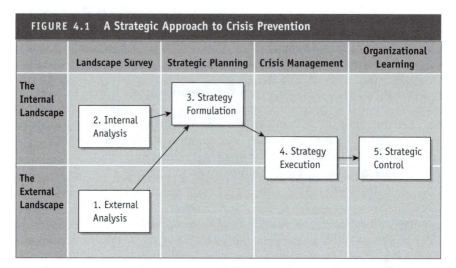

FIGURE 4.1 A Strategic Approach to Crisis Prevention

crisis events than others. For example, a strategy that emphasizes global expansion into less stable, emerging nations engenders a greater risk of crisis than one that has a strong domestic market orientation. This is not to suggest that potential crisis-laden strategies be avoided, but rather that they be evaluated closely within the strategic decision-making process.

The final step involves strategic control. Here, organizations take action to counter undesirable or unanticipated outcomes that emanate from the strategy's implementation. When a strategy is executed as planned, control may be minimal. When execution difficulties exist or unforeseen problems arise, however, the nature of strategic control may emphasize crisis prevention or even crisis response. Monitoring mechanisms must be established so that corrective action can be initiated when necessary. Strategic control is useful in crisis management because it often signals that a problem may be forthcoming. For example, accounting controls can signal if there is embezzlement taking place in the organization. Figure 4.1 depicts how these five strategic steps fit within the crisis management framework. Note that Chapter 3 provided the foundation for the first step in the process—examining the external landscape. This chapter builds on that discussion and also focuses on Steps 2 and 3. Steps 4 and 5, execution and control, are addressed in later chapters of the book.

Managing Environmental Uncertainty

Chapter 3 discussed a number of external sources of crises, including political–legal, economic, social, and technological forces. Preventing crises would probably not be an insurmountable process if the top management team always had perfect information. Unfortunately, this is not the case. Hence, the first step in the strategic management process—analyzing the external environment—presents one of the most critical challenges for preventing crises: managing environmental uncertainty.

Managers must develop systems to obtain information about the organization's environment. Ideally, top managers should be aware of the variety of external forces that influence an organization's activities. Uncertainty occurs when decision makers lack current, sufficient, reliable information about their organization and cannot accurately forecast future changes. In practice, decision makers in any organization must be able to make decisions when environmental conditions are uncertain.

Environmental uncertainty is influenced by three key characteristics of the organization's environment. First, the environment may be classified along a simple–complex continuum. Simple environments have few external factors that influence the organization and the strength of these factors tends to be low. Complex environments are affected by numerous external factors, some of which can have a major influence on the organization. Most organizations fall somewhere between these two extremes.

Second, the environment may be classified along a stable–unstable continuum. Stable environments are marked by a slow pace of change in the nature of external influences. City and county municipalities typically fall under the category of stable environments. Unstable environments are characterized by rapid change, such as when competitors constantly modify strategies, consumer preferences change quickly, or technological forces are developing continuously. The computer hardware and software industries reside in unstable environments.

Finally, environmental uncertainty is a function of the quality or richness of information available to decision makers (Starbuck, 1976). This information function usually does not present a problem for established firms operating in developed countries. In these settings, information sources are of higher quality and richness; they include business publications, trade associations, and well-developed governmental agencies. In emerging economies, however, reliable data on items such as market demand, economic forces, and consumer preferences may not be as readily available.

Considering these three environmental characteristics, uncertainty is lowest in organizations whose environments are simple and stable, and where the quality of available information available is high. In contrast, uncertainty is highest in organizations whose environments are complex and unstable, and where the quality of information is low (Duncan, 1972). The relationship between uncertainty and the prevalence of organizational crises can now be seen: As uncertainty increases in organizations, so does the likelihood of crises. Hence, organizations whose core competencies are tied closely to technology tend to experience the greatest complexity and instability. Following the terrorist attacks of September 11, 2001, airlines could be added to this category because of increased regulatory pressure and fears of further attacks.

Organizations in environments marked by low uncertainty should be managed differently from those marked by high uncertainty. When uncertainty is low, greater formality and established procedures can be implemented to increase predictability, improve efficiency, and lessen the frequency of crisis events. When uncertainty is high, however, procedures are difficult to develop because processes tend to change more frequently. In this situation, decision makers are often granted more freedom and flexibility so that the organization can adapt to its environment as it changes or as better information on the environment becomes available. While this freedom and flexibility may be necessary, it can create a crisis-prone environment. Figure 4.2 depicts the relationship between complexity, change, and the potential for crisis events.

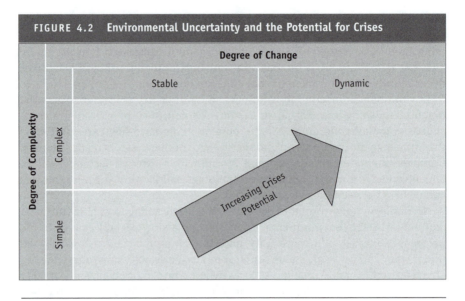

FIGURE 4.2   Environmental Uncertainty and the Potential for Crises

Source: Adapted from Robbins & Coulter (2007).

A number of techniques are available for managing uncertainty in the environment. The first consideration, however, is whether the organization should adapt to its environment or, in some cases, attempt to influence or change it. Urban hospitals represent a classic example of adapting to their environments when the surrounding neighborhoods where they are located become crime ridden, a common problem for many urban facilities. Moving the hospital is usually not an option since, geographically, it is located to serve a specific community. In some cases, the hospital could move if it were not bound to the local community, as in the case of a research hospital, but moving it to another location is usually not feasible. To keep the hospital safe from the crime in the external neighborhoods, measures are taken to ensure the safety of the buildings and the patients. Employing extra security guards, installing perimeter lighting, using security cameras, and utilizing metal detectors are all methods of adapting to the environment.

Sometimes a company can actually change its environment to protect it from a crisis. Nissan has an unusual method for dealing with a specific type of crisis that is prevalent in its environment: hail. In this example, Nissan attempts to modify its environment, literally. The company has a plant in Canton, Mississippi, with a storage area of 140 acres. Obviously, hail is a concern because of the body damage it can cause to an automobile. To respond to this threat, Nissan installed an anti-hail system. Using weather-sensing equipment, when conditions are right for hail, a sonic wave is fired into the air every five and a half seconds to prevent the forming of hail (Foust & Beucke, 2005).

Other techniques for managing uncertainty can also be used. One is buffering, a common approach whereby organizations establish departments to absorb uncertainty from the environment and thereby buffer its effects (Thompson, 1967). Purchasing departments, for example, perform a buffering role by stockpiling resources for the organization, lest a crisis occur if they become scarce. Establishing a crisis management team and engaging in formal planning is also a form of buffering. If a crisis occurs, the team takes on a mitigating role by managing the ordeal.

Another technique is imitation, an approach whereby the organization mimics a successful key competitor. Presumably, organizations that imitate their competitors reduce uncertainty by pursuing "safety in numbers." Imitating the successful crisis management techniques of other organizations can be advantageous as well. The crisis management plans for many universities and government agencies are publicly available. Imitation can restrict an organization's ability to develop its own distinctive competence, however. Managers must account for the specific internal and external factors unique to their own organizations. Imitating an ineffective strategy or structure can also reduce the effectiveness of crisis management (Bertrand & Lajtha, 2002).

Environmental Scanning

Keeping abreast of changes in the external environment that can lead to crises presents a key challenge. Environmental scanning refers to collecting and analyzing information about relevant trends in the external environment. A systematic environmental scanning process reduces uncertainty and organizes the flow of current information relevant to organizational decisions while providing decision makers with an early warning system about changes in the environment. This process is also an important element in risk identification. Because members of an organization often lack critical knowledge and information, they may scan the environment by interacting with outsiders, a process known as boundary spanning.

Environmental scanning is future oriented by nature. Unfortunately, the results of environmental analysis are often too general or uncertain for specific interpretation (Kumar, Subramanian, & Strandholm, 2001). The need for *effective* environmental scanning to produce information relevant to the firm is critical (Groom & David, 2001). Although managers may possess information that could mitigate a crisis or prevent it from occurring, they still need to act on that information and make the appropriate decisions.

The infamous crisis that erupted between Royal Dutch/Shell and the environmental activist group Greenpeace illustrates that important cues can still be ignored by management. In fact, this incident has since been labeled a "predictable surprise," one that had plenty of warning indicators, yet still caught the company off guard (Watkins & Bazerman, 2003). The incident involved Shell's plan to sink an obsolete oil platform, the *Brent Spar,* in the North Sea. On April 29, 1995, however, Greenpeace activists boarded the platform and announced they would block its sinking because of radioactive contaminants that were stored on the structure. Shell responded by blasting the protestors and their boats with water cannons, a move that turned out to cause a public relations crisis for the company. Opposition to Shell's plans soon grew in Europe, leading to a boycott of Shell service stations in Germany. Protestors even damaged 50 German gas stations, firebombing two of them and riddling one with bullets (Zyglidopoulos, 2002). Less than 2 months after the initial Greenpeace protest, Shell gave in and abandoned its plan to sink the *Brent Spar.*

Watkins and Bazerman (2003) note that Royal Dutch/Shell was surprised by the turn of public opinion against them. This occurred, in spite of the fact that Shell had an abundance of information indicating that not only were protests by Greenpeace likely, but that they would involve physical occupation of the platform. Even other oil companies protested Shell's plans. The case illustrates that misreading external signals can still occur, even when those signals prove to be reliable.

Environmental scanning should also be viewed as a continuous process (Herring, 2003). Top managers must plan for and identify the types of information the organization needs to support its decision making. A system for obtaining this information is then developed. Information is collected, analyzed, and disseminated to the appropriate decision makers. Their feedback concerning the usefulness and timeliness of the information should influence the type of information required by the organization. This feedback becomes especially important in preventing a potential crisis, as the A. H. Robbins case illustrates.

In the early 1970s, A. H. Robins manufactured the Dalkon Shield, a plastic intrauterine contraceptive device (IUD). Over 4 million IUDs were implanted in women by doctors who were swayed by the optimistic research reports offered by the company (Hartley, 1993). However, warnings from the external environment began to surface almost immediately after the product was introduced to the market. Women were afflicted with pelvic infections, sterility, septic abortions, and in a few cases, death (Barton, 2001; Hartley, 1993). A reading of the environment would have prompted most companies to shut down production of the IUD, but not A. H. Robins. It continued to promote the device as safe, even though management knew there were problems. In the end, the company was sued by thousands of victims. Eventually, the firm's poor financial standings resulting from lawsuit payoffs led to a sale of the company to American Home Products in 1989 (Barton, 2001).

Large organizations may engage in environmental scanning activities by employing one or more individuals whose sole responsibility is to obtain, process, and distribute important environmental information to their organization's decision makers. These individuals constantly review articles in trade journals and other periodicals, and watch for changes in competitor activities. They also monitor what is being said about the company on the Internet. Alternatively, organizations may contract with a research organization that offers environmental scanning services and provides them with real-time searches of published material associated with their organizations, key competitors, and industries. In contrast, decision makers at many smaller organizations must rely on trade publications or periodicals such as the *Wall Street Journal* to remain abreast of changes that may affect their organizations.

A potential lack of objectivity can be a concern when managers evaluate the external environment, because they perceive selectively through the lens of their own experiences and organization. Managers with expertise in various functional areas tend to be more interested in and elevate information pertaining to their functions. The problem with this viewpoint is that key elements from the environment may be ignored, elements that may pose future risks that could develop into a crisis. For example, cutting the budget of a human resource (HR) department to trim overall costs may sound tempting to the CEO, but lapses in HR can lead to poor training and loosely enforced safety rules, both of which can lead to industrial accidents (Sheaffer & Mano-Negrin, 2003). Perhaps the key problem associated with environmental scanning is determining which available information warrants attention. This is why developing sensitive indicators that trigger response(s) is so important. Consider the December 2004 Asian tsunami. Although an earthquake had been detected, scientists were unsure of the exact size of the resulting tsunami and were unable to share their observations with countries that would soon be affected since the governments in those countries lacked environmental scanning systems (Coombs, 2006).

Assessing Crisis Vulnerability

While it is important to take steps to prevent crisis events, it is equally important to assess crisis vulnerabilities specific to the organization. This process, known as crisis vulnerability assessment (CVA), involves the collection of data and perspectives from various stakeholders. The data are then integrated into an overall assessment of specific crisis threats that appear to be most prominent. Typically, each threat is ranked in terms of its likelihood and potential impact on the organization. Those crisis threats at the top of the list become the focus of prevention and mitigation efforts.

Assessing crisis vulnerability in the strategic decision-making process is a key to anticipating and preventing crises. Indeed, the probabilities of a crisis vary among organizations, so each must be considered individually. To facilitate effective strategic decision making and prevent crises from occurring, many organizations identify potential crises (sometimes called worst-case scenarios). Chemical companies, for example, typically prepare for chemical spills, while airlines prepare for an air disaster. Consequently, top managers must anticipate events unique to their organizations and industries.

By definition, worst-case scenarios tend to focus on the most severe crises that could occur in an organization. Although planning for extreme crises is critical, they are often less likely to occur than those of moderate intensity. Hence, crisis planners should broaden their scope in assessing potential events by including *less than worst* case scenarios as well. Crisis management teams at chemical companies might also consider the effects of crises such as labor strikes or a severe drop in demand for a chemical-related product due to environmental, safety, or health concerns. By doing so, the team would not only consider and plan for the most devastating possibilities, but also those of lesser severity that are more likely to occur.

In strategic planning, a "SWOT" analysis listing the organization's strengths, weaknesses, opportunities, and threats is often used as a tool in planning the organization's long-term strategy. The SWOT analysis should also be used to assess crisis vulnerability. Typically, internal strengths would not be thought to contribute to a potential crisis. In practice, though, this is not necessarily true. For example, the Chalk's Airways accident described earlier in this chapter occurred because the seaplanes were very old and had flown in an environment with salt-laden water and air for more than 50 years. These conditions no doubt contributed to the structural fatigue problems in the aircraft that eventually led to the loss of the right wing. However, Chalk's had a strong differentiating feature, which was one of its strengths, flying amphibious planes to the Bahamas in an

TABLE 4.1 Examples of Internal Organizational Strengths and Potential Crisis Events	
Internal Strength	*Corresponding Potential Crises*
Extremely fast company growth	Loss of managerial control over operations can occur, particularly when the company has multiple locations over a wide geographic area. This condition can eventually result in defective products and/or poor service quality.
Unique differentiating product or service characteristic	If the product or service offering is new, its uniqueness could later result in a product or service defect. For example, some types of elective or unique surgeries (such as gastric bypass) can later lead to physical problems.
Charismatic organizational leader	Some charismatic leaders have led their organizations into financial ruin because they were not challenged by the Board. In more extreme cases, some leaders become so influential that they take on a godlike status whereby they are not challenged by any of their followers. Religious cults exemplify this behavior.
A long history of successful performance	Simply being a successful company will draw criticism from many stakeholders. For example: • Employees may feel they are not compensated enough if the company is hugely successful. • Environmentalists will look for any evidence that the company is harming the environment, simply because making an example of a successful company generates a lot of publicity. • Socially minded citizens will feel the company does not share its wealth enough with the local community. • Stockholders will feel they should be receiving a greater share of wealth on their investment. • The government will watch the company closer and look for ways that it may be illegally hiding income. • Lawmakers will look for *any* wrongdoing on the part of the company so they can establish a reputation among their constituents.

old-style setting. The appeal of the aircraft and the convenience of landing away from an airport, closer to one's final destination, made this little airline popular for many years. It was differentiation that led to its success and, ultimately, to the crisis that resulted in its failure. Table 4.1 provides examples of internal organizational strengths that could conceivably result in organizational crises.

Crisis sources can also originate from the internal environment—that is, from inside the organization. Weaknesses listed in the SWOT analysis may point to organizational deficiencies with direct or indirect crisis possibilities. For example, an emphasis on the human resource management (HRM) function is directly related to the potential for crisis events in the organization (Lockwood, 2005). Specifically, when good human resources practices are ignored by an organization, a crisis is more likely to occur. The infamous Rent-A-Center case

TABLE 4.2	Examples of Internal Organizational Weaknesses and Potential Crisis Events
Internal weaknesses	*Corresponding Potential Crises*
Poorly trained employees	Industrial accidents in the workplace and poor service to the customer. In manufacturing settings, defective products could also result.
Poor relationship with the union	Labor strikes during contract negotiations as well as a larger amount of grievances resulting from day-to-day operations. Both of these can lead to a secondary crisis: negative publicity in the media.
Poor ethical orientation of top management	White-collar crime and cash flow problems. If the organization is large, publicity problems will also result.
Aging production facilities and equipment	A greater number of machine breakdowns, resulting in lost productivity and higher operating costs. Industrial accidents and poor product quality are also likely.
Understaffed or nonexistent Human Resource Department	Discrimination and sexual harassment charges are likely. Higher operating costs due to industrial accidents (a result of poor training), employee absenteeism, and turnover.
Haphazard safety inspections	Industrial accidents coupled with increased workplace injuries. Again, the larger the organization, the more likely negative publicity may follow.
Employee substance abuse	Increased industrial accidents, workplace injuries, and product quality problems.
Lack of a crisis management team and plan	Slow and ineffective response to crisis events. Negative public perception because the firm is seen as being unprepared.

illustrates how the link between HRM and employee lawsuits can develop. In this example, Rent-A-Center eliminated its HR department when its new CEO, J. Ernest Talley, took over in August 1998. The company also changed to a less female-friendly workplace, according to depositions from more than 300 company officials over a 47-state region. Talley's own anti-female policy became well known within the company, including several quotes indicating that women should not be working at Rent-A-Center (Grossman, 2002).

Without an HR department, women who felt discriminated against no longer had anyone to turn to. Charges of discrimination began to increase, plunging the company into a class action lawsuit on behalf of female employees, eventually resulting in a $47 million verdict against Rent-A-Center (Grossman, 2002). Table 4.2 provides additional examples of internal weaknesses that could conceivably result in organizational crises.

A SWOT analysis also looks at the organization's opportunities that exist in the external environment. While it may not seem readily apparent that

TABLE 4.3 Examples of External Organizational Opportunities and Potential Crisis Events	
External Opportunity (and accompanying strategic responses)	*Corresponding Potential Crises*
Expand product availability by moving from a brick-and-mortar to a "brick-and-click" arrangement	Offering products online can lead to denial-of-service cyberattacks by hackers. Note that though such hackers are usually external to the organization, they could also be internal if there is a disgruntled employee in the workforce.
Expand company manufacturing facilities to another part of the world	This arrangement means that the company still manufactures its own products. While the quality and process can be controlled better than if using a licensing approach, there is also the risk of outside interference from the host country. In some cases, companies have been taken over by the host country's government and become state owned.
Outsourcing manufacturing to another company outside the host country	Because domestic jobs may be lost in the process, the company could incur negative publicity from external stakeholders, particularly former employees and municipalities that hosted the business. If the outsourcing is through a licensing agreement, there is the possibility that proprietary information may be pirated by parties in the host country. The product from the outsourced company may be defective. This situation creates a two-pronged crisis. First, the defective product itself creates problems when installed or added to the final product that it is a part of. Second, there is the public image problem because of the firm's decision to outsource overseas in the first place.

organizational opportunities could be a potential source of crises, a closer examination suggests otherwise. Opportunities include activities a company may pursue to expand its market share. Problems can surface and escalate into a crisis, particularly as the firm considers globalization options. Table 4.3 outlines three possible scenarios where a strategic response to opportunities may breed a crisis.

External threats are a common source of crisis. One such threat concerns the organization's location. For example, in parts of the United States such as Florida, weather concerns such as hurricanes are included as part of the risk assessment (Kruse, 1993). Other regions of the United States such as California are vulnerable to earthquakes. Urban areas of any country can be subject to crises that are different from less populated areas. Events such as riots, power outages, and bad weather can be especially hard on more populated regions. Because of the uniqueness of urban locales, new crisis research agendas are being encouraged (Medd & Marvin, 2005). Table 4.4 overviews various external threats that can evolve into a crisis.

TABLE 4.4 Examples of External Organizational Threats and Potential Crisis Events	
External Threat	*Corresponding Potential Crises*
Changing demographics of surrounding neighborhoods	The organization may become a target for crime, such as vandalism or robbery.
Severe weather	The building and facilities where the organization is located may be damaged by wind, snow, or flooding. Sales revenue may be interrupted while the building is being repaired.
Dysfunctional customers or other individuals	There could be an incident of workplace violence.
Poor-quality components from a supplier	The components that are assembled into the final product will cause that product to be defective as well.
Consumer activism due to poor products or some other activity of the company	Consumer lawsuits may develop in the case of poor-quality products. Boycotts of the company's products and services can result.
Extortionists	Product tampering may occur. Online extortionist may threaten the company's Web site with a denial-of-service (DoS) attack.
Earthquake, wildfire, or other natural disaster	Structural damage to the building and information technology capabilities. Injuries and fatalities could occur to employees and customers.
Rumors	Loss of revenues due to boycotts and negative company publicity. Negative coverage could appear on the Internet through hate sites and blogs.
Terrorism	Direct physical attacks on buildings resulting in damage, injuries, and fatalities. Attacks outside the organization may disrupt the supply chain, in addition to the items mentioned above.

Organizational Culture and Crisis Planning

Despite the fact that crisis planning is an important part of the strategic manage-ment process, not all managers are convinced that its role is important. In other words, being diligent about crisis planning involves a cultural shift. As a result, organizations often do not have effective crisis management plans because their managers have not cultivated a mindset that values this process. Many executives are engrossed with "putting out today's fires" and may not believe they have time to plan for tomorrow's contingencies. Therefore, they have not developed the critical tools needed for a comprehensive crisis management plan (Simbo, 2003).

Thus, not all establishments have adopted a culture of crisis preparedness. At one end of the scale, many managers carry an "it can't happen to us" mentality

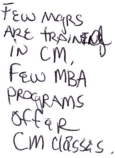
Few mgrs are trained in CM, few MBA programs offer CM classes.

(Nathan, 2000; Pearson & Mitroff, 1993). Other managers are reactive concerning crisis events by contemporaneously planning and managing as the problems unfold. Still other managers are more proactive in their conduct. They plan for future potential crises by presupposing what could be their worst-case predicaments. Yet another group of managers includes battle-scarred victims who have experienced an organizational crisis and are now involved in proactive planning so they can manage a future crisis more effectively.

Indeed, there is a "way of thinking" and a "way things are done" in every organization. Long-term members understand it well and newcomers usually learn it quickly. Organizational theorists refer to this phenomenon as organizational or corporate culture. *Culture* refers to the commonly held values and beliefs of a particular group of people (Weitz & Shenhav, 2000). Organizational culture is a more specific concept in that it refers to the shared values and patterns of belief and behavior that are accepted and practiced by the members of a particular organization (Duncan, 1989).

The first and most important influence on an organization's culture is its founder or founders. The founder's core values and business beliefs serve as the basis for the organization's activities (Schein, 1983). For instance, a key influence on McDonald's culture was the fast food company's founder, Ray Kroc. Although he passed away in 1984, his philosophy of fast service, assembly-line food preparation, wholesome image, cleanliness, and devotion to quality are still central facets of the organization's culture (Love, 1995). Likewise, Sam Walton's influence on the Wal-Mart culture can still be seen today even though he passed away in 1992. Wal-Mart is still passionate about providing products at the lowest price possible. Founding members and key organizational leaders such as the CEO therefore need to embrace crisis planning. Without their example, it is doubtful that a full crisis-planning program will be successful in the organization.

An organization's culture exists at two levels. At the *surface level,* one can observe specific behavior of the culture, such as accepted forms of dress and rituals or ceremonies. These artifacts reflect a deeper, *underlying level* that includes shared values, belief patterns, and thought processes common to members of the organization (Schein, 1990). The underlying level is the most critical to understand. Because it cannot be seen, it is often inferred by studying the surface level. Embracing a culture of crisis planning must occur at the underlying level first before it will be evident at the surface level. Indeed, as crisis expert Timothy Coombs (2006) put it, crisis management must become the DNA of the organization.

Because each organization develops its own unique culture, even organizations within the same industry will exhibit distinctly different ways of functioning. The organizational culture enables a firm to adapt to environmental changes and to coordinate and integrate its internal operations (Rouse & Daellenbach, 1999). Ideally, the values that define a culture should be clear, easy to understand by all employees, embodied at the top of the organization, and reinforced over time. "Adaptive cultures" are innovative and encourage initiative, whereas "inert cultures" are conservative and encourage maintenance of existing resources. Neither form is necessarily more prone to crises or better equipped to prevent them.

An organization's culture serves as the basis for many day-to-day decisions in the organization. For example, members of an organization whose culture values innovation are more likely to invest the time necessary to develop creative solutions to complex problems than their counterparts in organizations whose culture values short-term cost containment (Deal & Kennedy, 1982). An innovative organization is more likely to "do its homework" and take the steps necessary to prevent crises from occurring. This homework includes setting up crisis management teams, developing plans, and practicing mock disasters, which are drills to help the organization learn how to manage a crisis more effectively.

Sometimes there is universal agreement among an organization's members concerning its values, norms, and behavior. At other times, however, this is not the case. Cultural strength refers to the extent to which organizational members agree about the importance of certain values (Arogyaswamy & Byles, 1987). Strong cultures—such as 3M's strong emphasis on innovation and Southwest Airlines' strong emphasis on delivering value in a friendly manner—can lead to success, but a culture strong in all respects may not be appropriate for all organizations. Colleges and universities, for example, value diversity of thought and expression among faculty and students. As such, a culture strong in the sense that all members place a high value on freedom of expression and differences of opinion may be appropriate.

In the realm of crisis management, there appear to be "crisis-prepared" cultures that support crisis planning, as well as those that do not, sometimes labeled "crisis prone" (Pearson & Mitroff, 1993). Managers should seek to develop and support crisis-prepared cultures in their organizations.

Summary

Managers at all levels must understand both the sources of crisis events and the specific steps that can be taken to prevent crises, or at least reduce the likelihood that they will occur. Crises rarely occur without warning signs, which often emerge gradually, giving decision makers at least some time to address the problem in its early stages before it becomes a crisis.

Crisis prevention requires a *strategic* mindset or perspective. The first step in the strategic management process—analyzing the external environment—presents a critical challenge for preventing crises: managing environmental uncertainty. Uncertainty occurs when decision makers lack current, sufficient, reliable information about their organization and cannot accurately forecast future changes. Uncertainty is lowest in organizations whose environments are simple and stable, and where the quality of available information is high. It is highest in organizations whose environments are complex and unstable, and where the quality of information is low. Crises are more likely to occur when uncertainty is high.

Environmental scanning refers to collecting and analyzing information about relevant trends in the external environment. A systematic environmental scanning process reduces uncertainty and organizes the flow of current information relevant to organizational decisions while providing decision makers with an early warning system for changes in the environment.

Many organizations perform crisis vulnerability assessments to identify those events the organization should be prepared for. Sometimes crises are not prevented, however, because the culture of an organization is not supportive of crisis planning.

Questions for Discussion

1. What types of warning signs precede crisis events? Give examples of specific warnings and crises that you have experienced.

2. How is quality information important to crisis prevention? Provide examples.

3. How can crisis planning be part of the strategic management process?

4. What is environmental uncertainty? How can it be managed? Why is managing it important for crisis prevention?

5. Why do you think some managers believe that a crisis cannot happen in their organization?

6. In what ways can a crisis prevention mentality be embedded in the organizational culture?

Chapter Exercise

Identifying potential threats to the organization can be a highly effective means of preparing for and preventing future crises. Form teams of three or four students and consider the college or university that you are attending. Perform a crisis vulnerability assessment of your institution.

Using the SWOT analysis described in the chapter, identify potential crises that reside in each of the four areas of strengths, weaknesses, opportunities, and threats. Assess each crisis threat in terms of its likelihood and potential impact.

MINI CASE

INBEV, ANHEUSER-BUSCH, AND SPYKES

Prior to InBev's acquisition of the company in 2008, Anheuser-Busch owned almost 50% of the beer market in the United States. It is one of the largest brewers in the world. Best known for its Budweiser and Bud Light brands, Anheuser-Busch produces about 160 million barrels of beer each year.

Anheuser-Busch sought growth not only through global expansion, but also through the production of beverages that complement its strong beer brands, including nonalcoholic beers, beer mixers, malt liquor, and energy drinks. Many of its products have been quite innovative. In 2006, Anheuser-Busch introduced Peel, a fruit juice and alcoholic beverage marketed to women.

Anheuser-Busch's new parent company, InBev, faces a difficult challenge: attempting to respond to shifts in alcoholic beverage consumption patterns while maintaining a socially responsible image. Following a decade of reduction in beer's share of the overall U.S. consumption of alcoholic beverages, Anheuser-Busch teamed up in 2005 with notable Harvard epidemiologist Meir Stampfer to tout the potential medicinal benefits of beer consumption. Stampfer cited a number of studies suggesting that moderate alcohol consumption may reduce the risk of heart attack, diabetes, and other ailments.

In January 2007, Anheuser-Busch introduced Spykes, a 2-ounce beverage with 12% alcohol, caffeine, ginseng, and guarana. Spykes was available in eight flavors such as "hot chocolate" and "spicy lime." Anheuser-Busch faced opposition for its marketing of Spykes almost immediately. In April, the Center for Science in the Public Interest joined other critics, urging the company to discontinue production, referring to the marketing plan as a shameful effort to sell malt liquor to children.

In the beginning, Anheuser-Busch defended Spykes. Officials noted that Spykes had a relatively low alcohol content. The Web site promoted Spykes as a beer additive or a beverage that could be consumed as a shot. According to Anheuser's vice president of marketing, Michael Owens, the company was simply trying to deliver a variety of products to meet changing adult beverage consumption patterns.

Also in April, the U.S. Alcohol and Tobacco Tax and Trade Bureau found that the brewer's health warnings contained 41 to 47 characters per inch, exceeding the limit of 40. The backgrounds on three of the flavors made the warnings hard to read. Anheuser-Busch had to halt production for a week to bring its labels up to code.

In early May, 30 state attorneys general sent a letter to Anheuser-Busch CEO August Busch IV, expressing concern about the company's promotion of caffeine-infused alcoholic beverages like Spykes. Pressure continued to mount, and on May 17 Anheuser-Busch announced that it would abandon Spykes. The company continued to defend its product and reputation for fighting alcohol abuse and underage drinking, rejecting critics' claims and blaming the decision on poor sales.

Looking back on the incident, it appears that Anheuser-Busch could have avoided the situation if it had conducted a crisis vulnerability assessment prior to the introduction of Spykes. Several years earlier, consumer groups had begun to attack producers of alcoholic beverages sold in small quantities, suggesting that they facilitated consumption by teens. The company was certainly aware of the code mandating minimum character sizes on the warning labels. Hence, the Spykes crisis might have been avoided—or at least minimized—if top managers had "done their homework" more effectively.

Sources

Hellier, K., & Ellison, S. (2005, December 9). Anheuser wants world to know beer is healthy, *Wall Street Journal*, pp. B1, B4.

Kesmodel, D. (2007a, May 18). Anheuser abandons Spykes drink, citing sales and rejecting critics. *Wall Street Journal*, p. B3.

Kesmodel, D. (2007b, May 11). Label ruling temporarily halted Anheuser drink. *Wall Street Journal*, p. B4.

References

Arogyaswamy, B., & Byles, C. M. (1987). Organizational culture: Internal and external fits. *Journal of Management, 13*, 647–659.

Barton, L. (2001). *Crisis in organizations II*. Cincinnati, OH: Southwestern Publishing Company.

Bertrand, R., & Lajtha, C. (2002). A new approach to crisis management. *Journal of Contingencies and Crisis Management, 10*(4), 181–191.

Brookes, W. (1990). The wasteful pursuit of zero risk. *Forbes, 145*(9), 160–172.

Carpenter, M. A. (2002). The implications of strategy and social context for the relationship between top management heterogeneity and firm performance. *Strategic Management Journal, 23*, 275–284.

Coombs, W. (2006). *Code red in the boardroom: Crisis management as organizational DNA*. Westport, CT: Praeger.

Das, T. K., & Teng, B. (1999). Cognitive biases and strategic decision processes: An integrative perspective. *Journal of Management Studies, 36,* 757–778.

Deal, T. E., & Kennedy, A. A. (1982). *Corporate cultures: The rites and rituals of corporate life.* Reading, MA: Addison-Wesley.

Duncan, R. B. (1972). Characteristics of perceived environments and perceived environmental uncertainty. *Administrative Science Quarterly, 17,* 313–327.

Duncan, W. W. (1989). Organizational culture: "Getting a fix" on an elusive concept. *Academy of Management Executive, 3,* 229–236.

Foust, D., & Beucke, D. (2005, October 5). Heading off storms. *Business Week,* No. 3953, p. 16.

Groom, J. R., & David, F. (2001). Competitive intelligence activity among small firms. *SAM Advanced Management Journal, 66*(1), 12–29.

Grossman, R. (2002). Paying the price. Events at Rent-A-Center prove that when employers don't respect HR today, they'll pay tomorrow. *HR Magazine Online, 47*(8). Retrieved August 8, 2008, from http://www.shrm.org/hrmagazine/articles/0802/0802covstory.asp

Hartley, R. (1993). *Business ethics: Violations of the public trust.* New York: John Wiley.

Hellier, K., & Ellison, S. (2005, December 9). Anheuser wants world to know beer is healthy. *Wall Street Journal,* pp. B1, B4.

Herring, J. (2003). The future of competitive intelligence: Driven by knowledge-based competition. *Competitive Intelligence Magazine, 6*(2), 5.

Kesmodel, D. (2007a, May 18). Anheuser abandons Spykes drink, citing sales and rejecting critics. *Wall Street Journal,* p. B3.

Kesmodel, D. (2007b, May 11). Label ruling temporarily halted Anheuser drink. *Wall Street Journal,* p. B4.

Kruse, C. (1993). Disaster plan stands the test of hurricane. *Personnel Journal, 72*(6), 36–43.

Kumar, K., Subramanian, R., & Strandholm, K. (2001). Competitive strategy, environmental scanning, and performance: A context specific analysis of their relationship. *International Journal of Commerce & Management, 11,* 1–33.

Lebovich, J. (2007, October 20). Fort Lauderdale Airport may boot Chalk's: Chalk's International Airlines said it plans to catch up on its rent at Fort Lauderdale-Hollywood International Airport before Broward County commissioners. Retrieved 11/9/2008, from http://www.airportbusiness.com/online/article.jsp?siteSection = 1&id = 15068&pageNum = 1

Lockwood, N. (2005). Crisis management in today's business environment: HR's strategic role. *SHRM Research Quarterly, 4*(4), 1–9.

Love, J. F. (1995). *McDonald's: Behind the arches.* New York: Bantam.

Medd, W., & Marvin, S. (2005). From the politics of urgency to the governance of preparedness: A research agenda on urban vulnerability. *Journal of Contingencies and Crisis Management, 13*(2), 44–49.

Miller, A., & Gleizes, F. (1990, February 26). Perrier loses its fizz. *Newsweek, 115*(9), 53.

Nathan, M. (2000). The paradoxical nature of crisis. *Review of Business, 21*(3), 12–16.

O'Rourke, M. (2008). Some say tomato, some say jalapeno. *Risk Management, 55*(9), 14–16.

Parnell, J. A. (2008). *Strategic management: Theory and practice* (3rd ed.) Cincinnati, OH: Atomic Dog Publishing.

Pauchant, T., & Mitroff, I. (1992). *Transforming the crisis prone organization.* San Francisco: Jossey-Bass.

Pearson, C., & Mitroff, A. (1993). From crisis prone to crisis prepared: A framework for crisis management. *Academy of Management Executive, 71,* 48–59.

Perrier relabeled. (1990). *FDA Consumer, 24*(6), 2.

Preble, J. (1997). Integrating the crisis management perspective into the strategic management process. *Journal of Management Studies, 34*(5), 769–791.

Robb, D. (2005). Defending against viruses, worms and DoS attacks. *Business Communications Review, 35*(12), 24–27.

Robbins, S., & Coulter, M. (2007). *Management* (9th ed.). Upper Saddle River, NJ: Pearson-Prentice Hall.

Rouse, M. J., & Daellenbach, U. S. (1999). Rethinking research methods for the resource-based perspective: Isolating sources of sustainable competitive advantage. *Strategic Management Journal, 20,* 487–494.

Schein, E. H. (1983). The role of the founder in creating an organizational culture. *Organizational Dynamics, 12*(Summer), 14.

Schein, E. H. (1990). Organizational culture. *American Psychologist, 45,* 109–119.

Sheaffer, Z., & Mano-Negrin, R. (2003). Executives' orientations as indicators of crisis management policies and practices. *Journal of Management Studies, 40*(2), 573–606.

Shrivastava, P. (1995). Industrial/environmental crises and corporate social responsibility. *Journal of Socio-Economics, 24*(1), 211–217.

Simbo, A. (2003). Catastrophe planning and crisis management. *Risk Management, 40*(2), 64–66.

Smith, D. (1990). Beyond contingency planning: Towards a model of crisis management. *Industrial Crisis Quarterly, 4*(4), 263–275.

Smith, D. (1992). Commentary: On crisis management and strategic management. In P. Shrivastava (Ed.), *Advances in strategic management* (pp. 261–269). Greenwich, CT: JAI Press.

Spillan, J. E., & Crandall, W. R. (2004). Crisis planning in the lodging industry: A response to the "It can't happen to us" mentality. *Mountain Plains Journal of Business and Economics,* 5, Article 4—General Research. Retrieved November 4, 2006, from http://www.mountainplains.org/general/2004 general.html

Starbuck, W. H. (1976). Organizations and their environments. In M. D. Dunnette (Ed.), *Handbook of industrial psychology* (pp. 1069–1123). Chicago: Rand McNally.

Thompson, J. D. (1967). *Organizations in action.* New York: McGraw-Hill.

Vines, M. (2007). Intelligence. *Business & Commercial Aviation, 101*(1), 13–26.

Watkins, M., & Bazerman, M. (2003). Predictable surprises: The disasters you should have seen coming. *Harvard Business Review, 81*(3), 72–80.

Weitz, E., & Shenhav, Y. (2000). A longitudinal analysis of technical and organizational uncertainty in management theory. *Organization Studies, 21,* 243–265.

Zhang, J. (2008, June 12). Food-safety measures faulted. *Wall Street Journal,* p. A4.

Zyglidopoulos, S. (2002). The social and environmental responsibilities of multinationals: Evidence from the Brent Spar case. *Journal of Business Ethics, 36,* 141–151.

CHAPTER 5

Forming the Crisis Management Team and Plan

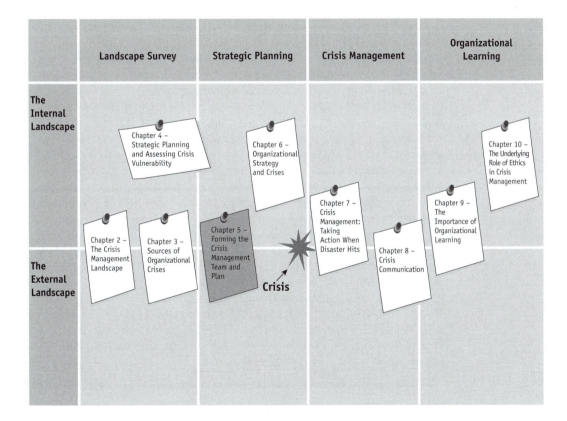

Concord College

Concord College is a small, picturesque school located on top of a mountain in the southern part of West Virginia. The quaint campus of almost 3,000 students, also known as the "campus beautiful," is located in the small town of Athens, West Virginia. In December 1995, the school administrators met and decided to form a crisis management team. Although little had happened in the past to indicate a need for such a team, they knew that was no guarantee that a major crisis could not occur.

After the team was formed, a crisis management plan was developed over the next year. Thereafter, the team met regularly for training and updates on the latest happenings in the world of crisis management. The crisis team remained diligent throughout the rest of the 1990s. One of the busiest years was 1999, when preparations were being made to manage the Y2K problem, a widespread fear that computers would malfunction when they recognized the year 2000. A couple of years later, the team was activated during the September 11 ordeal, after reports that some of the college's international students might have been threatened.

During the fall of 1996, an event did occur that brought the college an array of excitement and frantic activity. On September 26, emergency medical personnel descended on the campus, accompanied by two local fire departments, the local media, and a host of curious onlookers. Radio scanners throughout the county were closely following the events that were unfolding at this small rural college. It was reported that eight students were trapped in a building that had just experienced a large boiler explosion. Emergency crews were inside the building, attempting to extract the victims. Resident assistants (RAs) from student housing had been called to set up a perimeter around the affected building and control the crowd that was forming. A triage area was set up as the victims came out of the building. One victim was confirmed dead; the other seven were still alive, but with various injuries. At one point, a distraught student watching the ordeal tried to break through the perimeter to find a friend who was trapped inside. Student RAs blocked his path and tried to calm him down. As the injuries became more known, a medical evacuation helicopter was requested and instructed to land on the football field, the only flat area of the campus safe enough for such a landing. A reporter barged into the command center and asked for the name of the victim who had died. The president of the college, who was closely monitoring the radio in the center, located at the campus police department, was also still trying to find out that information.

The ordeal continued for about 4 hours, and then suddenly came to an abrupt halt. The injured and the dead victim suddenly got up and went back to their residence halls. The police, firefighters, RAs, and the crisis management team met for pizza at the command center. The strange ordeal finally came to an end. Concord College had just conducted its first mock disaster (Crandall, 1997).

The crisis management team (CMT) and the crisis management plan (CMP) are the core of an organization's crisis planning efforts. The team meets together first, and then develops the plan. Later, the plan can be tested through mock disaster drills and refined as needed. This chapter explores all three of

FIGURE 5.1   Goals of the Crisis Management Team (CMT)

	Landscape Survey	Strategic Planning	Crisis Management	Organizational Learning
The Internal Landscape		2. The CMT develops the crisis management plan.		
The External Landscape	1. The CMT identifies the crisis threats the organization is facing.	3. The CMT leads training in the area of crisis management.	4. The CMT actively manages the crisis when one occurs.	5. The CMT leads the postcrisis evaluation so that learning can occur.

Crisis

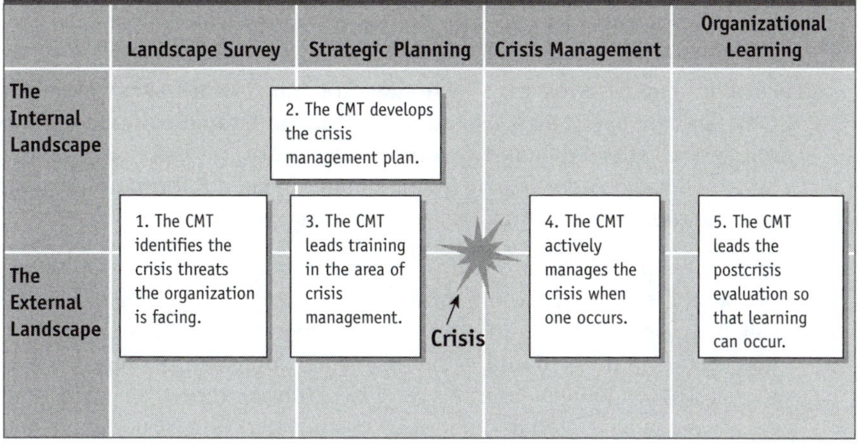

these processes in detail. We begin with the mechanics involved in forming the crisis management team. Next, the crisis management plan is outlined. We close the chapter with some comments on conducting mock disasters.

Forming the Crisis Management Team (CMT)

Before any crisis planning can occur, the crisis management team (CMT) must be assembled. While some discussion about crises can take place at any time without a team, the CMT is the most effective and formal starting point for serious crisis planning.

Goals of the CMT

The CMT plans for prospective crises and helps manage those that do occur. But the actual charge of the team is more comprehensive and should be presented as such. Figure 5.1 overviews the charge of the CMT.

1. *The CMF identifies the crisis threats the organization is facing.* Every organization faces threats that are unique to its industry. The CMT considers this as it weighs the specific risks that are likely candidates for a crisis. In planning for a crisis, the team cannot plan for everything, so it must be flexible (Clark & Harman, 2004). Most threats cluster into crisis families (Coombs & Holladay, 2001). This realization can simplify the threat assessment phase as crisis managers can look at potential families of crises first, and then develop their plans based on addressing the crisis families, as opposed to trying to plan for every potential crisis.

2. *The CMT develops the crisis management plan.* Based on the threats mentioned above, the CMT develops a crisis management plan that

addresses these threats. The plan also contains key contact information of vendors and other important stakeholders. In many cases, the plan is posted on the organization's Web site (Boyd, 2000). Some companies go a step further and create a special Web site ahead of the crisis that can be activated if a crisis occurs. Such sites are called "dark sites" (Snellen, 2003), and are specially designed to provide more rapid communication among the affected stakeholders. These types of Web sites allow concerned stakeholders to log in and obtain updated information on the details of the crisis and how it is being managed.

3. *The CMT leads training in the area of crisis management.* The CMT leads the training efforts in the organization. Two levels of training are made available, one for the team, and one for the organization members at large. Team training should occur at regular intervals, perhaps once a quarter. The content of training usually revolves around reviewing the crisis management plan and conducting simulated drills (Coombs, 2007; Wilsenbilt, 1989). Simulated drills are necessary because the team really does not know how well it can function in a crisis unless the plan is tested periodically (Clark & Harman, 2004; Crandall, 1997). Figure 5.1 illustrates how activities need to be coordinated between the internal and external landscapes. For example, when setting up a mock disaster drill, contacting stakeholders in the external landscape is necessary, such as fire departments and emergency medical service (EMS) organizations.

4. *The CMT actively manages a crisis when one occurs.* When a crisis does occur, the CMT will be activated and placed in charge of managing the event. This phase of the team's experience is most crucial because it reveals performance levels in two areas: (1) How well was the crisis handled, and (2) how well did members of the team work together? The evaluation of these two areas is addressed in the fifth goal, mentioned next. Figure 5.1 illustrates that learning input is needed from both the internal and external landscapes.

5. *The CMT leads the postcrisis evaluation so that learning can occur.* After the crisis, a postevaluation session is recommended to determine how well the crisis was managed. Specifically, the CMT seeks to find answers to the following questions:
   - What did we learn from this crisis that will help us prevent a similar one in the future?
   - If the same crisis did occur again, what could we do differently?
   - What weaknesses existed among the CMT?
   - Do any changes need to be made within the CMT?
   - What aspects of the crisis response were performed well?
   - What aspects of the crisis response need improvement?

The postcrisis evaluation phase is most important in terms of scheduling the evaluation sessions. Such sessions must be held soon after the event while the details of the crisis are still familiar to everyone. Waiting too long can lead to a state of forgetfulness (Kovoor-Misra & Nathan, 2000).

TABLE 5.1	Personal Characteristics for Crisis Team Members
Personal Characteristic	*Manifestation in a CMT Setting*
Stress tolerance	Employees react to stress in different ways. Some do not tolerate stress well. For CMT members, however, stress should be a motivator, a sort of adrenaline shot that makes them want to manage a crisis environment.
Ambiguity tolerance	We always prefer to make decisions with all needed information readily available. However, in a crisis situation, decisions may have to be made in the absence of complete information. Ambiguity tolerance is that unique characteristic that allows a decision maker to be effective, even when desired information is not available.
Listening skills	Crisis team members need to be able to listen well to the many stakeholders and victims presenting their sides of the story. Listening for what is said is important, but being intuitive and listening for the untold story is equally critical.
Cooperation	CMT members must like people and enjoy working in a group. This is not an assignment for an employee who prefers to work on projects independently.
Communication apprehension	This is one characteristic a team member should NOT have. All CMT members should be able to express how they feel without any hesitation or concern over rejection from other team members. Indeed, there will be times when team members do not always agree with each other.
Verbal clarity	Good speaking skills are a must. Some of the team members may be assigned to talk to the media, an assignment that requires excellent verbal skills. Among team members, communication intentions should also be clear. This ability goes back to stress tolerance, as some team members may not communicate as well verbally when they are under stress.

Source: Chandler, R. (2001). Crisis Management: Does Your Team Have the Right Members? *Safety Management, 458,* 1–3.

Team Member Characteristics

CMT members should be able to think under pressure (Clark & Harman, 2004). To accomplish this difficult task, a team approach is necessary, one whose composition is diverse and includes members from different parts of the organization (Barton, 2001). See Table 5.1 for personal characteristics recommended by Chandler (2001).

Team Composition

Within the crisis management literature, there is general agreement that team members should represent the major functional areas of the organization (Coombs, 2007). Representatives from the following areas are recommended:

Company CEO or President

In smaller organizations, this person would be on the CMT. In larger organizations, a vice president for administration or operations may serve as the representative of upper management (Barton, 2001). Podolak (2002) advocates that this person should also serve as the team leader. The CEO does not always serve as the company spokesperson during a crisis, although that is certainly an option. This role is often held by a member of the public relations department or the designee who typically communicates with the media. Pines (2000) notes that it may not even be necessary for the CEO to address the media if a better trained staff person is available: "Only in the most egregious of crises—when lives are lost, when the story remains on the front pages for days—does the media and the public even expect to see the CEO" (p. 15).

Human Resources (HR)

It is important for several reasons that this area be represented. First, HR serves as the liaison on behalf of the employees. Employees can be affected by a crisis in a number of ways, and HR is there to ensure their interests are represented in the crisis management process (Lockwood, 2005). Second, HR has knowledge areas that can be useful during a crisis. These areas include next-of-kin details, number of employees in each site of the facility, and language and cultural barrier knowledge that is especially important if the company operates globally (Millar, 2003). HR should also have a network of trauma counselors on contract in the event of a major crisis involving injuries and/or a loss of life.

Finance

A crisis can have a major influence on cash flow and stock valuations. There may also be a need to secure funds quickly for relief operations. This accountability becomes particularly critical if funds need to be disbursed to overseas locations.

Security

The head of the organization's security or police force should be a member of the CMT. Many crises will involve the services of this department, such as in the case of a workplace violence incident. This department also serves as a liaison with law enforcement departments outside the company, whose help may be needed.

Public Relations

This functional area goes by different names in different organizations. Some organizations refer to it as Public Information, Public Affairs, or Community Outreach. The charge of this department during the crisis is to express the information and viewpoints of the organization to its public stakeholders. The department also works to help predict public perception of the organization and issues related to the specific crisis at hand. Usually, these departments have established ties with the various media outlets so that a crisis event is not the first time the spokesperson and the media will have met.

Legal Counsel

The organization's attorney should be a member of the CMT. This person is needed for legal expertise, particularly in reference to deciding how much information should be disclosed to outside stakeholders during a crisis. With this in mind, the legal counsel and public relations director must work together and be in agreement about how much disclosure is appropriate.

Operations

The core operations of the organization should be represented on the team. In a manufacturing facility, the plant manager would be the logical choice. At a major university, several core areas require representation, including food service, housing, registrar and records, the director of plant and facilities, and the academic departments.

Crisis Consultant

Some organizations may opt to employ an outside consultant during the initial start-up of the CMT and the subsequent plan. In other cases, there is often a crisis "champion" within the organization who can initiate efforts to start the team and the plan.

Virtual Crisis Management Teams

In some cases, not all of the CMT members can meet together in one room at the command center during a crisis. If the organization is dispersed over a wide geographic area, then members will have to be linked electronically in order to communicate. Most virtual teams are partially distributed teams whereby part of the team meets in one command center while the rest of the group is dispersed in various locations (Hiltz, 2006).

Virtual teams still require a central command center, however. But what if the command center becomes inoperative? This situation actually occurred during the September 11 terrorist attack when the New York City Office of Emergency Management lost its state-of-the art center. After the first tower caught fire and collapsed, the emergency operations center was unusable because of its location across the street from the tower (Davis, 2002). Because of this type of dilemma, there may be times when the crisis management team will need to operate outside of the confines of the command center. In emergency operations management, the usual response has been the creation of a virtual emergency operations center (VEOC). This arrangement allows team participants to interact with the operations center from remote locations and make decisions as necessary.

Initially, the military and municipal emergency operations centers were the first to embrace VEOC. The private sector is slowly coming on board, however. Cisco and AT&T were two of the first high-profile companies to use VEOC commercial software (Davis, 2002). Other companies do not always use software, but they are still linked through their own intranet and Internet-based communication systems. Cell phones, conference calls, and fax messages supplement these virtual approaches.

Potential Problems

As in any group or team that works together, problems can arise. Care should be taken to select team members who have good interpersonal skills and can work well with each other. "If a team is dysfunctional before a crisis occurs, that team will have a dysfunctional response during an incident" (Barton, 2001, pp. 17–18). A number of problems can occur within the CMT. Bertrand and Jajtha (2002) summarize the more common problems cited in the literature:

Not Understanding the Symbolic and Sacred Aspects of a Crisis

A crisis is more than just an event; it is an attack on a specific stakeholder or institution, whether inside or outside the organization. Crises are perceived as "symptoms of underlying problems" and, as such, can be viewed as "policy fiascos" (Bovens & 't Hart, 1996). Crises "challenge the foundation of organizations, governmental practice and even societal cohesion" (Lagadec, 2004, p. 167). As a result, stakeholders feel threatened by these events and perceive them to have deeper significance. For example, when a large company is involved in an environmental accident, it is not just "an accident." It is perceived to be a big corporate giant exploiting the natural environment for its own gain. Bertrand and Jajtha maintain that CMT training needs to include understanding the symbolic impact of a crisis. When the media and the community appear to act irrationally, there is at least a semblance of a reason why they appear to act that way.

Not Being Able to Make Decisions Because of a Lack of Information

Many managers are effective at making some decisions without sufficient information. While complete information is preferred, the real world of operating a business demands the ability to operate with incomplete information. When the organization is thrust into a crisis, complete information is not always available to the CMT. Although nobody wants a lose-lose situation, team members must act even without the ideal amount of information. Crisis team members need to accept this as a fact of life, a part of the charge that comes with their service on the CMT.

The Lack of Interest and Involvement of Senior Management

It is difficult to promote a crisis preparedness atmosphere if the senior managers are not on board. As Bertrand and Lajtha (2002) lament, "Why do many top managers devote so little time to crisis management planning and training when the return on the small investment may be huge—and even commercially life-saving?" (p. 185). Because crisis management is a key part of the strategic management process, top management must be involved.

The Lack of Psychological Preparation Provided to CMT Members

Crisis team members bring their own emotional baggage to the meetings. Some are more adept than others at handling the stresses and fears of working on the team. The fatigue factor will also play a role, earlier for some members, later for others. In most cases, however, there is no forewarning as to what the CMT is about to face. Training for the psychological aspects of these assignments should be included.

In summary, "Crises are characterized by the absence of obvious solutions, the scarcity of reliable information when it is needed, the lack of adequate time to reflect on and debate alternative courses of action" (Bertrand & Lajtha, 2002, p. 185). While it is easy to list the functional departments that should be represented on the CMT, it is much more sobering to realize the intensity of the challenges team members must face.

Several other problems can surface with the CMT, including groupthink, operating in different time zones, verbal aggressiveness, and the presence of a Machiavellian personality.

Groupthink

Janis (1982) was the first to identify groupthink as a problem in the decision-making process of groups and teams. Groupthink occurs when the team does not take into consideration viable alternatives to the problem. Ironically, group cohesiveness can foster an atmosphere of groupthink. The rationale is that group members, unwilling to speak up and question the status quo, remain passive so as not to upset the equilibrium of the group. In the crisis management literature, Lintonen (2004) discusses how groupthink influenced the European Union's (EU) adopting sanctions against Russia during the Chechnya crisis.

Practicing in Different Time Zones

When a crisis spans times zones, coordination problems can surface. For the multinational corporation with locations worldwide, it is necessary to negotiate different time zones and languages. Perhaps a key factory has been hit by a typhoon, or a facility on the other side of the world has caught fire. Coordinating relief efforts to get the facility back on line is made more difficult because of the obvious logistic and time complications. One remedy is using the partially distributed or virtually distributed crisis management team discussed above.

Verbal Aggressiveness

Chandler (2001) warned of team members who can become overbearing or even hostile. Such people should be screened out as CMT candidates early in the team selection process as they can obstruct group decision making and hamper open communication.

Machiavellian Personality

This person's main goal is simply trying to look good and advance his or her personal agenda. Chandler (2001) also recommends avoiding this person and instead looking for a team player who has the heart for solving problems.

The Crisis Management Plan (CMP)   *No plan survives first contact...*

Once the CMT is in place, efforts can be made to construct a crisis management plan (CMP). The CMP is a plan, but it is also meant to be a way of thinking about a crisis. In managing a crisis, flexibility is favored over dogmatically following a step-by-step procedure. In technical operations, step-by-step procedures are necessary for the diagnosis and remedy of certain problems. In a crisis, however, where human, technical, and other unknown elements are integrated, some degree of flexibility is required to discern and act on the situation.

Plans should not be compiled just for the sake of meeting a compliance regulation (Bertrand & Lajtha, 2002). While this provides motivation to write the plan, it does not put the right spirit into crisis management. Ultimately, a plan should encourage the crisis team to "think" about what could happen, and plan for mitigation efforts for a crisis that does occur. The problem with writing a plan just to have one is that it may not be reviewed on a regular basis, if at all. The only updating that occurs to such plans is when they are subject to revision.

Basic Components of the Plan

The CMP today is likely to be found on the organization's Web page, as well as in a hard copy notebook. The degree of detail will vary, but a concise plan is usually preferable to a longer one (Barton, 2001; Coombs, 2007). Again, this ensures that an element of flexibility is present in the crisis response. The following components are recommended for the CMP.

Cover Page

The cover page includes the name of the organization, general contact information, date of distribution, and the company logo. The page also labels the document as the crisis management plan. A disclaimer may be added stating that the document is confidential and unauthorized use is prohibited.

Table of Contents

Although the document should not be too lengthy, a table of contents should be included. Crisis plans that are located on the organization's Web site should link hard copy page numbers to sections of the virtual document.

Crisis Management Team Members

Team members should be listed along with their respective departments and contact information, including e-mail address and office phone, home phone, and cell phone numbers.

Team Member Responsibilities

This section will vary in its degree of detail. Larger and more complex organizations such as a research university will include more detail than a small organization such as a local high school. While it is important to have some idea of who does what during a crisis, team members are selected from their functional areas of the organization, so it is expected they will be operating within their areas of expertise during the crisis. Two decisions that need to be determined before a crisis are: (1) Who is in charge of the team, and (2) who are the designated company spokespersons to the media? It is also important to keep the team format flexible so it can adapt to the particular crisis at hand.

Activation of the CMT

Some crisis plans may include procedures for activating the CMT. While some may view this as a formality, it is important to plan even this part of the event. Usually, the team will be activated by a team member or at the request of a key internal stakeholder. It is important that employees in the organization know who the crisis management team members are, as well. In some cases, employees may contact a team member instead of the police if they are not sure if an event is really a crisis.

Command Center Locations

The command center is a prearranged meeting location where the CMT gathers in the event of a crisis. The plan should clearly label both this location and the alternate command center in case the primary one is damaged in some way—perhaps due to weather or a fire—and therefore unusable. Care should be taken not to locate the alternate center too close to the primary one. Proximity in the event of a major fire could cause both centers to be unusable.

If the crisis involves a crime or physical damage to some aspect of the building facilities, an incident command center may be set up near the location of the actual crisis. This would be the case when emergency response providers are working a particular event while the CMT is meeting in the command center. With this type of arrangement, clear communication links will be needed between the incident command center and the CMT. Such a scenario could occur if there is a hostage situation in one location of the complex while the CMT is meeting in another part. It is common for these types of separate command center arrangements to occur on college and university campuses due to the sprawling complex of buildings that exist.

Response Plans for Specific Crisis Situations

The CMP will have a list of prospective crisis events that could likely occur at the organization. In this section, these events are addressed in general terms as to how they would be managed. The plan should list the potential crisis at the top of the page, and then follow with a series of bulleted steps on how to manage that event.

The length of the response plan will vary according to the crisis. Individuals who write response plans should attempt to be thorough, yet concise, remembering that too many steps in the response plan will limit the ability to remain flexible. Table 5.2 lists common crisis events addressed in CMPs at colleges and universities.

TABLE 5.2 Potential Crises for American Colleges and Universities	
Potential Crisis	*Past Examples*
Fires	2007—An off-campus fire at an Ocean Isle, NC, beach condominium kills seven university students during their fall break. 2000—A Seton Hall University residence hall fire kills three students.
Athletics scandals	2006—Three members of the Duke University lacrosse team are falsely accused of sexual offenses against a young woman at a team party. Although the charges were unfounded, the scandal proved damaging to the university and the students. 2004—The University of Colorado football program is plagued with a scandal involving sex, drugs, and alcohol for new recruits.
Major crimes	2007—Four Delaware State University students are shot, three fatally, in a schoolyard near the university. 2007—Virginia Tech massacre results in 32 fatalities; victims include both faculty and students.
Natural disasters	2003—Floods cause almost $2 million worth of damage at the University of Georgia's College of Veterinary Medicine. 1977—A flood ravages Toccoa Falls College, also in Georgia, killing 39 people and injuring another 60.
Contagious diseases	College and university students are commonly cited for being at a higher risk for influenza and meningitis because of the close living conditions associated with residence halls.
Building mold	A number of colleges and universities throughout the United States have been affected by building mold problems.
Weather-related crises	2005—A number of colleges and universities in New Orleans, LA, and the surrounding region are closed long-term after Hurricane Katrina devastates southern Louisiana and Mississippi.
Alcohol-related deaths	A major problem at many colleges and universities is the abuse of alcohol among students, sometimes resulting in binge-related deaths.

Distribution of the CMP

The CMP should be made available throughout the organization. There was once a time when the plan was distributed only to team members, but with the convenience of the Internet, many organizations also post their plans online. Some companies distribute their CMP to outside stakeholders as well. General Motors (GM) distributes its crisis plan to its suppliers (Armstrong, 2004). Although GM does not mandate that its suppliers have a plan, they are strongly encouraged to develop one. "We estimate that 70 percent of suppliers don't even have a plan in place," says Andrew Cummins, executive director of the Automotive Industry Action Group. He further speculates that the other 30% are not reviewed regularly (Armstrong, 2004).

Crisis Management Training

The CMT is charged with the oversight of training in the area of crisis management. Training can range from simple meetings that review the CMP, to providing classroom instruction on certain aspects of crisis management. Training can also include conducting smaller disaster drills that test a segment of the crisis response, to taking part in elaborate mock disasters where a crisis is simulated so the team can practice its response.

Regular CMT Meetings

The CMT should meet regularly throughout the year. Such meetings provide training opportunities as well as chances for team members to interact and bond. Potential training activities that can be held during such meetings include reviewing the CMP, conducting tabletop exercises, and presenting new material on crisis management.

Reviewing a Part of the CMP

Reading through the CMP refamiliarizes team members with the material. In addition, if editing errors are discovered, they can easily be corrected during the meeting if the document file is projected on a screen for all to see.

Conducting Tabletop Exercises

This type of training is conducted in the meeting room and involves a discussion of how the team would respond to a specific crisis. It is a form of a disaster drill, but without the realistic scenarios that are characteristic of a mock disaster. The advantage of a tabletop exercise is that it can be an inexpensive way to rehearse for a real disaster (Careless, 2007).

Workshops may last for several days and address a specific type of crisis. More recently, workshops combined with tabletop exercises have been used for training against coastal terrorism (Richter et al., 2005). Cognitive mapping has also been used as a tabletop exercise. In this exercise, participants are asked to draw spatial maps of a developing crisis and then develop scenarios for managing the event (Alexander, 2004). Such an exercise is useful for those involved in disaster response activities.

Presenting New Material on Crisis Management

This training approach can be flexible. A video can be shown, a guest speaker brought in, or the team can take part in a video conference. The objective is to learn new material that will assist the team in its response to a crisis.

Disaster Drills

While a mock disaster is more comprehensive and tests the overall team response, a disaster drill is a smaller exercise that addresses one aspect of the crisis response (Coombs, 2007). Perhaps the most common disaster drill is the standard fire drill that tests the evacuation of personnel from a building.

Drills are meant to test a part of the crisis response. Several examples of drills include:

• Sending an emergency phone message and e-mail to all the employees in the organization. This drill is practical because an alert of a crisis may need to be sent at a moment's notice. Perhaps a tornado has been spotted in the area or an individual with a gun is seen in the facility.

• Testing a procedure that is unique to the facility. A library is an example of a facility with unique crisis scenarios. A common crisis scenario for a library is the loss of documents and books due to water damage. In light of this possibility, some libraries practice unique water drills. The Stetson University Law Library held a drill scenario in which a water sprinkler head had malfunctioned and was spraying water onto shelves of books. The personnel practiced draping the shelves with plastic tarps as quickly as possible (Rentschler & Burdett, 2006).

• Accessing and using fire suppression equipment. Such equipment is required in all buildings, but training employees to use the equipment properly may be spotty. Local fire departments are usually happy to provide such training on site. In addition, the fire department can also learn more about the unique features of the building, helping it compile a "preplan," a prearranged response to a fire in that particular building.

• Conducting a lockdown drill. Lockdown drills involve securing the classroom(s) or building by locking the doors and requiring students to stay inside, rather than exiting the building as in a fire drill. The intended purpose of a real lockdown is to protect the occupants of the room (building) in the event of a shooting or related incident. Lockdown drills became more frequent after the Columbine massacre (Kass & Marek, 2005), and their practice will most likely increase as a result of the Virginia Tech massacre and other incidents of school violence. Such drills are not limited to schools, however. Incidents of workplace violence also require that employees be in a secure place in the event of a shooting. Thus, a lockdown drill would be advisable in nonschool settings as well.

A variation of the lockdown drill involves not only securing the building, but moving occupants to a more central location for added protection. In the United States, this type of drill, called "sheltering in place," has been practiced in school systems close to the nation's ports (Jacobson, 2003). Ports have been identified as potential terrorist targets, and population centers near these ports need to be prepared. Sheltering-in-place drills can include the shutting down of heating and air-conditioning systems, as well as sealing air inflow openings near windows. Such a move would be likely in response to a chemical or biological terrorist attack.

The Mock Disaster

A mock disaster is a scenario that is re-created so that a number of crisis management participant–stakeholders can respond to it. It operates in real time, in a setting that is as realistic as possible to a real crisis. A mock disaster is more comprehensive than a disaster drill. Mock disasters are widely recognized as essential in testing an organization's disaster plan (Perry, 2004).

Purpose of a Mock Disaster

A mock disaster can serve a number of purposes. Its practicality is enhanced by the number of people who can participate, the media attention that is usually received, and the usefulness of testing the organization's crisis response. The following section explains the intended purposes of the mock disaster:

To activate and test the working of the CMT. This type of exercise involves the full activation of the CMT. In fact, one of the most important goals is to ensure that the CMT is alerted to a crisis in a timely manner. The working dynamics of the team can also be evaluated. Do team members work well together? Are there any interpersonal problems that need to be addressed? Is there anyone who is not really cut out to serve on the team?

To test communication networks and equipment. A mock disaster should test the communication systems that will be used during an actual crisis. Phone systems, mobile radios, the intranet, and the Internet should all be activated and used. In addition, local fire and police departments may have special equipment they want to test. For example, robots are used in certain firefighting situations and in bomb removal and detonation. A mock disaster is an excellent opportunity for testing this type of specialized equipment.

To test the suitability of the command center. If the command center has never been used for an actual crisis, it should be activated during the mock disaster. In the opening vignette, the original command center designated by the CMT was found to be unsuitable in the event of a real crisis. The problem was that all radio communications were funneled into one large room, the same general area where the media were also assembling. When mock reporters heard the reports coming in from the incident command center, they demanded an explanation from the president of the college, who just happened to be listening to the same reports in the command center (Crandall, 1997). After the drill, a new command center in a different building was designated with a separate room for media briefings.

To develop working relationships with local fire and police departments. In the event of a real emergency, the local fire and police departments will be the first responders to the event. Developing relationships with these agencies before a crisis occurs is recommended. The mock disaster is an excellent vehicle for accomplishing this goal.

To build team cohesiveness and camaraderie. A CMT may actually function quite well in a noncrisis setting. Regularly scheduled meetings and training sessions are low-stress contact points. A mock disaster, however, adds a sense of urgency and purpose to the working relationships of the CMT. After working together in a large-scale exercise, which can be physically and emotionally challenging, team members may find they are more cohesive and appreciative of each other.

To let the CMT know where the organization's crisis response is weak. A well-designed mock disaster should test the key areas of crisis response, and be strenuous enough to expose weak points. The opening vignette showed the CMT several weak points in their response. One key area was the inability to notify grief counselors in a timely manner. After the exercise, the CMT made improvements so counselors could be contacted in a more expedient manner (Crandall, 1997). At the Stetson University Law Library, the mock disaster discussed previously revealed that response times to a water leak emergency needed to be improved (Rentschler & Burdett, 2006). A mock disaster at the Arco Chemical plant in South Charleston, West Virginia, revealed that media briefings were being rushed; not a good situation given the fact that this particular drill involved a sinking barge full of chemicals spilling its contents into the Kanawha River (Swift, 2004).

A mock disaster can also let the CMT know where additional training is needed (Zoltak, 1998). All mock disasters should involve calling a press conference and answering reporters. Training company employees in addition to the official spokesperson is recommended. There is always the possibility that the company spokesperson may not be available during a crisis that would require a response to the media. Mock disasters can be useful in determining how "polished" these backup spokespersons are and whether they need additional training.

Guidelines for Setting Up a Mock Disaster

A mock disaster should be planned like any other project. There should be a person in charge, a delegated list of duties, and a timeline for scheduling the drill. Specific considerations are discussed next.

Determine the objectives of the drill. A mock disaster tests some response systems, but not the organization's entire crisis response capability. The CMT should determine several key areas that need to be tested and include those in the plan. All mock disasters should test communication capabilities and interviews by the media.

If specific equipment is part of the crisis response, then it should be tested as well. The *Exxon Valdez* oil spill in Alaskan waters is known for the massive amounts of oil that damaged the environment. What is less well known is that Exxon had a response plan for an oil spill in that area. Unfortunately, the boat that was designated to set up perimeter booms around the spill was being repaired at the time of the spill (Hartley, 1993). The role of equipment, then, is paramount in certain areas of crisis response. Testing that equipment should be part of the mock drill.

Develop a scenario that represents a potential crisis at your organization. As mentioned earlier in this book, crisis assessment activities will reveal potential crisis events that could occur in the organization. Some of these crises have geographic considerations, such as earthquakes along the whole west coast of the United States, volcano activity at Mount St. Helens and Mount Rainier, hurricanes in the southeastern United States, terrorism at various targets throughout the world, and wildfires in drier locations in the western United States. Some potential crises are industry specific: chemical spills (production industries), *E. coli* outbreaks (food industries), school violence (education), and computer hacking and viruses (any industry that depends on online sales).

Be sure the top leaders in your organization are supportive and involved in the drill. Without their support, the project is dead. Support and participation in the mock disaster shows employees that management takes these activities seriously. In the opening vignette, the president of the college was an active participant on the CMT and in the mock disaster described. His enthusiasm helped carry the drill through to a successful implementation and completion. It also showed that he cared about instilling a culture in the organization that supported crisis planning.

Include as many parties as possible in planning the mock disaster. Despite their seriousness and intensity, mock disasters also have a social aspect to them in that larger groups of people are working together on a common project. This is not to imply that such drills are meant to be festive or partylike, but they are a social gathering, even if the objective is serious. Because of this factor, including as many individuals as possible who have a link to the drill is advisable. Enthusiasm for the drill can be high because participants are taking part in a social exercise while engaging in activities outside of their normal routines.

Include local police, fire, and other emergency services. Fire and police departments spend a great deal of time in training activities. Most are receptive to taking part in a mock disaster as it serves as a training opportunity for their departments as well. It is also beneficial in that CMT members can become acquainted with some of the key players within the emergency services departments.

Use mock reporters. Mock reporters are standard in any disaster exercise of this scope. The realistic scenario of being interviewed by the media can be unexpected and intimidating. Local university journalism students make a good source of mock reporters, as many will be working for the media in the future.

Sometimes the experience of working in a disaster exercise can lead to working on a real disaster. Mock reporters are used regularly at Syracuse University in disaster training. In 2002, however, the simulated chemical spill that was supposed to occur was replaced by the real thing. Two hours before the mock disaster, a real crisis developed when brown puddles of unknown origin formed inside the university's biological research center. The real crisis resulted in the building being evacuated and the arrival of a hazardous-material team, along with police and fire personnel (Strupp, 2002).

Use mock victims. Including mock victims with injuries is also useful in this type of exercise. Once again, local colleges and universities may be helpful (Crandall, 1997). The drama/theater department can supply "victims" who can be made up to look injured. This activity provides useful practice for these students who work both on and off stage.

Invite the media to come to your drill. In addition to using mock reporters, inviting the local media is an excellent idea as well. The training event can be featured in the local newspaper and on the television evening news. The publicity generated is usually well received as it shows the organization is being proactive in its crisis management efforts. In addition, local reporters can offer advice from their perspectives, some of which may be quite useful to the CMT.

Be sure all of the employees and local community are aware of the drill. The mock disaster should be well publicized to all employees and the local community. It is important to make sure that citizens do not mistake the drill for a real crisis. One of the authors lives near a large military base that occasionally runs mock exercises in the community. One such drill involved the use of a military team descending on an abandoned motel in the community. Helicopters were flying overhead and soldiers were maneuvering around the facility. The drill was so extensive that spectators gathered across the street to watch. Fortunately, advance notice had been given to the community and many were expecting this event as a form of entertainment for the evening. Several years later, the local fire department burned the entire facility down in a dramatic blaze as a training exercise. Again, the community knew to expect a spectacular fire that night. During the mock disaster in the opening vignette, radio transmissions were interrupted every few minutes by a voice that informed residents listening on their police scanners that what they were hearing was only a drill.

Guidelines While the Mock Disaster Is in Progress

Planning a mock disaster is an extensive process. The actual drill should run well if the above guidelines are applied. In addition, it is important that care be taken not to create a real crisis during the drill. Such events do occur and can result in injuries. If the fire department is involved, they will likely have a safety officer who helps ensure that injuries do not occur. Nonetheless, problems can develop and anyone planning such an exercise should be aware of such possibilities. Recently, an elaborate search and rescue drill involving about 400 people was held off the coast of Newfoundland. The objective of the drill was to respond to a scenario in which a ferry was on fire. The drill involved evacuating passengers from the ferry and into lifeboats. The drill took a realistic turn, however, when several passengers on one of the lifeboats were overcome by exhaust fumes and had to be airlifted by helicopter to a hospital (Brautigam, 2007).

A second consideration during a mock disaster is to remember that mistakes will be made during the drill. This is not a bad thing as long as serious damages and injuries are avoided, as one of the purposes is to identify response weaknesses. Those involved should record any mistakes and discuss them during the debriefing meeting held after the mock disaster.

A third guideline, which may be useful for catching mistakes, is to have the drill videotaped. In the opening vignette's disaster, two individuals videotaped the drill. One cameraperson was at the incident command center, where the actual disaster scenario took place. The other videotaped the meetings in the main command center, where most of the CMT was meeting. This arrangement was later useful for evaluation as CMT members at the command center could view what was happening at the incident area, and vice versa.

Guidelines for After the Mock Disaster

Immediately after the drill, food and refreshments should be provided for all of those who participated. This step is highly recommended, as most participants will be exhausted. This social gathering also gives individuals time to reflect, relax, and build camaraderie.

Within 1 week of the drill, it is recommended that a debriefing meeting be held to discuss what was learned. Some teams may choose to debrief immediately after the mock disaster. This may be feasible if the drill did not last too long. Otherwise, it may be better to debrief on another day when the CMT is refreshed and mentally alert. Care should be taken not to wait too long after the event, however, lest team members forget some of the finer learning details of the drill. The lessons learned from the mock disaster may result in changes to the crisis management plan. These changes should be made soon in the master document, and in any additional associated locations such as the organization's Web site.

Summary

This chapter emphasized the importance of forming the crisis management team (CMT) and the crisis management plan (CMP). The CMT is charged with developing a list of threats that face the organization; this is also known as crisis vulnerability assessment. The CMP revolves around addressing these threats, as well as providing other guidelines for how the organization should respond to a crisis.

The CMT also leads the training needed for crisis response. Regular meetings should be held to keep members familiar with the crisis plan, as well as to provide training for specific crisis events. Testing the crisis response of the organization is also important. Short training-response drills should be held several times a year. A more comprehensive drill, the mock disaster, should be conducted once every other year. All of these exercises fine-tune the CMT so that it is ready when a crisis does occur.

Questions for Discussion

1. Discuss how groupthink can be a problem for a crisis management team.

2. How are problems with the crisis management team different from the problems of a standing committee?

3. If you were the crisis management team leader, how would you ensure that the team members regularly review the crisis management plan?

4. How can the crisis management team ensure that the crisis plan is kept up to date?

5. Why is it a good idea to require your suppliers to have a crisis management plan?

6. What types of disaster drills are regularly practiced at your place of employment? If none are used, what would you propose for a disaster drill exercise?

7. What scenarios would make a good mock disaster where you work or go to school?

Chapter Exercise

All students and practitioners in the area of crisis management should be able to compile a crisis management plan (CMP). In addition, the ability to organize a training program and a mock disaster is desirable. This course exercise is designed to be a comprehensive project that accomplishes each of these goals.

General Guidelines

1. Students in the class should be assigned to teams of four to six members. Each team should contact a local organization and, working with the management team, compile a crisis management plan (CMP) for that organization.

2. Employed students already have an entry into their organizations. These are potential companies for the project. Your instructor may also have suggestions of organizations that may be desirable to contact.

3. Each team should design a mock disaster for that particular organization. Keep in mind that the purpose of this drill is to test the organization's CMP and its crisis response capabilities.

4. Each team should recommend a crisis training program for the organization. Indicate how often meetings should be held and what training modules should be provided. Designate which training is for the CMT and which can be made available on a company-wide level.

5. Each team should present its CMP and mock disaster to the class.

Specific Guidelines

1. In organizing the CMP, remember that many such plans are already posted on the Internet. College and university plans are readily available for review and can provide useful insights on how set up your team's plan. In addition, the Appendix at the end of this book provides an outline of areas that should be addressed in your CMP.

2. Remember that a landscape survey of the internal and external environment is necessary to assess that organization's crisis vulnerability. Include this information in the plan as well.

3. Be sure the plan is realistic for the organization you have selected. Do not address crisis scenarios that are not likely to occur at that organization.

4. Designate a backup command center in your plan and explain how a virtual command center would be arranged.

5. Be sure to prepare a timeline for the mock disaster. Identify what should occur 2 months before the drill, 1 month before, 2 weeks, 2 days, and so on. Use a timeline that is feasible for your particular mock disaster.

MINI CASE

(handwritten: MARY WASHINGTON UNIVERSITY PRESIDENT DWI)

UNIVERSITY OF COLORADO HIT WITH CRISES CONCERNING FOOTBALL SCANDALS AND A "FREE SPEECH" PROBLEM

If an award was given to the university that experienced a string of closely occurring crises, the University of Colorado would likely receive it. In 2004, the football team was hit with allegations of using sex, drugs, and alcohol to lure football recruits to the university. In 2005, Ward Churchill, a professor in the Department of Ethnic Studies, became a household word when it was learned that a 2001 essay he wrote referred to victims of the September 11 terrorist attack as "little Eichmanns," a derogatory reference to Adolf Eichmann, a key figure behind the killing of Jews during the Holocaust. In both instances, various critics had called for the firing of the football coach, Gary Barnett, and of Professor Churchill.

At the center of the controversy was the university's president, Elizabeth Hoffman. President Hoffman had many successes during her 5-year tenure as head of the university. She had increased the endowment by almost $100 million. Major strides had been made in the area of technology. Two professors had won Nobel Prizes. But her handling of the football scandal and the Ward Churchill crisis drew sharp criticism from key stakeholders. Although the Board of Regents supported Ms. Hoffman, she lost the support of the governor, Bill Owens, and of state lawmakers who were looking for ways to cut the budget.

What makes this situation particularly difficult is the nature of the two crises. Athletics are major priorities for many stakeholders, both within and outside a university. Free speech, on the other hand, is an internal priority, primarily for faculty. In fact, nearly 200 professors at the university signed a letter supporting Churchill's right to free speech, even if his viewpoints were controversial.

(Continued)

(Continued)

But firing offensive remarks at September 11 terrorist victims was more than what the average American could tolerate. Criticism from outside the university was widespread and solidly against Churchill as well as the university for supporting his right to free speech.

President Hoffman later resigned her post when it became apparent she could no longer weather the crisis and lead the university effectively. Her critics said she was too soft, on the athletic department officials, and for not firing Ward Churchill. Ironically, Churchill was later fired for other concerns related to academic misconduct during the term of the new president, Hank Brown.

Sources

Adams, J. (2005, March 16). Colorado University caught in fracas over professor's remarks. *Indian Country Today*.

Fain, P. (2005, March 18). Under fire on 2 fronts, University of Colorado chief resigns. *Chronicle of Higher Education, 51*(28).

Gravois, J. (2007, August 3). Colorado regents vote to fire Ward Churchill. *Chronicle of Higher Education, 53*(48), 1.

Jacobson, J. (2004, May 28). Panel blasts University of Colorado for handling of scandal. *Chronicle of Higher Education, 50*(38).

Kantrowitz, B., Springen, K., & Toime, P. (2005). Game over in Colorado. *Newsweek, 145*(12), 52–53.

References

Adams, J. (2005, March 16). Colorado University caught in fracas over professor's remarks. *Indian Country Today.* Retrieved November 4, 2007, from http://www.indiancountry.com

Alexander, D. (2004). Cognitive mapping as an emergency management training exercise. *Journal of Contingencies and Crisis Management, 12*(4), 150–159.

Armstrong, J. (2004, February 9). General Motors introduces crisis management plan to supplier, dealers. *Automotive News, 78*(6079), 24.

Barton, L. (2001). *Crisis in organizations II.* Cincinnati, OH: South-Western College Publishing.

Bertrand, R., & Lajtha, C. (2002). A new approach to crisis management. *Journal of Contingencies and Crisis Management, 10*(4), 181–191.

Bovens, M., & 't Hart, P. (1996). *Understanding policy fiascos.* New Brunswick, NJ: Transaction Publishers.

Boyd, N. (2000). Crisis management and the Internet. *Ivey Business Journal, 64*(3), 1–4.

Brautigam, T. (2007, September 28). Mock disaster turns real. *Toronto Star,* p. A03.

Careless, J. (2007). Practice, practice, practice. *Mobile Radio Technology, 25*(3), 46–49.

Chandler, R. (2001). Crisis management: Does your team have the right members? *Safety Management, 458,* 1–3.

Clark, J., & Harman, M. (2004). On crisis management and rehearsing a plan. *Risk Management, 51*(5), 40–43.

Coombs, W. (2007). *Ongoing crisis communication: Planning, managing, and responding* (2nd ed.). Thousand Oaks, CA: Sage.

Coombs, W., & Holladay, S. (2001). An extended examination of the crisis situation: A fusion of the relational management and symbolic approaches. *Journal of Public Relations Research, 13,* 321–340.

Crandall, W. (1997, April). How to choreograph a disaster. *Security Management,* pp. 40–43.

Davis, S. (2002). Virtual emergency operations centers. *Risk Management, 49*(7), 46–52.

Fain, P. (2005, March 18). Under fire on 2 fronts, University of Colorado chief resigns. *Chronicle of Higher Education.* Retrieved November 12, 2008, from http://chronicle.com/prm/weekly/v51/i28/28a00101.htm

Gravois, J. (2007, August 3). Colorado regents vote to fire Ward Churchill. *Chronicle of Higher Education, 53*(48), 1.

Hartley, R. (1993). *Business ethics: Violations of the public trust.* New York: John Wiley.

Hiltz, S. (2006, June). *Partially distributed teams: A tutorial, hands-on experience, and discussion of their use in emergency response.* Paper presented at ISCRAM-TIEMS 2006 Summer School, Tilburg, the Netherlands.

Jacobson, J. (2004, May 28). Panel blasts University of Colorado for handling of scandal. *Chronicle of Higher Education, 50*(38).

Jacobson, L. (2003, April 30). Disaster drills emphasize plans to "shelter" pupils at school. *Education Week, 22*(33), 6–7.

Janis, I. (1982). *Groupthink—Psychological studies of policy decisions and fiascoes* (2nd ed.). Boston: Houghton Mifflin.

Kantrowitz, B., Springen, K., & Toime, P. (2005). Game over in Colorado. *Newsweek, 145*(12), 52–53.

Kass, J., & Marek, A. (2005). What happened after Columbine. *U.S. News & World Report, 138*(12), 28–29.

Kovoor-Misra, S., & Nathan, M. (2000, Fall). Timing is everything: The optimal time to learn from crises. *Review of Business,* pp. 31–36.

Lagadec, P. (2004). Understanding the French 2003 heat wave experience: Beyond the heat, a multi-layered challenge. *Journal of Contingencies and Crisis Management, 12*(4), 160–169.

Lintonen, R. (2004). Understanding EU crisis-making: The case of Chechnya and the Finnish presidency. *Journal of Contingencies and Crisis Management, 12*(1), 29–38.

Lockwood, N. (2005). Crisis management in today's business environment: HR's strategic role. *SHRM Research Quarterly,* no. 4, 1–10.

Millar, M. (2003, October 28). HR must be at forefront of crisis management plans. *Personnel Today,* p. 7.

Perry, R. (2004). Disaster exercise outcomes for professional emergency personnel citizen volunteers. *Journal of Contingencies and Crisis Management, 12*(2), 64–75.

Pines, W. (2000). Myths of crisis management. *Public Relations Quarterly, 45*(3), 15–17.

Podolak, A. (2002). Crisis management teams. *Risk Management, 54*(4), 54–57.

Rentschler, C., & Burdett, P. (2006, Spring). Mock disaster at Stetson Law Library prepares staff for a real one. *Florida Libraries,* pp. 13–15.

Richter, J., Livet, M., Stewart, J., Feigley, C., Scott, G., & Richter, D. (2005, November). Coastal terrorism: Using tabletop discussions to enhance coastal community infrastructure through relationship building. *Journal of Public Health Management Practice,* pp. S45–S49.

Snellen, M. (2003). How to build a "dark site" for crisis management. *SCM, 7*(3), 18–21.

Strupp, J. (2002, September 2). Chemical scare tests reactions. *Editor & Publisher, 135*(31), 4.

Swift, K. (2004). Crisis stage. *ABA Journal, 90*(1), 75.

Wilsenbilt, J. (1989, Spring). Crisis management planning among U.S. corporations: Empirical evidence and a proposed framework. *SAM Advanced Management Journal,* pp. 31–41.

Zoltak, J. (1998). Facility managers urged to run disaster drills. *Amusement Business, 110*(35), 2–3.

CHAPTER 6

Organizational Strategy and Crises

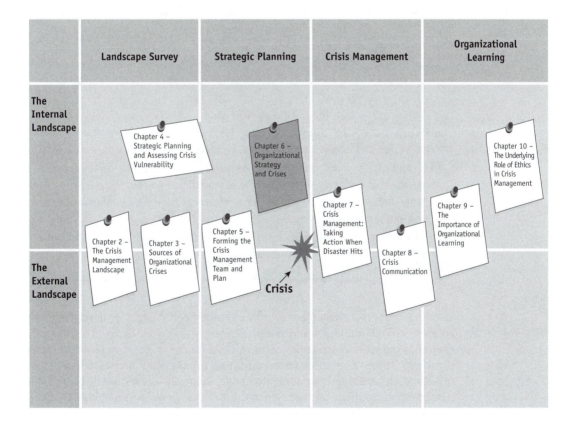

	Landscape Survey	Strategic Planning	Crisis Management	Organizational Learning
The Internal Landscape	Chapter 4 – Strategic Planning and Assessing Crisis Vulnerability	Chapter 6 – Organizational Strategy and Crises		Chapter 10 – The Underlying Role of Ethics in Crisis Management
			Chapter 7 – Crisis Management: Taking Action When Disaster Hits	Chapter 9 – The Importance of Organizational Learning
The External Landscape	Chapter 2 – The Crisis Management Landscape Chapter 3 – Sources of Organizational Crises	Chapter 5 – Forming the Crisis Management Team and Plan **Crisis**	Chapter 8 – Crisis Communication	

Frontier Hotel

The Frontier Hotel in Las Vegas, Nevada, was once a colorful spot on the famous Strip. The Frontier had once been owned by Howard Hughes, and in its heyday saw the likes of such famous musicians as Liberace, Elvis Presley, and The Supremes. But from September 21, 1991, to late January 1998, the hotel's owners staged an infamous battle with the unions representing its employees. For 6-1/2 years, what became the nation's longest strike wore on as the owners, Margaret Elardi and her two sons, stubbornly fought to keep the unions out of their hotel. Their strategy was unusual and perplexing, especially since the majority of hotel workers who are employed on the Las Vegas Strip are unionized. Their bitter strategy failed and cost them the hotel, which they eventually sold to a new owner, Kansas City businessman Phil Ruffin.

The 550 employees at the time of the strike were represented by five different unions, including the Hotel Employees & Restaurant Employees International and the International Brotherhood of Teamsters. Labor leaders argued the owners were using a union-busting tactic by eliminating the pension plan and cutting wages. Executives at other hotels on the Strip supported the strike. One Las Vegas hotel, Circus Circus, began providing food for the strikers on the picket lines. CEO William Bennett said his company was feeding the workers in hopes that would put pressure on the Elardis to resolve the strike (Serwer, 1992).

During the ordeal, the hotel was faced with round-the-clock pickets, negative publicity, rallies and arrests, charges of spying on union sympathizers, and condemnation from human rights leaders (Berns, 1998). Ending the strike would have been strategically simple if the Frontier owners had chosen to offer contracts to the employees that were consistent with those of other hotels on The Strip.

When Ruffin took over the hotel, he quickly negotiated new contracts with the unions and reopened the business under the New Frontier name. Ironically, almost 10 years after this labor crisis ended, the hotel was demolished in a dramatic implosion to make room for a newer and larger hotel/casino.

Effective crisis management requires a strategic mindset; top managers must be alert to vulnerabilities and potential events that may occur. This chapter examines the various strategies organizations follow and their relation to crisis planning. There is a somewhat reciprocal relationship between these two functions. On one hand, we argue that crisis management should be part of the strategic management process. On the other hand, we acknowledge that the strategies a firm chooses to implement can be a factor in the frequency and types of crises that are faced. This chapter begins by examining the link between strategy and crises. Of particular importance is how the intended and realized strategies of a firm can emerge, thus leading to a number of problems. We then proceed to a discussion of the role of strategic control and the prevention and mitigation of crisis events.

Strategy and Crises

Strategy refers to top management's plans to develop and sustain competitive advantage so that the organization's mission is fulfilled. *Strategic management* is a broader term and involves top management's analysis of the environment the organization operates in, as well as the plan for implementation and control of the strategy (Parnell, 2008). Much of this analysis is similar to what must be done to heighten crisis preparedness in an organization. Hence, there is a strong and necessary link between strategic management and crisis management (Pauchant & Mitroff, 1992; Preble, 1997; Smith, 1992).

The prevalence of organizational crises can be related to a firm's strategy. Simply stated, some strategies are more crisis prone than others. Airlines that fly international routes are more likely to face acts of terrorism than those limited to domestic routes. Distribution centers located in southern coastal regions of the United States are more likely to face hurricanes than those located farther inland. Hence, a firm's strategy can foreshadow the type of crisis that may occur, as seen in the Frontier Hotel example in the opening vignette.

The Dilemma of Intended and Realized Strategies

The link between strategies and crises emanates from the fact that strategies are not always implemented as originally planned. Henry Mintzberg (1988) introduced two terms to clarify the discrepancy that often occurs between the time a strategy is formulated and the time it is executed. An intended strategy (i.e., what management originally planned) may be realized just as it was planned, or in a modified form, or even in an entirely different form. What is hoped is that the strategy that management intends is actually realized in its original form. For example, a newspaper with a union representing its production employees may have the intended goal of operating its delivery route personnel with nonunion labor. If this functional goal is attained, then the realized and intended strategies are one and the same.

In most instances, however, the intended strategy and the realized strategy (i.e., what management actually implements) differ, at least to some extent (Mintzberg, 1988). The gap between the intended and realized strategies often results from an unforeseen environmental or organizational event, or as this book would say, a crisis. Suppose, for example, that the union representing the production workers "encourages" management to use only union labor in delivering the newspapers. During the next set of contract negotiations, this issue comes up as the union wants to include the delivery drivers in a separate bargaining unit. This threat to the intended strategy could represent a crisis for management, particularly if the union is able to post pickets in support of this move. Suppose now that the union is successful in including the delivery drivers in the contract. In this instance, the intended strategy and realized strategies are now distinct from each other, at least from management's point of view.

Although it is important for managers to formulate responsible strategies based on a realistic and thorough assessment of the firm and its environment, circumstances invariably change along the way. Hence, it is not uncommon for a gap between the intended and realized strategies to exist, creating the need for constant strategic action if a firm is to stay on course. Instead of resisting modest strategic changes when new information is discovered, managers should search for new information and be willing to make such changes when necessary. It is at this point that a vulnerability exists and a crisis can emerge. The problem is that larger gaps may create uncertainty and unpredictability, a breeding ground for organizational crises. The Frontier Hotel strike illustrates this gap. When the owners of the hotel saw that their strategy of fighting the unions was not succeeding, a new strategy should have been pursued. Instead, the conflict went on for over 6 years, and in the end, the owners were worse off for it.

Sometimes a company purposely creates a gap between their intended and realized strategies, and in the process, creates its own crisis. Beech-Nut Nutrition Corporation found itself in this predicament in the 1980s when it changed to a lower cost supplier of apple juice concentrate. At the time, Beech-Nut had just been newly acquired by Nestlé and was under significant pressure to generate positive cash flows (Traub, 1988), a goal that was becoming more difficult for the company. Subsequently, its intended strategy was to use a legitimate supplier that could offer apple juice concentrate at a low cost. This strategy necessitated changing its long-time supplier of concentrate to a less expensive one based in New York. The new supplier, Interjuice Trading Corporation, offered its product at 25 percent below the market price (Hartley, 1993). Beech-Nut later discovered that the concentrate was unfortunately not 100 percent apple juice, a claim that Beech-Nut made on its product. Instead, the product was a blend of synthetic ingredients, informally dubbed a "chemical cocktail" by an investigator (Welles, 1988). In other words, Beech-Nut found itself dealing with a supplier that was selling a fraudulent product. Thus, a gap was created between its intended strategy, working with a low-cost supplier that was legitimate, and its realized strategy, dealing with a supplier that was selling counterfeit apple juice concentrate. This gap represents a crisis that must be addressed. Figure 6.1 depicts the relationship between intended and realized strategies, and the crisis that can result.

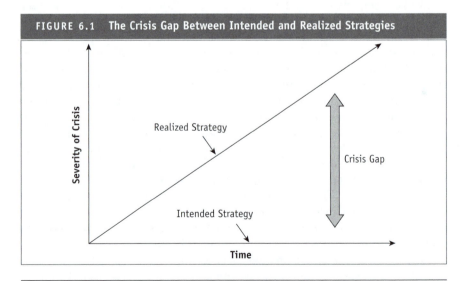

FIGURE 6.1   The Crisis Gap Between Intended and Realized Strategies

Source: Adapted from Carroll, A., & Buchholtz, A. (2003). *Business & Society: Ethics and Stakeholder Management.* Mason, OH: Thomson South-Western, p. 14.

At this point in the story, it would probably make sense to most readers to make a strategic change by suing the current low-cost supplier for damages and switching to a new one. But Beech-Nut did not see it that way. It continued using the supplier and ran a phony apple juice scam, creating an ethics crisis that is now one of the classic cases of white-collar crime. In the final analysis, this event cost Beech-Nut an estimated $25 million in fines, legal fees, and lost sales (Hartley, 1993). Clearly, this crisis should never have happened.

The Multiple Levels of Strategy

Organizational strategy can be examined from multiple levels. The corporate strategy (also called the firm strategy) reflects the broad strategic approach top management formulates for the organization. The business strategy (also called the competitive strategy) outlines the competitive pattern for a business unit— an organizational entity with its own mission, set of competitors, and industry. Competitive strategies are crafted so that each business unit can attain and sustain competitive advantage, a state whereby its successful strategies cannot be easily duplicated by its competitors (Cockburn, Henderson, & Stern, 2000; Parnell, 2008). As we will see, the choice of strategies can influence the types of crises the organization may face.

Corporate Strategies

There are two steps involved in developing the corporate strategy. The first is to assess the markets or industries in which the firm operates. At the corporate level, top management defines the corporate profile by identifying the specific industry(s) in which the organization will operate. Three basic profiles are possible: operate within a single industry; operate in multiple, yet related industries; or operate in multiple, unrelated industries. Each profile brings with it the potential for different types of crises.

An organization that operates in a single industry can benefit from the specialized knowledge that it develops by concentrating its efforts in one business area. McDonald's, for instance, constantly changes its product line, while maintaining a low per-unit cost of operations by concentrating exclusively on restaurants. Wal-Mart benefits from discount retail expertise derived from keeping its cost structures low, as well; a benefit that is passed on to consumers. Both of these companies are successful and play leadership roles in their respective industries. However, a drawback to their success is that they are easy targets for critics and, as a result, can be subject to negative public opinion. For McDonald's, critics in the 1990s pointed to bulky packaging practices (Sethi & Steidlmeier, 1997), and more recently, to unhealthy food in general (Adams, 2005). Wal-Mart's insistence on low costs has resulted in criticism aimed at its relationships with suppliers and employees (Fishman, 2006).

Because firms operating in a single industry are more susceptible to sharp downturns in business cycles that cannot be offset by other business units in the firm, one might argue that they are also more prone to economic crises. As such, an organization may operate in more than one industry in order to reduce uncertainty and risk. It may diversify by developing a new line of business, or acquire other businesses with complementary product or service lines, a process known as related diversification. The key to successful related diversification is the development of synergy among the related business units. Synergy occurs when the two previously separate organizations join to generate higher effectiveness and efficiency than each would have generated separately.

While it is true that related diversification can result in synergies, there can also be a potential crisis associated with certain types of acquisitions. Dow Chemical found this out when it acquired Union Carbide back in 1999. Union Carbide's Bhopal gas leak disaster in 1984 created a "guilt by association" crisis for Dow, which has found itself the target of protests from groups that want the old Bhopal facility cleaned up because groundwater in the area is being contaminated (Baldauf, 2004).

A business may choose to operate in unrelated industries because its managers wish to reduce company risk by spreading resources across several markets. These firms pursue an unrelated diversification strategy by acquiring businesses not related to its core domain. In terms of potential crises, this strategy also has its problems. By expanding their core competencies, firms may find themselves in unfamiliar territory, resulting in the potential for a crisis. This scenario happened to the once-respected A. H. Robins Company when it departed from its core product line to pursue the marketing of the ill-fated Dalkon Shield, an IUD or intrauterine contraceptive device. The product was later associated with health problems in women and was withdrawn from the market. The legal fallout was so devastating that A. H. Robins had to enter bankruptcy and was later bought out (D'Zurilla, 1998).

Table 6.1 illustrates the relationship between corporate profile and crisis likelihood and severity. From a likelihood perspective, operating in a single industry may minimize the number of potential crises by competing in only a single business environment. Should a crisis occur, however, its severity could be greater because it will affect all of the firm's business activities. From a diversification perspective, unrelated diversification may increase the likelihood a firm will encounter a crisis because it is operating in multiple business environments simultaneously. On the other hand, it may also minimize the severity of a crisis if it can be contained to a single business unit. Unrelated diversification, however, can make it more difficult for managers to stay abreast of market and technological changes in the various industries. Hence, unrelated diversification—as opposed to related diversification or operating a single business unit—does not necessarily make a firm less prone to crises, but rather enables it to buffer the effects of a crisis on a single business unit by shielding it from other businesses.

Table 6.1 also indicates that the link between the corporate profile and crisis prevalence depends on the degree of relatedness among a firm's business units and the ability of the firm to develop synergy across the businesses. A firm like Yum Brands, with high synergy across tightly related businesses (e.g., Pizza Hut, KFC, Taco Bell, A&W, and Long John Silver's), is likely to share the crisis characteristics of firms operating in a single industry. In contrast, firms whose businesses are not as closely related and those that have not been able to create synergy across their business units are likely to share the crisis characteristics of firms operating in unrelated industries.

After an organization's corporate profile is determined, its corporate strategy must be established. Simply stated, the corporate strategy reflects a firm's

TABLE 6.1 Corporate Profile and Crisis Prevalence			
Corporate Profile	Likelihood of Crises	Severity of Crises	Net Effect
Operates in a single industry	May minimize the number of crises through specialization in only one industry.	Could increase crisis severity because a crisis that affects one business unit cannot be buffered by other business units.	Fewer crises but more severe in terms of impact to the total organization
Operates multiple businesses in related industries (related diversification)	The link between corporate profile and crisis prevalence depends on the degree of relatedness among a firm's business units and the ability of the firm to develop synergy across the businesses.		
Operates multiple businesses in unrelated industries (unrelated diversification)	May increase the number of crises by exposing the firm to multiple business environments.	Could minimize crisis severity because crisis events can often be contained to a single business unit in the firm.	Greater frequency of crises but less severe in terms of impact to the total organization

intentions concerning growth. Three possibilities exist: An organization may attempt to increase its size significantly, remain about the same size, or become smaller. A growth strategy seeks to increase an organization's revenues or market share significantly. This strategy can be realized in several ways. Internal growth is accomplished when a firm increases revenues, production capacity, and its work force. This type of growth can occur by expanding the business or creating new ones. External growth is accomplished when an organization merges with or acquires another firm. Mergers are generally undertaken to improve competitiveness by sharing or combining resources.

In addition to the crisis potentials mentioned in Table 6.1, growth strategies also carry with them the potential for becoming an extortion target because the firm is larger and more visible. The Wendy's severed finger incident, described in Chapter 3, illustrates such an extortion attempt. Unfortunately, even though no extortion payment was made, Wendy's was still the victim of a 2.5% decline in sales for the quarter (Langston, 2006).

Another type of crisis can occur when a company enters into a strategic alliance as part of its growth strategy. Strategic alliances—often called partnerships—occur when two or more firms agree to share the costs, risks, and benefits associated with pursuing new business opportunities. Such arrangements include joint ventures, franchise/license agreements, joint operations, joint long-term supplier agreements, marketing agreements, and consortiums. Strategic alliances can be temporary, disbanding after the project is finished, or can involve multiple projects over an extended period of time (Parnell, 2008).

The late 1990s and early 2000s witnessed a sharp increase in strategic alliances (Reuer, Zollo, & Singh, 2002). There are many examples of partnerships, especially where technology and global access are key considerations. IBM and Apple Computer have exchanged technology in an attempt to develop more effective computer operating systems. General Motors (GM), Ford, and Chrysler are jointly conducting research to enhance battery technology for electric and alternative fuel cars powered by electricity, hydrogen, and other sources of alternative energy. Perhaps the most dramatic example of strategic alliances is occurring in China, where every major automobile manufacturer in the world is working with firms in the Chinese auto market to build vehicles (Casey, Zamiska, & Pasztor, 2007).

From one perspective, strategic alliances represent a conservative strategic approach by enabling a firm to expand its reach into new markets while utilizing the expertise of partner firms and sharing the risk with them. Yet, strategic alliances can also be vulnerable to crises, especially if the partner firms do not agree explicitly on the contribution each will make to the alliance or if they do not have a common agreed-upon approach to identify vulnerabilities and an action plan to address crisis management. For example, in 2000, Amazon.com and Toys "R" Us signed a 10-year deal to join forces in a strategic alliance. Amazon agreed to devote a portion of its Web site to Toys "R" Us products, while the toy retailer agreed to stock certain items on the virtual shelves. Although the arrangement was touted as an example of how Internet retailers can work effectively with their traditional counterparts, the deal deteriorated several years later and ended up in court in 2006. Toys "R" Us argued that Amazon broke its original commitment to use their company as its sole provider of toys and related products, while Amazon contended the toy retailer did not maintain an appropriate selection of toys (Mangalindan, 2006).

Business or Competitive Level Strategy

Whereas the corporate strategy concerns the basic thrust of the firm—which industries the company will compete in—the business strategy addresses the competitive aspect—how the company will compete in the industries in which they have chosen to compete. Business strategy focuses on who the company should serve, what needs should be satisfied, and how a business should develop core competencies and be positioned to satisfy customer needs. The challenging task of formulating and implementing a strategy for each business unit is based on a number of factors (Parnell, 2008).

The first step in formulating a business strategy is to select a broad or generic approach to competing with rivals (Kaplan & Norton, 2000). It is then necessary to fine-tune this basic approach—often called the generic strategy— to accentuate the organization's unique set of resource strengths (Campbell-Hunt, 2000). Porter's (1980) generic strategy framework serves as a good starting point for assessing business strategies. According to Porter, a business unit must address two basic competitive concerns. First, managers must determine whether the business unit should focus its efforts on an identifiable subset of the industry in which it operates or seek to serve the entire market (i.e., the industry) as a whole. For example, many specialty clothing stores in shopping malls adopt the focus concept and concentrate their efforts on limited product lines primarily intended for a small market niche. In contrast, most chain grocery stores seek to serve the "mass market"—or at least most of it—by selecting an array of products and services that appeal to the general public as a whole. Second, managers must determine whether the business unit should compete primarily by minimizing its costs relative to those of its competitors (what Porter calls a "low cost strategy") or through differentiation, distinguishing itself by offering unique and/or unusual products and services (Parnell, 2006).

Each business strategy has its own crisis-related vulnerabilities. A business emphasizing a low cost strategy, for example, may be susceptible to price competition from other firms, particularly large rivals. This constant pressure to reduce costs may cause a firm to "cut corners," ultimately leading to a crisis situation. Consider the case of Mattel in the late 2000s. Following a string of defective toys imported from China, Mattel issued recalls for millions of Chinese-made toys, many of which contained small magnets or lead paint. Shortly after announcing one of the recalls, an owner of a Chinese toy factory involved in much of the production committed suicide at a factory warehouse (Casey et al., 2007).

Dell computer laptop mother-boards, fire defect.

Most global manufacturing experts attest to the fact that quality has never been a recognized strength of Chinese manufacturing. China has been recognized largely for its ability to produce products at low costs, a view largely supported by a number of studies (Buehlmann, Bumgardner, Lihra, & Frye, 2006). Quality has improved markedly over the past 2 decades, thanks to modernization in both equipment and production practice. Nevertheless, product defects in toys, tires, and agricultural products underscore the fact that quality challenges remain.

Mattel initially blamed faulty Chinese workmanship, but later accepted responsibility for the problems and suggested that a design flaw was a contributing factor. Critics charged that Mattel's excessive efforts to control costs placed children at risk. Although this might be an overstatement, it is clear that the cost control dimension of Mattel's competitive strategy created a breeding ground for this type of crisis.

Alternatively, businesses emphasizing differentiation may be more threatened by abrupt shifts in consumer tastes. When oil prices spiked in 2008, consumer preferences shifted away from sport utility vehicles (SUVs), large cars, and trucks to smaller, more fuel-efficient alternatives. Carmakers like Ford and GM developed and emphasized vehicles that were stylish and fun to drive, not necessarily fuel efficient. When the average price of gasoline hit four dollars a gallon in the United States in 2008, they faced a strategic crisis. At the same time, venture capital began pouring into startup firms around the world racing to develop vehicles that consume less gas or utilize alternative, cleaner, and cheaper fuels (Stewart, 2008; Taylor, 2008).

In the example above, we would argue that this is not just a strategic event, but a crisis that fits the definition that we set forth in Chapter 1. Recall that a crisis is:

An event that has a low probability of occurring, but should it occur, can have a vastly negative impact on the organization. The causes of the crisis, as well as the means to resolve it, may not be readily clear; nonetheless, its resolution should be approached as quickly as possible. Finally, the crisis impact may not be initially obvious to all of the relevant stakeholders of the organization.

The sudden spike in gas prices in mid-2008 was a low-probability event. What would not have been as surprising is a gradual increase in the price of oil over a period of time. The causes of the sudden price increase have been widely debated. Corporate critics blamed the oil companies, while others pointed at the falling U.S. dollar and speculation buying. More likely, though, is the fundamental increase in Asian demand for oil, coupled with price controls and some production capacity problems (Peckham, 2008). The crisis had a negative impact on homebuilders and automakers, who were suddenly faced with short-term and costly decisions about how to address the problem. In the long term, it is apparent that in the automotive industry, a move away from inefficient vehicles and toward fuel-efficient and alternative-fuel vehicles is needed. But again, the short-term uncertainty resulted in the crisis situation.

The Strategic Control Process

The gaps that emerge between intended and realized strategies, as well as the crises that develop as a result of these gaps, can be monitored through an ongoing process called strategic control. This process consists of determining the extent to which the organization's strategies are successful in attaining its goals and objectives. The strategy implementation process is tracked and adjustments to the strategy are made as necessary (Picken & Dess, 1997). It is during the process of strategic control that gaps between the intended and realized strategies (i.e., what was planned and what really happened) are identified and addressed. When a crisis event occurs, strategic control often takes the form of activating the crisis management plan. While crisis prevention efforts should be made whenever feasible, managers should recognize that some crises are not preventable and must simply be managed as effectively as possible.

Consider the prevalence of floods, whether they be the seasonal kind that frequently occur in southern China or the less frequent but equally powerful floods that occur along the banks of the Mississippi River in the United States. In the case of the former, firms should plan accordingly and minimize risks by securing assets and avoiding building facilities in flood-prone areas. In the case of the latter, however, avoiding the region is a less attractive option because the level of risk in any given year is relatively low (Zamiska, 2008). In this situation, crisis management teams must consider the possibility of major flooding—albeit low—and be prepared to take steps in the days preceding a flood to minimize losses. Taking such action constitutes strategic control.

The process of strategic control can be likened to that of steering a vehicle. After the accelerator is pressed (which we will call strategy), the control function ensures that everything (the organization) is moving in the right direction. When a simple steering adjustment (managerial decision) is not sufficient to modify the course of the vehicle, the driver can resort to other means, such as applying the brake or shifting gears (other managerial decisions). In a similar manner, strategic managers can steer the organization by instituting minor modifications to prevent crises or resort to more drastic changes in response to an ongoing crisis, such as altering the strategic direction altogether (Parnell, 2008).

Strategic control can be exercised either as a means of crisis prevention by heeding the warning signs of a potential crisis, or as a means of crisis response by directly addressing the source of the problem. For example, a pressure gauge on a tank holding a lethal chemical is a mechanism for control. When the gauge indicates that the pressure is above the normal range, the operator must make a decision about how to prevent the release of the chemical that is in the tank. Several options are available: The temperature of the tank can be lowered, or the chemical can be moved to another tank.[1] Control as a prevention tool can eliminate the release of the dangerous chemical. Now suppose that the same scenario exists, except in this instance, the temperature of the chemical starts to rise and there is no way to move the chemical or alter the temperature of the tank. After a period of time, the tank pressure release valve opens and the dangerous chemical spews into the open atmosphere. At this point, strategic control enters a more acute phase where the factory must now contain the leak, protect the employees, and notify the public in the surrounding area of what has happened.

Following this analogy, strategic control is often viewed as the process of "keeping or getting the organization back on track." From our perspective, strategic control occurs when the organization's steering wheel is moved to keep the vehicle going in the right direction. Strategic control becomes crisis management when the driver must react quickly to avoid a head-on collision or to minimize injuries and damage when a flat tire sends the vehicle across an embankment. In this respect, strategic control and crisis management are quite similar, with the former suggesting an ongoing, maintenance perspective and the latter suggesting a sporadic, reactive orientation. While it is not difficult to distinguish between the two in theory, the overlap in practice is considerable.

Strategic control usually emphasizes continuous improvement whereby strategic managers seek to improve long-term efficiency and effectiveness throughout the organization. In other words, control is not viewed as an action necessary only when a firm is in crisis. Rather, managers should think critically when considering strategic control and look for opportunities to enhance performance even when things seem to be going well. In this regard, crisis management can be viewed as an outgrowth of strategic control. In Chapter 9 we will discuss an outgrowth of this type of strategic control: organizational learning.

The notion of strategic control highlights the link between a firm's strategy and the subsequent crisis events that may occur. When a crisis occurs, the top management team should not only address the situation but should consider strategic changes that may lessen the likelihood or severity of similar crises in the future. Hence, the public relations dimension is important when a crisis occurs, but a serious look at the appropriateness of existing strategies is also in order (Guiner, 2008).

The need for strategic control—and ultimately crisis management—is brought about by two key factors, the first of which is the need to know how well the firm is performing. Without strategic control, there are no clear benchmarks and ultimately no reliable measurements of how the company is doing. A second key factor supporting the need for strategic control is uncertainty, a concept discussed earlier in the text. Because managers are not always able to forecast the future accurately, strategic control serves as a means of accounting for last-minute changes during the implementation phase. A five-step strategic control procedure can be employed to facilitate this process (Parnell, 2008):

1. Top management determines the focus of strategic control by identifying internal factors that can serve as effective measures for the success or failure of a strategy, as well as outside factors that could trigger responses from the organization.

2. Benchmarks are established for internal factors with which the actual performance of the organization can be compared after the strategy is implemented.

3. Management measures or evaluates the company's actual performance, both quantitatively and qualitatively.

4. Performance evaluations are compared with the previously established standards.

5. If performance meets or exceeds the standards, corrective action is usually not necessary. If performance falls below the standard, then management must take remedial action.

First, strategic control has external and internal dimensions. Although individual firms usually exert little or no influence over the external environment, these macroenvironmental and industry forces must be continuously monitored because shifts in the macroenvironment can have strategic ramifications for the company. The purpose of monitoring the external environment is to determine whether the assumptions on which the strategy is based remain valid. In this context, strategic control consists of modifying the company's operations so it can defend itself more effectively against external threats that may arise or become known before a crisis emerges. External dimensions have been mentioned previously in the book and include other variables besides economic ones. These include globalization, the use of the Internet, the threat of terrorism, environmental concerns, and unusual weather patterns. A major shift in one or more of these factors can alter the strategy of the firm and, therefore, its crisis management preparedness.

From an internal standpoint, top management must assess a strategy's effectiveness in accomplishing the firm's mission and goals: If the firm seeks to be the industry's low-cost producer, for example, its managers must compare its production efficiency with that of competitors and determine the extent to which the firm is attaining its goal. In the broad quantitative sense, management must assess the strategy's effectiveness in attaining the firm's objectives. For example, management can compare a firm's 4% market share with its stated objective of 5% to determine the extent to which its strategy is effective. While it is unlikely that a discrepancy of 1 percentage point would constitute a crisis, examining the underlying reasons for the discrepancies can help managers head off potential crisis situations that could occur if modest corrective action is not taken.

Assessing performance accurately can help identify early warning signs that a crisis may be looming. Firm performance may be evaluated in a number of ways: Management can compare current operating results with those from the preceding quarter or year. A qualitative judgment may be made about changes in product or service quality. Quantitative measures may also be used, including return on investment (ROI), number of accidents in the workplace, employee turnover and tardiness, or number of customer complaints or quality problems. A key problem with performance measurement is that one measure can be pursued to the detriment of another. The common goals of growth and profitability versus safety concerns come to mind. Many crises in organizations are caused by accidents due to poor training and faulty equipment. Expenditures in these areas decrease short-term profits, yet a single accident can severely hurt the long-term viability of the firm or even close it down.

Because individual measures of performance can provide a limited snapshot of the firm, a number of companies have begun using a balanced scorecard approach to measuring performance; measurement is not based on a single quantitative factor, but on an array of quantitative and qualitative factors, such as return on assets, market share, customer loyalty and satisfaction, speed, and innovation (Kaplan & Norton, 1996, 2000). The key to employing a balanced scorecard is selecting a combination of performance measures tailored specifically to the firm. Including indicators that can predict potential crises such as level of customer satisfaction or product quality measures should be considered. A list of possible indicators is presented in Table 6.2.

TABLE 6.2 Balanced Scorecard Indicators and Potential Crises	
Indicator to Include on the Balanced Scorecard	*Potential Crises That It Represents*
Number of accidents in a work section, unit	Accident and safety issues; potential employee lawsuits
Absenteeism by employee in a work section, unit	Motivational problems; substance abuse; abusive supervision
Number of grievances (union setting)	Morale problems; abusive supervision; potential for workplace violence
Percentage of uninterrupted service of Web site	Stability of Web site and computer system infrastructure; denial-of-service (DoS) attacks
Machine, work section downtime	Major production interruption due to accidents, fire, or major machine breakdown
Percentage of defective product(s)	Potential for recalls; negative publicity
Negative media reports on the Internet	Adverse publicity; consumer boycotts
Customer complaints	Negative media attention; future loss of revenue
Returned or defective product rates	Negative media attention; injured customers

Identifying crisis events in the early stages is not always easy. Acknowledging the sales declines brought about by a product boycott is not difficult, for example, but seeing the early warning signals so that action can be taken to palliate its effect can be. Some warning signs are universal, such as product return rates. Others are more organization-specific, such as absenteeism levels and number of grievances.

Exercising strategic control requires that performance be measured, compared with previously established standards, and followed by corrective action, if necessary. Not meeting a performance indicator is often an early warning sign that a potential crisis may exist. Generally speaking, corrective action should be taken at all levels if actual performance is less than the standard unless extraordinary causes of the discrepancy can be identified, such as a halt in production when a fire shuts down a critical supplier. Whenever possible, it is most desirable for managers to consider and anticipate possible corrective measures *before* a strategy is implemented. Doing so lowers the likelihood that threats and problems turn into crises.

Retrenchment Strategies

Retrenchment strategies typically deal with decreasing the size of the organization in order to salvage the firm in some way. Although some might argue that a discussion of this nature really belongs solely in the realm of strategic management, not crisis management, we include it here for two reasons. First, our position is that crisis management should be an integral part of strategic management. To separate the two and treat them as unrelated strategies is a mistake. Second, it is quite probable that a crisis of some type may be the precursor for a retrenchment strategy. Certainly, an economic crisis, where sales are slumping, represents one such scenario. However, in this book we address the more acute crisis events that are sudden in nature and far reaching in impact. For example, a major fire, negative publicity, product recall, or a breach of ethics by management can all be factors that lead to a decrease in revenue and therefore the need to retrench.

When a major crisis looms, a retrenchment strategy may be appropriate. A retrenchment strategy is often accompanied by a reorganization process known as corporate restructuring, a planned change in the organization's structure to improve efficiency and firm performance. Even leading companies can experience crises emanating from product and economic cycles that require them to restructure. Fast food giant McDonald's, for example, posted a fourth-quarter 2002 loss of $344 million, its first in 37 years. The firm responded with a restructuring plan that included fewer new stores, greater product and marketing emphasis on existing outlets, and a number of store closings in 2003 in the United States and Japan, its two largest markets (Parnell, 2008).

An acute crisis can lead to retrenchment. On the extreme end of the continuum is Enron, a company that experienced a number of ethical problems at the top level. Enron eventually imploded, although one could argue the demise occurred in a series of stages, hence some degree of retrenchment was evident. But the more typical scenario involves a partial retrenchment in response to a crisis that does not lead to the ultimate dissolution of the company. Instead, after a period of retrenchment, a buyer may come along and rescue the company from its deteriorated condition. In the opening case, The Frontier Hotel was "rescued" after its 6-1/2 year demise due to the labor strike when it was bought by Phil Ruffin. Consider ValuJet, a budget airline that was one of the darlings of the market. In 1996, Flight 592 plunged into the Florida Everglades, killing all passengers and crew. Safety violations in the cargo area allowed the shipping of oxygen containers, which exploded in flight. In 1997, ValuJet merged with AirTran and adopted its name as part of its rebuilding effort to rebound from the crash (Beirne & Jensen, 1999).

Retrenchment may take any one of three forms: turnaround, divestment, or liquidation. A turnaround is the most conservative response to a crisis, whereas liquidation is the harshest response. The traditional view of a turnaround is that it seeks to transform the corporation into a leaner, more effective firm and includes such actions as eliminating unprofitable outputs, pruning assets, reducing the size of the workforce, cutting costs of distribution, and reassessing the firm's product lines and customer groups (Garry, 1994). From a crisis management perspective, however, turnaround strategies can involve any move that management deems necessary to get the company back on track. Denny's restaurants illustrate how a company not only can withstand a crisis, but can benefit from it in the long run. "A decade ago, the restaurant chain Denny's was nearly synonymous with racism," according to Ray Hood-Phillips, Chief Diversity Officer at Denny's. After a devastating $54 million racial discrimination lawsuit, the company viewed its turnaround as requiring "a holistic approach to diversity" (Brathwaite, 2002, p. 28). This move involved changing the culture of the company through intensive diversity training, better recruiting practices, and a more valid performance appraisal system.

Some crisis events may result in a loss of revenue and a reduction in the size of the workforce. If layoffs are implemented, management must be prepared to address their effects on both departing employees and survivors. Employees may be given opportunities to leave voluntarily—generally with an incentive—to make the process as congenial as possible. When this situation occurs, those departing can be the top performers who are most marketable, leaving the firm with a less competitive workforce. When layoffs are simply announced, morale is likely to suffer considerably. For this reason, turnarounds involving layoffs are often more difficult to implement than anticipated (Murray, 2001).

When layoffs are necessary, however, several actions can help to ease some of the negative effects. Specifically, top management is encouraged to communicate honestly and effectively with all employees, explaining why the downsizing is necessary and how terminated employees were selected. Everyone, including the "survivors," should be made aware of how departing employees will be supported. Employees should also be encouraged to partake of services available to them, and special efforts should be made to ensure that such programs are administered in a clear and consistent manner. Although these measures will not eliminate all the harsh feelings associated with layoffs, they can help keep the process under control.

A number of executives are widely recognized as "turnaround specialists" and may be brought in as temporary CEOs to lead the process and orchestrate such unpopular strategic moves as layoffs, budget cuts, and reorganizations. In addition, crisis management consulting firms are abundant and can advise on the specifics of crisis management planning and communicating with the media. Robert "Steve" Miller, also a major player in the Chrysler turnaround, has served as CEO of Waste Management and the automobile parts supplier Federal-Mogul, as well as a consultant on turnaround issues to such companies as Aetna. According to Miller, the CEO in a company seeking turnaround should be honest with employees from the outset and seek their input. He or she should also spend time with customers. As Miller put it, "Listen to your customers. [They] are usually more perceptive than you are about what you need to do with your company" (Lublin, 2000).

Divestment—selling one or more business units to another firm—usually occurs when a firm's leaders believe the organization is facing a crisis, although this is not always the case. Divestment may be necessary when the industry is in decline or when a business unit drains resources from more profitable units, is not performing well, or is not synergistic with other corporate holdings. In a well-publicized spinoff, PepsiCo divested its KFC, Taco Bell, and Pizza Hut business units into a new company, Tricon Global Restaurants, Inc., in 1997. The spinoff was designed to refocus PepsiCo's efforts on its beverage and snack food divisions. Tricon's name was officially changed to Yum Brands in 2002.

Liquidation is the strategy of last resort; it terminates the business unit by selling its assets. Liquidation is by definition a last-ditch response to a severe crisis. In effect, liquidation is a divestment of *all* the firm's business units and should be adopted only under extreme conditions. Shareholders and creditors experience financial losses, some of the managers and employees lose their jobs, suppliers lose a customer, and the community suffers an increase in unemployment and a decrease in tax revenues. Hence, liquidation should be considered only when other forms of retrenchment are not feasible.

Summary

A *strategy* is a top management plan to develop and sustain competitive advantage so that the organization's mission is fulfilled. The prevalence of organizational crises can be directly related to a firm's strategy. A firm may operate in more than one industry to reduce uncertainty and risk. Although some strategies may be more crisis prone than others, each firm-level and business-level strategy has its own crisis-related vulnerabilities.

Organizations often change strategies when a crisis occurs. Maintaining strategic flexibility and pursuing a change in strategy is not always advisable, however, even in the midst of a crisis. Strategic control can be exercised either as a means of crisis prevention by heeding signs warning of poor performance, or as a means of crisis response by directly addressing the source of the problem. The need for strategic control—and ultimately crisis management—is brought about by the need to know how well the firm is doing and the need to address uncertainty. Assessing performance accurately can help identify early warning signs that a crisis may be looming. When a major crisis looms, a retrenchment strategy may be appropriate. Retrenchment can take the form of turnaround, divestment, or liquidation, the most extreme crisis response.

The strategic control process consists of determining the extent to which the company's strategies are successful in attaining its goals. Control can be exercised either as a means of crisis prevention by heeding the warning signs of poor performance, or as a means of crisis response by directly addressing the source of the problem. From a crisis standpoint, effective strategic control is important because it embodies the crisis response efforts.

Questions for Discussion

1. What is the relationship between crisis management and strategic management?

2. Are some strategies more crisis prone than others? Explain.

3. In general, should organizations change strategies or "stay the course" when a crisis looms? Explain.

4. How are the concepts of strategic control and crisis management similar and different?

5. What are some examples of where controls failed in an organization and a crisis erupted?

6. What forms of retrenchment are available to firms facing a serious crisis situation? When should each be employed?

Chapter Exercise

Firms that operate in a single industry tend to experience fewer but more serious crises. In contrast, firms that diversify into multiple industries are open to a wider range of crisis events. Because these firms spread their resources over several industries, however, the effects of each crisis may be less severe. Consider Ford Motor Company. Currently, Ford competes primarily in a single industry, automobiles. What if Ford diversified its business by purchasing Burger King, Nike, Kroger, and Marathon Oil? How would this alter Ford's exposure to crises?

MINI CASE

DON IMUS

Radio personality Don Imus launched the program *Imus in the Morning* on WABC in New York in 1979, a show that was to endure 28 years on the air. For the last dozen years of the show, Imus's program was syndicated to 60 stations across the country via CBS's Westwood One network and was simulcast on cable television network MSNBC. From the beginning, Imus was known for satire, parodies, and off-color humor. Initially known as a "shock jock," Imus shifted attention to politics and commentary as the program matured. Guests on the show in its later years regularly included senators, congressional representatives, and other well-known politicians.

(Continued)

(Continued)

During the past decade, Imus was the center of a number of controversies stemming from on-air remarks. In 1998, Imus referred to *Washington Post* writer Howard Kurtz as "that boner-nosed . . . beanie-wearing little Jew boy." In 2004, he referred to publisher Simon & Schuster as "thieving Jews," later calling the remark redundant. In 2006, Imus referred to the Jewish management at CBS as "money-grubbing bastards."

His remarks on April 4, 2007, reached a new low. On that day, substitute sportscaster Sid Rosenberg reported on the University of Tennessee's women's national championship victory over Rutgers University. While MSNBC aired highlights of the game, Imus said, "They're some rough girls from Rutgers . . . they got tattoos . . . [they're some] nappy-headed hos . . ." Within 24 hours, several notables called for Imus's resignation. MSNBC and CBS were facing a serious publicity crisis.

Although there was little if any defense for Imus's comments, listeners—and Americans in general—were divided on whether or not the show should be eliminated. Some argued that his comments were overtly racist and should not be a part of any radio show. Others, however, argued that listeners should be the final arbiters of Imus's fate, fearing a chilling effect of free speech if Imus were not allowed to continue his show. Imus issued multiple apologies, appeared on civil rights leader Al Sharpton's radio show, and met with the Rutgers women's basketball coach and team to apologize as well.

CBS initially suspended Imus from its radio program for 2 weeks. MSNBC followed shortly thereafter by canceling its television simulcast of the program after firms began to pull their advertising from the show and consumers threatened boycotts of other firms and the networks. Several days later, CBS fired Imus from the radio show, marking an end to the crisis. In the end, pressure on the show's advertisers—not the moral argument—seemed to place the networks in a difficult situation. CBS suffered financially as a result of the crisis, with net income falling 5.9%, partially due to Westwood One's problems with Imus.

One can debate CBS's reluctance to respond when Imus made offensive remarks on numerous occasions preceding his comments about the Rutgers women's basketball team. In the end, however, Imus was removed and CBS was faced with the task of recovering from the crisis.

Sources

Barnes, B. (2007, April 10). Imus suspended over race slurs. *Wall Street Journal,* p. A16.

Barnes, B., & Ovide, S. (2007, May 4). CBS's radio woes drag down profits. *Wall Street Journal,* p. C6.

Bauder, D. (2007, April 10). Racial slur gets Imus 2-week suspension. *WashingtonPost.com.* Retrieved December 2, 2008, from http://www.washingtonpost.com/wp-dyn/content/article/2007/04/09/AR2007 040900098.html

CBS statement on Imus firing. (2007, April 12). *Wall Street Journal Online.*

McBride, S., & Steinberg, B. (2007, April 16). Finding a replacement for Imus won't be easy. *Wall Street Journal,* p. B1.

Steinberg, B., Barnes, B., & Steel, E. (2007, April 12). Facing ad defection, NBC takes Don Imus Show off TV. *Wall Street Journal,* p. B1.

Steinberg, B., & McBride, S. (2007, April 11). P&G, others pull Imus ads. *Wall Street Journal,* p. B3.

Note

1. Based loosely on the 1984 Union Carbide Bhopal gas leak incident.

References

Adams, R. (2005). Fast-food, obesity, and tort reform: An examination of industry responsibility for public health. *Business and Society Review, 110*(3), 297–320.

Baldauf, S. (2004). Bhopal gas tragedy lives on, 20 years later. *Christian Science Monitor, 96*(111). 7.

Barnes, B. (2007, April 10). Imus suspended over race slurs. *Wall Street Journal,* p. A16.

Barnes, B., & Ovide, S. (2007, May 4). CBS's radio woes drag down profits. *Wall Street Journal,* p. C6.

Bauder, D. (2007, April 10). Racial slur gets Imus 2-week suspension. *Washington Post.com.* Retrieved December 2, 2008, from http://www.washington post.com/wp-dyn/content/article/2007/04/09/AR2007040900098.html

Beirne, M., & Jensen, T. (1999). AirTran continues its comeback. *Adweek, 40*(30), 4.

Berns, D. (1998). Frontier strike ends after sale. *Hotel & Motel Management, 213*(5), 3–4.

Brathwaite, S. (2002). Denny's: A diversity success story. *Franchising World, 34*(5), 28–29.

Buehlmann, U., Bumgardner, M., Lihra, T., & Frye, M. (2006). Attitudes of U.S. retailers toward China, Canada, and the United States as manufacturing sources for furniture: An assessment of competitive priorities. *Journal of Global Marketing, 20*(1), 61–73.

Campbell-Hunt, C. (2000). What have we learned about generic competitive strategy? A meta-analysis. *Strategic Management Journal, 21,* 127–154.

Carroll, A., & Buchholtz, A. (2003). *Business & society: Ethics and stakeholder management.* Mason, OH: Thomson South-Western.

Casey, N., Zamiska, N., & Pasztor, A. (2007, September 22). Mattel seeks to placate China with apology. *Wall Street Journal, 250*(70), pp. A1–A7.

CBS statement on Imus firing. (2007, April 12). *Wall Street Journal Online.* Retrieved November 13, 2008, from http://online.wsj.com/article/SB117641139629568191.html?mod=todays_free_feature

Cockburn, I. M., Henderson, R. M., & Stern, S. (2000). Untangling the origins of competitive advantage. *Strategic Management Journal, 21,* 1123–1145.

D'Zurilla, W. (1998). Reflections of a Dalkon Shield arbitrator. *Dispute Resolution Journal, 53*(1), 13–15.

Fishman, C. (2006). *The Wal-Mart effect: How the world's most powerful company really works—And how it's transforming the American economy.* New York: Penguin.

Garry, M. (1994, February). A&P strikes back. *Progressive Grocer,* pp. 32–38.

Guiner, T. (2008, May 25). Dealing with a PR crisis takes planning and truth. *Wall Street Journal,* Special Insert.

Hartley, R. (1993). *Business ethics: Violations of the public trust.* New York: John Wiley.

Kaplan, R., & Norton, D. (1996). *The balanced scorecard: Translating strategy into action.* Boston: Harvard Business School Press.

Kaplan, R., & Norton, D. (2000). *The strategy-focused organization.* Boston: Harvard Business School Press.

Kaplan, R. S., & Norton, D. P. (2000). Having trouble with your strategy? Then map it. *Harvard Business Review, 78*(5), 167–176.

Langston, R. (2006). Just good business. *Communication World, 23*(5), 40–41.

Lublin, J. S. (2000, December 27). Tips from a turnaround specialist. *Wall Street Journal,* p. B1.

Mangalindan, M. (2006, January 23). How Amazon's dream alliance with Toys "R" Us went so sour. *Wall Street Journal,* pp. A1, A12.

McBride, S., & Steinberg, B. (2007, April 16). Finding a replacement for Imus won't be easy. *Wall Street Journal,* p. B1.

Mintzberg, H. (1988). Opening up the definition of strategy. In J. B. Quinn, H. Mintzberg, & R. M. James (Eds.), *The strategy process* (pp. 14–15). Englewood Cliffs, NJ: Prentice Hall.

Murray, M. (2001, March 13). Waiting for the ax to fall. *Wall Street Journal,* pp. B1, B10.

Parnell, J. (2008). *Strategic management: Theory and practice* (3rd ed.). Cincinnati, OH: Atomic Dog Publishing.

Parnell, J. A. (2006). Generic strategies after two decades: A reconceptualization of competitive strategy. *Management Decision, 44,* 1139–1154.

Pauchant, T., & Mitroff, I. (1992). *Transforming the crisis-prone organization.* San Francisco: Jossey-Bass.

Peckham, J. (2008). Distillate demand growth, price controls explain global oil price spikes. *Diesel Fuel News, 12*(14), 30.

Picken, J. C., & Dess, G. G. (1997). Out of (strategic) control. *Organizational Dynamics, 26*(1), 35–48.

Porter, M. E. (1980). *Competitive strategy.* New York: Free Press.

Preble, J. (1997). Integrating the crisis management perspective into the strategic management process. *Journal of Management Studies, 34*(5), 669–791.

Reuer, J. J., Zollo, M., & Singh, H. (2002). Post-formation dynamics in strategic alliances. *Strategic Management Journal, 23,* 135–152.

Serwer, A. (1992). Feeding a strike. *Fortune, 126*(6), 14–16.

Sethi, S., & Steidlmeier, P. (1997). *Up against the corporate wall: Cases in business and society.* Upper Saddle River, NJ: Prentice Hall.

Smith, D. (1992). Commentary: On crisis management and strategic management. In P. Shrivastava (Ed.), *Advances in strategic management* (pp. 261–269). Greenwich, CT: JAI Press.

Steinberg, B., Barnes, B., & Steel, E. (2007, April 12). Facing ad defection, NBC takes Don Imus Show off TV. *Wall Street Journal,* p. B1.

Steinberg, B., & McBride, S. (2007, April 11). P&G, others pull Imus ads. *Wall Street Journal,* p. B3.

Stewart, J. B. (2008, May 28). Auto makers can find opportunity in $4 gasoline. *Wall Street Journal,* p. D3.

Taylor, E. (2008, May 6). Start-ups race to produce "green" cars. *Wall Street Journal,* pp. B1, B7.

Traub, J. (1988, July 24). Into the mouths of babes. *New York Times Magazine,* p. 37.

Welles, C. (1988, February 22). What led Beech-Nut down the road to disgrace? *Business Week,* p. 124.

Zamiska, N. (2008, May 20). Quake quiets the critics of China's human-rights record. *Wall Street Journal,* p. A8.

CHAPTER 7

Crisis Management

Taking Action When Disaster Hits

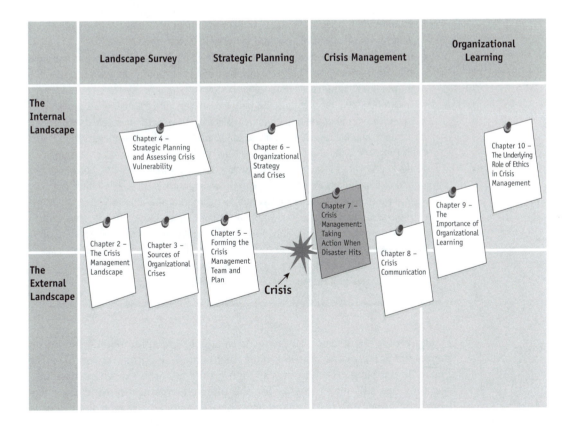

The Ferry Crisis

One of the most serious types of crisis that a maritime company can face is the sinking of a vessel. Ferry vessels carry both passengers and cars, which makes them especially vulnerable to a crisis in two ways. First, many ferries use a roll-on–roll-off design. This layout scheme provides for large openings located at either end of the ship, one to allow vehicles to "roll on," and one to allow vehicles to exit the other end of the ship (i.e., "roll off"). The roll-on–roll-off design has been questioned for decades in terms of its safety because it does not allow for an airtight compartment, common on most commercial vessels (Barnard, 1987; Talley, 2002). If water gets into the compartment where the vehicles are located, the ferry can list and capsize within 10 minutes (Talley, 2002).

This lack of warning in terms of time is not adequate to alert passengers, which leads to a second vulnerability unique to ferries. Unlike freight-laden sea vessels, a ferry typically transports a high number of passengers, making its sinking especially tragic since a large number of lives are usually lost in the accident. Several incidents are worth noting:

- In March 1987, the *Herald of Free Enterprise* ferry capsized just off the coast of Belgium, resulting in 191 fatalities. In this accident, the bow doors had been purposely left open to ventilate the compartment of exhaust fumes from the vehicles that had just driven onto the vessel (Roux-Dufort, 2007).
- In December of the same year, the *Dona Paz,* a ferry owned by Sulpicio Lines in the Philippines, sank. This accident, the worst peacetime sinking ever, resulted in over 4,000 fatalities ("Those in Peril," 2008).
- In October 2003, the Staten Island ferry in New York City crashed into a pier at 17 miles per hour after the ship's pilot fell asleep at the wheel. Ten people died in this accident, and the captain, Richard Smith, later attempted suicide (Gegax, 2003).
- In February 2006, the Egyptian-owned ferry M/V a*l-Salam Boccaccio 98* sank in the Red Sea after it caught fire and capsized in high winds. Over 1,000 passengers and crew members perished in one of the worst ferry disasters ever (Miller, 2006).
- In a more recent tragedy involving a ferry, another Philippines vessel, the MV *Princess of the Stars,* also owned by Sulpicio Lines, sank after it set sail in typhoon-whipped waves. Only 56 of the 850 on board survived the accident. In a secondary crisis, it was later discovered that 11 tons of pesticide were illegally on board the vessel, a risk that rescue divers were unaware of when they searched the area for survivors (Hookway, 2008).

[handwritten margin note: what was the cause of the ENRON CRISIS?]

High-profile events such as the terrorist attacks of September 11, the Enron scandal, and Hurricane Katrina have highlighted the importance of crisis preparedness. Most crises are not as high profile as these examples; nonetheless, they are still major events for the affected organization and the local geographic areas. As a result, many firms have changed their priorities and have begun to analyze their vulnerabilities. Indeed, anticipating and preparing for crises is much less traumatic and costly than experiencing an unexpected calamity without a plan for managing it. Assuming that a company will remain free from any type of a crisis is not an effective way to manage (Spillan &

[handwritten note: What is the cause of the CURRENT FINANCIAL CRISIS? GREED]

Crandall, 2004). For some organizational leaders, this may involve confronting "paradigm blindness," a condition "where people are unable to see information that threatens and disconfirms their worldview" (Wheatley, 2006, p. 18).

willful blindness

There are countless stories where the lack of a plan caused severe or even irreparable damage to a firm. Interestingly, however, there are also examples where proper planning and execution of a crisis plan not only kept the crisis under control but also resulted in positive changes for the business (Borodzicz & van Haperen, 2002; Sundelius, 1998; Wilderoter, 1987). This topic will be explored in depth in Chapter 9, "The Importance of Organizational Learning."

Most crises are, by their very nature, unexpected and unpredictable. A poorly managed crisis can severely damage a firm's reputation and profitability. Proactive organizations should develop crisis management responses for managing an event should it strike. Crises affect organizations in many different ways. Some businesses encounter "smoldering" crises that start internally and slowly create problems that can be difficult to resolve (Institute for Crisis Management, 2007). Other crises can occur externally and take the organization completely by surprise. Effective crisis management requires managers to develop strategies that are integrated with the annual corporate planning process (Preble, 1997). Its effectiveness can be enhanced if managers are able to identify a potential crisis and develop appropriate strategies to prevent it, or at least mitigate its effects.

This chapter focuses on the management practices and decision-making activities that should be implemented at the beginning, during, and conclusion of the crisis event. The first part of this chapter addresses the initial response actions that are critical in the assessment of the crisis. The next part discusses key issues relating to managing the crisis. Response and mitigation of the crisis are the major concerns here. In this stage, managers must make decisive decisions that will determine the success or failure of their crisis management efforts. The final part of the chapter discusses what happens after the crisis, including the issues of recovery, reentry, and business continuity. Ultimately, the organization must regroup and return to normal operations, or its survival may be in jeopardy.

The Beginning of the Crisis: Leadership, Strategies, and Activities

The response to a crisis depends on the nature of the event. Some crisis situations, such as a plant accident, the sudden death of a senior executive, the notification of a government investigation, or a chemical spill, can occur quickly and often with little or no warning. Others, such as a hostile takeover, union labor unrest, a boycott, or corporate embezzlement, develop over a longer period of time. The length of time managers have to react to a crisis is related to its impact on the organization and its stakeholders. Having a crisis management plan (CMP) makes it possible to think and act expediently during the first few hours of a crisis. The CMP is a key strategic organizational tool responsible for initiating the crisis decision-making process by helping to frame the problem, determine the parties responsible for implementing various actions, and develop justifications for the decisions that are made.

Leadership During the Crisis

Effective leadership is necessary during a crisis, both by the leader of the crisis management team (CMT) and by top management (Wooten & James, 2008). This team is responsible for making and implementing decisions that help the organization resolve the crisis. Three components of the CMT that must be present for crisis leadership to be successful are (1) the right leadership, (2) the structure and resources necessary to accomplish crisis response and containment, and (3) broad public support for the organization (Cavanaugh, 2003). Effective CMT leadership is also critical because of its influence on the rest of the team's performance (Flin, 2005).

In a crisis response, CMT members should not only be knowledgeable about their own specific responsibilities but also willing to accept suggestions presented by other members of the team who may be experts in other areas. The CMT leader must promote open communication, which includes defining goals and expectations. Some of the main attributes the leader must possess in a crisis are situational awareness, emotional stability, and emotional intelligence (Flin, 2005). Likewise, the leader must have an array of competencies related to decision making, situational assessment, delegating, prioritizing, team management, communication, and stress management (Crichton, Lauche, & Flin, 2005).

The CMT leader needs to use these competencies by taking charge of the situation, assessing the actual level of crisis seriousness, determining the level of resources needed, and then making the decisions that will resolve the crisis (Cavanaugh, 2003). Simultaneously, the leader should be in frequent communication with his or her team members to assess the implementation of the crisis plan. Within the context of this role, the leader must recognize and implement these actions while remaining visible and available. The leader must have the flexibility to move or respond to any situation that may emerge, and be able to communicate in a supportive manner.

How the team leader communicates can influence the final outcome of the crisis and can also affect the behaviors and reactions of the major stakeholders. Hence, the leader must have the ability to remain calm and focused on the crisis management process while making decisions under significant pressure. All crises create a level of tension and stress. In their study of incident command procedures, Crichton and colleagues (2005) found that acute stressors for the team included unfamiliar chaotic events, communication problems, time pressure, consequences and accountability, fear of failure, dealing with the media, and information problems including overload, missing, and/or ambiguous information. Maintaining control allows the leader to sustain an objective perspective and see the way through complex and confusing scenarios. Finally, the leader must quickly and methodically present an objective perspective for all the stakeholders (Rolston & McNerney, 2003).

One final note should be mentioned concerning the attributes of the CMT leader—there is no one best profile for success. As Schoenberg (2005) noted,

A crisis leader in one situation may be a follower in a different situation. A crisis leader in a natural disaster will need to demonstrate different skills than a crisis leader of a product recall. A crisis leader dealing with employee sabotage or violence faces an entirely different situation. (p. 3)

Initiating the Situational Analysis

One of the first acts of the CMT is to assess the situation so that decisions can be made on how to mitigate the crisis (Wilson, 2004). *Situational analysis* refers to the information processing and knowledge creation aspects of crisis management (Coombs, 2007). Endsley and Garland (2000) describe it as an awareness of knowing what is going on and then predicting how the crisis may evolve in later steps. For decision making, the initial situation assessment is an important starting point and includes not only problem identification, but also estimating the level of risk and the time available to make decisions (Flin, 2005). Situational analysis is critical to understanding the crisis and identifying its dimensions and intensity. Leaders should assess the crisis situation without delay and begin making decisions regarding resource allocations.

The Los Angeles riots in 1992 illustrate this need for timely assessment of the situation. The riot was rooted in the police beating of Rodney King, an African American motorist who had been stopped by police on March 3, 1991. King had led police on a high-speed chase before being pulled over, and then continued to resist arrest once he was out of his vehicle. Police officers struck King 56 times with batons, in addition to kicking him and stomping on his head (Miller, 2001). The riots commenced on April 28, 1992, shortly after 3:15 p.m., when police were found not guilty of using excessive force in the arrest.

Solomon (1992) overviewed the crisis response of various organizations in the areas where the rioting was worst. Because of the danger of physical harm to employees, companies needed to act quickly. Thrifty Corporation[1] operated 21 pharmacies in these areas. Four of the stores were burned to the ground and the other 17 stores were looted:

> Company executives gave guidelines to managers. If they felt that a group of people approaching the stored looked threatening, or if people came in hordes, they were to close down. In addition, if they could see that neighboring stores were having trouble, or if they could see fires anywhere around, they were to close down. (Solomon, 1992, p. 24)

The Los Angeles Police Department was widely criticized for its slow response in its assessment and containment of the riots. Miller (2001) pointed out that the 1965 Los Angeles Watts riots had provided ample lessons on the culture and dynamics of this particular area. Police were tentative in dealing with the riots in 1965, a lesson that indicated a quicker response and more forceful tactics would be needed in future riots. But these lessons were not heeded in 1992 as, once again, widespread damage occurred along with a number of fatalities.

Hospitals were also ill equipped to handle the patient loads, as injuries from the riots were staggering. On the other hand, ARCO service stations responded quickly by closing stations so underground gas tanks would not ignite. Employees were notified via a phone chain (e-mail was not available yet) not to report to work because of the danger. In addition, chain-link fences were quickly erected by ARCO around damaged stores (Solomon, 1992).

Whether a crisis involves human and/or physical resources, the crisis management leadership must ask several key questions to determine (1) the nature of the crisis, (2) the individuals involved, (3) the current status of the situation, and (4) the critical needs of the victims or of the physical location. While other questions may be required as well, these are important for the initial assessment stage so that urgent needs can be addressed. In the ARCO example, company headquarters were located 25 miles southeast of the riot area, but executives at the home office were updated continuously on the status of the riot (Solomon, 1992). To summarize, the leader of the crisis management team has a hierarchy of assessment he or she must make, one that requires asking the right questions and obtaining accurate answers. In addition, observation and inspection of the site or the situation can furnish a fair assessment of the intensity and status of the crisis. The leader's assessment of the situational analysis is a major factor in the success or failure of the crisis response.

The components of the situational analysis consist of the following elements (Flin, 2005, p. 8):

- Gathering information and advice from all potential sources including experts on the relevant technical issues
- Recognizing important cues, such as using historical information to build a mental model of the current situation
- Identifying the key elements in the situation
- Judging the degree of risk that is present in the crisis
- Reassessing the situation in response to new information that becomes available
- Predicting ahead to the potential consequences that may result
- Sharing information with relevant parties

Beginning the Mitigation Strategies

Once the situational analysis is completed, strategies for managing the crisis can be identified and implemented. Not all strategies will work initially, so care must be taken to reassess the situation on a regular basis. Flexibility must be maintained because a crisis situation can change on almost an hourly basis.

The Sheetz convenience store chain experienced such a crisis in July 2004. Hundreds of customers in western Pennsylvania became sick from salmonella. The source was later found to be Roma tomatoes that Sheetz procured from one of its produce suppliers. Sheetz executives immediately called a press conference to alert their customers and the media that the company would take full responsibility for the crisis. Shortly thereafter, the chain switched to a new type of tomato from a different supplier. In addition, the chairman of the company, Steve Sheetz, along with its president, Stan Sheetz, and its vice president, Travis Sheetz, personally visited stores to meet with customers, and offered to pay medical bills and lost wages to those who had become sick (Donahue, 2004). The company also posted a toll-free number on its Web site to field any questions that customers or other stakeholders might have. In this example, the mitigating strategies had to begin early and be sustained for several weeks until the crisis was brought under control.

The major goal at the beginning of a crisis is to minimize potential damage to the firm and its reputation. In some cases the objective may even be to turn any potential negatives associated with the crisis into positives for the organization.

For example, one of the first successful cases in crisis management involved the 1990 cruise ship fire aboard the *Crystal Harmony,* a luxury vessel owned by Crystal Cruises of Los Angeles, California. The company turned this crisis into a positive situation by immediately convening its crisis management team and implementing its 61-page crisis management plan (Sklarewitz, 1991). The first task was to conduct the situational analysis, which in this case involved ascertaining the damage to the ship and the extent of injuries. Fortunately, there were no injuries from the fire, which had started in an auxiliary engine room. However, because the ship had only minimal emergency power, it was not able to move itself in the water. With 920 guests and 540 crew members, it was necessary to transport the vessel back safely to port as soon as possible. The CMT arranged to have tugboats bring the ship back.

As mentioned previously, situational analysis is an ongoing process that proceeds throughout the duration of the crisis (Flin, 2005). In the case of the *Crystal Harmony,* the CMT later learned that the ship was able to regain 80% of its power, meaning the tugboats would no longer be needed. This example illustrates how initial mitigation strategies often change during the crisis. Once the safety of the ship was ensured, the CMT went to work preparing press statements for the media. The director of public relations, Darlene Papalini, managed the media proactively by issuing these press statements. Because of this forthcoming approach, media coverage of the event was minimal, which is what Ms. Papalini had desired (Sklarewitz, 1991). Meanwhile, another part of the CMT was managing the refunding process to the passengers. When guests finally disembarked from the ship, they received a full refund and were offered a $500 credit off any future cruise. The aggressive crisis management had a positive spin, as 280 passengers signed a letter expressing their appreciation for the way the company managed the event (Sklarewitz, 1991).

The initial mitigation strategies also begin the long-range quest for managing and surviving the crisis. Decision-making activities are similar to a number of other projects that employees may be part of. What is different here is the nature of the project. In crisis management, the goal is to contain the crisis quickly and return the organization to normal operations. Table 7.1 shows seven decision-making functions that should take place during the management of a crisis.

Utilizing a Spokesperson

Chapter 5 stressed the importance of designating a spokesperson who can manage organizational communications with the media. The major stakeholders in the crisis must be identified and informed, and given both an assessment of what exists and a sense of what is likely to occur next. In some cases, the organization may have to move quickly to make its first statements to the media. The Exxon Corporation, a company that has been through its share of crises, experienced a refinery fire in Baton Rouge, Louisiana, on August 2, 1993. The oil company reacted in less than 3 hours by issuing its first press release at 7:00 a.m. Follow-up statements were issued at 8:00 a.m., 9:00 a.m., 10:00 a.m., 12:15 p.m., 6:00 p.m., and 9:30 p.m. that same day (Duhe & Zoch, 1994). This crisis claimed the lives of three workers and had been preceded by a similar explosion and fire in December 1989, when two employees were killed. Chapter 8 focuses on this important aspect of crisis management.

TABLE 7.1   Decision Making During a Crisis
Step 1: Alert and assemble the crisis management team. As soon as the crisis is detected, the CMT should be activated.
Step 2: Collect all relevant information. Learn as much as possible about the situation, including what happened, who was involved, where it took place, and the current status of the crisis. This step not only occurs during the situational analysis but also throughout the duration of the crisis.
Step 3: Assign tasks and continue fact finding. The crisis management team should delegate duties, just like a project management team would.
Step 4: Develop solution alternatives. Identify possible solutions that are practical and capable of being implemented.
Step 5: Implement the chosen solution(s). Implementation is often the most difficult part of the process. It requires competent people, time, and money. Allocation of sufficient resources is important at this step.
Step 6: Communicate with the media. The organization should be proactive in meeting with the media and presenting its side of the story. If the organization does not communicate, the media must find the facts of the story elsewhere, a situation that takes control out of the hands of management.
Step 7: Review what happened. Evaluate the decisions that were made and the results that followed. What was learned, and how might such a crisis be handled differently in the future?

Source: Wilson, S. (2003). Develop an Effective Crisis-Management Strategy. *Chemical Engineering Progress, 99*(9), 58–61.

Establishing and Monitoring an Information-Gathering System

Managers and affected staff from all divisions of the company must share a common and systematic approach to obtaining and utilizing information (Coombs, 2006). It is important to monitor and evaluate the crisis and to make adjustments as needed. It can be difficult to know whether one is making the best decisions during a crisis, however. The CMT must recognize the importance of monitoring the opinions and behaviors of its key publics during a crisis and exercising its own influence when possible. It may be necessary to adjust the message being communicated, the stakeholders being addressed, and the manner in which the leader is communicating (Caponigro, 1998).

Three elements of information are essential in crisis management. First, it must be timely. Details of the crisis need to be made available to the CMT in a manner that is up to date. An interesting comparison between the private and public sectors before the arrival of Hurricane Katrina illustrates this point. Wal-Mart's emergency operations center began tracking the storm 6 days before it hit New Orleans. Wal-Mart reacted early to this timely information by sending bottled water, flashlights, batteries, tarps, canned tuna, and strawberry Pop-Tarts to those stores that were likely to be in the path of the storm (Olasky, 2006). Government agency responses were hampered by late information, slow response, and a general inability in deciding what to do.

Second, information must be accurate. It must include the exact location, description, and status of the crisis. The Sago Mine disaster in West Virginia illustrates how muddled communications and tired emotions triggered a wave of inaccurate information concerning the fate of 12 trapped miners. In this January 2006 crisis, a mine explosion trapped the miners. They were later found dead, save for one, some 40 hours later by rescuers. The original message originating from the rescuers simply said that "twelve individuals" had been found and one was alive. The radio message was transmitted through five underground relay stations and had to be conveyed through the rescuers' breathing masks, which they were wearing due to the carbon monoxide danger. Unfortunately, the message, muddied by all of the communication "noise," came out "twelve alive" (Langfitt, 2006). The wave of misinformation morphed into a frenzied celebration outside the mine, which would later be silenced by the news that 11 of the miners had in fact died.

Finally, information must be relevant. Information that may be timely and accurate but has nothing to do with the crisis event is of little value to decision makers. This was also exemplified in the Hurricane Katrina disaster. The media displayed a vast amount of information, much of it accurate and dramatic, and some of it useful to those in crisis management capacities. But decision makers seeking new information about the status of the damage or evacuations were often met with media reports of unfounded stories that were supposedly occurring. Some of these false stories actually hindered crisis response. In one instance, CNN reporter Sanjay Gupta detailed how two patients had died because rescue helicopters were grounded due to false media reports of sniper fire (Olasky, 2006).

Timely, accurate, and relevant information is vital to managing a crisis. In addition, crisis managers need systems and resources that ensure a continuous flow of appropriate information. Structures, procedures, and processes for gathering and monitoring information must be established and continuously monitored throughout the crisis. It may be necessary to restructure or modify the information-gathering process as the crisis evolves. Without a well-developed system of gathering information, the success of any crisis management effort is hindered.

In many cases, managers remain alert to the symptoms of a pending crisis. Over time they may have received indicators that certain areas of their organization may be vulnerable and subject to an event that would significantly interrupt operations and cause a major work stoppage and loss of revenue. Other managers, however, may be in denial. They believe that the organization is impervious to any major threat and that business insurance policies will mitigate the effects of any unanticipated crisis events (Spillan, 2003). Whether or not this assumption is completely accurate—and it usually is not—the manager will still be required to deal with the crisis as it unravels.

The Mid-Crisis Stage: Response and Mitigation

The mid-crisis stage represents a turning point for all affected stakeholders. Three potential scenarios may emerge at this point. The first is the belief that the crisis is under control and the damage can be contained. This is a positive sign that the business or organization may have a good chance for continuity. In the second scenario, however, control has not yet been attained, so crisis managers continue to assess the situation and take action to bring it under control. The third scenario suggests that the outcome is hopeless and managers should take steps to salvage whatever they can for the organization.

During the crisis, the CMT should monitor events to determine the following:

- Which of the three scenarios appears to be unfolding?
- What resources are available and how long will it take to deploy them?
- How long will it take to execute a decision or solution?
- Who and what are the victims of the crisis? (Leskin et al., 2004)

No matter what type of crisis occurs, the organization almost always incurs some type of damage. It is therefore important that the CMT do what is feasible to contain the damage inflicted on people, the reputation of the organization, and the property/assets. This task is the bottom-line goal for all crisis managers.

Damage Containment

Damage containment is the effort to keep the effects of a crisis from spreading and ultimately affecting other parts of the business (Mitroff & Anagnos, 2001). Management will need to gather resources such as capital and physical and human resources to help contain the damage (Pearson & Rondinelli, 1998). As a side note, it should be remembered that what we are calling crisis management within the four-phase framework of this book is actually the reactive part of the process. From this perspective, the four-step crisis management process is both reactive and proactive. Figure 7.1 illustrates this tradeoff within the four steps.

With the proper information flowing to the right stakeholders at the right time, damage to people and property can be minimized. In this regard, the main emphasis of crisis management should be focused on three major goals:

- Gaining complete control of the crisis
- Conducting frequent damage assessments
- Restoring normal operations to the organization

Communicating With Internal and External Stakeholders

Although Chapter 8 will address the subject of communication more deeply, we will introduce the topic briefly here. Because organizational crises usually have negative effects on internal and external stakeholders, truthful communication with both groups is crucial (Newsom, Scott, & Turk, 1992). Internal stakeholders include the employees and owners of the firm. External stakeholders include customers, suppliers, the local community, and any part of the general public that is impacted by the organization's crisis. A labor strike, for example, affects all of the stakeholders mentioned above. Suppliers in particular need to be

	Landscape Survey	Strategic Planning	Crisis Management	Organizational Learning
FIGURE 7.1	**Proactiveness and Reactiveness in Crisis Management**			
The Internal Landscape	**Proactive –** Seeks to determine the organization's internal weaknesses and environmental threats that can lead to a crisis.	**Proactive –** Seeks to formulate a crisis management team and a crisis plan that can be used to both prevent and mitigate potential crisis events.	**Reactive –** Seeks to respond to the crisis events that do occur. Emphasis is on containing the damage and restoring normal operations.	**Proactive –** Seeks to learn lessons from the crisis. Emphasis is on prevention of a future crisis and to function better as a crisis management team.
The External Landscape				

informed of a strike and any subsequent picket lines around the organization that may be set up by union members, as delivery trucks driving through these areas may be subject to vandalism (Crandall & Menefee, 1996). In some cases involving larger facilities, it may be necessary to inform suppliers of alternate delivery routes and gates that may be needed to ensure safe delivery. If any danger is present, such as rock throwing or gunshots fired in the area by strikers, then the organization must communicate these potential dangers to suppliers making deliveries (Herman, 1995).

Effective crisis communication should attempt to meet two goals. First, the organization experiencing the crisis should initiate communications with the media. This approach requires the CMT to anticipate the need to communicate and to prepare press releases for the media in advance (Barton, 2001; Williams & Treadway, 1992). This approach also requires a clear understanding of the issues and the selection of the appropriate response. Open communication requires the CMT to respond expediently by sharing relevant information concerning the crisis with the stakeholders (Williams & Treadway, 1992).

The second goal of effective crisis communication requires the organizational spokesperson(s) to restore and maintain stakeholder confidence. Sometimes, this task may simply involve being at the scene of the crisis and working at a grassroots level to ensure that recovery efforts are being maintained. California Governor Arnold Schwarzenegger presides over a state that has its share of crises, from earthquakes, and wildfires, to urban crime and gang problems. During a recent string of wildfires, the governor was out in the field encouraging firefighters with handshakes and consoling victims (Walsh, 2007). While he has certainly been controversial during his tenure, he has also earned praise during crisis events for being available to his constituents.

Evaluating What Is Going Right and What Is Not

The evaluation process is not an activity that occurs only after the crisis ends. Evaluation is a process that begins when the crisis commences and continues on an ongoing basis. The more managers can understand what is and is not working in the crisis response, the more easily they can adjust their plans both for the duration of the present crisis and for the managing of future ones. Because the evaluation process is so important, benchmarks are necessary. The following benchmarks can be helpful in understanding the effectiveness of strategies and tactics:

- How the crisis has affected the stakeholders' behaviors and opinions
- The extent to which sales or share prices have been affected
- Which crisis response strategies and tactics were effective and which were not

In the first benchmark, it is important to note that public opinion can work for or against the company. Human-induced crises are generally perceived more negatively by the general public than crises due to natural disasters. As a result, human-induced crises such as corporate scandals or other ethical violations can harm the reputation of the company (Pearson & Mitroff, 1993). In the case of a natural disaster, however, the public's perception is often that the company is the victim of an outside threat that could not be controlled. Therefore, public opinion may generally still favor the organization.

The second benchmark is important because revenues and shareholder values often decrease during a crisis (Coombs, 2006). Ralph Erben, CEO for Luby's Cafeteria, Inc., knew immediately after a gunman killed 23 people in a Killeen, Texas restaurant on October 16, 1991, that a massive selloff of Luby's stock would follow. On his flight to Killeen to address the crisis, he called the New York Stock Exchange and requested that stock sales be suspended (Barton, 2001). Revenues will most surely fall during a crisis. A fire at the Philips radio-frequency plant in early 2000 not only damaged the facility, but delayed delivery of its product. The snowball effect hit Ericsson, which was then in the cellular phone manufacturing business and using Philips as its supplier. The final impact was a $400 million revenue loss for Ericsson, and its exiting of the cell phone manufacturing industry (Rice & Caniato, 2003).

The third benchmark should be a reminder that not all crisis response strategies will be successful and that changes may be necessary. Even a strategy recommended by the CMP may need to be altered. In the Luby's case, the company's crisis management plan called for the marketing manager to speak with the media. However, due to the severity of the massacre, CEO Erben decided that it would be better if he served as the spokesperson (Barton, 2001).

Understanding how effective crisis management functions are performed requires the gathering of necessary information to use in the assessment process. To gather such information, managers need methods, instruments, and procedures. Major tools that can be used to obtain the information necessary include:

- Tracking sales and profits during and after the crisis
- Establishing a special communication avenue for stakeholders to call with questions and comments about the crisis and how it was managed
- Conducting focus groups to obtain information from key stakeholders
- Conducting surveys of external publics to determine their attitudes

- Documenting the information flow to and from the news media
- Documenting the information about those strategies that worked and those that did not work, and investigating why they were or were not effective (Caponigro, 1998)

The End of the Crisis: Where to Go From Here?

Bringing a crisis to its conclusion depends on how rapidly the initial incident(s) can be contained and resolved. Managing a crisis is not fun, and most of these events do not simply depart on their own. A crisis can leave behind a path of destruction and desolation, making recovery a difficult challenge. Employee morale might be low, sales could be down, and trust and credibility in the business might be shaken. How does the CMT know what adjustments to make in its crisis response strategy? What indicators signal the end of a crisis? How can the CMT measure its performance in managing the crisis? Such questions need to be answered (Caponigro, 1998).

Surviving a crisis provides an opportunity to establish a reputation for caring and competence. One of the critical steps management must take once the crisis has ended is to notify all of its stakeholders that the problem has been resolved. In addition, measures that will be taken either to prevent or to mitigate future crises should be communicated.

Assessment of the Damage

After the immediate crisis, the work of picking up the pieces and going forward begins. It is here that advanced planning, perhaps from the CMP, can help accelerate the recovery and minimize the long-term negative effects of the disaster. During the recovery, the CMT needs to take stock, assess the damage, and determine what resources are readily available to the organization. In some ways the struggle is similar to the startup phase for a business in that it must think strategically and take an entrepreneurial approach to solving future crisis matters (Munneke & Davis, 2004).

Business Continuity Implementation

Business continuity refers to the ability of the business to resume or continue activities regardless of the crisis it has experienced. Essentially, business continuity is about maintaining the important business functions during and after a crisis. Meeting customer demand is important, especially when a company is a key player in a supply chain network (Zsidisin, Melnyk, & Ragatz, 2005). A crisis can impact the core functional areas of marketing, accounting, financial management, human resource management, and manufacturing. When these functions are in trouble, the business begins to collapse because revenue is not being generated. In turn, the companies the business supplies may be severely impacted as well.

When the crisis is over and the immediate threat has passed, the firm moves from a crisis response mode to a crisis recovery posture. The recovery effort depends on the extent of the damage that has taken place. Some firms are closed for months because the business was totally destroyed by the crisis. Other firms that have experienced relatively minor damage may be able to open within a few hours or days. Some companies may remain open, but will have business units that are not operating because of localized damage, a common occurrence after a crisis such as a hurricane. Chain restaurants and retail stores are examples of companies that may have geographically specific damage.

Understanding the state of the business after the crisis will help determine its future. Managers must assess whether the firm has the ability to meet the needs of its stakeholders or not; this will likely depend on the severity of the crisis. This is both an operational decision and a strategic one. While the first impulse is to get the business functioning immediately, this may not always be possible. Munneke and Davis (2004) offered the following considerations:

- Does the firm have sufficient human, physical, and information resources to resume its business? If the disaster is severe, it is possible that the company may not have the resources to continue, even with some provision for insurance payouts.
- Is access to alternative facilities and support available? Some companies have alternate worksites prearranged for possible use in the event that a disaster takes down their primary operating facility. A hot site is a facility that has all of the backup equipment and electronic connections required to operate the business. A cold site is a facility that lacks such equipment but is ready to be equipped when needed. Somewhere in between these classifications are warm sites, which offer some but not all of the equipment and connections necessary to run the business (Bartlett, 2007).
- Does the firm have sufficient resources to support employees while income may be limited or lost altogether? When employees are out of work because of a disaster at the business, there is a good chance that they may not be able to return once the business is up and running. Employees need to support their families and are likely to secure employment elsewhere if their economic needs are great. As a result, some companies make the decision to keep displaced employees on the payroll, but this move is feasible only if the company has the resources to do so.
- Is it an appropriate time to reflect on the future of the business in the context of restructuring or rebuilding? If the company is able to continue, it may be desirable to upgrade certain components in the company's infrastructure. A new and more modern facility may be built, upgraded manufacturing equipment may be secured, and/or a new management information system (MIS) may be implemented.

While many organizations may need to apply a rapid approach to recover quickly, others may be able to pursue the reopening of their doors more methodically, with only minor modifications to their strategic plans and business model. A business that remains functional has a responsibility to provide products or service to its customers.

Summary

Taking action when disaster hits involves a three-stage approach. Certain responses and tactics are conducted when the crisis first hits, when the crisis is in full swing, and when the crisis is at a closing stage. At the beginning of the crisis, the CMT should meet and begin the situational analysis. As information about the crisis begins to unfold, strategies for how to manage the event can then be developed. Some of these strategies may originate from the crisis management plan, while others may have roots in the plan but need to be adjusted for use in the particular crisis at hand. The company spokesperson should be planning a strategy on what to say to the media outlets.

The mid-crisis stage is focused on response and mitigation. Efforts should be made to contain the damage and to respond to internal and external stake-holders' needs. Assessments should be made as to which crisis response strategies are working and which ones should be altered. As the crisis nears its end, the response is geared to assessing the damage and getting the organization up and running again.

Questions for Discussion

1. What elements of leadership are critical for successful crisis management?

2. What is meant by situational analysis in crisis management?

3. What role does a spokesperson/public relations person play in managing the communication during a crisis?

4. Why is it important to establish and monitor an information-gathering system?

5. What elements should a crisis manager monitor during a crisis?

6. What is damage containment and what are the major goals of this management function?

7. Why is it important to have consistent and continuous communication with the internal and external stakeholders?

8. Why is there a need to evaluate what is going right and what is going wrong in a crisis?

9. What is meant by business continuity implementation?

Chapter Exercise

For the following exercise, divide the class into groups of three to five students. Each group will represent a crisis management team that is addressing the following scenario:

Suppose a major snowstorm is about to hit your campus in the next 12 hours.[2] Weather information indicates that there will be widespread power outages and travel will be nearly impossible once the blizzard arrives. It is the first week of February and most students have been back on campus for several weeks following the holiday break. Convene your team and discuss the following questions.

1. What actions should be taken immediately, in other words, within 4 to 6 hours before the arrival of the storm? As you consider this question, consider the following:

   Who will be the key leader on campus during this crisis?

   Who will the communication spokesperson address and what messages should be conveyed?

   What type of information-monitoring requirements will your team need during the crisis?

2. During the storm, what actions should be taken? Be sure to consider the following items:

   How will you determine if damage has occurred to various locations across the campus? Keep in mind that some communication networks may be compromised due to power outages.

   What will be the main objectives of the CMT during the storm?

   How will you know if the crisis response strategies are effective or not?

3. After the storm has passed, what actions should the CMT take? Keep in mind the following items:

   What are the main priorities that must be addressed at this point?

   How will you assess the damage on campus?

   What messages should be communicated to the students, faculty, and staff?

   What messages should be communicated to the media?

MINI CASE

THE EXPLOSION IN TOULOUSE, FRANCE

On September 21, 2001, a large explosion erupted at an industrial facility in Toulouse, France. The accident at Atofina's Grande Paroisse fertilizer plant resulted in 30 fatalities, over 2,000 injuries, and damage to more than 4,000 homes and 80 schools (Scott, 2001). Shortly after the incident, around 12,000 families had to find alternate housing; 1,300 companies either had to shut down or scale back the number of employees they were using, resulting in 7,000 workers becoming temporarily unemployed (Dautun, Tixier, Chapelain, Fontaine, & Dusserre, 2008).

The emergency response to the incident was hampered by difficulties that impeded the progress of rescue and recovery. Several items noted by Dautun and colleagues include:

- The communication network that the emergency services utilize in the local area collapsed for 10 minutes.
- Communication networks in the rest of the town were unavailable for 8 hours.
- The firefighters who initially responded to the explosion were not adequately protected against the chemicals that were present. A toxic cloud was in the air and they had no adequate gas detectors to determine its danger.
- The communication networks that were operable were overloaded and therefore hampered in their abilities to aid emergency responders in their response to the situation (Dautun et al., 2008).

Local Stakeholder Reaction

The local community that housed the plant experienced the greatest reaction to the event. The explosion had occurred only days after the September 11 toppling of the World Trade Center in New York City, so local citizens were naturally living in a climate of fear, wondering if this had actually been a terrorist attack. Even before the explosion occurred, local residents had been calling for the plant to close. One week after the explosion, two groups mobilized to protest against the company. One group of 15,000 residents, which appropriately called itself "Never Again," formed a march through the town of Toulouse calling for the closure of all chemical plants in the area (Scott, 2001).

Indeed, the problem of chemical plants in urban areas was now being widely publicized. Unfortunately, the responsibility for this problem does not seem to reside squarely on the backs of the chemical plants. In many instances, the plants were originally built in rural areas, with urban sprawl spreading into the area years later. Such was the case with the Atofina plant, which was built 80 years before the accident, in rural, open countryside (Milmo, 2001). Ironically, the same situation existed with Union Carbide's ill-fated Bhopal plant that leaked the deadly methyl isocyanate gas into the atmosphere in December 1984. That plant, too, had been constructed originally in a rural region, but soon was surrounded by shacks and the poorest citizens in the area (Sethi & Steidlmeier, 1997).

At the company level, Atofina increased security at all of its plants across France. It had already begun a review of its security policies immediately after the September 11 terrorist attacks (Scott, 2001).

The Cause of the Blast

Initial press reports indicated that terrorism might have been behind the explosion (Scott, 2001). That this explosion happened soon after the September 11 attacks certainly prompted this speculation. However, an initial report by experts heading the inquiry into the cause of the accident indicated that negligence was more of a factor. The cause of the blast was more likely a reaction between ammonium nitrate and sodium dichlorisocyanurate, two chemicals that were stored in the same warehouse (Young, 2002).

Sources

Dautun, C., Tixier, J., Chapelain, J., Fontaine, F., & Dusserre, G. (2008). Crisis management: Improvement of knowledge and development of a decision aide process. *Loss Prevention Bulletin, 201*(1), 16–21.

Milmo, S. (2001). Toulouse accident raises questions of chemical sites near urban centers. *Chemical Market Reporter, 260*(15), 6, 28.

Scott, A. (2001). A case study in shaken confidence. *Chemical Week, 163*(43/44), 26–27.

Sethi, S., Steidlmeier, P. (1997). *Up against the corporate wall: Cases in business and society.* Upper Saddle River, NJ: Prentice Hall.

Young, I. (2002). "Negligence" led to Grande Paroisse blast. *Chemical Week, 164*(25), 18.

Notes

1. Thrifty operated about 1,000 pharmacies on the West Coast of the United States. In 1996, the company was acquired by Rite Aid.

2. If your campus is not in an area where snow is a problem, then substitute a torrential rainstorm in this scenario.

References

Barnard, B. (1987, March 10). Ferry loss raises questions: Concept of roll-on vessels faces spotlight again. *Journal of Commerce,* p. 16A.

Bartlett, N. (2007). Ready for trouble. *Credit Union Magazine, 73*(2), 38–42.

Barton, L. (2001). *Crisis in organizations II.* Cincinnati, OH: South-Western College Publishing.

Borodzicz, E., & van Haperen, K. (2002). Individual and group learning in crisis simulations. *Journal of Contingencies and Crisis Management, 10*(3), 139–147.

Caponigro, J. (1998). *The crisis counselor: The executive's guide to avoiding, managing, and thriving on crises that occur in all businesses.* Southfield, MI: Barker Business Books.

Cavanaugh, J. (2003). Coolness under fire: A conversation with James Cavanaugh. *Leadership in Action, 23*(5), 7.

Coombs, W. (2007). *Ongoing crisis communication: Planning, managing, and responding* (2nd ed.). Thousand Oaks, CA: Sage.

Coombs, W. T. (2006). *Code red in the board room: Crisis management as organizational DNA.* Westport, CT: Praeger.

Crandall, W., & Menefee, M. (1996). Crisis management in the midst of labor strife: Preparing for the worst. *SAM Advanced Management Journal, 61*(1), 11–15.

Crichton, M., Lauche, K., & Flin, R. (2005). Incident command skills in the management of an oil industry drilling incident: A case study. *Journal of Contingencies and Crisis Management, 13*(3), 116–128.

Dautun, C., Tixier, J., Chapelain, J., Fontaine, F., & Dusserre, G. (2008). Crisis management: Improvement of knowledge and development of a decision aide process. *Loss Prevention Bulletin, 201*(1), 16–21.

Donahue, B. (2004). True leadership in a crisis. *Convenience Store Decisions, 15*(9), 6.

Duhe, S., & Zoch, L. (1994). A case study: Framing the media's agenda during a crisis. *Public Relations Quarterly, 39*(4), 42–45.

Endsley, M., & Garland, D. (2000). *Situation awareness, analysis, and measurement.* Mahwah, NJ: Lawrence Erlbaum.

Flin, R. (2005). *Managing crises in the EU: A first assessment ESF SCSS* [Exploratory workshop]. Capacity for crisis management: Identifying core skills of crisis managers [Discussion Paper]. School of Psychology, University of Aberdeen, Scotland.

Gegax, T. (2003, October 27). No one behind the wheel. *Newsweek, 142*(17), 50.

Herman, M. (1995). When strikes turn violent. *Security Management, 39*(3), 32–35.

Hookway, J. (2008, June 30). World news: Ferry rules tightened after fatal crash. *Wall Street Journal,* A6.

Institute for Crisis Management. (2007). *Annual ICM crisis report: News coverage of business crises during 2006, 16*(1). Retrieved November 10, 2007, from http://www.crisisexperts.com/2006CR.pdf

Langfitt, F. (2006). Covering the Sago Mine disaster: How a game of "whisper down the coal mine" ricocheted around the world. *Nieman Reports, 60*(2), 103–104.

Leskin, G. A., Morland, L., Whealin, J., Everly, G., Litz, B., & Keane, T. (2004). *Factsheet: Fostering resilience in response to terrorism for psychologists working with first responders.* Washington, DC: American Psychological Association.

Miller, A. (2001). The Los Angeles riots: A study of crisis paralysis. *Journal of Contingencies and Crisis Management, 9*(4), 189–199.

Miller, P. (2006). Ferry disaster, tanker accident unlikely to affect marine renewals. *Business Insurance, 40*(7), 37–39.

Milmo, S. (2001). Toulouse accident raises questions of chemical sites near urban centers. *Chemical Market Reporter, 260*(15), 6, 28.

Mitroff, I., & Anagnos, G. (2001). *Managing crises before they happen.* New York: AMACOM.

Munneke, G., & Davis, A. (2004). Disaster recovery for law firms. In *The essential formbook:*

Comprehensive management tools for lawyers: Vol. IV. Disaster planning and recovery (pp. 59–67). Chicago: American Bar Association, Law Practice Management Section.

Newsom, D., Scott, A., & Turk, J. (1992). *This is PR: The realities of public relations* (5th ed.). Belmont, CA: Wadsworth.

Olasky, M. (2006). *The politics of disaster: Katrina, Big Government, and a new strategy for future crisis.* Nashville, TN: W Publishing Group.

Pearson, C., & Mitroff, I. (1993). From crisis prone to crisis prepared: A framework for crisis management. *Academy of Management Executive, 7*(1), 48–59.

Pearson, C., & Rondinelli, D. (1998). Crisis management in Central European firms. *Business Horizons, 41*(3), 50–59.

Preble, J. (1997). Integrating the crisis management perspective into the strategic management process. *Journal of Management Studies, 34*(5), 669–791.

Rice, J., & Caniato, F. (2003). Building a secure and resilient supply network. *Supply Chain Management Review, 7*(5), 22–30.

Rolston, L., & McNerney, D. (2003). Leading during times of crisis. *Innovative Leader, 12*(5), 1–2.

Roux-Dufort, C. (2007). A passion for imperfections: Revisiting crisis management. In C. Pearson, C. Roux-Dufort, & J. Clair (Eds.), *International handbook of organizational crisis management* (pp. 221–252). Thousand Oaks, CA: Sage.

Schoenberg, A. (2005). Do crisis plans matter? A new perspective on leading during a crisis. *Public Relations Quarterly, 50*(1), 2–6.

Scott, A. (2001). A case study in shaken confidence. *Chemical Week, 163*(43/44), 26–27.

Sethi, S., & Steidlmeier, P. (1997). *Up against the corporate wall: Cases in business and society.* Upper Saddle River, NJ: Prentice Hall.

Sklarewitz, N. (1991, May). Cruise company handles crisis by the book. *Public Relations Journal,* pp. 34–36.

Solomon, C. (1992, July). The LA riots: An HR diary. *Personnel Journal,* pp. 22–29.

Spillan, J. (2003). An exploratory model for evaluating crisis events and managers' concerns in nonprofit organisations. *Journal of Contingencies and Crisis Management, 11*(4), 160–169.

Spillan, J., & Crandall, W. (2004). Crisis planning in the lodging industry: A response to the "It can't happen to us" mentality. *Mountain Plains Journal of Business and Economics,* 5, Article 4—General Research. Retrieved November 10, 2007, from http://www.mountainplains.org/general/2004general.html

Sundelius, B. (1998). Conclusion: Learning from crisis experiences. In L. M. Newlove (Ed.), *Coping with value conflict and institutional complexity: International conference in an international perspective* (pp. 117–120). Stockholm: OCB.

Talley, W. (2002). The safety of ferries: An accidental injury perspective. *Maritime Policy Management, 29*(3), 331–338.

Those in peril. (2008, June 28). *The Economist, 387*(8586), 49.

Walsh, K. (2007). A film hero up to playing the real role. *U.S. News & World Report, 143*(18), 50–51.

Wheatley, M. (2006). Leadership lessons from the real world. *Leader to Leader, 41*(Summer), 16–20.

Wilderoter, D. (1987). Crisis management: A new plan is necessary. *National Underwriter (Property/Casualty/Employee Benefits), 91*(3), 34–35, 40–41.

Williams, D. E., & Treadway, G. (1992). Exxon and the Valdez accident: A failure in crisis communication. *Communication Studies, 43*(1), 56–64.

Wilson, J. (2004, June 21–July 11). Now the disaster's happened, what am I supposed to do? *Accounting Today,* pp. 24–25.

Wilson, S. (2003). Develop an effective crisis-management strategy. *Chemical Engineering Progress, 99*(9), 58–61.

Wooten, L., & James, E. (2008). Linking crisis management and leadership competencies: The role of human resource development. *Advances in Developing Human Resources, 10*(3), 352–379.

Young, I. (2002). "Negligence" led to Grande Paroisse blast. *Chemical Week, 164*(25), 18.

Zsidisin, G., Melnyk, S., & Ragatz, G. (2005). An institutional theory perspective of business continuity planning for purchasing and supply management. *Internal Journal of Production Research, 43*(16), 3401–3420.

CHAPTER 8

Crisis Communication

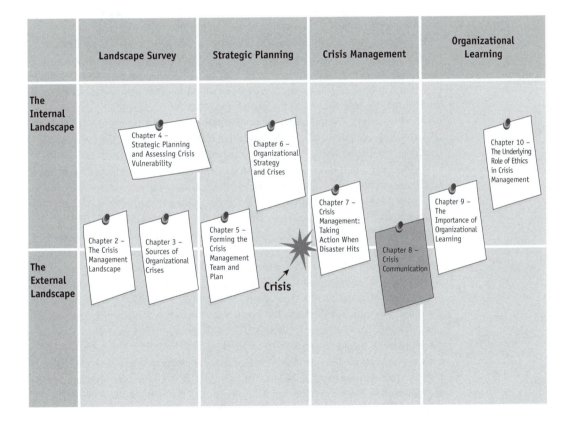

BCT Hotel

The BCT Hotel[1] is a beautiful 250-bed facility that operates near a tourist area of the city. It has been open for 25 years and caters to small meeting groups and families that come to visit the many historic sites around the city. It employs a management team consisting of the General Manager of the hotel, the Front Desk Manager, the Housekeeping Manager, the Foodservice and Catering Manager, and the Building Engineer. The management team also functions as the hotel's crisis management team (CMT).

In early October 2007, a variety of construction activities were in process. Most of the work focused on renovating the existing buildings and upgrading the hotel's electrical, plumbing, and phone line equipment. The construction seemed to go well for several weeks. Two and a half weeks into the renovations, however, the Front Desk Manager reported that intermittent power outages were becoming more frequent and causing concern among some of the guests. The General Manager of the hotel sent a letter to all of the guests apologizing for the inconvenience and assuring the guests that construction would be completed as soon as possible.

One night, however, around 2:00 a.m., the night security guard noted a hissing sound emanating from the basement of one of the guest buildings. Upon investigation, he discovered the entire basement was filled with thick black smoke. The hissing sound turned out to be electrical sparks coming from an old fan that was operating to keep some of the construction lights from emitting too much heat. Apparently, the fan had been left running after the construction crew left. The sparks from the old fan had ignited a dusty area of rags and newspapers that had been swept into the corner of the basement. The pile had been smoldering for hours, but had not yet created a sizable fire.

The security guard wondered why the fire alarm had not been activated, given the sizable amount of smoke. Upon opening the door, a strong breeze entered the room, giving the smoldering pile of rags enough oxygen to burst into flames. Without an operating alarm system, it was necessary to call 911 first, and then activate the fire alarms manually in the guest building. The fire department arrived within 10 minutes, but not in time to keep the fire from spreading into adjacent locations. Ten guests were treated for smoke inhalation, but nobody was seriously injured.

The entire management team arrived at the hotel within an hour and quickly convened as the crisis management team. The General Manager had been designated previously as the spokesperson to the media in the event of a major crisis at the hotel. Two major communication challenges lay ahead of the hotel's crisis management team: how to communicate to the guests and what to say to the media. Fortunately, the guests who had been displaced by the fire were quickly moved to other empty rooms in the complex, but media relations proved more challenging than anticipated. The immediate questions being posed were, how did the fire start and why were the fire alarms not working properly?

Effective communication strategies are necessary to successfully manage a crisis. Problems of conflicting information are often common. The crisis management team (CMT) needs accurate information in order to react quickly in its response to the crisis. Issues of fear, hostility, and anger can complicate an already complex situation, and communications can become distorted and inaccurate. These complexities often result in rumors and imprecise information that escalates the situation. Hence, creating a communication structure and flow of information that is objective, truthful, and timely is necessary for internal and external stakeholders to be informed of the crisis management activities. The more effective the communication, the better the prospects for resolving the crisis successfully. This chapter discusses crisis management communication practices, how they affect the respective stakeholders, and how the crisis communication function can be managed effectively.

Crisis management and crisis communication are intricately interlinked. As Scanlon (1975) put it, "Every crisis is also a crisis of information." He goes on to say, "Failure to control the crisis of information can ultimately result in a failure to control the crisis" (p. 431). The study of organizational crisis communication has resulted in a greater understanding of the role communication plays in both defining the origin of a crisis and launching the crisis recovery plan (Spillan, Rowles, & Mino, 2002/2003).

Communication strategies for crisis management are needed to explain the precrisis and postcrisis plans to all affected stakeholders (Coombs, 2007; Heath, 1997; Pauchant & Mitroff, 1992; Seeger & Bolz, 1996; Seeger, Sellnow, & Ulmer, 1998; Sturges, 1994). "Communication provides for the interpretation of the informational environment communally. It sets the stage for how those individuals outside the organization are likely to make sense of the crisis event" (Seeger et al., 1998, p. 235).

Because organizational crises can threaten stakeholders, information concerning how to mitigate negative effects is fundamental for organizational decision makers. Likewise, because communication's importance for organizational decision makers and stakeholders has been increasingly emphasized, this discussion further underscores the importance of using effective communication practices while managing an organizational crisis (Spillan, Rowles, & Mino, 2002/2003).

A distinction should be made between two types of crisis communication. A command and control mode is needed to communicate with the internal stakeholders—that is, the employees and the owners—particularly as plans are made for managing the crisis. The other area of crisis communication focuses on the external stakeholders, including the general public, suppliers, customers, special interest groups, and government agencies.

This chapter begins with a discussion of initiating the crisis communication process. Next we address the key areas of communicating with the internal stakeholders. This is followed by a close examination of crisis communication with external stakeholders, including a look at various communication strategies that have been utilized. We conclude the chapter with insights on the training needed for effective crisis communication.

Initiating the Communication Process

When a crisis commences, activating the crisis management team (CMT) is the first formal step in the successful management of the event. The CMT will serve a number of functions, including analyzing the situation, evaluating various options for solving the crisis, and communicating solutions and other key information to the key company stakeholders (Caponigro, 2000). The CMT will execute the crisis management plan (CMP), which contains communication strategies as part of the crisis response. This part of the plan can be thought of as the organization's crisis communication plan. Only through effective communication can the CMT implement its strategies successfully.

The purpose of a crisis communication plan is to develop procedures for effective communication with internal and external stakeholders and the media during a crisis. The long-term objective of any crisis plan is to minimize the effects of the problem. One way this objective is accomplished is by communicating with those affected by the crisis, telling them what happened and what plans are in place to address the crisis (Nelson, 2004). Rapidly establishing communication with key stakeholders is a primary objective. It enhances the credibility of the organization and builds trust. The communicated messages should satisfy the unique requirements of each audience and provide the tone, context, and consistency of all additional messages. The point to remember is that the objective and the key messages are consistent, while the detail and delivery methods may vary depending on the audience (Nelson, 2004).

Crisis Communication With Internal Stakeholders

When a crisis strikes the organization, there are two functions that must be addressed concerning communication with internal stakeholders. First, managing the crisis requires a command and control function that involves management, the owners, and selected employees. Second, the general employee population needs to be updated on the status of the crisis and how it has affected the organization, and what can be expected in the future in terms of its resolution. Each of these issues is examined in more detail below.

The Command and Control Function

The location of the command center and its accompanying facilities is important to the successful management of the crisis. The command center is the physical area where the company spokesperson and members of the media can communicate. In addition, the physical location should be equipped to disseminate information to stakeholders who are not in the immediate vicinity of the organization. Equipment such as telephones, computer connections, Internet access, appropriate seating facilities, and other infrastructure items are required. It is also possible that a mobile crisis response and communication system may be necessary. This would occur when the crisis is spread over a wide geographical area, such as when a major storm hits a region of the country. A mobile system is useful when the crisis involves coordination among multiple locations. Information can be monitored and reported to a central command center where it is assessed, and then it can be determined what strategies to follow to mitigate the crisis (Yuan & Detlor, 2005).

It is common for a large company with a designated corporate headquarters to experience a crisis "in the field" at the unit level. Such would be the case if a restaurant or retail chain experienced a crisis at one of its stores. Under these conditions, the crisis and communication response is typically directed from the home office. The Chi-Chi's hepatitis A illness, the Wendy's finger incident, and the Luby's Cafeteria murders (addressed in previous chapters) were all directed from locations above the unit level. This is not unexpected, since the home office is where the company resources of public relations and crisis expertise are located. Sometimes, however, the home office does not find out about the crisis until an inopportune moment arises. This situation should be avoided. Crisis communication within the firm must include the appropriate departments and outside plants. A common problem is that a crisis may strike one part of the organization, while the other parts are either unaware of the event or uninformed as to its status. This situation occurred with Bowater Incorporated during a weather event involving severe fog.

Bowater Incorporated's Southern Division, a newsprint manufacturer in Calhoun, Tennessee, experienced a horrific crisis on December 11, 1990. At 9:05 a.m. a massive 99-vehicle accident occurred on Interstate 75, about 2 miles from the plant. For years, complaints about industrial fog produced by the mill's aeration ponds had been directed at the company (McLaren, 1994). Ironically, the multivehicle accident started when a speeding car collided with one of the company's tractor-trailer trucks on the interstate. The resulting smoke, along with the already present fog, created a whiteout condition that made visibility impossible for drivers near the accident scene. The accident was the worst in Tennessee's history, with 12 motorists perishing in the resulting collisions and fires. Communication within the company was haphazard after the incident. The chairman of the board did not learn of the event until watching the evening news (Maggart, 1994). Internal communications within the company, which consisted of various mills in different locations of the southeast United States, was haphazard to nonexistent. Some of the other mills received telephone calls shortly after the wreck, unaware that the accident had even taken place. Special Case 8.1 overviews another incident where crisis communication within an organization was faulty.

SPECIAL CASE 8.1

The Town of Logan and Its College Welcomes the New Professor[2]

It was the fall semester of 1992. David Montcalm had been enjoying his new position as a professor in the local college's Hotel Restaurant Administration program. David, an accomplished chef and former gourmet restaurant operator, was well received in the program because of his ability to deliver culinary education in an area where few educators of his caliber existed. The town of Logan, the location of McDowell College, a small liberal arts school of 3,000 students, was nestled on a scenic mountaintop in a rural area of the southern Appalachian Mountains. Logan itself was a small town of barely 1,500, and had one full-time police chief and one town secretary who handled administrative matters in the office.

(Continued)

(Continued)

In mid-October, after David had been on the job for only 2 months, two uniformed police officers showed up on his doorstep. He lived in a modest house that was owned by the college and located one block from the president's home, directly adjacent to the Academic Dean's house. One officer was a local sheriff's deputy, the other an officer from the college. "You are under arrest," barked the sheriff's deputy. David could hardly believe his ears, while his wife stood nearby, visibly alarmed. The charge itself was equally unbelievable—a fine for not having the proper pet tag registration for David's dog; it had not been recorded as PAID at the local town office. Two weeks prior to David's arrest, his dog, Ashley, had run out of the house and been hit by a truck. The dog died, but an animal control officer, upon hearing of the event, issued David a fine because the dog did not have a collar with the proper tag registration (the tag was in the kitchen drawer when the dog was hit). David paid the fine, buried his dog, and went on with life, or so he thought, until the night of his arrest.

While sitting in a waiting area at the jail (the county jail deputy found the whole ordeal amusing and did not require David to sit in a cell), David's wife frantically called another new college professor and friend, Rich Beaver, for help. Rich drove to the jail and was prepared to pay David's bail. Six hours after David's arrest, the local magistrate arrived at 11:00 p.m. to begin his shift. Upon hearing the charge, he decided to release David on his own recognizance. "So that's how they treat new people around here," remarked Rich to David. "I don't understand this," said David. "I paid that fine the day after the officer wrote me up!"

The following day, at exactly 8 in the morning, the president of McDowell College, Dr. George Hinton, received a call from the local newspaper. The reporter, Ned Vale, normally would have called the school's Director of Public Information, but this story was too big, it had to go to the president first. "Dr. Hinton," asked Ned, "do you have a statement to make about the arrest of one of your professors last night?"

This was news to the president, who quickly told Ned he would call him back. "What arrest is he talking about?" thought Dr. Hinton. Soon the campus and the town of Logan was abuzz with rumors about the arrest. Apparently, the story circulating was that the "new professor" had been picked up with a 14-year-old girl. By noon, calls had come from concerned parents, the local television station, and a former president of the college who still lived in the area.

Communications to the General Employee Population

Employees are critical to the success of any crisis management communication. They are continuously on the front line of action and must also communicate with external stakeholders daily. In this role, they act as ambassadors for the company and thus should be kept abreast of what management is doing about the crisis (Weiner, 2006). It is also important to communicate with employees who are not directly involved in managing the crisis or responding directly to outside stakeholders. Indeed, employees must also respond to questions from friends, neighbors, and clients (Valentine, 2007). Depending on the crisis, some employees may be apprehensive and fear losing their jobs as a result of the crisis. Keeping them focused on the day-to-day operations during the crisis will offer reassurance and help maintain morale (Argenti, 2002; Reilly, 2008).

Utilizing the company Web site can be an excellent way to update employees. Setting up a discussion board just for employee access can be therapeutic and enable socialization to continue, especially if employees are geographically separated, say, for example, because of storm damage in the area (Premeaux & Breaux, 2007). Providing a toll-free number for employees to call to obtain updates is also useful. During Hurricane Katrina, McDonald's used its toll-free numbers to communicate with employees and also to account for any employees who might be missing as a result of the storm (Marquez, 2005).

One analogy that applies to employee communication during a crisis is the classic "mushroom" problem. Employees often complain that downward communication from management is often too infrequent or nonexistent when something goes wrong in the organization. This results in a situation where they feel like a mushroom—"they keep us in the dark and feed us garbage" (Reilly, 2008, p. 335). The remedy, of course, is to keep employees informed, even if the news is not always positive. Employees are generally concerned about their companies and want to be updated with frequent and candid summaries of the status of the crisis (Barton, 2001).

One area that may be overlooked in many crisis management plans is how to address the issue of pay and compensation should the organization go off-line for an extended period of time. Such an event could occur when the crisis involves a natural disaster such as a hurricane. Communicating this information to employees is important and may actually hold some advantages in terms of reopening. Premeaux and Breaux (2007) describe how a credit union in southeast Texas was able to reopen its offices more rapidly than other businesses in the area after Hurricane Rita struck the region. Many businesses were shut down, but the credit union promised its employees that it would continue to pay them even while the organization was not operational. This promise allowed the credit union to retain its employees and reopen more quickly than other organizations in the area.

Sometimes rapid communication is required, as in the case of a workplace violence incident. The Virginia Tech massacre illustrates such a need. The April 2007 incident, which is discussed in other sections of this book, was actually two separate attacks approximately 3 hours apart (Reilly, 2008). What is troublesome in terms of communication is that students were still going to classes several hours after the first shooting (Madhani & Janega, 2007). In response to this crisis, as well as other types of sudden calamities that can hit a university campus, many institutions have installed rapid communication systems that can alert faculty, staff, and students of an impending event such as a tornado or a serious crime that is in progress.

Finally, employees should be reminded not to respond on their own to reporters' questions but should refer all inquires to the organization's designated spokesperson (Barton, 2001; Wailes, 2003). Using one designated spokesperson helps ensure the organization's message is consistent. Updating employees regularly on the progress and the status of the crisis through internal reports can help maintain a sense of normalcy in day-to-day operations. It also has a major effect on decreasing the flow of rumors and inaccuracies seeping out to the media (Wailes, 2003).

Crisis Communication
With External Stakeholders

Communicating with external stakeholders requires designating a spokesperson skilled at interacting with various media outlets and public groups. Communication must also follow a strategy that fits the severity of the situation. Each of these is discussed below.

Designating a Spokesperson

Two contact people must be designated, preferably before a crisis commences. The first individual manages the organization's crisis response and serves as the principal decision maker. There is no set policy on who this person should be, except that it should be consistent with the hierarchy and culture of the organization. The appointed person may vary according to the type of crisis encountered. A crisis in the production sector of the company may be headed up by a production/manufacturing member of the CMT. Likewise, a problem with information technology (IT) may be led by a crisis team member from that department in the company.

One question that must be addressed is, when should the CEO be in charge? Again, that can vary, but generally, the more severe the crisis, the more likely the CEO should be in control and visible to the public. The classic case that supports this adage is the 1989 *Exxon Valdez* oil spill. CEO Lawrence Rawl chose to remain at Exxon headquarters rather than personally visit the oil-drenched Alaskan coast himself. Instead, he sent lower-level executives to manage the situation, creating the impression that he thought the crisis was trivial (Vernon, 1998).

The second contact person is the spokesperson for the organization. Although this position and the CEO could be assumed by the same person, this is not always the ideal. The spokesperson should be a member of the senior staff who is articulate and can speak convincingly and with empathy. In many larger organizations, this person comes from public relations or a similar department. Once the manager in charge of the crisis establishes the command center, the spokesperson can begin meeting communication needs during the crisis.

Centralized communication is necessary for developing a chain of command. Several personal characteristics should be considered when selecting a spokesperson. First, the spokesperson should have credibility with the audience, be articulate, understand the media, and know the details behind the technical aspects of the crisis at hand (Pines, 2000). Barton (2001) illustrates this necessity with an example from the 1999 Columbine High School shootings. The initial spokesperson was in that role by virtue of his seniority. Unfortunately, he lacked technical knowledge of the dynamics of the incident and was soon replaced by a more knowledgeable spokesperson. However, rank alone should not be the sole consideration when choosing a spokesperson.

Another essential trait in a spokesperson is the ability to remain calm under pressure. During a crisis, the organization may be criticized, often unfairly, by the media, by elected officials, or by customers. Such was the case for Connective Power Delivery, a distributor of electric power in the mid-Atlantic region including areas of New Jersey, Maryland, and Delaware. In September

2003, Hurricane Isabel swept through the area and knocked out power to 400,000 customers. Although the company worked hard to restore power quickly, some criticism was received from external stakeholders, yet Connective Power Delivery president Tom Shaw took the "high road" and focused on restoring power instead of worrying about unwarranted criticism (Brown, 2003, p. 32). The spokesperson should also be able to appear pleasant on camera, answer questions effectively, present crisis information clearly, and have the ability to answer difficult questions (Coombs, 2007). With this list of qualities, it is not surprising that many recommend media training for the spokesperson(s).

The spokesperson should be able to communicate a sense of compassion and concern for the victims of a crisis. The restaurant chain Chi-Chi's stopped operating in the United States in 2004, due partly to a crisis it faced in September 2003. An outbreak of hepatitis A, stemming from a shipment of green onions used in salsa, resulted in three deaths and over 600 illnesses (Veil, Liu, Erickson, & Sellnow, 2005). The first official public response by the company was made by a divisional vice president on November 4, 2003. In looking for the compassion and concern of the company's communication response, Veil and colleagues noted:

> In this first public comment the spokesperson was not reported as being regretful for the outbreak or compassionate for the hundreds of victims. In effect, the message failed to characterize the company as caring or willing to serve the public need, and thus lacked the essence of character. (p. 20)

In contrast, Exxon was successful in communicating concern after its August 1993 refinery fire in Baton Rouge, Louisiana. Instead of waiting weeks to make a response, as in the Chi-Chi's crisis, Exxon made its first press release within 3 hours of the fire and then followed up with six subsequent press releases throughout the day. Overall, the company communicated that it was concerned for the victims and families, and that it was taking responsibility for the accident (Duhe & Zoch, 1994).

It is also important that the organization arrange backup spokespersons in case the designated one is not available (Barton, 2001; Coombs, 2007). The organization must still speak with one voice, even if more than one spokesperson is designated. Such could be the case if the primary spokesperson is out of town when a crisis commences. Alternate spokespersons may also be needed if the crisis lingers on for several days.

Communication Strategies: The Coombs Framework

Effective crisis communication can be a difficult endeavor because each crisis is different. Some events require strong and aggressive communication with stakeholders, whereas others do not necessarily require that details be shared with all of the primary publics. Such a communication may cause more problems than it alleviates.

Determining how to communicate during and after a crisis is one of the most important strategic decisions managers can make. Setting a strategy can determine the difference between a quickly resolved crisis and one that remains a management problem for a number of days—or longer. The type and level of communication directly relates to the crisis's complexity. To address this issue it is essential to identify quickly, both before and during a crisis, the stakeholders that are affected by the event (Caponigro, 2000).

Coombs (2006b) offers a four-strategy framework in terms of communication postures during a crisis. These are overviewed next.

Denial Posture

This set of communication strategies seeks to disassociate any connection between the organization and the crisis. Three subcategories of this posture are attacking the accuser, denial, and scapegoating. Attacking the accuser launches an offensive against the party that is threatening the company. Denial simply explains that no crisis exists, while scapegoating places the blame for the crisis unto another party.

Diminishing Posture

These communication strategies try to picture the organization as having little control over the crisis. Excusing and justification are two subcategories of the diminishing posture. Excusing seeks to frame the organization as having little to no control of the crisis or the events leading up to it. Justification tries to minimize the perception of damage resulting from the crisis.

Rebuilding Posture

These strategies seek to rebuild the reputation of the organization that has experienced or caused the crisis. Compensation and apology are two subcategories of the rebuilding posture. Compensation communications state that the organization will provide some type of financial resources to the victims of the crisis. The apology communication strategies seek to show that the company feels responsible for the crisis and also that it seeks forgiveness from its stakeholders.

Bolstering Posture

Coombs (2006b) maintains that the bolstering strategies are meant to supplement the aforementioned strategies. The goal of bolstering is to frame the organization and its connection with its stakeholders in a positive light. Three subcategories of bolstering strategies are reminding, ingratiation, and victimage. Reminding communications reinforce the good works that the organization has done in its past. Ingratiation makes statements that seek to compliment the organization's stakeholders. Victimage communications frame the organization as a legitimate victim of the crisis.

The use of the various types of communication strategies will vary according to the situation at hand. Table 8.1 overviews suggested uses for these strategies.

Communicating With Customers

Customers are the lifeblood of any business or organization. They are free to abandon their relationships with the organization because they have their own

TABLE 8.1   Recommended Uses of Various Communication Strategies

Strategy Posture	Suggested Applications
Denial	Use if the crisis is a rumor
	Use if the organization is faced with an accusation or challenge that has no merit to it
	Do not use with diminishing or rebuilding strategies
Diminishment	If the crisis involves an accident,[3] use when there is no previous crisis history or unfavorable organizational reputation
	Can be used in combination with rebuilding strategies
	Use if the organization is subject to a victim crisis[4] and does have a previous crisis history or unfavorable prior organizational reputation
Rebuilding	Use for any crisis that is preventable
	Use if the crisis involves an accident and the organization does have a previous crisis history or unfavorable prior reputation
	Can be used in combination with diminishment strategies
Bolstering	Use to supplement the previous three strategies

Source: Coombs, W. (2007). *Ongoing Crisis Communication: Planning, Managing, and Responding* (2nd ed.). Thousand Oaks, CA: Sage.

goals and objectives to achieve. Companies can keep the loyalty of customers by telling them the truth and giving them the proper information concerning the crisis. When the facts around a crisis are properly explained, customers tend to understand and are more likely to continue their relationship with the organization. However, when a customer has not been given an appropriate explanation of a crisis problem, credibility issues arise and he or she may search for other vendors.

Poor communication may result in unpleasant consequences for any organization that does not appreciate its proper implementation. Utility companies are especially cognizant of the importance of customer communications since they must communicate to a customer base that is already without power. Customers can be especially irate when they have been without power for an extended period of time. Matt (2004) illustrates this dilemma with the story of a utility that had a company repair truck beaten by customers armed with baseball bats when power had not been restored after a hurricane.

The methods of communicating with customers are varied. In the Internet age, the most logical method of communicating is via the company's Web site. The Internet can be an effective means of communicating with employees and other stakeholders (Ulmer, Sellnow, & Seeger, 2007). Details of the crisis and its effects on consumers, employees, and the community can be posted. Press releases can also be archived on the Web site for all to view. As an example, school systems use this approach to alert students and parents about class cancellations due to inclement weather and other factors.

Some companies actually prepare special Web sites that can be added to the regular Web site during a crisis. These sites, called "dark sites," contain information that someone could access to obtain the latest information on a crisis (Snellen, 2003). Included in most dark sites is a prearranged space for questions and answers about the crisis. This section needs to be updated when a real crisis commences. Potential questions might include where to return a defective product, what the safety record is for the company, or the latest status on a recall effort. This section is the most customized as it must relate to the specific crisis at hand. Procter & Gamble used a Web site successfully when it was suggested that its scent freshener product Febreze could kill pets. To refute these rumors, the Febreze Web site included an addition that addressed these charges. It also provided a link to an urban legend Web site that elaborated on the nature of the rumor (Coombs, 2006a).

It is easy to assume that all customers will automatically access the organization's Web site when a crisis occurs, but there is still a segment of the population that is on the other side of the digital divide, and for various reasons does not use the Internet. They might be reached by full-page ads that the company places in newspapers to update the public about a crisis matter.

Communicating With the News Media

One of the mistakes many managers make is to assume the media are the enemy and out to discredit the organization when a crisis occurs (Sherman, 1989). This is not always the case, as the media can be beneficial by enabling the company to reach important audiences (Weiner, 2006). Members of the news media are more likely to misrepresent a situation when they lack the facts. The result depends on what the organization does or says in the first few hours following the crisis. The essential rule is to cooperate with the media and understand that journalists are trained to be inquisitive (Barton, 2001; Sherman, 1989; Wailes, 2003). Updating them periodically provides them the means to keep the media informed so they in turn, can keep the public informed. When developing the media message, the organizational spokesperson should be trained to deliver the message in a consistent fashion. In some instances, detractors—and perhaps competitors—will find "experts" who can demonstrate blame against the company. Organizations should be prepared to confront these claims. Crisis communication preparedness includes utilizing publicly recognizable third-party experts who are capable of addressing the media to support the organization's position and endorse its response to the crisis (Wailes, 2003).

In order to ensure that the news media obtain a consistent message from a responsible spokesperson, news conferences should be held. News conferences need to be arranged and managed by those experienced in press relations. Table 8.2 offers guidelines for the organization's spokesperson in preparing for a news conference.

One phrase that should be avoided when addressing the media is "no comment." The crisis communication literature is consistent in making this recommendation for several reasons. First, "no comment" implies that the company is hiding something. Members of the media, as well as the general public, are skeptical when they hear this statement. There are certainly some situations where certain information cannot be divulged initially. For example,

TABLE 8.2	Guidelines for News Conferences

1. The spokesperson should continually practice and rehearse, based on potential questions that may be asked by the media.

2. The spokesperson should seek to develop rapport and be candid with members of the media.

3. The spokesperson should avoid canned speeches, and instead strive for a presentation that is more conversational and spontaneous.

4. Technical experts should be used if necessary to clarify to the public details about the crisis. This person can also serve to field technical questions from reporters that may be beyond the scope of the regular company spokesperson's knowledge.

5. The spokesperson should maintain a sense of calm and concern, and not resort to anger over questions from reporters.

6. The spokesperson should always report the truth. No attempt should ever be made to mislead the press.

7. The media should be alerted 3 to 4 hours before a news conference is held. Late morning or early afternoon conferences are ideal since they give management time to review its information, and also provide ample time for reporters to prepare their story for the evening news.

Source: Barton, L. (2001). *Crisis in Organizations II*. Cincinnati, OH: South-Western College Publishing.

there may be an ongoing criminal investigation and revealing details of the inquiry may damage the case. Also, the identity of employee victims of a workplace accident resulting in injury or fatality will be withheld until the next of kin are notified. Under these circumstances, the spokesperson must inform the media that some information must be withheld until it is authorized for release (Valentine, 2007).

A second reason "no comment" should not be used is that it shows a lack of concern on the part of the organization. Such a terse comment is a sure sign of disrespect to victims and to the media. Third, a "no comment" response means the media must obtain their information from some other source (Barton, 2001; Coombs, 2007). When this happens, the company loses control of the information flow. In many cases, the media will then find sources among stakeholders who may already have an unfavorable view of the organization.

Monitoring the Internet

It is increasingly important to monitor what is being said about the organization on the Internet. Using search engines such as Yahoo! and Google can help management determine what is being said about the organization on the Internet. Blogs, hate sites, discussion forums, YouTube, and other Internet outlets may reveal negative comments. In some cases, companies have discovered that a product they offered was defective only after reading about it on the Internet. Such was the case for Kryptonite, a maker of heavy duty locks for bicycles and motorcycles. In 2004, negative Internet publicity resulted when it was revealed, via an online video, that the locks could be opened by using the cap of a Bic ballpoint pen. In just a few weeks, the company faced enormous negative publicity, resulting in a recall of the product and millions in lost sales revenue (Moore, 2005). The lesson is clear: Monitor the Internet on a regular basis for potential crisis events involving your organization.

Evaluating the Success of the Crisis Communication Process

Chapter 9 focuses exclusively on the organizational learning that must take place after a crisis. In this section, however, we briefly address the assessment of the organization's crisis communication responses. The evaluation process provides information and facts that build a knowledge base that promotes learning. This process of evaluation and organizational learning is critical to efficient and effective policy development and decision making because it determines which decisions and actions were effective and which were not. Hence, the reality of crisis management is that some aspects of implementation may be successful, while others will be unsuccessful (Pearson & Clair, 1998).

In this section, we focus on the successes and failures of the crisis communication process. For example, after the severe hurricane season of 2005, a number of retail chains began reassessing their crisis communications. The successes and failures in this area have led management to implement changes in how communication takes place during a crisis. Some retailers now utilize sophisticated technological applications, including GPS (global positioning systems) and satellite telephones, so they can stay in touch with employees during a crisis (Amato-McCoy, 2007).

Debriefing/Postcrisis Analysis

After a reasonable interval following the crisis, the CMT should meet to evaluate its role and to assess the outcome of and response to the crisis. The CMT should also provide a report that provides an assessment of internal and external communications. This report should include an evaluation of how the company communicated to the media, as well as how the media portrayed the company.

Representatives from the CMT should collect feedback from affected audiences and include a report from each impacted area. The team should analyze the effectiveness of the implementation of the crisis management response and make recommendations for future implementation of the plan. The team should provide feedback on the individual plans maintained by units/departments and recommend changes in company policies and procedures as necessary. Bovender and Carey (2006) provide an excellent summary of how HCA's (Hospital Corporation of America) Tulane University's hospital assessed its crisis responses and communications after Hurricane Katrina. Key observations made during this hurricane concerning telephone usage included:

- Cell phones may not work after a disaster such as a hurricane.
- Cell phones seeking to call area codes outside of the disaster area might work better than those cell phones calling area codes inside the disaster area.

- Digital phone lines will go down when a building loses power; therefore some analog phones should be kept on hand.
- Amateur radio operators can often fill the void when other types of technical communication systems fail.
- Communication between headquarters (in this case, HCA is based in Nashville, TN) and the field office (Tulane Hospital is in New Orleans, LA) needs to be arranged on a regular schedule. In this case, hourly phone calls were made during the most critical period of the crisis.
- As strange as it may seem, making a successful phone call across town was impossible, while making long distance calls was easy (Bovender & Carey, 2006).

The evaluation process leads to conclusions that will help management convert the experiences gained into revised plans, instructions, routines, and exercises that can be used in future crisis communication preparations and activity.

Crisis Communication Training

The CMT is responsible for coordinating the training efforts needed to ensure that relevant organizational members have the necessary knowledge of crisis management procedures. Medium-sized and larger organizations with human resource management departments should take advantage of the training expertise these departments can offer. Specifically, the training and development resources are needed to achieve the organization's overall crisis management capabilities (Reilly, 2008; Roemer, 2007).

Communication efforts to be undertaken by the team include:

- Posting the crisis management plan and information about what to do in the event of a crisis on a designated link within the organization's Web site;
- Developing and disseminating user-friendly "emergency guides" with basic guidelines for the types of crisis the organization may encounter. For example, many companies are sending out special memos on guidelines to follow in regard to a potential outbreak of avian influenza (bird flu);
- Conducting information sessions with appropriate groups throughout the organization to familiarize them with the crisis management plan.

Media Training

Media training prepares a spokesperson to communicate effectively with various members of the media, such as newspaper, magazine, and television reporters. Media training consists of four basic modes of instruction: (1) discussion and staging, (2) instruction, (3) simulation and drama, and (4) evaluation (Caponigro, 2000).

Discussion and Staging

This training involves viewing videos and reading news reports with the intention of comparing effective and ineffective spokespersons. The emphasis here is on the effects their comments have on the audiences.

Instruction

Modules in this segment instruct the participants about the "behind the scenes" activities in a news organization. These lessons help crisis spokespeople understand media needs and the deadlines that they must meet. As such, the spokesperson can learn to express what the CMT needs to communicate, while simultaneously providing the media with the information they need.

Simulation and Drama

This part of the training occurs in a private television studio where participants become accustomed to the basic tools and techniques used in a television interview. This role-playing portion involves a mock interview where the level of questioning intensifies. This approach can be a challenge to even the best speaker.

Evaluation

This element of the training focuses on areas that need improvement. Learning from past successes and mistakes is an important part of becoming an effective media spokesperson (Caponigro, 2000).

A key skill spokespersons must learn is how to limit comments to a few well-chosen key messages. Media training instructs the participants to identify those key messages correctly and then to articulate them successfully. It shows the spokesperson how to confront a succession of different questions that might arise in print and broadcast interviews (Wailes, 2003). Generally, however, it is suggested that this type of training take place every 9–12 months (Caponigro, 2000).

Summary

Implementing crisis communication strategies allows organizational decision makers to respond proactively throughout a crisis situation. The company spokesperson must be credible, have some technical knowledge of the crisis, and must always tell the truth. Being truthful about the causes and accompanying events of a crisis helps contain speculation and any negative perceptions stakeholders may develop. It also strengthens an organization's positive reputation, both in general and during a crisis.

Involving organizational stakeholders and the general public means consistently and effectively sharing accurate information about the crisis. Moreover, evaluating the plan's effectiveness when dealing with an actual crisis will assist in adjusting communication strategies and their implementation.

Effective crisis communication involves listening to the organization's stakeholders. Crisis managers must communicate early about the crisis, acknowledge uncertainty, and assure stakeholders that the crisis management team will maintain contact with them about current and future risks. Above all, the company must show concern, empathy, and compassion for the victims of the crisis. As the crisis progresses, communication to stakeholders moves from reducing feelings of uncertainty to resolving the crisis, and then to moving beyond the ordeal.

Finally, effective communication necessitates learning from the crisis. Organizations should be changed by a crisis. If an organization has not been affected emotionally and functionally by a crisis, then there is a strong possibility that it can experience a similar event in the future.

Questions for Discussion

1. How can effective crisis communication aid in managing the crisis in a more favorable manner?

2. How does communicating to internal stakeholders differ from communicating to external stakeholders?

3. What problems can occur with crisis communications directed to internal stakeholders (i.e., within the organization)?

4. What examples of the "mushroom analogy" of communication have you witnessed in organizations that you have been a member of?

5. What traits are needed in a company spokesperson? What examples of poor spokespersons have you seen in the news?

6. Under what circumstances would a denial communication strategy be advisable?

7. What examples of bolstering strategies have you seen in the media?

8. How would you prepare for a news conference if you were the spokesperson and your organization had just been involved in a serious industrial accident?

9. How can the crisis management team evaluate the effectiveness of its communications?

Chapter Exercise

This is a role-playing exercise where a select group of students will pose as the crisis management team (CMT) and give an account to the press on the fire that was described in the opening vignette of this chapter.

1. Select one group of five students to serve as the crisis management team (CMT) of the hotel. Decide which students will serve as the following managers: the General Manager, the Front Desk Manager, the Housekeeping Manager, the Foodservice and Catering Manager, and the Building Engineer. The team responsibilities are as follows:

   • Hold a press conference with the media where the CMT presents a written press release to the media. Have the spokesperson for the CMT read the statement.

- After the written statement has been issued, hold a press conference in which the members of the class who represent the two groups described below ask questions of the General Manager. The rest of the CMT should sit with the manager during the conference and offer their input as needed.

2. The rest of the class will serve as two different groups that exist outside of the hotel. Designate students who will serve in the following capacities:

   - Representing members of the media. These students will ask relevant questions during the press conference.
   - Representing members of families who are calling the hotel, trying to determine the status of family members who are guests at the hotel.

3. Preparation for this class exercise should take place outside of the scheduled class period. Assign the roles during one class session and then select another class session to carry out the exercise.

Questions for Discussion

Review the Special Case: The Town of Logan and Its College Welcomes the New Professor and answer the following questions.

1. How should the president's office proceed in finding the truth of what really occurred? Which parties should be contacted within the college? Which parties should be contacted outside of the college?

2. Given that the president eventually learns the truth of the matter, what information should be communicated to the internal stakeholders, that is, the faculty, staff, and students of the college? What is the best way to communicate this information?

3. How should the college address its external stakeholders, that is, the media, the concerned parents, and the local citizens of the town?

The Rest of the Story

The town's sole police officer, not the arresting county deputy, looked into the matter and discovered that the fine had been paid as David said, but not properly documented in the files by the town secretary. Because of that mistake, David had spent an evening at the county jail. Furthermore, neither the president of the college nor anyone else in the college, save for Rich, knew of the incident, despite the fact that the arrest took place on campus property and that a campus police officer "assisted" in the arrest. Furthermore, David was a full-time employee of the college. Rich, himself a student of crisis events, pondered the outcome of this strange incident. "Wouldn't that have been enough to get someone in the college administration involved so that this whole fiasco need never have occurred? Clearly, there was a communication breakdown in the college," Rich thought.

MINI CASE

THE "ACCIDENTAL" HOMICIDE

On October 7, 2001, an 18-year-old Western Washington University freshman died in his residence hall room. The student, who was in the presence of two friends, had become agitated after an adverse reaction to the recreational use of cold medication and marijuana. His friends physically restrained him after he tried to jump from his third floor dormitory room. In the process, they held him down and put pressure on his chest and neck. At 4:14 a.m. university police arrived at the scene, where they observed the student had already stopped breathing. At 4:43 a.m. he was declared dead despite CPR efforts by the police and fire departments.

The university had a crisis plan that had been updated within the past year. The crisis team convened and began addressing the event. Immediately, efforts were made to notify the victim's family. An initial press release was prepared and distributed to the appropriate stakeholders.

The investigation into the death involved an autopsy and an examination of the victim's room. Drug paraphernalia, a small amount of marijuana, and over-the-counter cold medication were found. On the fourth day of the crisis, the medical examiner issued the details surrounding the student's death: "Preliminary autopsy results indicate that an adverse reaction to recreational abuse of an over-the-counter cold medicine complicated by marijuana use resulted in acute, excited delirium. Intervention on the part of the two friends who were with him and a restraining struggle with pressure on the chest and neck led to manual asphyxiation and death. In view of the circumstances, the manner of death is certified as homicide" (Duke & Masland, 2002, p. 32).

The challenge to the university crisis management team was to become familiar with the State of Washington's definition of *homicide* and why this specific word was used by the medical examiner. Clearly, the two friends' intention was not to kill or even injure the victim. According to the state statute, homicide is defined as the killing of a human being, but it does not have to be intentional. In other words, *homicide* meant that a death had occurred at the hands of another party, but this did not mean the persons involved had any intention of harming their friend. Nonetheless, the word "homicide" was in the examiner's report, and the crisis management team had to communicate this situation clearly to the campus and local community. The challenge was to communicate that homicide was not the same as murder, a distinction that is not always clear in the minds of many.

The University Police Chief was later called in to explain it to reporters in this manner: "Review of the investigation reveals that the intent of the friends' actions was only to protect their friend. It is important to note that the fact of classification of homicide does not require intent to harm" (Duke & Masland, 2002, p. 33).

Sources

Duke, S., & Masland, L. (2002). Crisis communication by the book. *Public Relations Quarterly, 47*(3), 30–35.

Morse, K. (2001, October 18). President Karen W. Morse Fall State of the University Address to the Staff, Western Washington University. Retrieved August 23, 2008, from http://www.wwu.edu/president/docs/Speeches/fallstafftalk2001.PDF

Student used cold medicine, marijuana before death. (2001, October 12). *Seattle Times.* Retrieved August 23, 2008, from http://community.seattletimes.nwsource.com/archive/?date=20011012&slug=dige12m

. what campus in America is drug free?
. what happens when WWU is listed as a top party school as in SDSU?

Notes

1. This fictitious vignette is written to illustrate how a crisis can create communication challenges. The end of the chapter exercise will use this vignette as a basis for discussion.

2. This story is based on a true incident. All names have been changed to protect the innocent stakeholders.

3. Coombs classifies accidents as having low attribution (i.e., some degree of blame) to the organization.

4. Coombs classifies victim crises as having little attribution to the organization. Examples would include natural disasters, rumors, or workplace violence.

References

Amato-McCoy, D. (2007). Ensuring continuity. *Chain Store Age, 83*(6), 50.

Argenti, P. (2002). Crisis communication: Lessons from 9/11. *Harvard Business Review, 80*(12), 103–109.

Barton, L. (2001). *Crisis in organizations II.* Cincinnati, OH: South-Western College Publishing.

Bovender, J., Jr., & Carey, B. (2006). A week we don't want to forget: Lessons learned from Tulane. *Frontiers of Health Services Management, 23*(1), 3–12.

Brown, T. (2003, Winter). Powerful crisis communications lessons: PR lessons learned from Hurricane Isabel. *Public Relations Quarterly,* pp. 31–33.

Caponigro, J. R. (2000). *The crisis counselor: A step-by-step guide to managing a business crisis.* Chicago: Contemporary Books.

Coombs, W. (2006a). *Code red in the boardroom: Crisis management as organizational DNA.* Westport, CT: Praeger.

Coombs, W. (2006b). The protective powers of crisis response strategies: Managing reputational assets during a crisis. *Journal of Promotion Management, 12*(3), 241–259.

Coombs, W. (2007). *Ongoing crisis communication: Planning, managing, and responding* (2nd ed.). Thousand Oaks, CA: Sage.

Duhe, S., & Zoch, L. (1994). A case study: Framing the media's agenda during a crisis. *Public Relations Quarterly, 39*(4), 42–45.

Duke, S., & Masland, L. (2002). Crisis communication by the book. *Public Relations Quarterly, 47*(3), 30–35.

Heath, R. L. (1997). *Strategic issues management: Organizations and public policy challenges.* Thousand Oaks, CA: Sage.

Madhani, A., & Janega, J. (2007, April 17). Slow reaction spurs anger. *Chicago Tribune,* p. A1.

Maggart, L. (1994). Bowater incorporated: A lesson in crisis communication. *Public Relations Quarterly, 39*(3), 29–31.

Marquez, J. (2005). The best-laid disaster plans are merely works in progress. *Workforce Management Online* (October 10). Accessed December 15, 2007, from http://www.workforce.com/archive/feature/24/18/05/index.php

Matt, M. (2004). Crisis communication in the eye of the hurricane. *Electric Light & Power, 82*(7), 30, 39.

McLaren, J. (1994). Bowater's Calhoun Mill at center of fog-related highway pileup dispute. *Pulp & Paper, 68*(8), 79–80.

Moore, A. (2005, Autumn). Are you prepared for the power of the blogosphere? *Market Leader, 30,* 38–42.

Morse, K. (2001, October 18). President Karen W. Morse Fall State of the University Address to the Staff. Western Washington University, Retrieved August 23, 2008, from http://www.wwu.edu/president/docs/Speeches/fallstafftalk2001.pdf

Nelson, J. (2004, July), Crisis communication, coordination in the program. *Security, 41*(7), 68.

Pauchant, T., & Mitroff, I. (1992). *Transforming the crisis prone organization.* San Francisco: Jossey-Bass.

Pearson, C., & Clair, J. (1998). Reframing crisis management. *Academy of Management Review, 23*(1), 59–76.

Pines, W. (2000). Myths of crisis management. *Public Relations Quarterly, 45*(3), 15–17.

Premeaux, S., & Breaux, D. (2007). Crisis management of human resources: Lessons from

Hurricanes Katrina and Rita. *Human Resource Planning, 30*(3), 39–47.

Reilly, A. (2008). The role of human resource development competencies in facilitating effective crisis communication. *Advances in Developing Human Resources, 10*(3), 331–351.

Roemer, B. (2007). *When the balloon goes up: The communicator's guide to crisis response.* Victoria, British Columbia, Canada: Trafford.

Scanlon, J. (1975). *Communication in Canadian society.* Toronto, Ontario, Canada: B. D. Singes.

Seeger, M. W., & Bolz, B. (1996). *Technological transfer and multinational corporations in the Union Carbide crisis Bhopal, India.* In J. A. Jaksa & M. S. Pritchard (Eds.), *Responsible communication: Ethical issues in business, industry and the professions* (pp. 245–265). Cresskill, NJ: Hampton Press.

Seeger, M. W., Sellnow, T. L., & Ulmer, R. R. (1998). Communication, organization and crisis. In M. E. Roloff & G. D. Paulson (Eds.), *Communication yearbook* (Vol. 21, pp. 231–275). Beverly Hills, CA: Sage.

Sherman, S. (1989, June 19). Smart ways to handle the press. *Fortune,* pp. 69–75.

Snellen, M. (2003). How to build a "dark site" for crisis management: Using Internet technology to limit damage to reputation. *SCM, 7*(3), 8–21.

Spillan, J. E., Rowles, M. S., & Mino, M. (2002/2003). Responding to organizational crises through effective communication practices. *Journal of The Pennsylvania Communication Association* (Pennsylvania Communication Association Annual), *58/59,* 89–103.

Student used cold medicine, marijuana before death. (2001, October 12). *Seattle Times.* Retrieved August 23, 2008, from http://community.seattletimes.nwsource.com/archive/?date=20011012&slug=dige12m

Sturges, D. L. (1994). Communicating through crisis: A strategy for organizational survival. *Management Communication Quarterly, 7*(3), 297–316.

Ulmer, R. R., Sellnow, T. L., & Seeger, M. W. (2007). *Effective crisis communication: Moving from crisis to opportunity.* Thousand Oaks, CA: Sage.

Valentine, L. (2007). Talk is not cheap. *ABA Banking Journal, 99*(12), 38–41.

Veil, S., Liu, M., Erickson, S., & Sellnow, T. (2005). Too hot to handle: Competency constrains character in Chi-Chi's green onion crisis. *Public Relations Quarterly, 50*(4), 19–22.

Vernon, H. (1998). *Business and society: A managerial approach* (6th ed.). New York: Irwin McGraw-Hill.

Wailes, C. (2003). Crisis communication 101. *Business & Economics Review, 50*(1), 13–15.

Weiner, D. (2006, March/April). Crisis communications: Managing corporate reputation in the court of public opinion. *Ivey Business Journal,* pp. 1–6.

Yuan, Y., & Detlor, B. (2005). Intelligent mobile crisis response systems. *Communications of the ACM, 48*(2), 95–98.

CHAPTER 9

The Importance of Organizational Learning

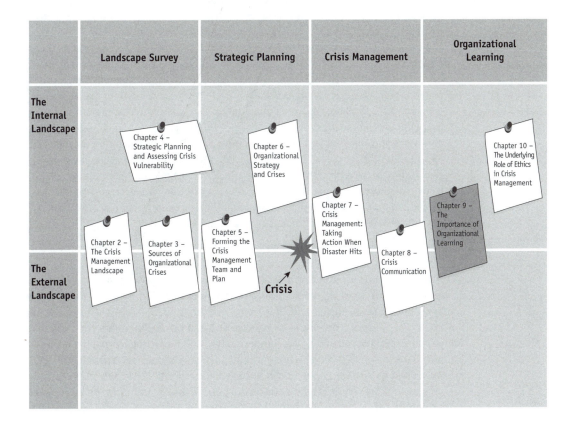

TEDA Dynamics

TEDA Dynamics[1] analyzes and tests electrical component parts for power generation facilities around the world. The business is located in a small town in the Midwestern United States. Its physical facilities consist of two 2-story buildings. In the first building, the top floor is organized to accommodate the administration and business operations of the company. The lower floor and basement contain the laboratories and mechanical operating segments used to complete the analysts' work on various parts that are constructed or reconstructed. The second building is arranged almost identically to building one. The basement, first, and second floors are primarily for the analytical testing and construction of component parts. One segment of the second floor is used for research and development activities.

The potential for fire, electrical explosion, or chemical emission is high in both buildings. Analysts must wear protective clothing and use special chemical detection devices to work with certain components. All employees are instructed repeatedly to be cautious when handling components and about exposure of the chemicals to areas outside the laboratory. The expert technical staff has a solid understanding of the consequences of accidents in the facilities.

Despite management's constant discussion about being careful, TEDA Dynamics had experienced four incidents in the first 4 years of existence. At this point, TEDA has completed its nineth year of operation with no additional incidents since year 4. The CEO attributes this safety accomplishment to developing a comprehensive crisis planning process and a crisis management plan. He also believes that his management team was able to build a learning organization that quickly took charge of finding long-term solutions to the problems that caused the four major crises in the company's early years. Now that the business is considering a major expansion into an allied field to integrate the electrical testing with computer algorithmic development and chemical heat induction, there is a need to develop the crisis management plan further. Because there are many new professionals who will become part of the organization, the CEO wants to make sure that the concept of a learning organization is maintained and expanded throughout the company.

Although it is common to think of a crisis as a negative event, it can also be an opportunity for learning and change in the organization (Wang, 2008). New perspectives can be developed that hedge the organization against future crisis attacks. The Chinese concept of a crisis views it as both a dangerous situation and an opportunity (Borodzicz & van Haperen, 2002). Not learning from a crisis brings to mind the adage that those who ignore history are doomed to repeat it, and thus to be visited by similar crises in the future (Elliott, Smith, & McGuinness, 2000).

Unfortunately, some organizations do not even take initial steps to prepare adequately for a crisis. Perhaps human nature prevents many of us from addressing a crisis until it has actually arrived (Nathan, 2000). When an event does occur, learning from a crisis can be haphazard at best, often depending on the crisis in question. In addition, the organizational research that addresses crisis learning is relatively sparse (Lalonde, 2007). Table 9.1 conveys the idea that learning success can vary among several ranges of outcomes.

TABLE 9.1 Levels of Learning Outcomes After a Crisis			
	Failure Outcomes	*Midrange Outcomes*	*Success Outcomes*
Degree of learning	No learning occurs.	Learning occurs, but its applications are sporadic.	Learning occurs throughout the organization.
Future impact on the organization	The organization continues to make the same mistakes when similar crises occur.	Some areas of the organization may change for the better while others remain the same.	The organization changes its policies/procedures. Learning is applied to future crisis events.
Strategy posture toward crisis management	Reactive; unwilling or unable to learn.	Reactive; willing to learn, yet not ably equipped to learn.	Proactive; willing to learn and take the knowledge to the next step for application.

Source: Adapted from Pearson, C., & Clair, J. (1998). Reframing Crisis Management. *Academy of Management Review*, 23(1), pg. 68.

The concept of degrees of success in crisis management outcomes was first discussed by Pearson and Clair (1998). One of the items they considered was organizational learning from a crisis. Table 9.1 depicts three levels of outcomes: failure, midrange, and success. Each outcome is further distinguished by degree of learning, future impact on the organization, and strategy posture toward crisis management. Companies that experience mostly failure outcomes in the crisis management process have not learned from past events. It is not surprising that these organizations continue to make the same mistakes each time a similar crisis erupts. Such organizations are reactive in nature, and therefore unable to learn because they are always in a state of surprise or perhaps, nonchalance.

Some companies will experience limited degrees of success in their crisis management practices, and thus show some capacity for learning. A degree of learning is possible, but its applications will be sporadic. Therefore, certain areas in the organization will change for the better while others might remain the same. In terms of a strategy posture, the firm is still reactive, but shows some willingness and ability to learn.

The ideal, of course, is a total learning organization. Companies that experience success outcomes in this area are willing and able to learn. The result is that policies and procedures are changed as needed. The hope is that in the event of future crisis events, the new learning will enable the organization to respond more effectively.

An optimum time to learn from a crisis is shortly after it has occurred. Waiting too long to extract lessons from the crisis could cause the sense of urgency for learning to wane (Kovoor-Misra & Nathan, 2000). Organizational learning is key, as there is a clear opportunity to learn from the experience and, in so doing, to decrease the likelihood of another crisis and to mitigate any that do occur. As a result, the organizational learning phase must be a well-managed process (Henry, 2000).

In recent years, there has been much attention on the concept deemed "the learning organization." Management writers Robert Kreitner and Angelo Kinicki (2007) have defined the learning organization as one that "proactively creates, acquires, and transfers knowledge throughout the organization" (p. 549). This chapter discusses how organizations can apply learning to the overall crisis management process.

Levels of Learning

Learning from a crisis can occur at several different levels. At the most basic level, learning can be realized in such a way that new methods of dealing with a crisis are addressed. Simon and Pauchant (2000) call this behavioral learning: It seeks to change the external controls of the organization so that crises are less likely to occur, and are less serious if they do occur. The application of behavioral learning changes standard operating procedures, rules, regulations, and technological systems. In their analysis of the Hagersville tire fire in Canada, Simon and Pauchant noted the changes in techniques firefighters used to extinguish a tire fire. Such fires are difficult to extinguish, but at Hagersville, the fire was broken down into smaller sections and then extinguished with water and foam (Simon & Pauchant, 2000).

Learning can also occur at a deeper level, one that challenges the values and assumptions of the organization. Such learning usually occurs after a process of thoughtful reflection (Kolb, 1984). This type of learning changes the organizational culture and the cognitive arrangement of the company. Thus, the occurrence of a crisis can change the belief system of the organization. "Based on an inquiry or some form of crisis, the organization's view of the world will change and, so, stimulate a shift in beliefs and precautionary norms" (Stead & Smallman, 1999, p. 5). Such a change in beliefs can cause organizational leaders to rethink the "it couldn't happen to us" mentality whereby managers feel immune to a crisis (Elliot et al., 2000, p. 17). As Stead and Smallman point out, this evaluation–rethinking process has come to be known by different terms, including "double loop learning" (Argyris, 1982), "un-learning" (Smith, 1993), and "cultural readjustment" (Turner & Pidgeon, 1997). When these deeper learning processes are applied to crisis learning, the perception that a crisis cannot occur and that the organization is invulnerable usually diminishes.

Organizational Learning From a Crisis

Above all, organizational learning cannot occur unless there is feedback (Carley & Harrald, 1997). After a major crisis occurs, managers should reevaluate their crisis management plans based on feedback received during the event. They must be able to determine who knew what and when, to understand why specific decisions were made during the crisis. Mechanisms such as debriefings, stakeholder interactions, and technology enable managers to capture and share information with members of the crisis management team (CMT). This information can be used in follow-up discussions to learn lessons and develop best practices. Neglecting to perform this task can have a major impact on the reputation of the organization.

The process of determining what went right and what went wrong is the initial step in the learning process after a crisis. Managers cannot move forward in developing new crisis plans without first understanding previous successes and failures. This step cannot be taken lightly; it must have substantial rigor and it must be timely. Management must quickly assemble a debriefing team that can sift through substantial amounts of information and put it into proper context. Managers therefore need to organize their staff to assist in this effort.

One facet of this process is to determine the extent of injuries and/or fatalities among any of the employees or other individuals. This can be a difficult task because of emotional factors and the risk of error and omission. Using proper checklists to determine those involved must be implemented correctly. In addition, legal counsel must be included in any of the deliberations that are associated with crisis injuries or deaths. Numerous analyses of the Virginia Tech shooting in 2007 have traced the progression of the crisis. At each point along the way, investigators had a host of questions to answer to determine what went right and what went wrong.

Redesigning the Crisis Management Plan: The Learning Response

In many cases, analyzing "what went right and what went wrong" generates a variety of recommendations. Modifications may be suggested in terms of leadership changes, crisis management procedures, and resource allocations.

Leadership Changes

The "what went right and what went wrong" analysis could result in a call for a change in leadership. At the organizational or macro level, the president or CEO may be asked to resign. One of the authors of this book was close to a situation in a company that recently initiated a major leadership change. On three distinct occasions the comptroller of this company, with verification by the external auditors (CPA firm), found that the CEO had manipulated the company funding sources by allowing money to be used to construct a vacation home in a resort area of the country. The CEO claimed that the facility was constructed to provide a retreat and training center for company employees, but clear evidence that the CEO had moved money from company funds to finance this facility as a personal acquisition was presented to the board. The board could ask the CEO to resign, pursue criminal charges against the CEO, or both. The board chose the third option and commenced proceedings with the district attorney's office. This action obviously created significant turbulence within the organization and initiated the immediate implementation of the company's CEO succession plan. Fortunately, the board had learned long before that succession planning was a critical factor in organizational management. It was therefore relatively easy to move the appropriate individual into the CEO's position.

At the micro level, changes in the CMT leadership may also be necessary. The leader is the focal person, intricately involved in ensuring that all of the procedures are in place and operating harmoniously. He or she can play a substantial role in resolving a crisis effectively and minimizing its effects on the organization's stakeholders. The other members should also be evaluated periodically as to their effectiveness and fit on the team.

Crisis Management Procedures

Simply having a crisis management plan does not necessarily mean that the organization will execute it properly (Carley & Harrald, 1997). Debriefing on "what went right and what went wrong" is meant to reveal the gaps that were identified and what additional procedures have to be developed to protect the organization's human resources and property from a subsequent crisis. Procedures that worked well or poorly must be identified, followed by additions, deletions, or modifications to the crisis management process.

Resource Allocations

In most instances, financial resources can be used to acquire human and material resources to enhance the organization's capacity to respond to a crisis. In the Virginia Tech massacre crisis, communication was a critical factor. Many have commented that if better communications systems were in place, the number of fatalities might have been reduced (Reilly, 2008). Creating and implementing a communications system is an example of a resource application. In the Virginia Tech case, it would take substantial financial resources to build a system that would be workable, reliable, and effective during a similar crisis. Hence, it is management's responsibility to decide which resource allocations will meet the crisis needs and to ensure that there is a return on the investment.

Improving the Crisis Management Process

Learning from a crisis can occur in several ways. The remainder of this chapter looks at the improvement process from two different perspectives. The first section focuses on the strategic changes an organization can make to prepare for the next crisis. The concluding section looks at the process of learning in more detail and offers insights on how the organization can improve its ability to learn.

Identify Problems

After a crisis, it is likely that new problems related to crisis vulnerability will become apparent. Managers cannot make effective decisions unless they understand the problems, issues, and vulnerabilities associated with a crisis. Defining these new crisis challenges sets the stage for other decisions. To define and understand the problem, managers must analyze the procedures that exist in the organization. Debriefing after a crisis provides needed insight into crisis management challenges and vulnerabilities.

An organization can analyze its challenges through an internal investigation or (externally) by utilizing a crisis consultant, a more objective but potentially costly approach. Important tradeoffs should be considered when making this determination. Staff assigned to investigate a crisis incident may need to be borrowed from other projects or committees. One way or another, management must develop strategies for analyzing the challenges and vulnerabilities so that there is a clear definition of the new crisis management problems facing the organization. Once this task has been accomplished, appropriate strategic decisions should follow to position the organization to address future crises.

Reestablish Objectives

Objectives can be reestablished to account for changes in the crisis management plan after a crisis. This process includes focusing on results and outcomes that an organization needs to achieve during a subsequent crisis. Objectives provide clarity for the organization (Parnell, 2008). For example, a crisis management plan may include the objective of responding quickly and accurately to all public stakeholders. If this was difficult during the crisis, then it might be necessary to clarify what is meant by "public stakeholders." Is the current definition too broad? If so, the CMT may refine the plan to say they will respond to employees, the media, and suppliers within a reasonable time period. Alternatively, the original objective may have been sound but the means to carry it out flawed, in which case the crisis management processes need to be addressed. This is a topic discussed in the next section.

Redesign Processes

The information obtained from the problem definition process and the crisis debriefing sessions provide the basis for making decisions about needed infrastructure changes to amend the crisis management response. Once this input has been acknowledged, it is necessary to develop a blueprint that outlines the plans and specifications for the proposed solutions to the defined problem. A common approach is to redesign those systems that did not function correctly to achieve the established goals. This redesign process is completed by consulting with both internal staff members who work in the vulnerable areas every day, and with experts in the field about best practices in the industry so that the malfunctioning processes and procedures can be corrected. In the case of a crisis response design, managers must ensure that the change will better address the existing gaps and resolve the vulnerability issues that have been identified. For example, policy and procedure changes have occurred in the aviation industry in response to new security legislation (Birkland, 2004). Redesigning crisis response procedures is an ongoing process. Because all crisis plans can be improved, constant vigilance over how the plan functions, what it produces, and how it is managed will determine whether it adds value to the organization.

Recognize the Presence
of Interdependence in All Organizations

Success managing a crisis is often a function of the degree of cooperation and interdependence that exists among various departments within and across organizations (Carley & Harrald, 1997). Interdependence is important in resolving resource allocation issues and developing teamwork. When a crisis occurs, there should be a unified effort to focus on keeping the organization whole and sustainable.

A mold outbreak in a university building illustrates the degree of cooperation that must take place. This not too uncommon scenario[2] requires the redeployment of all personnel and activities from the building affected. A number of university departments are affected:

- The physical plant and maintenance department must work to set up the initial cleanup of the facility. The work is often contracted to outsourced firms, but the department must oversee all work and reconstruction. Any movement of materials or office supplies and furniture will also be coordinated by this department.
- The registrar's office plays a vital role in finding and assigning new classrooms for the courses being taught.
- Deans work at communicating new location information for classes and offices to the affected students and faculty.
- University computing and information systems departments communicate electronically relevant information to those who are able to receive the messages.
- The university's public information department can disseminate information to students and faculty, but its primary goal is to communicate important news of the crisis to the general public.

Coordinating communication and cooperation among these departments is important if the crisis is to be managed successfully. If there is any consolation, it is that weaknesses in the crisis management practices are exposed and can then be corrected. At that point, learning will be somewhat easier as participants try not to repeat their mistakes.

Build Resilience Through Redundancy

There is an old saying that "repetition is the mother of learning." The practice of redundancy in an organization's processes helps ensure that everyone understands their jobs and that there are backup systems for computers, files, and mechanical devices. Having a spare tire available for that one time when there is a flat is a common personal example of redundancy. At the organizational level, information technology (IT) professionals learned quickly and early that failure to back up their information systems can lead to disaster. The same is true in any organization. While redundancy is not necessary in every function, it is essential in those areas that are difficult to replicate. The organization that is prepared with backup systems can be resilient.

The same approach is appropriate in crisis management. When a specific process does not function well or at all, managers should have an alternate process that can substitute for the original. Redundancy in crisis management can be seen in the following examples:

- Methods of contacting the CMT in the event of a crisis should include cell phone, regular phone, and e-mail.
- The crisis management plan should be printed in hard copy as well as made available on backup storage sites and posted on the organization's Web site.
- The primary location of the command center should be backed up by a secondary command center, and perhaps even a third alternate site, lest the first command center become inaccessible during a crisis.
- A selection of alternate crisis team members can be designated, in case one or more of the original members are not available.

Many examples of redundancy already exist in crisis situations. Backup generators may be available when the primary power is offline. Additional counselors may be told to "be ready" after a significant event has taken place on a school campus, such as the death of a student. Battery-powered lights go on in the stairwells when the main power is unavailable. During the Y2K scare, many organizations brought in extra food, water, and sleeping mats, just in case.

Building a Learning Organization

The basic foundation or building blocks of a learning organization is ideas. New ideas promote insights and creativity throughout the organization. Employees are the carriers of the ideas and thus are the essence of the learning process. New ideas emanate from external sources and from internal investigations. Employees learn by sharing these ideas with each other. These new ideas become the catalyst for organizational improvement. Introducing a new idea is one aspect of the learning process; it should be followed by positive behaviors that lead to implementation.

Unfortunately, some organizations acquire knowledge but do not apply it effectively. General Motors, for example, has struggled over the years to upgrade its manufacturing practices even though many of its managers are already knowledgeable about lean manufacturing and JIT (just in time) production. Other companies like Honda, Corning, and General Electric have become accomplished at translating new knowledge into new ways of operating. They actively manage their learning process to ensure that it occurs by design rather than chance (Garvin, 1994).

Organizations are often reluctant to review past failures as a learning mechanism. This perspective is unfortunate, however, since knowledge gained from failures is often instrumental in subsequent successes. Indeed, failure is the ultimate teacher (Garvin, 1994). IBM's profitable 360 computer series was based on the technology of its failed predecessor. Johnson & Johnson switched from capsules to impenetrable caplets for its sabotaged product, Extra-Strength Tylenol. In addition, most makers of over-the-counter drugs eventually implemented tamper-proof containers that served a dual purpose: (1) Detection of tampering was easier, and (2) small children found it more difficult to open a potentially dangerous drug. Both the air travel industry and the federal government have learned from the September 11 terrorist attacks on New York City and Washington, D.C., and have since revised security practices for boarding passengers.

Organizational learning operates from two interconnected yet different concepts: the procedure of organizational learning and the configuration of the learning organization (Hult & Keillor, 1999). Organizational learning at its fundamental level involves the expansion of new knowledge or new perspectives that can influence behavior (Slater & Narver, 1995). Organizations learn and then exhibit new behaviors as a result of the knowledge and lessons that are gleaned from past events.

We cannot discuss the topic of organizational learning without acknowledging the work of Peter Senge and how it can relate to learning in a crisis management context. Senge (2006) describes the components of the learning organization as systems thinking, personal mastery, mental models, building shared vision, and team learning. Each of these is described next.

Systems Thinking

Everything that occurs in an organization is influenced by something else. Likewise, the events the organization initiates influence other items or systems. This interconnectedness forces managers to think conceptually: How does a decision made at one point in time impact other decisions that are made later?

As we have seen, a crisis is not merely a random event. Instead, it is caused by many other movements of systems that finally culminate in a trigger event that initiates the crisis. Recognizing that an organization is part of a larger flow of events helps the manager understand how crises emerge. Crisis events do not just occur; they evolve and are influenced by various systems.

Personal Mastery

Senge views personal mastery as a competency that can be developed. It is also an organizational skill set. At its heart is the ability to see reality in an objective manner. Without this ability, learning is not possible. Developing this ability takes time, effort, and a commitment to discovering the truth. For the crisis manager, personal mastery is a must because reality is not always attractive.

The concept of sensemaking occurs during a crisis as managers seek to assign meaning to the events that are transpiring. There are times, however, when a crisis is so bizarre that there is a collapse of sensemaking (Weick, 1993). This collapse can be caused by the loss of a frame of reference, because nothing similar has occurred in the past. The human response is one of fear and helplessness. As Weick (1993) describes it, "I have no idea where I am, and I have no idea who can help me" (pp. 634–635). Nonetheless, decision makers in charge of responding to a crisis should acknowledge their need to regroup to see the event as objectively as possible. This mindset can help the response to the crisis, and begin to let the organization learn from the event.

Mental Models

These are the sets of assumptions and viewpoints that we have. Such models are necessary because they help us make sense of the world. Organizations also have mental models that reflect the collective assumptions of their members. Mental models can be useful when they urge us to think creatively about problems being faced. Indeed, some managers thrive on thinking "outside the box," to quote a well-known phrase, because their minds are geared to seeing possibilities behind every problem.

Mental models can also hamper crisis response and, ultimately, organizational learning. When managers insist that a crisis "cannot happen here," they are exhibiting a mental model of denial. Destructive mental models can be seen even when crisis events occur repeatedly in the same organization. For example, scapegoating is a mental model that seeks to shift the blame to some other party. Again, such a model is a form of denial, not a healthy ingredient in an environment for learning.

Building Shared Vision

This ingredient of learning involves a collective agreement on the organization's mission and goals. The mission and goals cannot be held by only a few. They are a vision of how things are to be throughout the entire organization. Inherent is a passion that employees show for the projects they work on and the role their company plays in society. When a crisis occurs, the whole organization is hurt because the collective vision has been attacked. Likewise, efforts at confronting the crisis and getting back to business are embraced enthusiastically. This can explain how some communities immediately move into action when a disaster strikes. Cleanup crews hit the streets quickly, volunteers abound, and government visibility is heightened as everyone works together to overcome the crisis and return to a sense of normalcy.

In the absence of a shared vision, there is a higher vulnerability to the organization when a crisis does occur. A fragmented organization will not respond cohesively and may even attack itself as the crisis unfolds. Many professional sports teams experience this type of crisis from time to time. The scenario is usually predictable; the team has a bad season, the owners and coaches are confrontational with each other, and the players frequently complain about the owner, the coach, or fellow teammates. Ultimately, they just want to be traded. To make the crisis even worse, much of the players' "venting" often surfaces in the media. Thus, a public relations crisis is born as well.

Team Learning

Senge (2006) describes the familiar situation where an average group of managers can produce an above-average company. The opposite is also true; a group of above-average managers can produce a below-average company. Many crises originate because less-than-ideal dynamics occur among a group of otherwise competent professionals.

According to Senge (2006), the key to better performance, or team learning, is to acknowledge the presence of dialogue. Dialogue is a deeper form of discussion where new ideas originate from the group. Such ideas evolve from team dialogue. In the end, the team becomes the learning unit for the organization and is capable of reaching new levels of performance that a group of individual managers might not reach on their own.

This notion of dialogue is important from a crisis management perspective. CMTs are special units, capable of doing much more than just generating a list of potential threats and crisis plans. The crisis team is the unit that protects the organization, its mission, its values, and its reputation. Thus, the CMT is a strategic unit within the organization. Thinking of the CMT as just a committee or a staff department hampers its ability to promote true learning and long-term benefits for the organization.

Learning From a Crisis Event

Table 9.2 offers a framework for assessing the learning areas in crisis management. If learning is to be systematic, we must examine the four major areas of the crisis management framework, as well as the internal and external landscapes associated with each area.

TABLE 9.2	After the Crisis: Potential New Learning Areas in Crisis Management			
	Landscape Survey	**Strategic Planning**	**Crisis Management**	**Organizational Learning**
The Internal Landscape	Are there new vulnerabilities in our organization that we need to be aware of? Are there new methods of detection that we can use to sense an impending crisis?	Do we need to change the composition of our crisis management team? Are there new types of simulations that we can practice?	What warning signs did we miss that signaled the oncoming crisis? How can our communication networks improve so we can perform better during the next crisis?	What and how are we learning after a crisis event? Are we making good use of debriefing meetings? Is there an adequate use of paper and electronic recording during the crisis? Are we building systems that provide feedback?
The External Landscape	Are there new threats in the environment that can lead to a potential new crisis?	Are there training opportunities outside the organization that we can pursue?	How can we better partner with industry and government agencies in managing a crisis?	What can we learn from the best practices of those outside of our organization who have encountered similar types of crises?

Landscape Survey

The internal landscape survey looks inside the organization for emerging crisis vulnerabilities. Perhaps an equipment breakdown brought on the initial crisis. Have repairs been overlooked on other equipment? Perhaps the crisis occurred when a number of key personnel left the company. Their replacements were not adequately trained, and subsequently a production accident occurred. In this example, at least two problems should be identified: Why the high exit of employees, and why the poor training of new employees? These problems indicate that human resource issues may need to be addressed.

An analysis of the internal landscape may also reveal that new methods of detection should be used to sense an impending crisis. Perhaps new accounting and financial controls are needed to detect potential sources of employee embezzlement and other types of fraud. Taking a closer look at the existing controls may be necessary. The example in the chapter mini case illustrates a form of fraud that should have been detected by the Board of Directors.

The external landscape survey can also signal emerging vulnerabilities. A recent crisis might have been weather related; in fact, during the writing of this book a major drought occurred in the area where the authors reside. This situation created water shortages and low-running wells. In a highly agricultural area like the southeastern United States, such an event is not only a crisis for many organizations, but is a data point for a future crisis. To compound this crisis, an influx of new citizens is expected in this region, based on the growth of a nearby military base. Fortunately, learning is also taking place and new plans to satisfy water needs are being developed, even if droughts continue to occur in the future.

Strategic Planning

Changes in the internal landscape may necessitate a number of changes in crisis response plans. The composition of the CMT may require revision. Some members may not be suitable, while potential members in the organization may be excellent replacements. Crisis management training may also need revising. It may be that a previous crisis calls for experience in new types of training situations.

As discussed in Chapters 5 and 8, a *crisis management training program* places the staff in a realistic crisis scenario, customized to the particular organization. Instruction and proper use of communication tools for handling the crisis is a necessity in these training programs. Exercises are presented to improve a team's crisis management capability in high-pressure situations. Scenarios give staff and managers insight into operational threats and risks and training in crisis management, organization, group dynamics, leadership, and communication. Using scenarios in training also incorporates a strategic mindset, because scenarios are meant to match the potential threats the organization may face (Moats, Chermack, & Dooley, 2008).

Techniques and assumptions about managing the crisis should be reevaluated during such training. The reevaluation process is based on actual experience with a previous crisis. The goal is to take what has been experienced from the previous crisis, reflect on and learn from it, and then use it to plan for the next potential crisis. This facet of learning is also referred to as assessment, and more specifically, closing the loop (Martell, 2007). Striving for this stage is important because it facilitates continuous improvement in the way crisis managers can make the next crisis more manageable.

The external landscape can offer additional training opportunities that can fit the specific needs of the organization. For example, many workshops offered by government agencies and the private sector address the problem of workplace violence, an area that unfortunately is growing in presence. In other areas of crisis prevention, various agencies, colleges/universities, and consulting groups are useful because they offer expertise that the company itself may not possess.

Crisis Management

It is the acute stage of the crisis that will require management to learn the most to help them plan for the next "big one." The result of learning is what Simon and Pauchant (2000) referred to as the behavioral learning level. Inevitably, there are two areas of the crisis that management should reexamine in the learning process:

- What crisis warning signs were missed?
- How can communication networks improve so the organization can respond better during the next crisis?

No manager likes to be caught unaware or unprepared when a crisis hits. Missing the warning signs can be embarrassing and costly. The 2007 toy scandal where children's toys were coated with lead paint from outsourced companies in China provides such an example. The communication networks may falter as well. When the media pick up bits of information that cannot be substantiated, they may pass them on as breaking news. The unfortunate Sago Mine disaster in West Virginia illustrates how well-meaning journalists mistakenly reported that the trapped miners had been found safe when, in fact, all but one had perished (Lordan, 2005).

Managing a crisis is a formidable and supreme test for an organization and its leadership. The strength of the chain of command and the efficient flow of information will be challenged constantly, and loyalties will be tested regularly. After each crisis, both the chain of command and the analysis of information flow need to be reevaluated. One college realized after conducting a mock disaster that although its chain of command was sound, the flow of information was being impeded, particularly at the command center. The learning from this experience resulted in moving the command center to a more suitable location (Crandall, 1997).

The external environment can offer learning opportunities through better partnerships with industry and government agencies. At the community level, businesses can partner with their local emergency service providers. Training opportunities often exist where these providers conduct simulation drills at the business location. After a major disaster, two or more cities may partner and change their emergency response structures to better cover their geographical obligations. Such was the case after the 1997 Red River Flood in Grand Forks, North Dakota, an incident analyzed further in Chapter 11.

Organizational Learning

Within the internal landscape, the organization should learn from the crisis in a constructive manner (Lagadec, 1997). Specifically, how and what is the organization learning from the event, and what changes are being implemented for the prevention and mitigation of future crisis events? Holding debriefing meetings after the crisis has ended is a constructive venue for learning. Outside parties who can help management learn objectively from the crisis should also be invited. Depending on the crisis, this could include local fire, police, and emergency personnel, as well as a crisis management consultant.

Almost all organizations use technology to supplement their traditional paper-based processes. Word processing, e-mail, and other applications are used to facilitate electronic management of incidents and crises. While these have merit, they do not always lend themselves to effective real-time reporting or easy record keeping during a crisis. In the heat of a crisis, for example, it may be necessary to produce a status report on any aspect of the incident, regardless of whether it concerns people, premises, or press communications. Proper venues for recording information are necessary. The use of crisis management software can be helpful in this regard.

Within the internal landscape, there is another mechanism that should be utilized—providing adequate feedback to the rest of the organization. Without feedback, learning cannot occur. Feedback must be channeled back to the landscape survey, strategic planning, and crisis management phases. In Chapter 12 we will develop this concept in more detail.

The external landscape can yield numerous resources that can be useful to crisis managers. Books and articles on crisis management are one such resource. Books such as this one offer a framework for learning about crisis management, whereas articles tend to be more specialized and often highlight the best practices of specific companies. Many articles focus on lessons learned from a specific crisis. In addition to these outlets, some colleges and universities offer courses in crisis communications and crisis management.

Barriers to Learning

Learning is not necessarily a natural outcome of a crisis. In fact, many companies are actually reluctant to learn, and instead choose to return to the status quo as quickly as possible (Roux-Dufort, 2000). There are a number of reasons why this is so. In the next section, we examine the more common reasons organizational members, particularly those in management, may resist learning.

Too Many Programmed Decisions

Programmed decisions—those that are based on some type of decision rule or prearranged logic—can be useful in a number of situations. They tend to work well when management decisions are routine and repetitious, such as the reordering of inventory when levels reach a prespecified amount. Programmed decisions have also been factored into certain crisis management procedures.

For example, many organizations have a prearranged list of procedures to follow when there is a bomb threat. These are designed to methodically protect assets and people (usually by evacuating the occupants from the building) while seeking as much information as possible about the person making the threat (taking note of background noises, engaging the caller in conversation as long as possible to identify speaking patterns, etc.). Such programmed decisions are useful because they are systematic in their application.

There can be a problem, however, when there is too much reliance on programmed decisions: "The more programmed decisions are utilized by an organization, the more resistant to change it becomes" (Lester & Parnell, 2007, p. 177). This kind of situation can occur in companies where programmed decisions are used to promote efficiency. Because this mode of operation is usually effective, management may take on an attitude of complacency in seeking new ideas on running the operation. This complacency can carry over into the area of crisis management, especially when crisis planning is either not addressed or left to top management to handle (Nystrom & Starbuck, 1984).

Information Asymmetry
Between a Product Maker and Its Users

Learning from some types of crises can be difficult. This can happen when similar incidents occur over a wide geographic area involving the same technology (Boin, Lagadec, Michel-Kerjan, & Overdijk, 2003). The result is a problem of information asymmetries (i.e., different stakeholders with different information) that can exist between the manufacturer of the technology and the users. The Therac-25 incidents from 1985 to 1987 illustrate this (Leveson & Turner, 1993).

Therac-25 was a computer-controlled radiation machine that administered prespecified doses of radiation to cancerous tumors. The machines were offered by Atomic Energy Canada Limited (AECL), and were introduced in 1982. The machines operated flawlessly until a time period between June 1985 and January 1987. During this period, six incidents occurred where patients received massive overdoses of radiation while undergoing treatment. Several of these patients later died (Leveson & Turner, 1993). What made the crisis especially perplexing was the lack of information transfer that took place between the six medical centers using the Therac-25. Instead, each medical center reported the machine failure to the manufacturer. Figure 9.1 illustrates the information asymmetry that existed.

The figure shows four different medical centers that were affected by the overdoses of radiation caused by the Therac-25 machines. The incident that started the Therac-25 crisis occurred at Kennestone Regional Oncology Center in June 1985. The second incident occurred at Ontario Cancer Foundation in July 1985. Yakima Valley Memorial Hospital experienced incidents in December 1985 and in January 1987. East Texas Cancer Center experienced incidents in both March and April of 1986. The radiation overdoses resulted in three patients with serious physical injuries and three who died (Fauchart, 2006).

As Fauchart reports in his analysis of the case, communication took place between each medical center and the manufacturer, but not among the four medical centers. Thus, the manufacturer, AECL, had complete information but

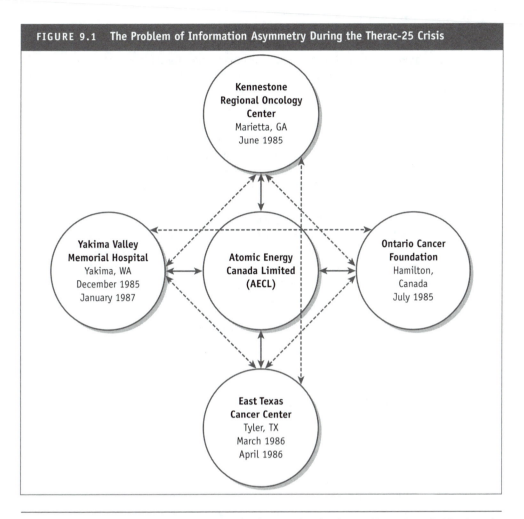

FIGURE 9.1   The Problem of Information Asymmetry During the Therac-25 Crisis

Source: Fauchart, E. (2006). Moral hazard and the role of users in learning from accidents. *Journal of Contingencies and Crisis Management, 14*(2), 97–106.

Note: Dark arrows indicate communication between Atomic Energy Canada Limited and the facilities experiencing problems with the Therac-25 machine.

Broken lines indicate potential communication avenues that were not utilized during the crisis.

the four medical centers did not. Learning at each of the four medical centers was therefore at a disadvantage. Fauchart (2006) maintains that this information asymmetry could have been avoided:

> The manufacturer should have informed all the users that a number of accidents had occurred, but he did not do so. Instead, he told every user who asked for information about other possible incidents that he was not aware of any. He thus used the information asymmetry to pretend that each accident was a one-off fluke. This clearly delayed the instauration of a learning process aimed at fixing the problem and preventing other accidents from occurring. (p. 101)

There Is a Culture of Scapegoating

Scapegoating hinders an organization from learning from a crisis (Elliott et al., 2000). It blames the crisis on another party, thus deflecting attention away from the organization. There are a number of problems with scapegoating that ultimately prevent learning in the organization. First, the organization is likely to become even more failure prone because key issues and warnings are not raised and addressed (Elliott et al., 2000). This scenario is likely because putting the blame on a scapegoat diverts attention away from the core problem. For example, manufacturers often blame their suppliers when a product is found defective. While this may actually be true, it still begs the question of why that particular supplier was used in the first place. The example mentioned earlier of toys manufactured in China that were decorated with lead paint and sold in the United States illustrates this supplier dilemma. The fact that there have been a number of recalls, even as this book was being written, indicates that toymakers are still learning about the pitfalls of outsourcing operations overseas.

Another problem with scapegoating is that it indicates a company's lack of ethics in running the business (Elliott et al., 2000). Scapegoating requires that blame be shifted, even if the company is at fault. Such an ethical stance is a form of denial, which is hardly a healthy atmosphere for organizational learning. The hindrance to learning is that the company's core belief system cannot be changed for the better if managers are in denial as to what went wrong at the outset.

There Is a Status Quo–Seeking Culture

A company's core beliefs are the foundation of its organizational culture. If the culture is entrenched in an unwillingness to change from the status quo, then organizational learning will be virtually impossible (Roux-Dufort, 2000). This type of belief system begins with the attitude that a crisis "cannot happen here" or "it can't happen to us" syndrome. When denial is present, there is a high likelihood that the organization can become crisis prone (Pearson & Mitroff, 1993). When a crisis does occur, the organization must either learn from it and move on, or transfer the blame to another party, thereby entering a state of denial.

Christophe Roux-Dufort studied a 1992 crisis involving a French airliner that crashed into the Saint Odile Mountain while making its final approach for landing. He interviewed a vice president for the airline and was surprised to learn that the executive did not consider the event a crisis. His reasoning was that the day after the accident, reservations for other flights with the airline had not changed (Roux-Dufort, 2000). The problem with this mindset is that the crisis is written off as just another event—something that happens when you conduct business—and nothing more. Deep learning and attempts to change the organization's culture are difficult to achieve when a company is in such denial.

Summary

Organizational learning is an integral component of a well-rounded crisis management program. To achieve the level of success required to make sure crisis management plans are ready and effectively implemented, senior managers must create a culture of organizational learning. This requires a shared vision, skill sets that can function in a changing and rapidly adapting environment, and the ability to think systematically. This is a tall order, because managers have many competing goals and activities that consume their time.

In essence, learning organizations constantly develop new ideas on how to adapt to changing environments, while ensuring that the staff shares the desire, enthusiasm, and willingness to prepare for the intense demands that a crisis will make. There is one certainty in this effort: If an organization does not learn, its ability to survive a future crisis diminishes dramatically. Hence, organizational learning should be built into the culture and made a strategic priority.

Questions for Discussion

1. Based on the information presented in this chapter, define organizational learning within the context of crisis management.

2. What is the role of leadership in the development of a learning organization?

3. What characteristics are needed to develop a crisis management program that is learning oriented?

4. How do Peter Senge's concepts of systems thinking, personal mastery, mental models, building shared vision, and team learning apply to crisis management learning?

5. How can learning take place within the four areas of the crisis management framework? Specifically, how does it occur in the landscape survey, strategic planning, crisis management, and organizational learning phases?

6. What examples of organizational learning have you seen where you work? Were any of these examples brought on by a crisis event? If so, explain how the crisis initiated the learning process.

7. What examples of barriers to learning have you seen where you work? How could these barriers be overcome?

Chapter Exercise

You have just been asked to lead the next meeting of the crisis management team of a medium-sized manufacturing facility located in a growing suburb of a large city. In your meeting you are going to discuss an incident that occurred last week in which an armed man entered the production building and threatened to kill his ex-girlfriend. The man in question came in through a back door and entered the employee cafeteria. He was agitated, verbally abusive, and had apparently been drinking. Two security guards restrained the man until police arrived. A loaded gun was found in his backpack.

The company has a newly formed crisis management team (CMT), and it genuinely wants to improve the safety of the workplace. You have been asked to facilitate the next meeting of the CMT. During the meeting, you want to help the new CMT learn from this event, as well as be positioned to become an effective learning unit. As you plan the meeting, you are thinking of how to address the following questions:

1. What can be learned specifically from this event involving the gunman?

2. How can the CMT address learning within the larger context of the landscape survey, strategic planning, crisis management, and organizational learning phases?

3. What barriers to learning should the CMT be made aware of?

MINI CASE

REPEATED VIOLATIONS

This case, involving a nonprofit organization (NPO), illustrates what can happen when internal controls are not monitored and unethical administrators exploit the system for their personal gain. The administrators in a New York state–based NPO manipulated operations through illegal real estate transactions. They also engaged in Medicaid fraud to set up lucrative tax-free funds for themselves. Specifically, the executive director established interlinking corporate structures that operated and leased back real estate properties that housed programs for the disabled for which he was chief administrator. The returns on these real estate investments were primarily for his own personal benefit.

These financial manipulations would have gone on indefinitely had not the New York state certification agency finally inspected this NPO. When confronted with numerous program deficiencies, the NPO's explanation for its noncompliance was that it lacked funds! Since it was a publicly funded and publicly licensed entity, this NPO had to account for the funding shortfall that prevented it from addressing the deficiencies. The web of closely held real estate holdings provided the administrators with tight control over the NPO's operations. Most important, it generated significant revenues for their private benefit.

The board of directors and the CPA that oversaw the NPO's finances appeared totally oblivious to the interlinked structure, as they were told that this was a means to provide better services to the clients housed in the NPO's programs. Not only was the board deceived, but they also failed to initiate or evaluate controls within the organization. The greed and impropriety of the administrators involved—along with the neglect of the board—drove this organization into managerial chaos and disrupted the genuine goal attainment function that the NPO was originally charged to execute.

Questions:

1. What can the board of directors learn from this crisis situation?

2. Which major stakeholders are affected by this ordeal?

3. What type of culture do you suppose exists in this organization?

4. What type of culture do you suggest needs to be developed so that this incident(s) does not occur again in the future?

5. What type of learning environment needs to be developed so that the board can identify and respond to crisis indicators?

Source

New York State Department of Social Services. (1996). *New York State Commission on Quality Care for the Mentally Disabled: Profit making in not-for-profit care: Part III: The case of Queens County Neuropsychiatric Institute, Inc.* [Available from New York State Commission on the Quality of Care for the Mentally Disabled]

Notes

1. TEDA Dynamics is a fictitious case. It illustrates the importance of organizational learning after a crisis.

2. Two of the authors of this book have seen this crisis occur at two different universities where they have worked.

References

Argyris, C. (1982). *Reasoning, learning, and action: Individual and organizational.* San Francisco: Jossey-Bass.

Birkland, T. (2004). Learning and policy improvement after disaster: The case of aviation security. *American Behavioral Scientist, 48*(3), 341–364.

Boin, A., Lagadec, P., Michel-Kerjan, E., & Overdijk, W. (2003). Critical infrastructures under threat: Learning from the anthrax scare. *Journal of Contingencies and Crisis Management, 11*(3), 99–104.

Borodzicz, E., & van Haperen, K. (2002). Individual and group learning in crisis simulations. *Journal of Contingencies and Crisis Management, 10*(3), 139–147.

Carley, K., & Harrald, J. (1997). Organizational learning under fire: Theory and practice. *American Behavioral Scientist, 40*(3), 310–332.

Crandall, W. (1997, April). How to choreograph a crisis. *Security Management,* pp. 40–43.

Elliott, D., Smith, D., & McGuinness, M. (2000, Fall). Exploring the failure to learn: Crises and the barriers to learning. *Review of Business,* pp. 17–24.

Fauchart, E. (2006). Moral hazard and the role of users in learning from accidents. *Journal of Contingencies and Crisis Management, 14*(2), 97–106.

Garvin, D. (1994). Building a learning organization. *Business Credit, 96*(1), 19–28.

Henry, R. (2000). *You'd better have a hose if you want to put out the fire.* Windsor, CA: Gollywobbler Productions.

Hult, G., & Keillor, B. (1999). Organizational learning and market orientation in international marketing education. *Journal of Teaching in International Business, 10*(3/4), 81–97.

Kolb, D. (1984). *Experiential learning: Experience as the source of learning and development.* Englewood Cliffs, NJ: Prentice Hall.

Kovoor-Misra, S., & Nathan, M. (2000, Fall). Timing is everything: The optimal time to learn from crises. *Review of Business,* pp. 31–36.

Kreitner, R., & Kinicki, A. (2007). *Organizational behavior* (7th ed.). New York: McGraw-Hill Irwin.

Lagadec, P. (1997). Learning processes for crisis management in complex organizations. *Journal of Contingencies and Crisis Management, 5*(1), 24–31.

Lalonde, C. (2007). Crisis management and organizational development: Towards the conception of a learning model in crisis management. *Organizational Development Journal, 25*(1), 17–26.

Lester, D., & Parnell, J. (2007). *Organizational theory: A strategic perspective.* Cincinnati, OH: Atomic Dog Publishing.

Leveson, N., & Turner, C. (1993). An investigation of the Therac-25 accidents. *IEEE Computer, 26*(7), 18–41.

Lordan, E. (2005, Winter). The Sago Mine disaster: A crisis in crisis communication. *Public Relations Quarterly,* pp. 10–12.

Martell, K. (2007). Assessing student learning: Are business schools making the grade? *Journal of Education for Business, 82*(4), 189–195.

Moats, J., Chermack, T., & Dooley, L. (2008). Using scenarios to develop crisis managers: Applications of scenario planning and scenario-based training. *Advances in Developing Human Resources, 10*(3), 397–424.

Nathan, M. (2000). The paradoxical nature of crisis. *Review of Business, 21*(3), 12–16.

New York State Department of Social Services. (1996). *New York State Commission on Quality Care for the Mentally Disabled: Profit making in not-for-profit care: Part III: The case of Queens County Neuropsychiatric Institute, Inc.* [Available through the New York State Commission on Quality of Care for the Mentally Disabled]

Nystrom, P., & Starbuck, W. (1984). To avoid organizational crises, unlearn. *Organizational Dynamics, 12*(4), 53–65.

Parnell, J. (2008). *Strategic management: Theory and practice* (3rd ed.). Cincinnati, OH: Atomic Dog Publishing.

Pearson, C., & Clair, J. (1998). Reframing crisis management. *Academy of Management Review, 23*(1), 59–76.

Pearson, C., & Mitroff, I. (1993). From crisis prone to crisis prepared: A framework for crisis management. *Academy of Management Executive, 7*(1), 48–59.

Reilly, A. (2008). The role of human resource development competencies in facilitating effective crisis communication. *Advances in Developing Human Resources, 10*(3), 331–351.

Roux-Dufort, C. (2000, Fall). Why organizations don't learn from crises: The perverse power of normalization. *Review of Business,* pp. 25–30.

Senge, P. (2006). *The fifth discipline handbook: The art and practice of the learning organization.* New York: Currency Doubleday.

Simon, L., & Pauchant, T. (2000, Fall). Developing the three levels of learning in crisis management: A case study of the Hagersville tire fire. *Review of Business,* pp. 6–11.

Slater, S., & Narver, J. (1995). Market orientation and the learning organization. *Journal of Marketing, 59*(3), 63–74.

Smith, D. (1993). Crisis management in the public sector: Lessons from the prison service. In J. Wilson & P. Hinton (Eds.), *Public service and the 1990s: Issues in public service finance and management.* London: Tudor Press.

Stead, E., & Smallman, C. (1999). Understanding business failure: Learning and unlearning lessons from industrial crises. *Journal of Contingencies and Crisis Management, 7*(1), 1–18.

Turner, B., & Pidgeon, N. (1997). *Man-made disasters* (2nd ed.). London: Butterworth-Heinemann.

Wang, J. (2008). Developing organizational learning capacity in crisis management. *Advances in Developing Human Resources, 10*(3), 425–445.

Weick, K. (1993). The collapse of sensemaking in organizations: The Mann Gulch disaster. *Administrative Science Quarterly, 38,* 628–652.

CHAPTER 10

The Underlying Role of Ethics in Crisis Management

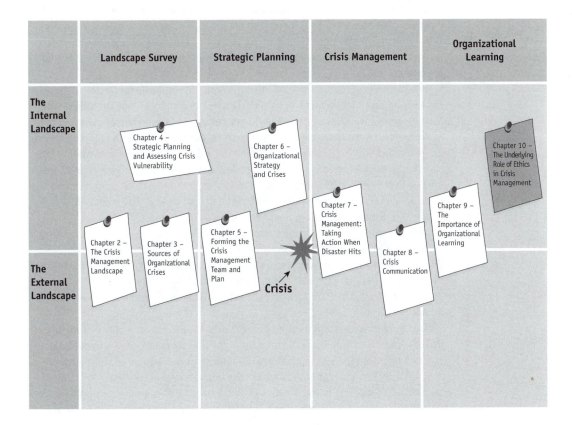

Hawks Nest

In southern West Virginia, there is an engineering feat that few people know about except for the locals and the tourists who happen to stop by the small roadside park overlooking the project. It is an underground tunnel, about 3 miles long, that carries water from a dam to a small hydroelectric plant perched securely on the side of a mountain. The purpose of the project was to supply electricity to the Union Carbide plant, then located in Alloy, West Virginia, about 6 miles away. The tunnel was built during the Great Depression, mostly by poor workers who migrated to the area seeking employment (Cherniak, 1986).

The project itself was somewhat ingenious because it solved a problem faced by Union Carbide. Additional electricity was needed to power its new plant, but the prospects of supplying it with hydroelectric power seemed bleak because the New River—one of only a few rivers in the United States that flow north—was (and still is) a slow-moving, narrow band of water that does not have enough force to power a hydroelectric plant in that location. The engineers came up with a clever solution: Construct a dam to build up water volume and then pitch it in a downward direction to give it force (Cherniak, 1986). A small hydroelectric building with four turbines was positioned where the water emerged with great force from the tunnel. The result was a facility that still makes electricity to this day (Crandall & Crandall, 2002).

But there is a darker side to this project. The tunnel contractor, Virginia engineering firm Rinehart and Dennis, drastically cut corners to save on project time and expenses. Workers were forced to go inside the dusty tunnel shortly after explosives had been detonated to begin clearing out the debris. Although engineers were supplied with respirators, those doing the manual labor were not. When silica rock was encountered, the resulting fine dust that the explosion had created was inhaled by the workers as they removed debris from the tunnel shaft. As a result, many of these laborers developed silicosis, a debilitating lung disease that eventually causes death. This disease is avoidable if respirators are worn.

Rinehart and Dennis also used another cost-cutting measure: dry drilling. Wet drilling should have been used to minimize dust levels. The downside is that wet drilling slows the extraction process, unlike dry drilling, which is faster but also creates more dust (Orr & Dragan, 1981; Rowh, 1981). The additional dust associated with the dry drilling, coupled with the lack of respirators, was another factor that led to sickness in these workers.

The number of deaths attributed to the Hawks Nest Tunnel can only be estimated because Social Security records did not exist at the time (Cherniak, 1986). The estimates vary depending on the source of information. Rinehart and Dennis submitted a figure of 65 total deaths, whereas Union Carbide, the ultimate user of the Hawks Nest tunnel, counted 109 fatalities. In his account of the Hawks Nest incident, Martin Cherniak estimates a total of 764 deaths. Regardless of the exact number, the figures are high relative to today's standards of industrial safety. As one might expect, the death estimates become more conservative as the source of information moves closer to the tunnel contractor (Crandall & Crandall, 2002).

Background

There is an underlying problem in many of the crisis events discussed in this book. This problem does not manifest itself in every crisis, but it is substantial nonetheless. Why do seemingly preventable crises happen again and again? The answer can be found with a firm's employees, particularly managers and top-level business executives and their desire to gain unfairly at the expense of another party. This problem appears in many forms, but the results are usually the same: an organizational crisis of some type, stakeholders that have been hurt, and prevention that would have cost pennies when compared to the damage done.

The Hawks Nest Tunnel incident was one of the first major industrial crises in the United States. Although the tunnel was a remarkable success, the human resource tragedy was enormous. The deaths of these workers were entirely preventable, but tunnel contractor Rinehart and Dennis seemed to decide that breathing protection and other safety measures be abandoned in order to maximize profits. The contractor did not escape unscathed, however. Within 5 years of the project, its assets were liquidated, a victim of bad publicity, lawsuits, and loss of revenue.

In an age when Enron, Arthur Andersen, WorldCom, Tyco, and Adelphia are more commonly known scandal-ridden companies, why focus on a human tragedy that occurred more than half a century ago? The Hawks Nest Tunnel incident clearly illustrates the fact that some crises have human roots that can be traced back to unethical or irresponsible behavior by key decision makers. In addition, such behaviors are not confined to any specific time period in history. Human-induced crises have always occurred and will continue to occur, an inescapable reality. However, we also know that some organizations seem to do better than others at avoiding these types of crises because they put an emphasis on promoting ethical behavior throughout their organizations. This fact also is inescapable, and a cause for hope.

In this chapter we examine human-induced crises more closely, specifically those linked to unethical behavior. We examine these types of crises through the crisis management framework presented in this book. The chapter begins with a brief review of the concept of business ethics. Next, we survey the landscape in which unethical behaviors reside. The discussion proceeds to the strategic planning phase where we will consider how organizations, industries, and ultimately government regulations seek to prevent unethical behavior. The crisis management phase involves the management of internal and external stakeholders during this acute segment of the crisis. We examine what works and does not work, using an ethical perspective. We conclude by considering the organizational learning phase and what should occur at the micro and macro levels when stakeholders seek to learn lessons from experiencing scandal-ridden crises.

What Is Business Ethics?

Business ethics looks at issues of right and wrong in a business context (Carroll & Buchholtz, 2003). A related but distinct concept is corporate social

TABLE 10.1	The Components of Corporate Social Responsibility (CSR)	
Component of CSR	Key Thought to Understanding	Manifestations
Economic	Be profitable	Maximize revenues Cut expenses Maximize profits Increase shareholder wealth
Legal	Obey the law	Abide by all legal regulations Stay within industry standards Maintain all contract and warranty obligations
Ethical	Avoid questionable practices	Go beyond just obeying the law, abide by the spirit of the law as well Avoid practices that may appear to be suspicious, even if they are legal Do the right thing, and be just and fair
Philanthropic	Be a good corporate citizen	Make financial contributions to stakeholders in the community Seek to be a good neighbor in the community by making it a better place to live Look for ways to support education, health/human services, and the arts

Source: Adapted from Carroll, A., & Buchholtz, A. (2003). *Business & Society: Ethics and Stakeholder Management* (5th ed.). Cincinnati, OH: Thompson South-Western, pp. 39–40.

responsibility (CSR), which maintains that businesses should seek social benefits for society as well as economic benefits for the business (Post, Lawrence, & Weber, 2002). A popular framework for looking at the two concepts of business ethics and CSR is shown in Table 10.1. In this framework, proposed by Carroll & Buchholtz, (2003), CSR is made up of our four parts: economic, legal, ethical, and philanthropic responsibilities. Above all, businesses must meet their economic responsibility by being profitable while operating within the confines of the law.

There is also a realm of business behavior that goes beyond obeying the law. Ethical responsibility seeks to avoid behaviors that are questionable though not necessarily illegal. Practically speaking, it is not possible to develop laws to prohibit every unethical business activity. Consider also that many companies sell products or services that are legal, but are considered by many to be unethical in some contexts. Hartley (1993) documents the now infamous PowerMaster Beer controversy in which malt liquor, a legal product, was heavily marketed to poor urban areas, markets where crime and youth despair were prevalent. This combination created an unethical situation in the eyes of many community stakeholders who saw this product contributing to even higher crime problems in urban neighborhoods. More recently, the mortgage crisis of the early 2000s that adversely affected an entire industry could have been avoided if individual lenders had simply refused to issue loans with terms that were likely to create a substantial repayment hardship down the road for borrowers. To their credit, several lenders—including BB&T, a regional banking company based in North Carolina—refused to issue such profitable loans on ethical grounds, a high road not taken by most in the industry (Parnell & Dent, in press).

Finally, it can be argued that companies have a philanthropic responsibility: the obligation to be a good corporate citizen. Some seek to fulfill this responsibility by contributing time and money to the communities in which they operate. Many businesses make financial contributions to school systems as well as colleges and universities. Others encourage their employees to volunteer in their communities and will often compensate these employees for their time invested in a civic cause.

Carroll and Buchholtz (2003) maintain that three CSR components—economic, legal, and ethical—are also the most closely tied in with business ethics. Considering organizational crises, it is clear that many are comprised of one or more of these components. In Table 10.2 we provide examples based on the assumption that business ethics crises are motivated by a desire to gain financially at the expense of another stakeholder. For example, at the heart of the economic component is the need to make a profit for the business. But doing so without regard to morality can result in breaking the law (the legal component) or taking part in questionable ethical practices (the ethical component), both of which can result in an organizational crisis.

Business Ethics and the Crisis Management Framework

Many of the ethically oriented crises that are discussed in this section are examples of what have been labeled "smoldering crises." The Institute for Crisis Management (ICM) notes that these crises start out small and can be fixed early on, but instead are allowed to fester until they become full-blown crises and known to the public (Institute for Crisis Management, 2007). What makes some smoldering crises ethically induced is that they do not have to occur in the first place. If such a crisis does occur, it can be mitigated through ethical decision making, although not all executives will proceed in that manner. Instead, some escalate the crisis by making additional unethical decisions, until the crisis spins out of control.

The Beech-Nut apple juice case (see Chapter 6) illustrates a smoldering crisis that should have been stopped early on. During the late 1970s, Beech-Nut Nutrition Corporation found out that it was the victim of a scam when it discovered its apple juice concentrate supplier was providing bogus apple juice. This discovery was especially troublesome because Beech-Nut advertised its apple juice as "100% fruit juice, no sugar added," a claim that was, in fact, not true, given the fraudulent supplier. At that point, Beech-Nut could have reported the incident, pleaded ignorance, and most likely escaped any prosecution since it was an innocent victim ("Bad Apples," 1989; Hartley, 1993). However, this particular supplier was providing its product at 25 percent below the market

TABLE 10.2	Ethical Crises Components	
The Basis for an Ethical Crisis	*Ethical Crisis Component*	*Examples of Crises* *Note*: Some of these company crises events may not be familiar to you. These will be examined in more detail in the chapter exercise.
Economic: The basic motive is a desire to gain financially, sometimes at the expense of another stakeholder.	**Legal:** These cases involve behavior on the part of company employees that violates the law.	Company misrepresents its accounting statements by hiding debt or overstating profits. Examples: Adelphia Communications Corporation (2002); Enron (2002); HealthSouth (2002); Qwest Communications International (2005) Company knowingly sells a defective product. Examples: the A. H. Robins Dalkon Shield (1984); Dow Corning silicone breast implants (1992) Company falsely advertises its product. Example: Beech-Nut apple juice (1982) Company violates safety standards in the workplace. Examples: BP Texas City Explosion (2005); Film Recovery Services, Inc. (1985); Warner-Lambert Company (1976)
	Ethical: These cases involve behavior on the part of company employees that is questionable, but does not necessarily violate the law.	Company sells a product that is legal but not necessarily beneficial to society. Examples: PowerMaster Beer (1991); the tobacco industry; Nestlé Infant Formula (1970s) Company is aware of safety changes it could make to its product, but decides to not to do so because of cost factors. Examples: Ford Pinto (1970s); GM Corvair (1960s) Company uses questionable means to obtain phone information. Example: HP (2006) Company compensates auto shop managers based on sales commission, resulting in higher customer bills for repairs not necessarily needed. Example: Sears Auto Centers (1992)

Sources: Carroll A., & Buchholtz, A. (2003). *Business & Society: Ethics and Stakeholder Management* (5th ed.). Cincinnati, OH: Thompson South-Western; Coombs, W. (2006). *Code Red in the Boardroom: Crisis Management as Organizational DNA.* Westport, CT: Praeger; Coombs, W. (2007). *Ongoing Crisis Communication: Planning, Managing, and Responding* (2nd ed.). Thousand Oaks, CA: Sage; Hartley, R. (1993). *Business Ethics: Violations of the Public Trust.* New York: John Wiley; Sethi, S., & Steidlmeier, P. (1997). *Up Against the Corporate Wall: Cases in Business and Society* (6th ed). Upper Saddle River, NJ: Prentice Hall.

rate, and the cost savings was too attractive for Beech-Nut executives to pass up. The incident escalated to a smoldering crisis where Beech-Nut top executives concocted an elaborate coverup scheme and continued using the supplier. From 1977 to 1983, Beech-Nut sold its juice as 100% pure when, in fact, it was nothing more than a "100% fraudulent chemical cocktail," according to an

TABLE 10.3	Crisis Management Framework			
	Landscape Survey	Strategic Planning	Crisis Management	Organizational Learning

The Internal Landscape	❑ The ethical environment and the board of directors
	❑ The safety policies of the organization
	❑ The extent of greed present among top executives and management
		❑ The enthusiasm for crisis management planning and training
		❑ The focus on the prevention of ethical breaches
			❑ The management of internal stakeholders
			  o Owners
			  o Employees
			
			Crisis
				❑ The evaluation of the ethical management process
				❑ The commitment to organizational learning

The External Landscape	❑ The degree of industry vulnerability
	❑ The vulnerability of the organization in the global environment
		❑ The fulfillment of existing government regulations
		❑ The fulfillment of current industry standards
			❑ The management of external stakeholders
			  o Customers
			  o Suppliers
			  o Government parties
			  o Local community
				❑ The benefits of industry renewal
				❑ The inevitability of new government regulations
				❑ The anticipation of new stakeholder outlooks

investigator close to the case (Welles, 1988, p. 124). What should have been a decision to change suppliers became an ethical misconduct crisis. Beech-Nut president Neils Hoyvald, and John Lavery, vice president for operations, were the main parties who instigated the coverup. When the crisis was finally over, both men were found guilty of violating federal food and drug laws. Hartley (1993) estimates the crisis that never should have happened cost Beech-Nut $25 million in fines, legal costs, and lost sales.

Table 10.3 depicts the crisis management framework in relation to business ethics issues. The next sections develop the four areas of the crisis management process.

Landscape Survey: Uncovering the Ethical Boulders

The landscape survey looks for clues in the organization's internal and external environments that may indicate the presence of an unethical event brewing. Potential crisis indicators include the ethical environment of the Board of Directors, the safety policies of the organization, the economic motives among top executives and management, the degree of industry vulnerability, and the vulnerability of the organization in the global environment. These indicators are discussed next.

The Ethical Environment and the Board of Directors

The ethical environment of the organization is an indicator of the potential for a future crisis. The founder of the company holds a considerable amount of influence in forming this ethical environment. For example, Enron, WorldCom, Adelphia, HealthSouth, and Tyco have all faced ethical scandals. What these firms had in common was that their founders, all hardworking entrepreneurs, were at the helm when the crises hit (Colvin, 2003). Furthermore, those in charge of these companies had at least three characteristics in common that led to the scandals. First, these companies had not learned to question the founder/CEO when necessary. Rather, their CEOs were powerful individuals who seemed to answer to no one. Second, the characteristic of greed was apparent at the top levels of these companies. It was as if an entitlement mentality prevailed, with those running the company receiving extraordinary amounts of compensation because they felt they deserved it. Finally, all of these companies had leaders who seemed to focus on short-term gains through increasing stock price, without regard to the sustainability of the company. The link between CEO compensation and stock price is an underlying factor in many of the scandals that hit these big corporations (Colvin, 2003).

This factor presents the corporation with a dilemma. On one hand, CEO compensation should be linked to firm performance; on the other hand, this linkage can be abused in favor of short-term performance versus long-term survival and growth. In response to this quandary, some firms have favored the balanced scorecard approach (Kaplan & Norton, 2001), an approach that has pushed the practice of accounting to track long-term as well as short-term performance results. Thousands of companies have now adopted this approach in the United States and abroad (Parnell & Jusoh, 2008; Post et al., 2002).

More scrutiny of corporate boards has also occurred, with boards facing more accountability and disclosure mandates (Thorne, Ferrell, & Ferrell, 2003). The situation at WorldCom is an example of a board that continually gave in to the desires of then-CEO Bernard Ebbers: "As CEO, Ebbers was allowed nearly imperial reign over the affairs of the company with little influence from the board of directors, even though he did not appear to possess the experience or training to be qualified for his position" (Breeden, 2003, p. 1). Two areas of questionable freedom were requested by Ebbers and approved by the board. The first involved the approval of the collection of $400 million in loans, and the second a rubber-stamping of his request to compensate favored executives to the tune of $238 million. The arrangement was made without standards or supervision and allowed Ebbers to compensate whomever he wanted and in whatever amount he wished (Breeden, 2003). Ultimately, these schemes, along with others, culminated in a crisis that resulted in the largest accounting fraud case in the United States.

Crisis cases like WorldCom illustrate why boards have to be more than just a rubber stamp for the CEO. In response, some boards are taking a more aggressive approach to holding the CEO accountable for ethical behavior. Case in point: Boeing's former CEO, Harry Stonecipher, lost his job after it was revealed he was having an affair with another Boeing executive (Benjamin, Lim, & Streisand, 2005). The relationship violated company policy. Ironically, Stonecipher, who agreed to come out of retirement to serve as CEO, was brought in to lead the scandal-ridden company out of its ethical quagmires (Levenson, 2005).

The Safety Policies of the Organization

Safety policies, or the lack of them, have a direct link to the ethical climate of the organization. Ultimately, the adherence to such policies can determine whether or not a major crisis occurs. An ethical stance on the part of management promotes an environment where all stakeholders (particularly employees) are safe from bodily and emotional harm. However, as every manager and top executive knows, safety costs money and can detract from the bottom line in the short run. In the long run, though, these expenditures can save the company millions and maybe even the company itself.

In looking back at industrial accidents, organizational researchers have never reached a conclusion that indicated too much money was spent on safety (Crandall & Crandall, 2002). Executives who have experienced a safety issue such as an industrial accident resulting in injuries or deaths probably wish they had spent more on safety. For example, in the 1983 Bhopal, India gas leak incident, Union Carbide and local government officials in India should have focused more on correcting safety problems that had already been widely documented at the plant prior to the accident (Sethi & Steidlmeier, 1997; Steiner & Steiner, 2000).

Safety measures involve short-term expenses but usually produce long-term savings by avoiding accidents. Hence, safety remedies need not always be viewed as "expensive." Money spent to prevent employee injury and death is not money wasted; it may well save the company millions in lawsuits, as well as the company's reputation, not to mention human lives. The Hawks Nest Tunnel contractor, Rinehart and Dennis, could have implemented at least three relatively low-cost measures to make working conditions safer and thereby prevent their workers from developing silicosis: better ventilation of the tunnel shaft, wet drilling, and providing respirators for workers. While it is difficult to determine the exact cost of these measures, it is clear that such measures might have saved many lives as well as the downfall the company experienced within 5 years of completing the tunnel.

The Economic Motives Among Top Executives and Management

Economic motives are often linked to unethical and illegal behaviors. As Table 10.2 indicates, the economic motive can be pushed to the point of greed becoming part of the process. The reason for this is actually easy to see. Management competence is measured by key performance indicators such as sales, profits, and market share, which can ultimately drive the price of the company's stock. Boards of directors typically reward the CEO when stock valuations increase, because this represents an increase in wealth for the shareholders. At first, this sounds like a win-win situation, but as many recent business crises indicate, abuses can occur that ultimately are not in the best interest of the corporation or its stakeholders. Two such abuses are hiding debt and counterproductive cost cutting.

Hiding debt creates the illusion that the firm is performing better than it actually is, which encourages a false sense of optimism and confidence in the stock. The result is that stock prices rise in the short term, and shareholder values increase. The CEO is also rewarded, because "on paper" the firm is doing well. This whole process is motivated by an attempt at excessive financial gain at the expense of other stakeholders. In the short run, this unethical strategy can actually produce financial benefits for the CEO and the shareholders. In the long run, however, it is a prescription for a major crisis. Enron will remain the poster child for this abuse as the company spiraled downward after its elaborate schemes for hiding debt became known. Technically, the mechanism for hiding its debt, a provision called special-purpose entities (SPEs), was legal, but such SPEs have trigger mechanisms that require repayment of the debt under certain circumstances (Henry, Timmons, Rosenbush, & Arndt, 2002). It was these trigger mechanisms that began the "visible" crisis at Enron even though the invisible part of the crisis, the part not known to stakeholders, actually took place well before, when the SPEs were originally developed.

Counterproductive cost cutting is the other abuse that can arise from unethical motives. Such cost cutting is actually the profit motive at work, and will cause some managers to do just about anything. Cutting costs delivers dollars to the bottom line, but doing so without regard for worker safety has resulted in many examples of industrial tragedies. In 1976, when Warner-Lambert was introducing a new line of chewing gum, it took shortcuts in the manufacturing area by allowing high levels of dust near the machinery. The company could have installed a dust collection system, a move that would have reduced dust levels significantly. The cost was seen as prohibitive, however, so the opportunity to buy the system was ignored. The result was a dust explosion that killed six employees and injured 54 others (Sethi & Steidlmeier, 1997).

Although cost cutting is a normal and necessary business activity, it was the major factor in the many deaths that resulted from building the Hawks Nest Tunnel. The use of dry drilling to expedite the project time was discussed earlier. Shortening the project time reduces expenses and increases the bottom line. The decision not to provide tunnel workers with respirators is especially troubling. The only explanation for this seems to be the additional cost that would have been incurred.

The Hawks Nest incident illustrates the connection between ethical decision making—doing what is just and fair for employees—and protecting worker safety. Perhaps the most famous abuse of worker safety in the United States was the 1911 Triangle Shirtwaist Company fire that occurred on the 10th floor of a factory in New York City. The fire spread rapidly due to the large amounts of linen and other combustible materials close by. One hundred forty-six employees died, most of them immigrant women, who were either burned in the blaze or jumped to their deaths. Sadly, the fire escape routes for these employees had been locked by management in order to prevent theft (Greer, 2001; Vernon, 1998). Some may argue that revisiting cases like Hawks Nest and the Triangle Shirtwaist fire is not necessary today. After all, labor unions, labor laws, safety inspectors, and various watchdog groups discourage this kind of behavior (Shanker, 1992). Unfortunately, history has a way of repeating itself.

On September 3, 1991, a fire erupted at the Imperial Food Products poultry plant in Hamlet, North Carolina. Before the day was over, 25 employees, most of them single mothers, would perish. "The plant had no sprinkler or fire alarm system, and workers who got to the unmarked fire exits found some of them locked from the outside. Imperial's management was using the same 'loss control' technique as the bosses at Triangle—and with the same results" (Shanker, 1992, p. 27). An $800,000 labor code fine was levied against the company. Fourteen months after the fire, a $16 million settlement was reached between the insurers and the claimants. Plant owner Emmet Roe was sentenced to 20 years in prison after pleading guilty to manslaughter (Jefferson, 1993). Eventually, Imperial went bankrupt. As these examples illustrate, unchecked greed comes in various forms and can hurt other stakeholders in the process.

The Degree of Industry Vulnerability

Certain industries are more vulnerable to crisis events. The airline industry remains the most crisis prone, according to the Institute for Crisis Management (ICM). This is due to the potential for terrorist attacks and aviation accidents, which are risk factors when operating in that industry. However, a crisis-prone industry does not mean that unethical decision making prevails. Some industries are just more susceptible to accidents, such as natural gas and petroleum refining, which ranked fifth and sixth, respectively in the top crisis-prone industries (Institute for Crisis Management, 2007).

Looking through the lens of ethical rationality (Snyder, Hall, Robertson, Jasinski, & Miller, 2006), the challenge is to determine if an industry is more vulnerable to a crisis because of a higher degree of unethical occurrences. The link between industry-specific factors and unethical behaviors has not been as widely addressed, although some attention has been focused on aircraft manufacturers. Both Lockheed and Northrop were found to have made improper cash payments to overseas sales agents in the 1970s in order to secure contracts to sell aircraft (Securities and Exchange Commission, 1976). More recently, Boeing has been plagued by a number of ethical problems, perpetuated by what has been called a "culture of silence" by Boeing general counsel Douglas Bain. The culture stems from a lack of speaking up on ethical issues, a problem that has plagued the company for a considerable amount of time (Holmes, 2006).

The Vulnerability of the Organization in the Global Environment

As a firm expands its international presence, its vulnerability to crisis may also increase. There is a greater potential for an ethical breach to occur as well. Three reasons for potential ethical problems include the temptation to make illegal cash payments, the possibility that a foreign contractor will supply a defective product, and the potential to be linked with sweatshop manufacturing.

The Temptation to Make Illegal Cash Payments

Major scandals often result in new legislation. As a result of the Lockheed bribery scandal, the Foreign Corrupt Practices Act was passed in 1977 (Hartley,

1993). The act prohibits offering cash payments to foreign government officials for the purpose of obtaining business (Carroll & Buchholtz, 2003). Critics often complain, however, that the act places American firms at a disadvantage when competing for foreign contracts where legal infrastructure requiring that all companies play by the same rules does not exist. In many parts of the world, offering bribes is an accepted way to conduct business. To further complicate the matter, the act does allow some cash payments, called grease payments—smaller amounts of cash used to encourage foreign officials to do what they are supposed to do anyway (Carrol & Buchholtz, 2003). A bribe, on the other hand, is a large cash payment used to entice a foreign official or agent to do something not normally done in the course of business, such as buying from a particular vendor.

As companies expand globally, the temptation to use illegal cash payments such as bribes increases. Recent enforcement by the U.S. Securities and Exchange Commission (SEC) and the U.S. Department of Justice (DOJ) indicates that the act is being violated to some degree. The year 2006 was a busy year for its enforcement, with charges leveled at four high-profile companies and a number of individuals. The DOJ promises that future enforcement of the Foreign Corrupt Practices Act will be carried out with "increased vigilance" (Warin, Blume, Bell, & McConkie, 2007, p. 2).

The Possibility That a Foreign Contractor Will Supply a Defective Product

Defective products originate from foreign contractors just like they do from domestic companies. However, the perception of citizens in the home country may be that the foreign contractor has acted unethically in some way, possibly by cutting corners in the manufacturing process. Furthermore, if jobs have been lost due to outsourcing, the home company is likely to experience a public relations problem.

The Potential of Being Linked With Sweatshop Manufacturing

Companies that outsource processes to overseas vendors may face potential association with sweatshops. This crisis can lead critics of outsourcing to be diligent in identifying companies that are using sweatshops for the manufacturing of their products. Sweatshops are manufacturing facilities that pay low wages, employ child labor, have poor working conditions, require long work hours, and use abusive supervision of workers. Their use has increased as companies seek to lower costs (Carroll & Buccholtz, 2003). Their use can also cause companies to be hit with a public relations crisis. Wal-Mart, Nike, Liz Claiborne, Disney, and McDonald's are large, high-profile companies that have been linked with sweatshops in the past (Post et al., 2002).

Sweatshops are the ultimate "guilt by association" crisis. Although some progress has been made in recent years to improve working conditions in developing countries, the issue will not go away anytime soon. Although a company can "require" its subcontractors to abide by certain working condition standards, the enforcement of these standards can be difficult. Typically, independent monitors are sent to investigate working conditions in plants that are supposed to be compliant with certain standards. Even companies with reputations for good ethics face such problems. The 2007 discovery tracing some of the clothing sold in Gap stores to sweatshops in India where children as young as 10 years of age work 16 hours a day is one such example (Hansen & Harkin, 2008).

Strategic Planning: Confronting the Ethical Boulders

The strategic planning process can generate efforts to improve the ethical climate of the organization. Improving this climate can reduce the company's vulnerability to an ethics-related crisis. Specific efforts should be directed to generating enthusiasm for crisis management and training, focusing on the prevention of ethical breaches, and abiding by both government regulations and industry standards.

The Enthusiasm for Crisis Management and Training

Neglecting to prepare for a crisis is in itself an ethical problem. Unfortunate events can eventually happen to an organization, and having a plan to meet these crises is expected by the company's stakeholders. The lack of a crisis management plan and the subsequent training that goes with it will only draw negative perceptions from employees, suppliers, customers, government agencies, and the general public when a crisis does occur.

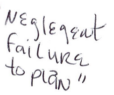
"Neglegent Failure to plan"

Simply forming a crisis management team and generating a crisis plan is not sufficient. Enthusiasm for the crisis management process and the accompanying training must also be present. For this reason, the organization should seek a crisis management champion from within who will spearhead the process toward an ongoing crisis management program. If the organization is new to crisis planning, an outside consultant should also be retained to assist the crisis management team in writing its first plan.

The Focus on the Prevention of Ethics Breaches

The best approach to dealing with an ethical crisis is to prevent it from happening in the first place. An ethical rationality approach seeks to address events in the life of the organization from a morally driven response perspective (Snyder et al., 2006). However, to a great extent the organizational culture dictates how ethical or unethical decision making will be in the company (Heineman, 2007; Vallario, 2007). For this reason, a cultural change in the organization is also necessary to improve ethical decision making.

Changing the culture of an organization is a large undertaking; culture is, after all, the prevailing belief system within the organization. Some cultures simply look the other way when an ethical breach occurs, whereas others are committed to ethical standards in any business decision. All cultures look to

TABLE 10.4	Measures Organizations Take to Change Their Ethical Culture
Measure Taken	*Description*
Code of ethics	Organization-wide ethical principles and behaviors are outlined in a pamphlet or manual. Managers and employees review the code on a regular basis and sign it, indicating their willingness to abide by the code.
Ethics training	Short classes and workshops that highlight ethical issues and how to respond to them are offered to employees.
Ethics hotline	Employees have a person or department they can report ethical violations to within their organization. A hotline can also offer guidance on specific ethical issues that an employee may be facing.
Top management sets the example	Executives in top positions in the company—the CEO, president, and vice presidents—need to realize that lower-level managers get their cues on ethical matters by watching those higher up. Thus, top managers are encouraged to set the right example.
Realistic goal setting	Goals set for managers are well conceived and realistic. Unrealistic goals encourage unethical decision making since managers feel they must cut corners to attain the goal.
Discipline for ethical violations	When an ethical violation is discovered, the company works quickly to correct the situation and punish the person responsible.
Ethics audits	As in a financial audit, the company periodically checks itself in a systematic manner to see if it is following proper ethical guidelines in its business processes.

Sources: Carroll, A., & Buchholtz, A. (2003). *Business & Society: Ethics and Stakeholder Management* (5th ed.). Cincinnati, OH: Thompson South-Western; Post, J., Lawrence, A., & Weber, J. (2002). *Business and Society: Corporate Strategy, Public Policy, Ethics.* New York: McGraw-Hill Irwin.

upper-level management for cues to right and wrong behavior in the organization (Trevino, Hartman, & Brown, 2000). Table 10.4 overviews other measures companies take to change their ethical cultures.

Abiding by Existing Government Regulations

Government regulations exist to protect employees, consumers, and the local community. Unfortunately, such regulations can sometimes be sidestepped by businesses, which can lead to catastrophic outcomes in the future. It is an ethical decision to abide by government regulations. The converse of this statement is also true: Ignoring regulations is also a decision, one that is conscious and deliberate. Many organizations find themselves in trouble with government regulations because of unethical/illegal decisions made by management or other key employees.

In 1997, the Andrew & Williamson Sales Company sold strawberries grown in Mexico to the U.S. Department of Agriculture (USDA). There was one problem with the deal. The USDA distributes food to public schools, and government regulations require that strawberries sold to school systems be grown in the United States. As part of a coverup, the San Diego–based firm submitted falsified certificates of origin that indicated the strawberries were grown domestically (Salkin, 1997). While the company thought its deed would go unnoticed, a major crisis soon erupted. A number of public school students in Michigan were stricken with hepatitis A, and the ailment was linked to the strawberries sold by Andrew & Williamson. Eventually outbreaks of the hepatitis A strain originating from the strawberries resulted in 213 cases in Michigan, 29 in Maine, and 7 in Wisconsin (Entis, 2007). What started out as an illegal scheme to move excess inventory out of the warehouse culminated in a major crisis across a number of states. When the ordeal ended, Frederick Williamson resigned as president and was sentenced to 5 months in prison, followed by 5 months of home detention. The company was also forced to pay $1.3 million in civil damages, as well as $200,000 in criminal penalties (Entis, 2007).

In the Hawks Nest incident, existing regulations were ignored in certain circumstances. For example, standard operating procedures required that wet drilling be utilized to keep dust levels to a minimum (Cherniak, 1986; Tyler, 1975). Testimony before the U.S. Congress revealed that employees were posted to watch for incoming mine inspectors (Comstock, 1973). With these arrivals "announced," wet drilling would begin until the inspectors had left the area, when dry drilling would resume to speed up the extraction process. Such sidestepping of regulations would provide short-term relief for the contractor, but in the long run it would come back to haunt them.

Abiding by Current Industry Standards

Industry standards are often set by associations for their members to follow. The intent is to set guidelines concerning a particular item, such as quality or safety, that can be viewed by member companies as a minimally acceptable standard (Vernon, 1998). Such efforts have also been referred to as self-policing (Becker, 2006) or self-regulation (Hemphill, 2006). Certain professions also have standards for their members; these professions include physicians, attorneys, college and university professors, engineers, pharmacists, and accountants.

Guidelines for ethical conduct can be proposed by industry associations. In 2001, an industry group of 14 Wall Street firms established ethical conduct standards governing compensation and stock ownership for analysts. This move was prompted by some of the industry leaders, including Goldman Sachs, Merrill Lynch, and Morgan Stanley Dean Witter, to address emerging ethical problems (Carroll & Buchholtz, 2003). In another example, Financial Executives International (FEI) requires all of its members to review and sign a code of ethics. They also recommend that the financial executive deliver the signed copy to the company board of directors. FEI has become a model for companies seeking to comply with Sarbanes-Oxley and New York Stock Exchange mandates (Vallario, 2007).

Several caveats should be offered concerning industry standards. First, requiring that member companies have a code of ethics is a step in the right direction, but it does not ensure all companies will have leaders who always make ethical decisions. Even Enron had a 62-page code of ethical conduct;

unfortunately, it was not an ingrained part of the Enron culture (Becker, 2006). Second, larger companies within associations attract more attention than smaller ones and thus are easier targets for critics. Case in point: A Google search on the company names Wal-Mart or Starbucks will inevitably reveal Web sites that are critical of these companies. Some of these sites even trump up false claims about the companies. Why? Large, successful companies are also seen as vulnerable targets by issue-oriented groups.

Crisis Management: Further Considerations During an Ethical Crisis

A crisis should be managed in an ethical manner. "Decision-makers who understand the needs of a wide range of stakeholders as part of their strategic decision-making will make more ethical decisions during a time of crisis" (Snyder et al., 2006, p. 376). Thus, ethical rationality is a habit that must be ingrained in the culture and daily operations of the organization (Fritzsche, 2005). This ethical rationality involves the careful management of the organization's internal and external stakeholders throughout the duration of the crisis.

The Management of Internal Stakeholders

Employees and owners are the internal stakeholders that must be managed with ethical integrity when a crisis occurs. Typically, it is the crisis communication function that must be approached in an honest, straightforward manner. Employees are often the forgotten stakeholder in the ordeal. It is important they receive truthful and expedient information updates as the crisis progresses.

On the other hand, the owners may suffer a direct consequence from a crisis in the form of financial loss. If the shareholders are geographically dispersed, the impact of the loss may not be felt until quarterly reports are distributed months after the crisis commences. If the company is a corporation with many stockholders, then they, too, like the employees, may be left in the dark on the details of the crisis at hand. This is not an ethical approach to informing these groups.

The organization's Web site is a strategic tool that can be used to communicate with these stakeholders. Updates on the state of the crisis should be made on a regular basis. Chapter 8 addressed the importance of maintaining a special "dark site," a link used to answer frequently asked questions (FAQs) on the nature of the crisis (Snellen, 2003). Both employees and stockholders should have ready access to these sites. In addition, the organization should use its managers and supervisors to communicate the details of the crisis to employees. To supplement this type of communication, an organization-wide memo or letter should be circulated to all employees. This is an excellent way to clarify misunderstandings or rumors that may be circulating about the crisis.

The Management of External Stakeholders

External stakeholders include customers, suppliers, the local community, the media, and affected government agencies. As with internal stakeholders, the ethical approach is to make sure that communication to these groups is honest and timely. For example, if the crisis is an untrue rumor, it should be addressed quickly and stated that it is untrue (Coombs, 2007; Gross, 1990). Again, the organization's Web site can be an excellent vehicle for updated information on the latest developments of the crisis.

Organizational Learning: Lessons From the Ethical Crisis

Lessons learned from an ethical crisis tend to be somber. Recovering from these types of crisis requires a commitment to pursue better behavior in the future. But not all individuals involved will take responsibility for their actions, and some of them will pay for their actions with prison time. Collectively, the organization must also speak with one voice and make it plain that it proposes to remedy the problems that led to the ethical incident to begin with, and to continue with aboveboard behavior in the future.

Evaluating the Ethical Management Process

Organizations guilty of a moral lapse are usually caught in the process. Unlike a crisis where the organization is an obvious victim (e.g., earthquake, torrential weather, or some other act of nature), an ethical crisis generates little public sympathy. Furthermore, sentiments often run against the company, even if it is not to blame for the actual crisis. For example, if damaging weather hits a company warehouse and knocks out its storage and operations, some critics will still question why the company was not more prepared.

Ethical decision making will anticipate not only how to handle the crisis, but what to do about the organization's critics. This is why Bertrand and Lajtha (2002) noted that every crisis can be interpreted as a sign of a loss of trust. In this example, stakeholders lose trust in the organization when something bad happens, whether or not it was caused by the organization. This is not a pretty scenario, but it is real. To witness this phenomenon, simply watch the comments section of any major online news Web site. Critics frequently emerge to blame just about anyone for a given calamity. When a company is in the midst of a crisis, it will often be perceived by others as blameworthy, even if it did not cause the crisis at hand.

As the company seeks to learn from the crisis they have just experienced, management should acknowledge the various viewpoints that exist. For some, there exists a strong anticorporate mindset. Such critics often feel they are the ethical standard-bearers and thus represent the collective consciousness of society. As a result, company management needs to communicate that it is doing everything it can to learn from each crisis, and to learn how to become better at making ethical decisions in the marketplace.

The Commitment to Organizational Learning

Chapter 9 focused on the process of organizational learning after a crisis. Crises involving ethical breaches should not be repeated. Once an ethical crisis has been resolved, the organization must commit itself to a learning process that seeks to avoid repeating the mistake. Unfortunately, crisis management history teaches us that some companies resort to a "defense-and-attack" mode (Nathan, 2000, p. 3), a tactic that in itself is unethical. The A. H. Robins company used this tactic to discredit the victims who used the Dalkon Shield, a contraceptive device that was surgically inserted into the uterus. When recipients of the Shield became sick, the company resorted to attacking the victims and questioning their sexual practices and partners (Barton, 2001; Hartley, 1993). This is no way to fight a crisis, and A. H. Robins paid dearly in the end by enduring an endless onslaught of consumer lawsuits.

What is expected by both internal and external stakeholders is a commitment by the company to "get it right" by abiding by the law and staying within ethical guidelines. This learning process may involve a number of measures, including getting rid of the executives and managers who caused the problem in the first place. New controls may need to be implemented as well.

The Benefits of Industry Renewal

Some industries seem to have more problems with ethical matters than others. This may sound odd, given that people, not an industry, commit the unethical acts. But some industries have had more "experience" in this area than others. The tobacco industry certainly falls in this category. Many question the ethics of selling a product that causes serious health problems. The industry maintained for many years that cigarettes were not harmful, even though illnesses from tobacco represented a heavy burden on the health care system. In 1998, however, 46 state attorney generals reached an agreement with the five largest tobacco manufacturers in the United States. The settlement required the companies to pay billions of dollars to the state governments each year to alleviate the burden on the state health care systems (Thorne et al., 2003). In terms of industry renewal, there has been a decline in advertising aimed at youth and teenagers, a problem that existed during the Joe Camel advertising days.

The catalyst for industry renewal in the tobacco industry was ultimately a push from state governments. Some industries try to change their ethical problems before the government has a chance to intervene. Marketing practices within the pharmaceutical industry represent one example of an industry establishing its own reforms. Prior to these reforms, gifts and other incentives were frequently lavished on physicians by representatives advocating the use of their company's drugs (Hemphill, 2006). The intent was to influence prescribing behavior, which in itself was not unethical, but the means to achieve this goal was of growing concern. In response, the American Medical Association (AMA) adopted ethical guidelines in 1990 on gift-giving practices. The initial responses were positive but, as Hemphill (2006) notes, a reappraisal of pharmaceutical marketing codes of conduct needs to be performed.

The Inevitability of New Government Regulations

After a major crisis, the government may step in to impose new regulations. This is especially true if the company is large and efforts at self-policing have not been effective. Self-policing refers to efforts on the part of an industry association to get its member organizations to abide by a certain set of standards. The intent of self-policing is to generate positive change without government mandates (Becker, 2006). Nonetheless, when self-policing is not successful, government regulations often follow. Hartley (1993) has noted a general progression from public apathy, to media attention, to public outcry, and finally to government regulation. Table 10.5 overviews this progression.

Today, we see numerous examples of how the government seeks to protect society through regulation. The Environmental Protection Act resulted from public outcry against the pollution crises. The Occupational Safety and Health Administration was a government response to safety inadequacies in the workplace. Sarbanes-Oxley legislation in 2002 was a government effort to improve financial accountability in corporations. Although the effectiveness of such government interventions can be debated, their links to previous crises is clear.

Anticipating New Stakeholder Outlooks

There is a sad irony in the realm of organizational crises events: A significant loss of human life often launches a company into immortality. Unfortunately, this is a stakeholder memory that is hard to erase. For many people from the baby boomer generation, just mentioning the word "Bhopal" immediately brings to mind Union Carbide, the company behind the accidental gas leak that killed thousands in India in 1983. Indeed, Googling "Union Carbide" produces many references to this disaster. The name and incident association is strong. Likewise, Hawks Nest Tunnel contractor Rinehart and Dennis will not be remembered for its previous successful engineering projects; instead, its name will forever be associated with the needless loss of hundreds of workers who died from silicosis.

There is an added irony to the Hawks Nest crisis. The company receiving the electricity that was produced by the tunnel project was Union Carbide. There has been some speculation as to how active Union Carbide was in the tunnel crisis. Some critics have assumed guilt by association, while others claim the company was not involved in promoting unsafe working conditions for the tunnel workers (Deitz, 1990; Jennings, 1997). Nonetheless, name recognition has a strong emotional component; it is associated with good products and services, but can also be associated with death.

There are other stakeholder outlooks that can result from crisis events. Consider the following crisis events and how they changed the viewpoints of many:

- The September 11 terrorist attacks forced air travelers to accept new forms of security that were previously not utilized. They have also created the mindset that the ethical thing for companies to pursue is the safety and welfare of their customers. In the past this viewpoint was implied, but today more and more is expected from companies in safeguarding their people.

TABLE 10.5 The Progression From Crisis to Government Regulation				
	Public Apathy ⟶	**Media Attention** ⟶	**Public Resentment and Outcry** ⟶	**Imposition of Government Regulations**
General Description	The general public is not too concerned about potential crises. Likewise, the company is not proactive in diffusing any potential crises.	The media focuses on a crisis event and brings it to the attention of the general public.	The general public reacts to the crisis by asserting that "something must be done" to correct the situation and keep it from reoccurring.	The government will wait for an appropriate period of time in hopes the company or industry will self-regulate. Government regulations will follow if self-regulation does not occur.
Example: The Hawks Nest crisis	The Great Depression was at its height and most people just wanted to work.	In the late 1930s, media attention highlights the abuses of workers who are now dying of silicosis.	Public sympathy is slow at first, but eventually builds momentum to the point that lawsuits and government investigations ensue.	Silicosis legislation is passed in 46 states.[1]
Example: GM's Corvair crisis	Cars were cool. The Corvair was a desirable low-cost sports car for the cost-conscious public.	Reports surface that the Corvair will roll over under certain steering conditions. Ralph Nader's book *Unsafe at Any Speed,* an exposé of the Corvair and GM, gains widespread attention.[2]	The public rallies for safer cars. In time, other safety issues arise with other vehicles, such as the Ford Pinto.	Today, the automobile is the most regulated consumer product in the United States. Focus areas include pollution emissions, fuel economy, and safety provisions.
Example: September 11, 2001 terrorist attacks	Although terrorist threats at airline targets were recognized by the government, passengers, and airlines, few anticipated that a jet airliner would be used as a terrorist weapon.	The attacks on the World Trade Center and the Pentagon are known immediately throughout the world. The Internet makes this news event unfold in real time and with an abundance of visual images.	Airlines' sales drop dramatically after the attacks. All airlines experience financial shocks and some eventually go into bankruptcy.	The government responds with the creation of the U.S. Department of Homeland Security and the Transportation Safety Administration (TSA).

Source: Adapted from Hartley, R. (1993). *Business Ethics: Violations of the Public Trust.* New York: John Wiley & Sons, pg. 26.

Notes: 1. Cherniak (1986); 2. Hartley (1993).

- As the manufacturing of goods is outsourced to overseas vendors, there is a feeling among many that firms are losing direct contact with the means of production (Bertrand & Lajtha, 2002). This anxiety rises when products shipped to the domestic country are flawed in some way, such as toys with lead paint. The question of ethics arises when those who have lost their jobs to outsourcing end up purchasing products—some of them defective—from other countries.
- Recent weather patterns suggest that global warming has occurred in recent years. Some scientists link global temperatures to human activity, namely the production of carbon emissions. The ethical viewpoint held by many is to reduce emissions into the atmosphere because this may be an issue of long-term survival.
- Hurricane Katrina and the ineffective government response prompted wide criticism. Many cite the poor communication and coordination among government agencies, which should have been trained to manage these types of problems. The ego and turf wars that existed among city, state, and federal branches of the government were also obvious and invited the scorn of many who felt let down when elected officials did not work in the best public interest.

Summary

Bertrand and Lajtha (2002) have concluded that all crises can be interpreted as signs of a loss of trust. If this statement is true, then the ethical repercussions are enormous. What this means is that no matter what the crisis is, some stakeholder(s) will feel a loss of trust in the organization.

Consider these common examples where the party obviously at fault is not included in the blame equation, and yet blame, or at least some sense of responsibility, is deflected back onto the organization. The countering questions that follow each event are often raised by the media, or can even be seen on blogs when similar events occur.

- A recently fired employee walks into his former place of work and kills his supervisor along with several other employees: Why was the employee allowed back on the premises? What did the company do to make this employee so agitated?
- An employee is killed on his factory job because he did not follow standard procedures in doing his job, thus leading to the fatal accident: Why did the company hire this person in the first place? How many similar accidents have occurred at this workplace? Why did the company not enforce its own procedures?

Responses like these are common when a crisis occurs. In an attempt to make sense out of what has happened, many people will cognitively distort the situation and assign an ethical cause to the crisis; in their minds, the cause is often the organization. Bertrand and Lajtha's comment about the loss of trust is based on a perception. Nonetheless, perceptions can influence behavior more than reality. Hence, ethical decision making must be at the forefront of all management actions.

Questions for Discussion

1. Give an example of an ethical problem that has occurred either where you currently work or have worked in the past.

2. Using the crisis management framework, conduct a landscape survey and determine the current status of potential ethical issues in your present organization (internal landscape). In your answer, be sure to address the following: the ethical environment and the board of directors, the safety policies of your organization, the extent of greed among top executives and management. (Note: On this question and the ones that follow, you may substitute a former employer if you like.)

3. Conduct a landscape survey to determine the current status of potential ethical issues in your organization's external environment (external landscape). In your answer, address the degree of industry vulnerability, and the vulnerability of the organization in the global environment.

4. Using the strategic management framework, discuss how prepared your current organization is address these potential ethical crises (internal landscape). In your answer, address the enthusiasm for crisis management planning and training as well as how focused your company is on the prevention of ethical breaches.

5. What is the current status of your organization in meeting government regulations and industry standards (external landscape)?

6. In terms of crisis management, how well did your company perform in managing its internal stakeholders during a recent crisis? How did it perform in managing the external stakeholders? Were there any ethical problems that were not addressed properly?

7. In terms of organizational learning, how did your company improve in its ethical decision making after the crisis was over (internal landscape)? Were there any changes in the industry or new government regulations that appeared as a result of this crisis (external landscape)?

Chapter Exercise

Table 10.2 lists a number of crisis events that the class may not be familiar with. Select several unfamiliar cases. Outside of class, research each case and write a one-page summary of what happened and the outcome of the case. Discuss these in class. Be sure to address the following topics:

- What crisis did the organization face?
- How did mismanagement contribute to the crisis?
- How was the crisis finally resolved and what legal implications were present (the settlement of lawsuits, etc.)?

MINI CASE

HP—WHERE "UNCOMPROMISING INTEGRITY" AND UNETHICAL BEHAVIOR COLLIDE

Hewlett-Packard (HP) built its reputation on "trust and respect for individuals" and "uncompromising integrity," two statements that are part of the "HP Way" doctrine (Barron, 2007, p. 8). From 2005 to 2006, however, an ethical crisis erupted that tarnished the integrity of the company.

The saga began when it was discovered in the early part of 2005 that a board member had leaked company information to the media. In an effort to find the culprit, an investigation using a private investigation firm was secretly authorized by then–Board Chairwoman Patricia Dunn. Investigators spied on HP employees by digging through their trash and using a practice called pretexting—a means of obtaining private information about a person by assuming a false identity (Ecker, 2006). In the HP investigation, pretexting was used to obtain phone records of journalists who were suspected of communicating with the "leaking" board member, who was later identified as George Keyworth, the longest serving HP board member (Barron, 2007).

One problem had been identified, but a second one was on the horizon. The use of pretexting in this case was deemed to be illegal, according to California Attorney General Bill Lockyer. A lengthy investigation ensued, and when it was over, HP agreed to pay a $14.5 million settlement and to reform its ethical practices (Woellert, 2006). Through it all, the company had to face a mountain of negative publicity and a humiliating crisis.

Diane Swanson, a Kansas State University business professor, sums up the problem well: "What kind of signal does [spying] send to other employees?" (Barron, 2007, p. 10). The carefully crafted HP Way doctrine had been put to the test—and failed.

Sources

Barron, J. (2007, January). The HP Way: Fostering an ethical culture in the wake of scandal. *Business Credit,* pp. 8–10.

Ecker, K. (2006). HP probe highlights investigation worst practices. *Insidecounsel, 16*(180), 94–96.

Woellert, L. (2006, December 8). Closing the doors on HP-Gate. *Business Week Online,* 6. Retrieved November 28, 2008, from http://www.businessweek.com/technology/content/dec2006/tc20061208_293484.htm

References

Bad apples: In the executive suite. (1989). *Consumer Reports, 54*(5), 294.

Barron, J. (2007, January). The HP way: Fostering an ethical culture in the wake of scandal. *Business Credit,* pp. 8–10.

Barton, L. (2001). *Crisis in organizations II.* Cincinnati, OH: South-Western College Publishing.

Becker, C. (2006). Police thyself. *Modern Healthcare, 36*(41), 28–30.

Benjamin, M., Lim, P., & Streisand, B. (2005). Giving the boot. *U.S. News & World Report, 138*(11), 48–50.

Bertrand, R., & Lajtha, C. (2002). A new approach to crisis management. *Journal of Contingencies and Crisis Management, 10*(4), 181–191.

Breeden, R. (2003, November/December). WorldCom: The governance lessons. *Corporate Board,* pp. 1–6.

Carroll, A., & Buchholtz, A. (2003). *Business & society: Ethics and stakeholder management* (5th ed.). Cincinnati, OH: Thompson South-Western.

Cherniak, M. (1986). *The Hawk's Nest incident: America's worst industrial disaster.* New York: Vail-Ballou.

Colvin, G. (2003). History repeats itself at HealthSouth. *Fortune, 147*(9), 40.

Comstock, J. (1973). 476 graves. *West Virginia Heritage* [Yearbook], *7,* 1–194.

Coombs, W. (2006). *Code red in the boardroom: Crisis management as organizational DNA.* Westport, CT: Praeger.

Coombs, W. (2007). *Ongoing crisis communication: Planning, managing, and responding* (2nd ed.). Thousand Oaks, CA: Sage.

Crandall, W. R., & Crandall, R. E., (2002). Revisiting the Hawks Nest Tunnel incident: Lessons learned from an American tragedy. *Journal of Appalachian Studies, 8*(2), 261–283.

Deitz, D. (1990, Fall). "I think we've struck a gold mine." A chemist's view of Hawks Nest. *Goldenseal,* pp. 42–47.

Ecker, K. (2006). HP probe highlights investigation worst practices. *Insidecounsel, 16*(180), 94–96.

Entis, P. (2007). *Food safety: Old habits, new perspectives.* Malden, MA: Blackwell.

Fritzsche, D. (2005). *Business ethics: A global and managerial perspective* (2nd ed.). New York: McGraw-Hill.

Greer, M. (2001). 90 years of progress in safety. *Professional Safety, 46*(10), 20–25.

Gross, A. (1990, October 11). How Popeye's and Reebok confronted product rumors. *Adweek's Marketing Week, 31,* pp. 27, 30.

Hansen, M., & Harkin, T. (2008, June 12). Gap's message on child labor. *Women's Wear Daily, 195*(124), 18.

Hartley, R. (1993). *Business ethics: Violations of the public trust.* New York: John Wiley.

Heineman, B., Jr. (2007). Avoiding integrity land mines. *Harvard Business Review, 85*(4), 100–108.

Hemphill, T. (2006). Physicians and the pharmaceutical industry: A reappraisal of marketing codes of conduct. *Business and Society Review, 111*(3), 323–336.

Henry, D., Timmons, H., Rosenbush, S., & Arndt, M. (2002, January 28). Who else is hiding debt. *Business Week,* pp. 36–37.

Holmes, S. (2006, March 13). Cleaning up Boeing. *Business Week,* pp. 63–68.

Institute for Crisis Management. (2007). *Annual ICM Crisis Report: News Coverage of Business Crises During 2006, 16*(1). Retrieved November 10, 2007, from http://www.crisisexperts.com/2006CR.pdf

Jefferson, J. (1993). Dying for work. *ABA Journal, 79*(1), 46–51.

Jennings, C. (1997, Spring). Was Witt Jennings involved? The Hawks Nest tragedy. *Goldenseal,* pp. 44–47.

Kaplan, R., & Norton, D. (2001). *The strategy focused organization.* Boston: Harvard Business School Press.

Levenson, E. (2005, December 12). The weirdest CEO moments of 2005. *Fortune, 152*(12), 30–31.

Nathan, M. (2000). From the editor: Crisis learning—Lessons from Sisyphus and others. *Review of Business, 21*(3), 3–5.

Orr, D., & Dragan, J. (1981). A dirty, messy place to work: B. H. Metheney remembers Hawk's Nest tunnel. *Goldenseal, 1*(7), 34–41.

Parnell, J. A., & Dent, E. C. (in press). Philosophy, ethics, and capitalism: An interview with BB&T CEO, John Allison. *Academy of Management Learning and Education.*

Parnell, J. A., & Jusoh, R. (2008). Competitive strategy and performance in the Malaysian context: An exploratory study. *Management Decision, 46*(1), 5–31.

Post, J., Lawrence, A., & Weber, J. (2002). *Business and society: Corporate strategy, public policy, ethics.* New York: McGraw-Hill.

Rowh, M. (1981). The Hawks Nest tragedy: Fifty years later. *Goldenseal, 1*(7), 31–33.

Salkin, S. (1997). Attn: School foodservice directors and other commodity purchasers. *Foodservice Director, 10*(7), 82.

Securities and Exchange Commission. (1976, May 12). *Report on questionable and illegal corporate payments and practices.* Exhibits A and B, submitted to U.S. Congress, Senate, Committee on Banking, Housing, and Urban Affairs.

Sethi, S., & Steidlmeier, P. (1997). *Up against the corporate wall: Cases in business and society* (6th ed.). Upper Saddle River, NJ: Prentice Hall.

Shanker, A. (1992). The Hamlet, N.C., fire: A postmortem. *New Republic, 206*(7), 27.

Snellen, M. (2003). How to build a "dark site" for crisis management: Using Internet technology to limit damage to reputation. *SCM, 7*(3), 8–21.

Snyder, P., Hall, M., Robertson, J., Jasinski, T., & Miller, J. (2006). Ethical rationality: A strategic approach to organizational crisis. *Journal of Business Ethics, 63,* 371–383.

Steiner, G., & Steiner, J. (2000). *Business, government, and society: A managerial perspective* (9th ed.). New York: McGraw-Hill.

Thorne, D., Ferrell, O., & Ferrell, L. (2003). *Business and society: A strategic approach to corporate citizenship.* New York: Houghton Mifflin.

Trevino, L., Hartman, L., & Brown, M. (2000). Moral person and moral manager: How executives develop a reputation for ethical leadership. *California Management Review, 42*(4), 128–142.

Tyler, A. (1975, January). Dust to dust. *Washington Monthly,* pp. 49–58.

Vallario, C. (2007). Is your ethics program working? *Financial Executive, 23*(4), 26–28.

Vernon, H. (1998). *Business and society: A managerial approach* (6th ed.). New York: McGraw-Hill.

Warin, F., Blume, R., Bell, J., & McConkie, J. (2007). The Foreign Corrupt Practices Act: Recent developments, trends, and guidance. *Insights, 21*(2), 2–10.

Welles, C. (1988, February 22). What led Beech-Nut down the road to disgrace? *Business Week,* pp. 124–128.

Woellert, L. (2006, December 8). Closing the doors on HP-Gate. *Business Week Online,* 6. Retrieved November 28, 2008, from http://www.business week.com/technology/content/dec2006/tc200 61208_293484.htm

CHAPTER 11

Chaos Theory

*An Alternative Paradigm
in the Study of Organizational Crises*

The Malden Mills Fire

The fire in Lawrence, Massachusetts on December 11, 1995, started out as an apparent boiler explosion at the Malden Mills complex. The plant made fleece, a textile component in clothing and upholstery fabric, and was operating with about 700 employees at the time. This single explosion led to a series of additional explosions, all of which were believed to be rupturing gas lines. These escalating events caused the fire to spread quickly. Under normal weather conditions, the fire would have been large but most likely contained within one building. Unfortunately, the winds were blowing in excess of 45 miles per hour, and near-zero temperatures limited water availability (Macko, 1995). Even a furniture repair store a quarter of a mile away caught on fire from embers that were blown from the Malden Mills complex (*Technical Series Report 110*—FEMA, 1995).

More than 200 firefighters responded to the fire, along with 67 engine companies, 22 truck companies, and four medical evacuation helicopters. Fortunately, there were no fatalities, but 33 people were injured, 8 seriously. When the fire was finally out, it was considered one of the worst in Massachusetts history (Macko, 1995).

This incident can be viewed through the lens of chaos theory. As we will see in this chapter, this crisis illustrates the concepts of (1) sensitive dependence to initial conditions, (2) the inability to predict occurrences for the long run, (3) the presence of bifurcations, (4) a phenomenon known as a strange attractor, (5) behavior that is nonlinear, and (6) the presence of positive feedback, all of which are important concepts in chaos theory.

Chaos theory has captured the interest of many management scholars, some of whom have attempted to use the framework as a lens for analyzing crisis events (Kiel, 1995; Sellnow, Seeger, & Ulmer, 2002; Verwey, Crystal, & Bloom, 2002). At first glance, its appeal seems intuitively obvious. Chaos becomes a metaphor for crisis, so why not apply the theory to the study of crisis events?

This chapter begins by looking at the components of chaos theory. Next, a discussion on why chaos theory appeals to social scientists is presented. Indeed, it is somewhat interesting to consider why some use chaos theory as a metaphor to explain social phenomena. We then devote the remainder of the chapter to the application of chaos theory to crisis events.

The Appeal of Chaos Theory

The bestselling book by James Gleick (1987) made chaos theory understandable to those outside the mathematics and physics disciplines. Shortly thereafter, social scientists, organizational scholars, and psychologists became interested in chaos theory. Finally, a nonlinear, dynamic framework could be used as a lens for understanding the complex social and psychological interactions that make up these disciplines.

The past decade has brought an interest in the application of complexity-based theories as a lens for viewing organizations. These theories seek to find order emerging in systems that may not exhibit a clear sense of cause and effect (Burns, 2004). Such work has been seen in the fields of psychology (Barton, 1994; Carver, 1997), social work (Bolland & Atherton, 1999; Hudson, 2000), strategic management (Dervitsiotis, 2004; Edgar & Nisbet, 1996), health care management (McDaniel, Jordan, & Fleeman, 2003), public relations (Murphy, 1996), corporate social responsibility (Frederick, 1998), career counseling (Bloch, 2005; Bright & Pryor, 2005; Duffy, 2000), public management (Farazmand, 2003), and the analysis of organizational crises (Kiel, 1995; Sellnow et al., 2002; Verwey et al., 2002).

The appeal of chaos theory has been likened to a romantic appreciation of disorder that accompanies a corresponding reaction against the scientific appreciation for order and symmetry (Friedrich, 1988; Smith & Higgins, 2003). One could understand that such a viewpoint stresses liberation from the constraints and bondage of a world obsessed with trying to bring order to every issue imaginable. As we will see, however, this perspective is not consistent with the context of chaos theory.

What is noteworthy about this particular interest in chaos theory is its application to the social sciences. In this case, the concepts associated with a specific mathematical state—chaos—are used as metaphors to explain organizational phenomena of a nonmathematical nature. The irony is that social scientists and organizational scholars do not use elaborate concepts from chemistry or physics to explain social behavior, so why the attention to chaos theory? The appeal of metaphors may be a starting point for this discussion.

Using metaphors to help explain the workings of an organization is not a new concept. Morgan (1997) was a key player in generating enthusiasm for the use of metaphors to explain organizational behavior. Following this lead, others have encouraged the use of chaos theory as a metaphor in the study of organizational phenomena (Bright & Pryor, 2005; Frederick, 1998; Hudson, 2000; Lissack, 1999).

Components of Chaos Theory

Chaos theory is rooted in mathematics and the natural sciences, not the social sciences. Chaos is a state whereby phenomena that appear to be unrelated actually follow an unknown or hidden pattern. This hidden pattern is called an attractor, and it can be visually discernable through the plotting of data in phase space. Chaotic systems possess two characteristics: sensitive dependence to initial conditions and unpredictability in the long run.

Sensitive Dependence on Initial Conditions

Lorenz (1993) noted that a slight change in the initial input of data can lead to vastly different results. This now famous occurrence led to the popular "butterfly effect" illustration. This effect states that the flapping of the wings of a butterfly, perhaps in some exotic part of the world like Hawaii, can influence air currents that eventually cause a hurricane in the United States. Of course, should the butterfly flap in a different direction, the hurricane could develop somewhere else, perhaps Cuba or Mexico. Herein lies the key to unlocking chaos theory: A slight change in initial conditions can lead to a vastly different outcome in the system.

Unpredictability in the Long Run

The behavior of a chaotic system cannot be predicted in the long run. At best, there may be some accuracy in short-term predictions. Weather is an example of a chaotic system that defies long-term prediction (Lorenz, 1993). These two characteristics describe the behavior of a chaotic system. The actual components of such a system are described next.

Bifurcations

A bifurcation is a point in the behavior of the system where the outcome can actually oscillate between two possible values in alternating time periods. Chaos theorists call this *period doubling*. The discovery of a bifurcation was made by Robert May, a biologist who was conducting a population model experiment (Gleick, 1987). May found that as he increased the parameter value in his model, the population would increase until it reached a critical point. At that point, the period doubling or bifurcation point, the population would then alternate values on a 2-year cycle, reaching a certain value the first year, followed by a lower value the next year, then returning to the original value the third year, and so on. As the parameter was increased again, another critical point was reached, this time a period-four or second bifurcation took place.

Now the population values alternated over a 4-year cycle. Increasing the parameters again led to still more bifurcations until the model reached a state where almost any value was possible. The system was now in chaos because the population did not seem to settle down to any predictable level. At this chaos point, the correlation among the study variables was nonexistent, as the potential outcomes could lie virtually anywhere.

Interestingly, May continued to increase the parameters even while the system (i.e., the population level) was chaotic. When a certain parameter value was reached, however, the system settled back down to a constant 3-year cycle. Increasing the parameters caused the phenomenon to repeat itself; following more bifurcations, the system returned to chaos. In fact, the system continued to move in and out of chaos as the parameter level increased. Figure 11.1 illustrates a simplified bifurcation diagram.

Attractors

In chaos theory, an attractor is a pattern that forms when the behavior of a nonlinear system is plotted in phase space (Lorenz, 1993), that is, the different states of the system through various points in time. Such systems may produce plots that resemble orbits. Thus, the behavior of the system follows a pattern through time.

Attractors range from fairly simple to vastly complex. Four types of attractors have been identified: point, pendulum, torus, and strange. Point attractors depict a simple system that constantly returns to a single point. Pendulum attractors swing between two points. The torus attractor is a more complex pattern that forms an orbit. Points near the center of the orbit show more similarity in the system state, while points toward the edge of the orbit are more varied. Finally, the strange attractor, sometimes referred to as a fractal, is a complicated pattern that emerges when the system is in chaos. Perhaps the

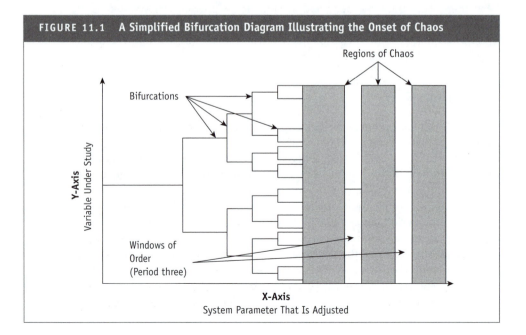

FIGURE 11.1   A Simplified Bifurcation Diagram Illustrating the Onset of Chaos

Regions of Chaos

Bifurcations

Y-Axis
Variable Under Study

Windows of
Order
(Period three)

X-Axis
System Parameter That Is Adjusted

most famous strange attractor is the Lorenz butterfly, so named because it resembles the wings of a butterfly when graphed. The significance of acknowledging the existence of a strange attractor is that it illustrates how a semblance of order can be found in the midst of a system that is in chaos.

Nonlinearity

Linear systems react in a proportional or linear manner. The concept of linearity implies that a change in one variable will result in a proportional change in another variable such that the relationship among the variables can be depicted as a straight line. In contrast, nonlinear systems have relationships among variables that are not linear and may be curvilinear, U-shaped, S-shaped, or any combination of these. Chaotic systems are nonlinear and do not have the predictability for variables that linear systems have. Since much of the natural world and the social world behave in a nonlinear fashion, chaos theory offers a suitable perspective for examining these systems (Smith, 2002).

Feedback

Two concepts of feedback must be presented: negative and positive. Negative feedback occurs when the system returns to a steady or normal state. For example, if one blows out a burning match, the flame is extinguished and the match returns to its beginning state, that is, unlit. Positive feedback, on the other hand, amplifies deviations until a chaotic state is reached. Assume now that the glowing match ignites paper in a trash can. Positive feedback transpires as the fire moves away from equilibrium (extinguished) to a rapidly burning state.

Self-Organization

This term describes the chaotic system's ability to change itself into a new form without intervention from forces outside the system (Loye & Eisler, 1987; Tasaka, 1999). The concept posits that a chaotic stage is necessary before a new system can emerge (Butz, 1997).

Chaos Theory and Organizational Crises

When using chaos theory as a crisis metaphor, it is tempting to assume that a crisis event equals a state of chaos. Indeed, managers may refer to a "chaotic" situation when a crisis hits. This assumption is not entirely accurate, however. Rather, it is more accurate to start with the assumption that all organizations currently reside in chaotic systems. This perspective is reflected by Pascale (1999), who noted that completely chaotic systems can be illustrated through such events as riots, stampedes, or even the early years of the French Revolution. In addition, Sellnow and Seeger (2001), in their discussion on crisis communication, viewed the 1997 Red River Valley flood in North Dakota and Minnesota as a chaotic episode. Both of these examples are correct in the sense that an acute event such as a crisis is part of a larger system that is displaying chaotic behavior. However, it would be incorrect to isolate the specific crisis as the specific example of chaos because chaos is more of a system of events rather than a single isolated event.

Consider the analogy to weather systems. The weather is a frequently cited example of a system in chaos, largely because it displays sensitive dependence to initial conditions and is unpredictable in the long run, two characteristics that also define chaos. In addition, weather is never in a state of equilibrium as it is constantly changing in every part of the world. Weather patterns include days of sunshine as well as turbulent events such as thunderstorms and hurricanes. It would be incorrect to say that the day of sunshine is the state of equilibrium while the thunderstorm or hurricane is the state of chaos because both weather conditions are part of a larger chaotic system. Likewise, referring to an industrial accident as an example of chaos is not accurate. Instead, the organization that experienced the accident already resides in a chaotic system, one that is subject to sensitive dependence to initial conditions and is unpredictable in the long run.

Sellnow and colleagues (2002) hold that chaos theory lends itself well to understanding complex systems. The rationale is that crisis events are complex and nonlinear, and thus are in need of more sophisticated methods of analysis. Chaos theory also allows researchers and managers to view the world as an elaborate system of flux and change (Kiel, 1995; Morgan, 1997). Implied in this thinking is the events leading up to a crisis, sometimes called "fluxes" (Prigogine & Stengers, 1984), are both complicated and interrelated. Butz (1997) also advocates the use of chaos theory to analyze crisis events because they are subject to small variances, the absence of predictability, and the element of surprise or unanticipated outcomes. The following discussion outlines how components of chaos theory can be used as a framework for analyzing crisis events.

Sensitive Dependence to Initial Conditions

Industrial fires offer an example of sensitive dependence to initial conditions. In many of these events, a small, almost insignificant factor can trigger a crisis. For example, under the right conditions, a sufficient amount of dust can serve as a trigger event. Warner Lambert experienced such an event in November 1976 when a fire and explosion shook its manufacturing site near New York City, resulting in a crisis that left 6 employees dead and 54 injured. The trigger event for the fire was thought to have been a stray electrical spark in the presence of magnesium stearate, a powdered lubricant used in the manufacturing of chewing gum (Sethi & Steidlmeir, 1997).

The concept of sensitive dependence suggests that the outcome of this event might have been dramatically different had something in the initial conditions been slightly different. For example, the stray spark is thought to have originated from a machine that was overworked due to its close proximity to liquid nitrogen, a factor that caused the machine to become too cold (Sethi & Steidlmeir, 1997). The spark could have been prevented if the machine had been operating at its designed temperature. Of course, the level of dust was also a factor. Had the level been lower, the chance of an explosion might have been reduced.

Many examples abound of crisis events that were propagated by sensitive dependence to initial conditions. The *Exxon Valdez* might not have made history with its oil spill if the tanker had been on a course slightly away from the reef that it hit. In the tragic 1996 ValuJet Flight 592 crash, oxygen canisters that were improperly loaded on the plane exploded in the cargo compartment, sending the airliner uncontrollably into the Florida Everglades (Greenwald & Hannifin, 1996). Aircraft successfully take off and land every day, but when an accident occurs, it is often because of a sensitive detail, a slight difference that sends the aircraft into the accident case files.

Unpredictability in the Long Run

Chaos theory maintains that predicting the long-range behavior of the system is impossible, although short-run predictions are possible. The fire at the Malden Mills complex in Lawrence, Massachusetts, on December 11, 1995, provides such an example. When it was over, 22 workers were hospitalized and the entire complex required reconstruction. While the facilities were being rebuilt, CEO Aaron Feuerstein decided that the employees should receive full pay and benefits (Moreno, 2003).

In the Malden Mills case, two short-run predictions were feasible: (1) The manufacturing facilities would be rebuilt; and (2) most of the employees would be kept on the payroll during the rebuilding. But there was also an unexpected occurrence. Malden Mills received positive publicity after the fire because of Feuerstein's decision to keep his employees on the payroll during the reconstruction. His move has been touted as a good model of employer–employee loyalty (Fisher, Schoenfeldt, & Shaw, 2003; McCurry, 1997). This result was neither expected nor predictable according to chaos theory.

Predicting the long-term future of the company proved to be even more elusive, as chaos theory posits. In the short run, the company experienced a devastating fire, an impressive recovery, and positive press on its human resource practices. In 2001, however, the company experienced bankruptcy, partly due to the $100 million debt it took on after the fire in 1995. But the onset of bankruptcy 6 years after the fire was also influenced by several unexpected, stray variables that impacted the system, including warm weather the previous year (which hurt product sales), the loss of a key customer, and an abundance of fleece knockoffs entering the market (Moreno, 2003). The resulting declines in sales and cash flow devastated the company while it was still reeling from the debt it had incurred after the fire. Chaos theory maintains that these events could not have been predicted in the long run.

Bifurcations

When used as a metaphor, bifurcations are considered as the defining moments in the life of the crisis episode (Sellnow et al., 2002). When they occur, the crisis escalates into a more serious event. Bifurcations can change the system suddenly, causing it to behave in a different way (Edgar & Nisbet, 1996). At the Malden Mills fire, a key bifurcation was the subzero weather and windy conditions that preceded the crisis (Crandall, 2007). These conditions resulted in frozen fire hydrants and winds in excess of 40 miles per hour, factors that hampered firefighters (*Technical Series Report 110*—FEMA, 1995). Another event that hampered fire suppression efforts was the extensive search and rescue effort that had to be completed prior to an aggressive attack on the fire. Altogether, 56,000 square feet of the mill complex had to be searched by a limited number of fire personnel, resulting in a 15-minute delay before fire suppression could commence (*Technical Series Report 110*—FEMA, 1995). A third significant bifurcation concerned the truck trailers that were in use for storage throughout the complex. Unfortunately, their locations blocked access to some of the fire hydrants; consequently, some of the trailers were engulfed by the fire as well.

The *Exxon Valdez* oil spill disaster illustrates another series of bifurcations that contributed to that crisis. Perhaps the most significant was the decision of the captain to give control of the ship to a junior officer in waters where regulations required a senior officer (Hartley, 1993). The role of CEO Lawrence Rawl was also a significant bifurcation in the crisis. Rawl chose not to go to Alaska to oversee recovery efforts at the local level. This evolved into a public relations nightmare because Rawl was in charge at the corporate level but not at the local level, a move that made him appear insensitive to the environmental needs of the area.

Attractors

Like bifurcations, strange attractors are usually discussed as metaphors when analyzing a crisis event. Management researchers and social scientists have assigned various descriptions to strange attractors. Murphy (1996) relates several studies that identify organizational culture as a strange attractor. Organizational culture is generally described as a set of beliefs and values that an organization ascribes to. For example, Johnson & Johnson's strong belief in a focus on the consumer has been identified as an example of the strange attractor that emerged during the Tylenol poisoning crisis (Murphy, 1996).

In the organizational realm, Dervitsiotis (2004) identified unique styles of management as attractors. Likewise, Frederick (1998) describes an organization's values as its strange attractor. From this perspective, values can be likened to an organization's culture. In other words, it is the organization's values that hold it together while it is going through the turmoil of a crisis.

In the crisis management literature, Sellnow and associates (2002) offer an example of using chaos theory to analyze a crisis. Their research looks at the 1997 Red River Valley flood. They propose that the U.S. National Guard and the Federal Emergency Management Agency (FEMA) were strange attractors, since both agencies were instrumental in bringing order to a situation that was in the midst of a crisis. Thus, Sellnow's viewpoint maintains that the strange attractor can literally bring stability to a situation that is in chaos.

Crandall (2007) suggested that Malden Mills CEO Aaron Feuerstein fulfilled the role of a strange attractor. During the crisis, Feuerstein, then 71, physically took part in fighting a part of the fire located in one of the other buildings on the complex. Although fire department officials felt that particular building could not be saved, Feuerstein led 28 employees into the structure and successfully prevented it from being totally destroyed (Moreno, 2003). After the conflagration was over, Feuerstein kept 1,400 employees on the payroll for

3 months while rebuilding efforts were under way. In addition, he extended employee health benefits by 9 months. When the complex finally reopened, 90% of the displaced employees returned to work (Skala, 1999). In this illustration, the example and guidance of the CEO kept the company together when the organization was in the midst of chaos.

The cause of a crisis is another area where the attractor can be applied. Rarely does one event cause a crisis. Instead, a series of steps leading up to a final event—the trigger event—commences the crisis activity. An example from weather helps illustrate this pattern. Lightning strikes are responsible for a number of accidents and fires. However, lightening cannot occur unless a precise set of atmospheric conditions are met. From a chaos perspective, a number of events precipitate the lighting strike, and these form a pattern of atmospheric behavior that is somewhat predictive in the short run. This pattern can be equated to a strange attractor.

Nonlinearity

The events in a crisis do not always transpire in a neat cause-and-effect manner. Sensitive dependence to initial conditions illustrates this nonlinear phenomenon. As the crisis progresses, events continue to unfold haphazardly and in a less than proportional manner. Small events may end up having a major impact during the course of a crisis. Politicians are well aware that saying the wrong word or phrase during a speech may offend or alienate certain groups. Industrial explosions and fires are often traced to small amounts of dust in the wrong places. In the restaurant industry, a single employee who does not wash his or her hands can cause a number of customers to become ill.

Nonlinearity also means that large, carefully planned interventions may sometimes have little or no effect during the crisis. Prior to the *Exxon Valdez* oil spill, containment booms were available in the town of Valdez. These buoy-like objects encircle oil spills during the initial stages of an accident. Despite this preparedness measure, the barge that was designated for bringing the booms out was inoperable at the time of the incident (Hartley, 1993).

The Malden Mills fire was also an event that displayed nonlinearity. Despite well-implemented efforts to contain the fire, progress was slow due to winds and cold weather. The end result was almost total destruction of the production facilities, even though massive resources in fire personnel and apparatus were utilized. But the decision to keep the employees on the payroll may have been the most far-reaching event of the crisis. Prior to the fire, Malden Mills was not a case study in management and human resource textbooks. After the event, however, Malden Mills and CEO Aaron Feuerstein were corporate heroes, an outcome that far exceeded the original intention of the decision.

Feedback (Positive and Negative)

Positive feedback involves the amplification (i.e., intensification) of deviations until a chaotic state is reached. Negative feedback seeks to correct those deviations and bring the system back to a state of equilibrium. When positive and negative feedback offset each other, the system is in equilibrium. On the other hand, when positive feedback is greater than the dampening effects of negative feedback, a crisis incident may arise. A crisis, then, is a "far-from-equilibrium" situation that launches the system (or organization) into chaos (Paraskevas, 2006, p. 903).

The situation at Malden Mills involved the interaction of positive and negative feedback, as a small event escalated into a large fire. Efforts to attack and control the fire through negative feedback interventions were hindered due to the winds and frozen hydrants. According to the Technical Series Report submitted through FEMA, the initial explosion occurred in a production building where flock operations were being conducted. The work environment was dusty and the fibers were subject to explosion under the right conditions. Previous fires had occurred in the flock operations, with a major fire resulting in injuries occurring in 1993 (Moreno, 1993). Escalation of the fire was rapid, and much of the production complex was engulfed in flames.

Self-Organization

Changes to the organization are usually inevitable after a crisis hits. From a practical point of view, self-organization prompts the question: How does the company look different from how it looked before the crisis? Malden Mills saw an upgrading of equipment in its newly rebuilt facility, resulting in a safer and more efficient factory. In addition, the physical structure and infrastructure of the mill were improved. The ordeal forced the company to install a new information technology system, one that had been needed for some time. As industry analyst Bruce Richardson put it, "Sometimes it takes a cataclysmic event like a major fire to bring about profound change in an organization, and that's clearly working here. . . . Left to their own devices, people usually don't make such sweeping changes" (Hamblen, 1997, p. 1).

The 1997 Red River Valley flood resulted in self-organization for the political units involved in disaster relief for that area. Murphy (1996) reminds us that chaos produces changes in the organization's system, changes that create a new order with positive dimensions. Sellnow and colleagues discuss how the 1997 flood prompted a reorganization of emergency services between the adjacent cities of Moorhead, Minnesota, and Fargo, North Dakota (Sellnow et al., 2002). On the positive side, the two cities were formerly rivals, but after the flood, cooperative structures emerged whereby crisis communication was centralized through Fargo's City Hall.

Implications for Research and Management

From a research perspective, chaos theory offers an alternate framework for analyzing organizational crises, one that can be used to supplement traditional (i.e., linear) perspectives in the study of crisis. Hence, chaos theory is an alternative way to look at problems that follow a nonlinear pattern. Similarly, linear deterministic thinking should not be abandoned, nor should systems theory (Bolland & Atherton, 1999). With this in mind, chaos theory should be viewed as one of a set of analytical tools, useful when complex phenomena such as crisis events are analyzed.

Chaos theory offers alternative practical perspectives that are useful in the planning and management of organizational crises. The following implications are offered.

1. *Little things do matter in relation to an organizational crisis.* For example, the former president of Rutgers University, Francis Lawrence, unintentionally insulted the African American community when he referred to genetics and heredity as a reason for low SAT scores among African Americans. Despite Lawrence's strong record in promoting affirmative action, the remark provoked a widespread protest charging racism against the president (Murphy, 1996).

Other crises, such as industrial accidents or plane crashes, are often traced to small changes that pushed the operating system into a crisis. The lesson to be learned for management is that the small and insignificant details can come back later to create a bigger-than-life crisis.

2. *Long-term predictions of future crises are difficult to make, but short-term predictions are more feasible and necessary for crisis vulnerability assessment.* Chaos theory maintains that making long-term predictions is impossible, due to the system nonlinearities that exist among the multiple variables in organizational life. However, there is value in planning for the short run, as system behavior can be anticipated to some degree. For example, it is difficult if not impossible to predict which organizations may be hit by a terrorist attack, a large magnitude earthquake, or employee violence. Yet in the short run it is useful to plan for the possibility of these events. Crisis vulnerability assessment dictates that organizations plan for certain events, and thus are able to maintain a level of alertness and competency for the occurrence of these crises, as well as others that may not have been planned for. Indeed, planning for specific events actually prepares organizations to handle other, unexpected events as well, those that are not on the worst-case scenario list (Mitroff, 1989).

Although chaos theory maintains that long-term predictions are impossible, this does not imply that standard operating procedures, often referred to as SOPs, are no longer necessary. Indeed, SOPs are still necessary, and should be written in detail when planning for potential crisis events. However, managers should adjust these procedures as necessary, given that every crisis is unique. This perspective is especially true in government organizations where rigid SOPs are often the norm. An example from Hurricane Katrina illustrates this point. FEMA was plagued by a number of inflexibilities in the managing of this crisis. Options to change SOPs were ignored in favor of a "going by the book" approach. In one example, hundreds of firefighters—complete with sleeping bags and lifesaving equipment—converged in Atlanta to wait for instructions from FEMA. Before they were permitted to work, however, they spent 2 days completing paperwork and taking courses on diversity and sexual harassment, thus delaying their response to the crisis (Olasky, 2006). This lack of flexible thinking and improvisation resulted in one of the worst report cards yet for FEMA.

3. *Bifurcations represent key turning points whereby the crisis can be brought under control or can escalate out of control.* From a managerial perspective, a bifurcation often results in a situation with positive or negative outcome possibilities. In addition, management must recognize that bifurcations can add to the complexity of the crisis. Management's responsibility is to recognize when

a bifurcation exists and respond in a manner that keeps the outcomes to a manageable level. This mindset is necessary because more potential outcomes entering a situation can reduce managerial control over the crisis event.

4. *There are hidden patterns (i.e., attractors) in almost everything, including the causes of a crisis and the way it is managed.* The attractor concept has intrigued researchers in the study of a chaos theory. Yet, attractors are not just unusual patterns that can be plotted in phase space. As a metaphor, they are the patterns that exist in the management of organizations, many times going undetected. At first, the practice may have been noticed, but after many repetitions, it becomes an unconscious habit, an attractor. For example, there are employees who may be taking hidden shortcuts in their work, totally unaware of the ramifications. The safety guard on a machine is left off, eye goggles are not worn in a restricted area, or a safety form is signed without being carefully reviewed. When an accident does occur, it can often be traced to a series of patterns (attractors) that had become habits in the work of the employee.

A concept related to attractors is self-similarity, the observation that what appears on one scale of the organization repeats itself in other parts of the organization. Self-similarity can exist in the form of organizational ethics and organizational culture. As a result, it is likely that the organizational culture at top levels is similar to that at lower levels. Likewise, top management's attitude toward ethics is often pervasive throughout the organization. The impact of self-similarity can be significant, particularly if unethical behavior exists at the top levels of the organization. When it does, the pattern of unethical behavior will often spread throughout the organization, as lower-level managers take their cue for correct behavior from observing the actions of their superiors (Carroll & Buchholtz, 2003).

5. *A certain amount of order and disorder is natural and even healthy for the organization.* Trials and tribulations are a natural part of organizational life. Organizations become stronger and more adaptable as they move through these ordeals and crises. Certainly, extreme crisis events where there is significant damage or loss of life are not welcome, but organizations can learn from these events and adapt more effectively as a result. The more likely scenario for organizations is to encounter a series of minor crises events that disrupt operations to some degree and have an impact on the entity, but do not necessarily cripple the organization. Weather events, power outages, and extreme sales fluctuations are some examples. Mitigation as opposed to prevention is the rule for these types of events.

A central theme for the organization as it moves in and out of disorder is to enable employees and departments to have the freedom to adjust standard operating procedures as necessary in order to best manage the crisis. Managers of flatter organizations have known for a long time that this ability is necessary to quickly adapt to changing conditions in the field.

6. *Finding the cause of a crisis may be more difficult than originally anticipated.* Isolating a single cause for every crisis is neither practical nor appropriate. For example, in cases where ethical standards and laws have been violated, there may not be a clear "smoking gun." On the contrary, chaos theory stresses that there may be multiple factors at work that contribute to the evolution of the crisis. This assertion is based on the nature of the behavior of

nonlinear variables in a crisis event. For instance, fog conditions have contributed to deadly traffic accidents in the past, including along a specific stretch of highway on Interstate 75 near Calhoun, Tennessee. The fog in this area, however, has been linked to the Bowater[1] newsprint plant's aeration ponds, which are located near the highway (McLaren, 1994). On December 11, 1990, 12 people were killed and 50 were injured when a 99-vehicle accident occurred during heavy fog. One of the initial vehicles involved in that crash was a Bowater tractor-trailer rig. It burst into flames after a car traveling more than 65 miles per hour hit it. The truck was moving at only about 35 miles per hour at the time (Maggart, 1994). What unfolded next was a chain reaction of collisions and subsequent fires, scorching cars within a quarter of a mile of the initial crash site.

But the question remains, which party was actually at fault? Was it the car traveling too fast, the Bowater truck, the fog, the Bowater plant management, or even the consumers who demand Bowater products? Depending on one's perspective and even political viewpoints, the potential causes could vary tremendously.

The media, management, motivated attorneys, and even human nature in general like to think in terms of finding a single cause for an accident. Nonetheless, a closer analysis usually reveals multiple factors at work in the initiation of an accident. Chaos theory maintains that small changes in the initial state of the system variables can lead to vastly different outcomes. An accident, for example, may occur when even one variable is slightly out of line from its normal operating state. For example, at least five factors can be observed in the analysis of the Bowater smashup. (1) Fog caused by natural weather events could have contributed to the accident. (2) The aeration ponds owned by Bowater possibly brought about the fog. (3) However, one could also argue that the car going 65 miles per hour in heavy fog started the accident. (4) Or, what about that truck going only 35 miles per hour on a major highway? Was that too slow? (5) Which came first, the Bowater plant, or the interstate? Indeed, this road was built 21 years after the Bowater facility opened in 1952 (McLaren, 1994). On this premise, one could even argue that the federal government played a role in the accident since it provided the resources to build the interstate. Chaos theory posits that a change in one or more of these factors, even a slight change, could have been enough to cause a large interstate disaster. Sensitive dependence to initial conditions is indeed an important consideration in analyzing crises from a chaos perspective.

The above example illustrates that preconditions exist before a crisis takes place. These factors can interact in ways that make it difficult to determine the exact cause of a crisis. Unfortunately, linear thinking—particularly in a litigious society—indicates that there must be a single or at least predominant cause for every incident. Chaos theory, with its implication for complexity, holds that such simplistic thinking is neither feasible nor correct.

7. *The concept of positive feedback in chaos theory is not a good thing. It means the crisis is getting worse because the outcomes become harder to predict.* All organizations operate with a set of positive and negative feedback mechanisms. Negative feedback helps keep the organization at equilibrium. A pressure relief valve is an example of a negative feedback mechanism. Without such a valve a gas tank may explode, sending metal and dangerous gases in all directions.

Another negative feedback mechanism is the quarterly budget report. Cost areas that are too high are brought to the attention of management, who can then work on reducing them. Hence, negative feedback serves the important function of bringing the organization back to safe operating levels.

On the other hand, positive feedback moves the organization away from equilibrium or safe operating levels. It amplifies deviations, moving the organization to a more complicated state, and potentially toward chaos. The rising temperature of a gas tank that holds a toxic substance is an example of positive feedback. Cooling neutralizes the dangerous effect of that gas, while a rise in temperature will cause that same gas to become volatile, possibly escaping beyond the confines of its metal casing. Such was the case at Union Carbide's Bhopal, India, plant in 1984, when a rise in the temperature of methyl isocyanate (MIC) caused the pressure of the gas to increase to dangerous levels. In this example, the negative feedback mechanisms, such as temperature and pressure gauges, steel tanks, and cooling units, were unable to withstand the positive feedback of water accidentally entering the MIC holding tank, causing a dangerous rise in pressure.

The lesson for management is to recognize that there are positive and negative feedback mechanisms in constant flux within and outside the boundaries of the organization. Organizational crises are replete with examples of such feedback mechanisms in battle with each other. The negative feedback mechanisms, usually implemented by management, represent the controls necessary to contain deviations to acceptable operating standards. The positive feedback mechanisms can occur from within or outside the organization. Sometimes a positive feedback force slips by an outdated or inadequate negative feedback mechanism (Reason, 1997). The manager, learning to be astute in recognizing crises, needs to be able to detect when positive feedback forces have entered the organization.

8. *Whether management realizes it or not, the organization is changing constantly.* The concept of self-organization reminds us that the organization is adjusting itself every day. On the positive side, it may be adapting to the turbulent changes that frequent the environment. Such adaptation makes it better able to deal with the next big crisis that comes its way. On the negative side, it may be holding on to tradition, the status quo, and slowly dying in the process. One major crisis could put the organization out of operation.

This self-organization process comes primarily from forces within the organization. Chaos theory holds that new forms of order will emerge after periods of chaos, but the type of order to emerge will depend on the priorities of management. From this viewpoint, change emerges from within the organization, but may be influenced by factors in the outside environment.

Limitations of the Use of Chaos Theory

There has been much enthusiasm for the use of chaos theory among social researchers. However, some of this enthusiasm has been overinflated and misdirected. Some have argued that chaos theory is vastly superior to current models. Others have been caught in semantic misunderstandings of the meaning of chaos. There is also a contingent that has put aside the long-held viewpoint that organizations should practice long-term strategic planning. Consequently, the following limitations are offered in rebuttal to these viewpoints.

1. *Chaos theory has been overly enthusiastically endorsed as a "cure-all" in organizational research applications.* Chaos theory has been offered by some as a superior perspective for understanding organizational events. The usual argument is that most of the world operates in a nonlinear manner; therefore, it should be analyzed using a nonlinear perspective (Farazmand, 2003). Certainly this contention has merit. However, there is a temptation to belittle the linear approaches in science and math that have been so useful heretofore. Much of the empirical research in management is based on these linear perspectives. To imply that chaos theory is somehow a superior or exclusive means suggests that previous research that used linear approaches is of diminished value.

There is another problem with this argument, however. Little empirical management research is available that validates chaotic conditions. For the management researcher, the use of chaos theory is usually as a metaphor, not a strict statistical tool that seeks to plot values in phase space. While metaphors are useful for understanding complex systems (Morgan, 1997), there is the danger of taking them too far. Andrew Smith (2002) summed up the problem well when he stated, "Some disciplines have already displayed a tendency to rely too heavily on purely conceptual applications of chaos theory. This is in danger of reducing chaos theory to a collection of metaphors, or worse still reducing it to just semantic innovation if the application is trivial" (p. 523).

This leads to a third problem, best stated as a question: Can chaos theory actually tell us much that cannot be explained with existing theories (Kincanon & Powel, 1995)? The answer to this question is, yes. Most likely, chaos theory will add to our body of knowledge in the study of organizational crisis. It can provide a useful metaphor, but not necessarily a superior perspective that outclasses all other approaches. As mentioned previously, chaos theory is one of several tools or perspectives available to the organizational researcher, but it is not one that should be assigned elevated status over any of the other perspectives.

2. *There are some significant semantic misunderstandings of the word* chaos. Perhaps the most significant limitation pertains to the apparent misunderstanding of the word *chaos.* Within the context of chaos theory, chaos refers to a system state characterized by sensitive dependence to initial conditions and unpredictability in the long run. However, some have employed the more familiar definition, a state of being where events are random or out of control. This comparison is incorrect (Kincanon & Powel, 1995), although one could see how the two meanings of chaos may be confused.

Chaos is typically used as a metaphor in relation to the study of crisis because mathematically the concepts of chaos and crises are dissimilar. This is not to say that the mathematical meaning of chaos may not be associated at all with a crisis. For example, when heartbeats display a chaotic pattern, a heart attack, which is a crisis, may be imminent. This mathematical example is not the same, however, as using chaos theory as a perspective metaphor in the analysis of crises.

3. *The inability to forecast long-term events does not mean standard operating procedures and strategic planning should be abandoned*. Because chaos theory maintains that only short-range predictions are possible, it has been suggested that SOPs and strategic planning may not be feasible (Singh & Singh, 2002). In crisis management, SOPs are based on the potential events the crisis management team has determined could confront the organization. Strategic planning examines the long-range plans of the organization and how it will choose to compete in the marketplace. The dilemma in chaos theory is that nonlinearity in systems makes such long-range planning difficult, a result of sensitive dependence to initial conditions. In other words, trying to determine exactly what the long-term future might entail is impossible.

This situation is not necessarily a death sentence for long-range planning; rather, chaos theory helps explain why long-range plans are not always productive (Singh & Singh, 2002). For managers, the freedom to adjust plans when warranted is crucial. Indeed, if managers can learn anything from chaos theory, it is the practicality of adjusting plans at a moment's notice. Rigid plans that do not allow for contingencies along the way are destined for failure. Perhaps an analogy from a number of popular software programs may help here. Many programs have a "wizard," a simplified application of the software that is adaptable to a smaller set of uses. Software wizards can be likened to long-range planning in that they are useful in a limited set of conditions but are relatively inflexible. But with the same software comes the option to customize uses as needed. Instead of using the wizard, the user customizes the software according to the needs of the new situation. When a different scenario is encountered, the user has the option to customize further or to keep the defaults previously used. The point is that software used in this manner is flexible and can be customized to meet current needs. Still, the software itself does not change, only its application.

Long-range planning should also have the option of customization as needed. Likewise, SOPs and other short-term management applications should also be adjusted as needed. SOPs are the foundation of crisis management plans, ways the organization has chosen to respond to its potential crises. But adjusting plans should always be an option when a new and unique situation presents itself. As we saw in the FEMA example given earlier, an unwillingness to deviate from standard operating procedures can slow disaster response efforts.

Summary

Chaos theory can be used as a lens for analyzing crisis events. Chaos theory maintains that chaotic systems are identified by two characteristics: (1) sensitive dependence to initial conditions and (2) unpredictability in the long run. Chaotic systems also display bifurcations, attractors, nonlinearity, positive feedback, and self-organization.

Crisis events are unique in that they are kindled by small changes in initial conditions, and their predicted outcome is difficult in the long run. The actual components of chaos theory are used in a metaphorical manner when analyzing a crisis. Hence, bifurcations are considered the defining moments in the life of the crisis episode. Attractors are the patterns that exist in chaotic situations. In this chapter, they were used to depict the culture, values, and even the careless safety habits that can emerge in a crisis. Nonlinearity means that crisis events do not always fall together in a neat cause-and-effect manner. Positive feedback depicts how events can move away from equilibrium into a crisis situation. Finally, self-organization reminds us that companies will respond to a crisis by reinventing themselves so they are better able to withstand the onslaught of future crises.

Questions for Discussion

1. Describe a crisis event that has occurred where you work that resulted from a very small change in initial conditions (e.g., a customer slipping on a small patch of ice in the parking lot).

2. What are bifurcations? What examples of bifurcations have you seen in your workplace that emerged during a crisis?

3. What attractors were present in the crisis you described in Questions 1 and 2?

4. Explain the difference between positive and negative feedback. Illustrate your answer with an example from a crisis setting (e.g., in positive feedback, if your car begins to skid, you may overcorrect by turning the wheel too far in the other direction).

5. Self-organization is an important concept in chaos theory. How was your organization different after it experienced the crisis you described in Questions 1 and 2?

Chapter Exercise

Select a crisis event of interest to you. Research that event by reading several articles that analyze it in detail. From a chaos theory perspective, answer the following questions.

1. What evidence do you see of sensitive dependence to initial conditions?

2. Why is this case an example of unpredictability in the long run?

3. What bifurcations do you see in this case?

4. What attractors can be seen in this case?

5. What variables in this case show evidence of nonlinearity?

6. What evidence of feedback (positive) do you see?

7. How did the company change as it went through self-organization?

MINI CASE

MINI CASE: COMAIR CRASH
SHOWS THAT DETAILS MATTER

It was supposed to be a routine, early morning commuter flight to Atlanta, Georgia. Comair flight 5191 taxied to the runway at Blue Grass Airport in Lexington, Kentucky, just after 6:00 a.m. on August 27, 2006, and began its acceleration for takeoff. There was just one problem—the jet was on the wrong runway, a mistake that turned fatal for 49 people onboard the flight.

Flight 5191 should have been on Runway 22, a 7,000-foot-long stretch that was more than adequate for the commuter jet's takeoff. Instead, it was on Runway 26, a 3,500-foot length of asphalt that was supposed to be used only for private aircraft. The runway was too short for the Bombardier CRJ-100 jet to gain adequate speed for its ascent. Under normal conditions, this particular commuter jet, fully loaded, requires at least 5,800 feet for takeoff (Perez & Pasztor, 2006).

The ill-fated flight, unable to gain adequate lift, crashed and burned beyond the end of the runway, killing two crew personnel and 49 passengers. Only the copilot survived the disaster. It was the worst air mishap in the United States since the November 2001 crash of an American Airlines flight in New York.

Chaos theory tells us that a small change in initial conditions can alter the outcome of an event. In this crisis, the two runways at Blue Grass Airport were close to each other but very different in their uses and lengths. To get to Runway 22, the intended runway, it was necessary to taxi across Runway 26, the one designated for smaller aircraft. In the predawn hours of the morning of the crash, visibility may have been a factor in the confusion. The crash would not have occurred had the correct runway been used.

There is one other disturbing note in this crisis. Even after the plane began its acceleration down Runway 26, the copilot noted that the runway had no lights working. "Dat [sic] is weird with no lights," said copilot James Polehinke, the sole survivor of the crash. This transcript comes from the flight recorder, but the copilot, who suffered brain damage, has no recollection of what happened that morning.

The presence of two runways also represents a bifurcation, both literally and figuratively, in chaos theory. The use of the wrong runway was a key bifurcation or turning point in this crisis. But were there others? At least one newspaper, the *Washington Post,* reported that the pilots had actually first boarded the wrong plane, a mistake caught by a gate worker (Wilber, 2007). The *Post* reported that once they realized their mistake, the crew seemed embarrassed and chuckled. Was fatigue also a key bifurcation that caused the pilots to cross the line?

Could alcohol have been a factor? Although that was not likely, it was noted that copilot Polehinke had consumed two beers at 6:30 p.m. the night before the flight, thus violating the airline's 12-hour limit (Wald, 2007). Could the fact that only one air traffic controller was on duty and was busy have been a factor? After the flight was cleared for takeoff, the lone controller turned to attend to some paperwork and did not see the plane taxi to the wrong runway (Wald, 2006). Had this been noted, the disaster would have been averted. Investigators later learned the air traffic controller had slept only 2 hours the night before. Again, was fatigue a factor?

Another facet of chaos theory is the presence of positive feedback, which accelerates the situation into a crisis instead of pulling it back into equilibrium. Consider the decision by the pilots to continue the takeoff down Runway 26, even though the lights were off. Aborting the takeoff would have been an example of negative feedback. The aircraft would have reversed engines and eventually come to a halt, a halt back to equilibrium—and safety. So why was the decision made toward positive feedback? At the time of this writing, the Federal Aviation Administration's (FAA) investigation is still ongoing.

Chaos theory also notes that self-organization will take place after a crisis. In this incident, the Blue Grass Airport was later staffed with two controllers. Unfortunately, this particular tower was supposed to have two controllers anyway. The FAA later acknowledged it had violated its own policy by allowing only one controller on duty at the time of the accident (Wald, 2007).

Sources

Perez, E., & Pasztor, A. (2006, August 28). Jet that crashed my have used a short runway. *Wall Street Journal,* p. A2.
Wald, M. (2006, September 3). The loneliness of the air traffic controller. *New York Times,* p. 4.2.
Wald, M. (2007, January 18). Crew sensed trouble seconds before crash. *New York Times,* p. A16.
Wilber, D. (2007, January 18). Pilots noted lack of runway lights before Kentucky crash. *Washington Post,* p. A13.

Note

1. The Bowater incident was introduced briefly in Chapter 8.

References

Barton, S. (1994). Chaos, self-organization, and psychology. *American Psychologist, 49*(1), 5–14.

Bloch, D. (2005). Complexity, chaos, and nonlinear dynamics: A new perspective on career development theory. *Career Development Quarterly, 53,* 194–207.

Bolland, K., & Atherton, C. (1999). Chaos theory: An alternative approach to social work practice and research. *Families in Society: The Journal of Contemporary Human Services, 80*(4), 367–373.

Bright, J., & Pryor, R. (2005). The chaos theory of careers: A user's guide. *Career Development Quarterly, 53,* 291–305.

Burns, B. (2004). Kurt Lewin and complexity theories: Back to the future? *Journal of Change Management, 4*(4), 309–325.

Butz, M. (1997). *Chaos and complexity.* Washington, DC: Taylor & Francis.

Carroll, A., & Buchholtz, A. (2003). *Business & society: Ethics and stakeholder management* (5th ed.). Cincinnati, OH: Thompson South-Western.

Carver, C. (1997). Dynamical social psychology: Chaos and catastrophe for all. *Psychological Inquiry, 8*(2), 110–119.

Crandall, W. (2007). Crisis, chaos, and creative destruction: Getting better from bad. In E. G. Carayannis & C. Ziemnowicz (Eds.), *Rediscovering Schumpeter four score years later: Creative destruction evolving into "Mode 3."* Basingstoke, UK: Palgrave Macmillan.

Dervitsiotis, K. (2004). Navigating in turbulent environmental conditions for sustainable business excellence. *Total Quality Management, 15*(5–6), 807–827.

Duffy, J. (2000). The application of chaos theory to the career-plateaued worker. *Journal of Employment Counseling, 37*(4), 229–236.

Edgar, D., & Nisbet, L. (1996). A matter of chaos— Some issues for hospitality businesses. *International Journal of Contemporary Hospitality Management, 8*(2), 6–9.

Farazmand, A. (2003). Chaos and transformation theories: A theoretical analysis with implications for organization theory and public management. *Public Organization Review, 3,* 339–372.

Fisher, C., Schoenfeldt, L., & Shaw, J. (2003). *Human resource management* (5th ed.). Boston: Houghton Mifflin.

Frederick, W. (1998). Creatures, corporations, communities, chaos, complexity: A naturological view of the corporate social role. *Business and Society, 37*(4), 358–389.

Friedrich, P. (1988). Eerie chaos and eerier order. *Journal of Anthropological Research, 44*(Winter), 435–444.

Gleick, J. (1987). *Chaos: Making a new science.* New York: Viking.

Greenwald, J., & Hannifin, J. (1996). Tragedy retold. *Time, 148*(25), 57.

Hamblen, M. (1997). Mill disaster fires up planned IS overhaul. *Computerworld, 31*(3), 1, 28.

Hartley, R. (1993). *Business ethics: Violations of the public trust.* New York: John Wiley.

Hudson, C. (2000). At the edge of chaos: A new paradigm for social work? *Journal of Social Work Education, 36*(2), 215–230.

Kiel, L. (1995). Chaos theory and disaster response management: Lessons for managing periods of extreme instability. In G. A. Koehler (Ed.), *What disaster response management can learn from chaos theory.* Sacramento: California Research Bureau, California State Library. Retrieved November 28, 2008, from http://www.library.ca.gov/CRB/96/05/over_12.html

Kincanon, E., & Powel, W. (1995). Chaotic analysis in psychology and psychoanalysis. *Journal of Psychology, 129*(5), 495–505.

Lissack, M. (1999). Complexity: The science, its vocabulary, and its relation to organizations. *Emergence, 1*(1), 110–126.

Lorenz, E. (1993). *The essence of chaos.* Seattle: University of Washington Press.

Loye, D., & Eisler, R. (1987). Chaos and transformation: Implications of nonequilibrium theory for social science and society. *Behavioral Science, 32*(January), 53–65.

Macko, S. (1995). *Conflagration in northern Massachusetts.* Emergency Response and Research Institute: Fire Operations Archive. Retrieved 8/30/2008, from http://www.emergency.com/massfir.htm

Maggart, L. (1994). Bowater Incorporated: A lesson in crisis communication. *Public Relations Quarterly, 39*(3), 29–31.

McCurry, J. (1997). Loyalty saves Malden Mills. *Textile World, 147*(2), 38–45.

McDaniel, R., Jordan, M., & Fleeman, B. (2003). Surprise, surprise, surprise! A complexity view of the unexpected. *Health Care Management Review, 28*(3), 266–278.

McLaren, J. (1994). Bowater's Calhoun Mill at center of fog-related highway pileup dispute. *Pulp & Paper, 68*(8), 79–80.

Mitroff, I. I. (1989, October). Programming for crisis control. *Security Management,* pp. 75–79.

Moreno, K. (2003). Trial by fire. *Forbes, 171*(8), 92.

Morgan, G. (1997). *Images of organization* (2nd ed.). Thousand Oaks, CA: Sage.

Murphy, P. (1996). Chaos theory as a model for managing issues and crises. *Public Relations Review, 22*(2), 95–113.

Olasky, M. (2006). *The politics of disaster: Katrina, big government, and a new strategy for future crisis.* Nashville, TN: W Publishing Group.

Paraskevas, A. (2006). Crisis management or crisis response system? A complexity science approach to organizational crises. *Management Decision, 44*(7), 892–907.

Pascale, R. (1999). Surfing the edge of chaos. *Sloan Management Review, 40*(3), 83–94.

Perez, E., & Pasztor, A. (2006, August 28). Jet that crashed may have used a short runway. *Wall Street Journal,* p. A2.

Prigogine, I., & Stengers, I. (1984). *Order out of Chaos: Man's dialogue with nature.* New York: Bantam Books.

Reason, J. T. (1997). *Managing the risks of organizational accidents.* Ashgate, UK: Aldershot.

Sellnow, T., & Seeger, M. (2001). Exploring the boundaries of crisis communication: The case of the 1997 Red River Valley flood. *Communication Studies, 52*(2), 153–168.

Sellnow, T., Seeger, M., & Ulmer, R. (2002). Chaos theory, informational needs, and natural disasters. *Journal of Applied Communication Research, 30*(4), 269–292.

Sethi, S., & P. Steidlmeir, P. (1997). *Up against the corporate wall* (6th ed.). Upper Saddle River, NJ: Prentice Hall.

Singh, H., & Singh, A. (2002). Principles of complexity and chaos theory in project execution: A new approach to management. *Cost Engineering, 44*(12), 23–33.

Skala, K. (1999, March). Balancing the human equation. *Workforce,* pp. 54–59.

Smith, A. (2002). Three scenarios for applying chaos theory in consumer research. *Journal of Marketing Management, 18,* 517–531.

Smith, W., & Higgins, M. (2003). Postmodernism and popularization: The cultural life of chaos theory. *Culture and Organization, 9*(2), 93–104.

Tasaka, H. (1999). Twenty-first century management and the complexity paradigm. *Emergence, 1*(4), 115–123.

Technical Series Report 110. (1995). United States Fire Administration, FEMA. J. Gordon Routley, Editor, and Scott M. Howell, Investigator. Retrieved November 23, 2008, from http://www.interfire.org/res_file/pdf/Tr-110.pdf

Verwey, S., Crystal, A., & Bloom, E. (2002). Chaos and crisis: The Swiss bank case study. *Communicatio, 28*(2), 28–42.

Wald, M. (2006, September 3). The loneliness of the air traffic controller. *New York Times,* p. 4.2.

Wald, M. (2007, January 18). Crew sensed trouble seconds before crash. *New York Times,* p. A16.

Wilber, D. (2007, January 18). Pilots noted lack of runway lights before Kentucky crash. *Washington Post,* p. A13.

CHAPTER 12

Emerging Trends
in Crisis Management

The New Madrid Earthquake Fault

I n August of 2001, a FEMA emergency training session drew agreement from
participants that the three most likely disasters to strike the United States would
be a New York terrorist attack, a major California earthquake, and a hurricane
strike on New Orleans (Olasky, 2006). Ironically, two of those three events occurred
shortly thereafter. The third event, a California earthquake, is widely considered to be
inevitable. In fact, of the three disasters, predicting an earthquake is probably the most
certain because of what geologists know about earthquake faults.

An earthquake fault exists in the United States that is not widely known but is
capable of inflicting major damage. The New Madrid fault lies in a path between
St. Louis, Missouri, and Memphis, Tennessee. From 1811 to 1812, it produced a series
of earthquakes at 7.5 magnitude on the Richter scale that altered the course of the
Mississippi River. Scientists predict a 7%–10% chance that an earthquake of similar
magnitude will occur within the next 50 years (Green, 2003). Because of the high
population now in the area of the fault, a potential crisis has emerged in this part of
the country.

The field of crisis management has grown rapidly over the past 20 years. No
doubt this trend will continue as new knowledge is added to the field, as well as
new types of crises that have yet to be encountered. This chapter looks at the
emerging trends in crisis management, and how these trends may affect your
career in the future. We use as a foundation the crisis management framework
presented in this book, highlighting emerging trends within each of four areas.
Table 12.1 presents an overview of the chapter contents.

TABLE 12.1	Emerging Trends in Crisis Management			
	Landscape Survey	**Strategic Planning**	**Crisis Management**	**Organizational Learning**
The Internal Landscape	• Enthusiasm for crisis management planning will increase within organizations. • Crises will increasingly be seen as moral failure on the part of the organization.	• Crisis management plans will move from bound, static notebooks, to dynamic electronic documents. • Crisis management planning will become part of the organization's regular strategic planning process.	• Contingency responses to specific crisis events will become more common. • The organization's website will become the chief communications tool during a crisis. **Crisis**	• Organizational learning will increase in importance because of its role in providing the important feedback loop back to strategic planning. • Organizational learning after a crisis will lead to the abolishment of the existing status quo.
The External Landscape	• Victims of crises will become more visible and powerful as stakeholders. • An organizational crisis will be increasingly seen as a trust issue.	• Crisis management teams will be interacting more with crisis teams from outside their organization. • The focus efforts of crisis management will expand to include a wider range of stakeholders.	• The Internet will become more powerful in its ability to influence the outcome of a crisis. • The general public will play a more active role in crisis communication through the use of social networking tools.	• Crisis management frameworks and models will become more complex and sophisticated. • Crisis research will become more empirically rigorous. • Crisis research will take on a long-range perspective.

The Landscape Survey

Throughout the book, the landscape survey process has examined the organization's environment and identified the trends therein. Now we will consider trends that may appear on the horizon.

The Internal Landscape

The internal landscape considers the state of the organization and its ability to withstand—or even cause—a crisis. What follows is an identification of emerging internal landscape trends, and how you may be affected.

*Enthusiasm for crisis management
planning will increase within organizations.*

Figure 12.1 shows how interest in crisis management has grown in recent years. The figure depicts the number of articles published on crisis management on a yearly basis. Article counts (more formally called bibliometric data) are often used as a proxy for interest in a particular area of management (Crandall, Crandall, & Ashraf, 2006). Figure 12.1 shows that the number of articles on crisis management was steady from 1980 to 1992. From 1993 to 2001, there was a slow but steady increase in number of articles published. From 2002 to 2006, however, the number of articles increased dramatically. This figure also distinguishes between mainstream and academic articles. Mainstream articles target a broader audience of managers and other working practitioners. Academic articles are written mainly by and for those who conduct research on crisis management. The figure shows a higher number of mainstream articles than academic articles. In addition, the number of mainstream articles rose sharply while the number of academic articles rose more gradually.

One reason for this escalation in articles may involve the typical manager's attitude toward vulnerability. The traditional view of an organizational crisis was simple—"it can't happen to us" (Barton, 2001; Pearson & Mitroff, 1993). Many of these managers felt that even when a negative event occurred in an industry, it always happened to the other guy (Lockwood, 2005).

With the recent sharp increase in interest in crisis management, the prevailing viewpoint is changing to a more cautious "it might happen to us"

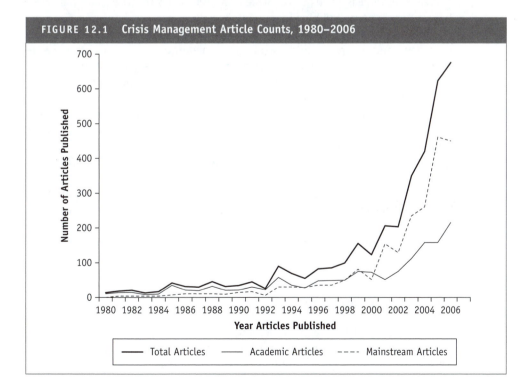

FIGURE 12.1   Crisis Management Article Counts, 1980–2006

mentality. Certainly, the September 11 terrorist attacks on New York and Washington, D.C., and Hurricane Katrina in August 2005 showed managers that a single crisis can affect a large number of stakeholders. Although many organizations did not suffer a direct hit from the terrorist attacks or the hurricane, a large number were adversely affected by their association with those organizations that were directly affected.

Never before in modern history has there been a more focused interest on crisis management. Both new and experienced managers must learn the basics of crisis management practices. We label this an emerging trend because many organizations are not currently prepared for a crisis. They do not have crisis management plans or teams, and they have not thought through their crisis vulnerabilities.

Crises will increasingly be seen as
moral failure on the part of the organization.

Some have taken the viewpoint that crisis events can be likened to moral failures on the part of one or more stakeholders in the organization, inferring that the crisis is human induced. Dan Millar (2003), senior consultant for the Institute for Crisis Management, has noted that the majority of organizational crises are human induced, with management initiating more than 53% of all crises, while employees account for 28%. Millar further classifies crises according to a category called "smoldering." Such crises start out small, internal, and manageable, but escalate into crises that are visible to the public. A greater emphasis needs to be placed on addressing these smoldering crises before they become full blown.

In this book we have discussed several examples of smoldering crises that were not properly addressed by management. Many of these were due to ethical breaches in the organization. Adequate attention was not focused on remedying the core problem, and the situation became a crisis. Based on the nature of human behavior and the record of ethical breaches leading to crisis, such breaches will likely continue despite the best efforts of business schools, religious leaders, and management writers. What does appear to make a difference in reducing such moral shortcomings in a given organization is the example set by upper management (Carroll & Buchholtz, 2003).

The implication for management is to set the ethical tone of the organization at the top levels of the company. In the absence of knowing what to do, employees will look one level higher for cues on how to respond in a certain situation. Promoting good business ethics can go a long way in preventing an organizational crisis.

The External Landscape

In the external landscape, emerging issues are focusing in two areas: the growing power of victims of a crisis and the eroding trust stakeholders experience when an organization goes through a crisis.

Victims of crises will become more visible and powerful as stakeholders.

In the past, victims of crisis events have been acknowledged to some degree, but were eventually forgotten. Indeed, certain victims, particularly those of natural disasters, are often poor and considered outcasts in society. As a result, they are not long remembered. Patrick Lagadec (2004) makes this observation in looking at the fatalities from the killer heat waves in France (2003) and Chicago (1995). In both events, those who died were often the poor, the elderly, and those who were isolated to some degree from society.

Recently, however, victims have become more vocal, visible, and noticed ('t Hart, Heyse, & Boin, 2001). After Hurricane Katrina, victims of the storm began to receive much media attention. One of the reasons why these victims were heard was because of the ineptness of government agencies in properly responding to this disaster. Managers should realize that all parties affected by a crisis are viable stakeholders. Furthermore, if the organization's response to the crisis is weak, public sympathy will move away from the organization, and to the victims. Organizational ineptness in handling a crisis is not an option.

An organizational crisis will increasingly be seen as a trust issue.

The traditional view of a crisis is that the organization is the victim of that crisis. This mindset would particularly hold true in the event of a natural disaster, but less so if the crisis was human induced from within the organization. Events such as hurricanes, fires, and earthquakes are viewed as things that "happen to" the organization.

Any crisis can be an issue of trust, however (Bertrand & Lajtha, 2002). This viewpoint maintains that the organization shares some of the blame for the crisis, either in terms of causing the crisis or in how it managed the crisis response. Even in the event of a natural disaster, the organization can be blamed if it was not adequately prepared. Hence, organizations get the blame they deserve, and this in proportion to their degree of unpreparedness. While such an attitude does not always seem fair, the onslaught of media attention that accompanies crisis events certainly seeks a scapegoat. Whether valid or not, a scapegoat mentality does help add meaning to an otherwise meaningless situation. Even if an organization is not to be directly blamed for the results of a crisis, a loss of public confidence is still a likely outcome (Bertrand & Lajtha, 2002).

Management is a symbol of trust that the organization has with its stakeholders. Internally, management must be trusted by its employees to manage the crisis in the best manner possible. Employees also expect that management will not induce a crisis, such as in the area of worker safety. Such a crisis would be a trust issue if management made ill-advised cuts in safety training or equipment. Should an employee be injured due to a cutback of this sort, then employee trust in the organization would be compromised.

External stakeholders also trust the organization to prevent crises when possible and mitigate them when they do occur. As we have discussed previously, the media, the community, and the customers are often critical of the organization when it does not manage a crisis effectively. Simply stated, the issue of trust is becoming more important. If stakeholders lose trust in the organization, its ultimate survival may be in jeopardy.

Strategic Planning

Strategic planning is the proactive stage when management has a chance to plan for future crisis events. The trends and implications in this important area are discussed next.

The Internal Landscape

Crisis management plans will move from bound, static notebooks to dynamic electronic documents.

A crisis plan typically includes a selection of potential vulnerabilities and how the organization should respond if they occur. In addition, contact information for the organization's key stakeholders is included. The opening vignette discussed the New Madrid earthquake fault. Because of the danger it poses, crisis management plans in the Memphis, Tennessee, region include contingencies for how to manage through the aftermath of an earthquake.

Prior to the availability of the Internet, crisis management plans were kept in bound guidebooks. Such notebooks were similar to other standard operating procedure (SOP) materials that organizations kept on their bookshelves. Today, increasing numbers of organizations are posting these plans on their Web sites. This approach makes the plan readily available to all stakeholders with Internet access, and its general distribution ensures the plan can be accessed in a wider geographic context. It also enables crisis planners to evaluate other published plans when formulating or revising their own. Finally, because these plans are electronic documents, they can be easily changed and redistributed, unlike bound documents in notebooks, which take more effort to change.

One implication of this change is that the organization's information technology (IT) department must be actively involved in the distribution of the crisis management plan. This relationship is actually a welcome one, since IT is an integral part of crisis recovery anyway. Another implication is that all employees must be Web savvy and comfortable reviewing electronic documents. Part of crisis management, then, is not just preparing for a crisis, but preparing employees to learn new things, such as accessing and working with electronic documents on the organization's Web site.

why?

Crisis management planning will become part of the organization's regular strategic planning process.

The planning process for a crisis has traditionally been carried out by crisis management teams (Barton, 2001; Penrose, 2000). Such teams have typically operated outside of the strategic management process (Preble, 1997). Team members usually include representatives from the key functional units of the organization. Planning is usually focused on the development of crisis vulnerabilities and contingencies for dealing with these potential crises.

An important emerging trend is to make crisis management planning an actual part of the strategic planning process (Chong, 2004; Coombs, 2006; Parnell, 2008; Preble, 1997), a theme consistent with this book. The advantage of this approach is that it makes crisis awareness an ongoing process that is reviewed in conjunction with the organization's long-range plans. Crisis vulnerability planning is incorporated into the strengths, weaknesses, opportunities, and threats (SWOT) analysis component of planning. The implication for management is that it must ensure that the entire crisis management process does not take place in a far corner of the organization, away from the main players who need to be part of the process. Crisis management should be part of an ongoing strategic planning process, not a separate activity that occurs only occasionally.

The External Landscape

In the strategic planning area, one of the main trends we see is the interaction of the crisis management team with teams outside of the organizational unit.

Crisis management teams will be interacting more with other crisis teams from outside their organization.

Traditionally, one crisis team is organized for each organizational unit. For example, a large company with several plants may have one crisis team for each manufacturing facility. In addition, there may also be an overall team for the entire organization. This type of arrangement works well when the crisis event is relatively minor.

In crises that are more complicated and geographically diverse, organizational crisis management units must interact with similar teams from other organizations. In addition, a host of government agencies may also be involved in this network of crisis teams. These interlinking crisis teams that form during an event have been called *hastily formed networks* (Denning, 2006). Hurricane Katrina led to the formation of a number of hastily formed networks among aid agencies, crisis management teams, military units, emergency response teams, and local governments.

The implication of this trend is important. Crisis management team leaders must begin to network with their counterparts in other organizations. There are opportunities for knowledge transfer, as well as the planning of disaster drills. The time to interact with these groups is before the crisis occurs. In this way, crisis team members are familiar with their counterparts and have already developed working relationships.

The focus efforts of crisis management will expand to include a wider range of stakeholders.

The traditional focus of crisis management has been on media relations ('t Hart et al., 2001; Marra, 1998). A good relationship with the media will ensure that the public sees the company in the best light.

The scope of crisis management outreach is also beginning to adopt a broader stakeholder approach. This approach advocates meeting the needs of the multiple groups that have distinct vested interests in the organization (Carroll & Buchholtz, 2003). Certainly, employees are one such stakeholder (Barton, 2001; Lockwood, 2005). This sometimes forgotten group needs to know both the good and the bad news that occurs during a crisis. Employees are a key resource and can help pull the firm through a perilous time.

Other stakeholders that may be affected by a crisis include shareholders, customers, the local community, suppliers, and social activist groups (Carroll & Buchholtz, 2003). The response by several large private-sector companies to Hurricane Katrina in New Orleans and the surrounding areas provides an example. Wal-Mart, Home Depot, and FedEx tracked the hurricane and moved aggressively to meet community needs after the storm hit (Olasky, 2006). Their goal was to generate business, but more importantly, they were poised to fill a humanitarian role in the aftermath of the storm.

The implication for crisis decision makers is to expand the scope of response of the organization to include helping local stakeholders where possible. Such a move is especially welcomed when a local geographical area has been the victim of a natural disaster. This response will vary according to the type of business services offered by the company. Several applications become apparent:

- Food service establishments can offer food and beverages during times when these items may be scarce in the community. Offering these items for free or at a reduced cost may be feasible. Raising prices to reflect scarcity will be viewed by many as a form of inappropriate opportunism and will create community ill will that can last long after the crisis subsides.
- Retailers can ensure that adequate supplies of staple items such as flashlights, batteries, and portable stoves will be available. Purchasers must be able to anticipate the kind of emergency items that will be needed and order accordingly. Again, opportunistic price increases will create bad feelings in the community. Although legal in many instances, doing so in a time of need is bad business ethics and can create an unnecessary public relations crisis for the organization.
- Organizations with access to automotive or van fleets may be able to offer transportation for the elderly or needy. This could be accomplished by offering pickup and delivery for needy citizens to local stores, similar to what a bus service would offer in a city. While even offering this type of service may sound preposterous to some managers, doing so on a temporary emergency basis will be appreciated and well received by the community.

To summarize, planning for a crisis means considering the interests of both the company and the stakeholders in the community.

Crisis Management

Crisis management is the reactive phase of the four-stage model outlined in this book. Specifically, it is the stage where the organization responds to a given crisis. Emerging trends within the internal landscape are discussed next.

The Internal Landscape

*Contingency responses to specific
crisis events will become more common.*

The reliance on crisis management teams and plans is a good step in moving an organization toward a firm base in formalized crisis planning. Conventional crisis planning has followed a standardized procedure format in addressing incidents. As a result, most crisis plans contain specific procedures to follow in a particular event. For example, bomb threats are common crisis events that are addressed, and plans for these usually contain a step-by-step procedure for responding. Another example is the evacuation of a building, a procedure that should be carried out in an organized, methodical fashion. Responding to complex crises, however, will also involve contingency approaches. This line of thinking maintains that there may not be one best approach to addressing every crisis.

Shrivastava (1993) noted the beginning of a shift from procedures to broader based crisis skills in the early 1990s. Included in this skill set are "decentralized decision making" and "managerial autonomy and flexibility" (p. 28). While procedures are important in managing a crisis, this skill set recognizes that flexible contingencies may be required along the way. Bertrand and Lajtha (2002) refer to this ability as the "breaking of inflexible mindsets" or "training oneself to deal with the unexpected" (p. 186).

The implications for management are twofold. On one hand, crisis planners need to address specific events and how they should be managed. These are the potential crisis vulnerabilities that have been discussed in this book. On the other hand, managers should maintain flexibility in their responses to more complex situations. Making adjustments along the way is part of contingency thinking, and this in itself is both an art and a science. Crisis response, then, requires a set of plans that become the backbone for managing the event. Crisis response also requires a degree of improvisation, an ability to create new responses in light of new information that the crisis may reveal.

*The organization's Web site will become
the chief communications tool during a crisis.*

Internet technology has expanded the communication tools that are available during a crisis (Vielhaber & Waltman, 2008). At the top of the list is the organization's Web site. The Web site can become the key contact point between the organization and its stakeholders during a crisis. Unfortunately, some crises have actually caused a Web site to "go down," rendering it useless. Union University, a small private college in western Tennessee, experienced this in February 2008 when a tornado hit the campus, damaging buildings and causing the Web site to become unavailable for several hours. On the other hand, Virginia Tech was able to remain online by loading a simplified "light version" of its Web site after the April 2007 shooting rampage by student Seung-Hui Cho (Joly, 2008). The Web site became the key communication device with the public during the ordeal. Following the shootings, the Web site received up to 150,000 visits per hour. It normally transfers 15 gigabytes a day, but on the day of the shooting the Web server transferred 432 gigabytes (Carlson, 2007).

There are several implications for crisis managers. First, the organization's emergency Web site arrangements should not be compiled in a vacuum by the IT department. The crisis management team must be available to share information and also receive advice on how the Web site should be maintained during a crisis. One thing is certain: The Web site will need to be scaled down considerably so that it can absorb the high amount of traffic that will descend on it with users wanting an update on the crisis. A second implication is to consider partnering with another organization in a "co-location arrangement" for operating the Web site (Joly, 2008, p. 62). This means that one organization can piggyback off the other if their Web site goes down, and vice versa. Among institutions of higher education, Duke and Stanford have such an arrangement (Joly, 2008). If a major emergency renders the Web site of one of the schools inoperable, the other school will host and maintain the Web site until the crisis is over.

The External Landscape

The Internet will become more powerful in its ability to influence the outcome of a crisis. The Internet began to influence crisis planning shortly after its use became widespread in the early 1990s. One of the first companies directly affected by an Internet-related crisis was Intel, when its flawed Pentium chip surfaced in 1994. The crisis began rather innocently when math professor Thomas Nicely at Lynchburg College in Virginia found a computer error when he was working on a math problem. He e-mailed a colleague about the matter, and soon his spreadsheet problem showing how the Intel chip could incorrectly calculate certain problems was all over the Internet (Weiss, 1998). Intel had thus become one of the first victims of substantial negative Internet publicity, a phenomenon known as flaming.

As the Intel example illustrates, the Internet can *intensify* the crisis. At least three types of this crisis are evident: (1) when an organization's Web site is compromised due to a hacker intrusion or virus, (2) when negative Web sites or blogs surface that criticize an organization, and (3) when evidence from the Internet incriminates a party. The 2006 crisis involving Congressman Mark Foley illustrates this third manifestation. In this case, damaging e-mails and chat messages surfaced concerning Foley's inappropriate behavior regarding student pages (Lueck, 2006).

The general public will play a more active role in crisis communication through the use of social networking tools.

One of the more interesting outgrowths of social networking tools is their use in crisis communication. Such tools consist of blogs, instant messaging services, photo sites, and interactive maps. Social networking tools were used during the October 2007 wildfires in Southern California. The advantage they offered was an ability to communicate news that was not available on national or even local news outlets. News such as the progression of the fires, the availability and location of emergency shelters, and the opening or closing of businesses and schools was available in almost real time through social networking outlets (Palmer, 2008).

Social networking offers the advantage of being able to disseminate information, even if the organization's Web site becomes inoperable. Such was the case after the Union University tornado, discussed above. The university did not have a Web site, so a blog was set up at blogspot.com to provide updates on the damage and recovery. In addition, the university was able to use its Facebook page to share updates, photos, and videos (Joly, 2008).

The implication for crisis managers is the importance of educating themselves about the various social networking tools available. Unlike Web sites, which often need people with specialized skills to set up and operate, social networking tools are easy to use and manage.

Organizational Learning

Organizational learning after a crisis is necessary so that the company's crisis response will be more effective when the next incident arrives. Learning also helps to prevent certain types of crises from reappearing in the future.

The Internal Landscape

Organizational learning will increase
in importance because of its role in providing
the important feedback loop back to strategic planning.

Traditionally, organizational learning has focused on improved planning for future crises and mitigating the impact of the ones that do occur. Much has been written on the need for effective crisis detection interventions (Elsubbaugh, Fildes, & Rose, 2004; Mitroff & Anagnos, 2001; Pearson & Clair, 1998). Preventing crises before they occur makes economic sense and reduces the possibility of human and physical damage to the organization.

Although traditional crisis management acknowledges the need for organizational learning after an event, most research continues to focuses on pre- and midcrisis planning. This mindset will need to change. A number in the crisis management field have called for a renewed focus on the postcrisis stage, where learning and evaluation need to take place (Bertrand & Lajtha, 2002; Chong, 2004; Kovoor-Misra & Nathan, 2000; Pearson & Clair, 1998). What is significant about organizational learning is that it initiates the feedback loop that is necessary in the strategic management framework. Figure 12.2 illustrates this feedback loop as it moves back to the landscape survey, strategic planning, and crisis management stages. In each stage, feedback can be useful as the organization prepares for the next round of crises. The external landscape link is also depicted, showing that organizations and industries also utilize feedback to protect from crises.

The implication of this emerging trend is significant and remains a central theme of this book—the crisis management process, from landscape survey to organizational learning, needs to be an integral part of the organization's strategic planning process. The days when crisis management consisted of a small, select group of managers who wrote the crisis plan and met occasionally

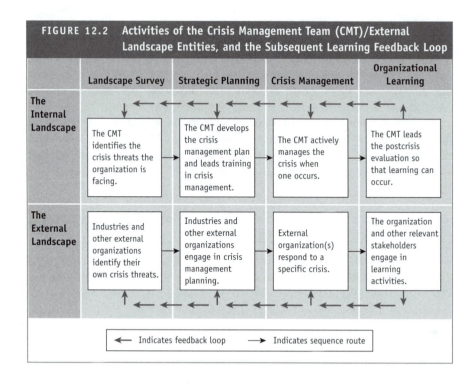

FIGURE 12.2 Activities of the Crisis Management Team (CMT)/External Landscape Entities, and the Subsequent Learning Feedback Loop

are gone. Crisis events impact strategy in the long run; therefore the planning, managing, and learning from these events must be carried out within the strategic management framework.

Organizational learning after a crisis will lead to the abolishment of the existing status quo.

Preserving the current state of affairs in an organization and returning to "business as usual" has been the traditional mindset of many organizations following a crisis. However, a crisis offers an opportunity to change or even abolish the status quo. "Crises are, by their very nature, an invitation to abandon standard ways of doing things. They offer an opportunity to think and work laterally and to de-compartmentalize/break down encrusted silos in the company" (Bertrand & Lajtha, 2002, p. 186). Inherent in this mindset is the notion that a crisis can trigger the forces of renewal in an organization (Dynes, 2003; Olshansky, 2006). Chaos theorists who study crises call this self-organization, a process that occurs when an organization passes through a crisis and transforms into a more adaptable organization (Murphy, 1996). For example, the Red River Valley flood of 1997 and the subsequent organizational renewal that took place was analyzed through the lens of chaos theory. The local government of Fargo, North Dakota, emerged as a new leader in that geographic area, taking over the lead in emergency response management from the county, which had formerly carried out this function. In other words, the status quo of how emergencies had been managed in the past was now broken and replaced with a better system (Sellnow, Seeger, & Ulmer, 2002).

The implication for crisis managers/strategic planners is one of hope. Although crises are negative events, they can engender positive change. However, for this positive change to occur, the learning process must be tied back to the strategic planning process. Managers need to be cognizant of their role as potential change agents in their organizations.

The External Landscape

In the external landscape, learning extends into areas outside of the organization. The following are emerging trends in the field of crisis management research.

Crisis management frameworks and models will become more complex and sophisticated.

Frameworks of crisis management have traditionally been simple, with most depicting a sequential format for understanding the evolution and resolution of a crisis. The most basic framework consists of a precrisis, crisis, and postcrisis sequence as overviewed in Chapter 1. Smith (1990) and Richardson (1994) utilized this approach in their studies. Four- and five-stage frameworks have also been proposed (see Fink, 1996; Hosie & Smith, 2004; Myers, 1993; Pearson & Mitroff, 1993); this book uses a four-stage approach. Frameworks have also been offered for types of crisis categories as well as crisis management communication strategies. Such strategies were examined in Chapter 8.

In the future, frameworks will examine new areas that have not yet been researched. For example, an area that has been mostly untouched is the relationship between crisis management and sustainable development (Crandall & Mensah, 2008). These two areas are actually closely related because an environmental crisis triggered by an organizational decision can quickly consume sustainable resources. Framework development in this area is needed.

Although frameworks offer a general approach to understanding the components of crisis phenomena, models are designed to examine the different variables that interact with each other before and during a crisis. Some progress has been made in the area of organizational crisis model building. Shrivastava, Mitroff, Miller, and Miglani (1988) offered one of the first industrial crisis models. Sheaffer, Richardson, and Rosenblatt (1998) studied the 1995 collapse of Barings, a conservative and once solid British bank, and proposed two models, a crisis–causal antecedents model and an early-warning-signals model. Pearson and Clair (1998) looked at the crisis management process and proposed a success–failure outcomes model. More recently, a crisis preparedness model has been proposed by Elsubbaugh and colleagues (2004). In the future, continued progress in model building can be expected.

Another emerging trend in the area of frameworks and models is the inclusion of complexity and chaos theory as a means of offering enriched understanding of the complexity of crisis events. As previously mentioned, Sellnow and colleagues (2002) examined the 1997 Red River Valley flood using the framework of chaos theory. Smith (2005) looked at the phases of a crisis event utilizing concepts from chaos theory. Paraskevas (2006) offered a complexity science approach to organizational crises. More recently, Crandall (2007) utilized chaos theory to examine the Union Carbide Bhopal gas leak and the 1995 Malden Mills textile fire in Massachusetts. Chapter 11 introduced the paradigm of chaos theory as a means of studying crisis events. We anticipate that complexity models such as chaos theory will continue to be used in the study of crises.

Crisis research will become more empirically rigorous.

Crisis management research has been dominated by the case approach. Indeed, much can be gleaned from examining a past crisis in detail. In the 1980s, Union Carbide's Bhopal disaster, Johnson & Johnson's Tylenol cyanide sabotage, and the *Exxon Valdez* oil spill were well documented. A number of high-profile events made valuable case studies in the 1990s, including the bombing of the Murrah Federal Building in Oklahoma City, the crash of ValuJet Flight 592 in Florida's Everglades, and the Luby's Cafeteria massacre in Killeen, Texas. Since the beginning of the millennium, the September 11 toppling of the World Trade Center Towers, Hurricane Katrina, the Asian tsunami of December 2004, and the 2008 China earthquake (also known as the Great Sichuan Earthquake) have been subjects for case studies.

More sophisticated statistical techniques are being utilized in crisis research. In one of the earlier empirical studies, Marcus and Goodman (1991) looked at the impact on the stock market made by corporate announcements pertaining to crises. Greening and Johnson (1996) used regression analysis to discover how management teams and strategies correspond to catastrophic events. More recently, Sheaffer and Mano-Negrin (2003) used factor analysis to examine executive orientations to crisis management policies and practices. More rigorous empirical models are emerging and therefore a wealth of research opportunities to develop and test these models is available.

Crisis research will take on a long-range perspective.

The traditional approach in crisis management research is to analyze short-term events, typically single-event crises. The study of these events includes an analysis of the various phases of the crisis from the precrisis stage to the learning stage. However, the long-term effects of these crises have not been widely evaluated. Revisiting the sites and stakeholders involved in a crisis to determine what learning and policy changes have been implemented is often appropriate ('t Hart et al., 2001). A long-term view of crisis also looks at the precursors of these events. Analyzing variables such as the organizational culture and other mini-steps that led to the crisis can yield useful information to both researchers and managers.

Although the research changes that occur in the external landscape may appear to have little significance for students of crisis management, or for practicing managers, for that matter, nothing could be farther from the truth. Research data are drawn from the activities and experiences of practicing managers whose organizations engaged in crisis management. It is quite possible that in the future you may be called on to answer questions for a research study that is being conducted to learn more about organizational crises and their management. Researchers often collect data through surveys. If you have an opportunity to participate in such a survey, you can do so knowing that you are helping other managers in your field, as well as management researchers, who are attempting to learn how organizations can respond more effectively to a crisis. In some cases, you may even be asked for an interview. Perhaps your organization experienced a crisis and the researchers want to learn more about how your crisis management team responded. Granting an interview to a researcher will help that person gain insights that are not possible through a survey.

Summary

This chapter examined the emerging trends in the field of crisis management. One of the key trends mentioned is also a central theme of this book—that crisis management should be seen as an integral part of the strategic management process. In the past, much of what we call crisis management planning existed in a vacuum, away from the strategic planners who guide the future of their organizations. The next decade is likely to be as turbulent as the last. Hence, a change in this type of thinking is required.

Questions for Discussion

1. Why do you think crisis management has not always been heavily emphasized in the strategic management process?

2. Hastily formed networks are an emerging trend in crisis management, particularly in the area of disaster management. If a major storm were to hit your local area, what groups do you think should be part of the network to coordinate crisis and disaster relief?

3. Looking at the positive side of a crisis might seem contradictory, and yet that is an emerging trend. What positive outcomes can you see that resulted from a crisis in an organization in your area or perhaps where you have worked?

4. Much has been written on the importance of business ethics, and yet it continues to cause many crises in businesses. Why do you think ethical violations continue to be a source of crises in organizations today?

5. Crisis management research is a developing field. What areas do you think need to be researched more in the future?

Chapter Exercise

When it comes to looking at the future, the threat of earthquakes is a very real concern in the United States. The opening vignette mentioned the New Madrid fault as a potential threat for two major cities along the Mississippi River: St. Louis, Missouri, and Memphis, Tennessee.

The University of Memphis offers an informative Web site on earthquake research and the New Madrid fault. The Center for Earthquake Research and Information can be found at www.ceri.memphis.edu.

Take some time to visit the Web site and familiarize yourself with the mission of the Center and the different resources that are available. Now, suppose you have been asked to advise a retail clothing business headquartered in New York City on how to prepare for a potential earthquake on the New Madrid fault. The company is planning on opening three stores in the Memphis area, two in shopping malls and one in a strip mall. What advice would you give this company?

MINI CASE

THE GREAT MOLASSES SPILL

It may seem odd to end a chapter on the future of crisis management with a case that is one of the earlier industrial crises in the United States. But a close look at this rather unusual incident will reveal many concepts that have been covered in this book, plus some items that have an eye for the future.

The scene is Boston, Massachusetts, on January 15, 1919. In an industrial area of town, just off Commercial Street, was the United States Alcohol Company, the owner of a large tank that housed the ill-fated molasses. The huge structure measured 58 feet tall and 90 feet in diameter and was at that moment filled to the brim with 2.5 million gallons of the dark sugary liquid (Mason, 1965). Molasses was a key product in making rum, which explains its presence at this particular factory. Without warning, around lunch time, the tank split open and proceeded to spew its contents onto the local firehouse, an elevated train, numerous houses and buildings, and innocent bystanders. Visualizing the disaster is almost unfathomable. Imagine a heavy sludge, 15 feet deep, moving at around 35 miles per hour, sucking up people and knocking over structures along its way. When the casualties had been tallied, 21 people were dead and another 150 had been injured (Park, 1983). Some of the victims had been crushed to death in the fallen building, while others literally drowned in the molasses.

The cause of the disaster was a structural flaw in the tank. The company blamed Italian anarchists, while the other main theory was that U.S. Alcohol was negligent in maintaining the tank (Puleo, 2003). After the court hearings, the verdict went against the company, citing it for not keeping the tank in a safe operating condition. Inadequate inspections by company personnel were most likely the reason for the structural fatigue not being detected (Park, 1983).

This case is one of the first documented crises that show how corporate greed and negligence can threaten public safety. Stephen Puleo notes in his book on the disaster, *Dark Tide*, that the company responded to existing leaks in the tank by painting the tank brown so the molasses seepage would not be detected. The outcome of this crisis and the court hearings that resulted was that large companies would be held accountable for their actions. This attitude continues to this day. In fact, the lesson from this case from almost 100 years ago is relevant to a modern-day audience. First, organizational crises do occur, sometimes quite by accident; other times the company will be at fault. In either case, crises do occur and anticipating them is important, as this book points out. Second, many crises can be prevented. Certainly the molasses spill was an example of a preventable event, but instead of acting wisely, the company chose to neglect adequate safety and maintenance procedures. Finally, this case shows us that the burden of proof will always be on the company when something goes wrong. The fact is that the media, outside stakeholders, and elected officials will call on any company to explain itself when a crisis occurs. Guilt is often presumed until innocence is proven. Crisis management is real, and should be part of every manager's repertoire of skills.

Sources

Mason, J. (1965, January). The molasses disaster of January 15, 1919. *Yankee Magazine,* pp. 52–53, 109–111.
Park, E. (1983). Without warning, molasses in January surged over Boston. *Smithsonian, 14*(8), 213–230.
Puleo, S. (2003). *Dark tide: The great Boston molasses flood of 1919.* Boston: Beacon.

References

Barton, L. (2001). *Crisis in organizations II.* Cincinnati, OH: South-Western College Publishing.

Bertrand, R., & Lajtha, C. (2002). A new approach to crisis management. *Journal of Contingencies and Crisis Management, 10*(4), 181–191.

Carlson, S. (2007, August 3). Emergency at Virginia Tech shows the power of the Web, says campus official. *Chronicle of Higher Education, 53*(48).

Carroll, A., & Buchholtz, A. (2003). *Business & society: Ethics and stakeholder management.* Mason, OH: Thomson South-Western.

Chong, J. (2004). Six steps to better crisis management. *Journal of Business Strategy, 25*(2), 43–46.

Coombs, W. (2006). *Code red in the boardroom: Crisis management as organizational DNA.* Westport, CT: Praeger.

Crandall, W. (2007). Crisis, chaos, and creative destruction: Getting better from bad. In E. G. Carayannis & C. Ziemnowicz (Eds.). *Rediscovering Schumpeter four score years later: Creative destruction evolving into "Mode 3."* Basingstoke, UK: Palgrave Macmillan.

Crandall, W. R., Crandall, R. E., & Ashraf, M. (2006). Management fashion: An examination of seven life cycles and the problem of scholarly lags. *Proceedings of the 2006 Academy of Management Meeting,* Atlanta, GA. [Available from William "Rick" Crandall, School of Business, University of North Carolina at Pembroke]

Crandall, W. R., & Mensah, E. C. (2008). Crisis management and sustainable development: A framework and proposed research agenda. *International Journal of Sustainable Strategic Management, 1*(1), 16–34.

Denning, P. (2006). Hastily formed networks: Collaboration in the absence of authority. *Communications of ACM, 49*(4), 15–20.

Dynes, R. (2003). Noah and disaster planning: The cultural significance of the flood story. *Journal of Contingencies and Crisis Management, 11*(4), 170–177.

Elsubbaugh, S., Fildes, R., & Rose, M. (2004). Preparation for crisis management: A proposed model and empirical evidence. *Journal of Contingencies and Crisis Management, 12*(3), 112–127.

Fink, S. (1996). *Crisis management: Planning for the inevitable.* New York: American Management Association.

Green, M. (2003). Study: Scientists re-evaluate New Madrid earthquake risk. *Best's Review, 103*(11), 63.

Greening, D., & Johnson, R. (1996). Do managers and strategies matter? A study in crisis. *Journal of Management Studies, 33*(1), 25–51.

't Hart, P., Heyse, L., & Boin, A. (2001). New trends in crisis management practice and crisis management research: Setting the agenda. *Journal of Contingencies & Crisis Management, 9*(4), 181–188.

Hosie, P., & Smith, C. (2004). Preparing for crisis: Online security management education. *Research and Practice in Human Resource Management, 12*(2), 90–127.

Joly, K. (2008, April). It's 2008: Is your 911 Website ready? *universitybusiness.com.* Retrieved November 23, 2008, from http://www.universitybusiness.com/viewarticle.aspx?articleid = 1044

Kovoor-Misra, S., & Nathan, M. (2000, Fall). Timing is everything: The optimal time to learn from crises. *Review of Business,* pp. 31–36.

Lagadec, P. (2004). Understanding the French 2003 heat wave experience: Beyond the heat, a multi-layered challenge. *Journal of Contingencies and Crisis Management, 12*(4), 160–169.

Lockwood, N. (2005). Crisis management in today's business environment: HR's strategic role. *SHRM Research Quarterly,* (4), 1–9.

Lueck, S. (2006, October 4). Ex-pages exposed Foley's explicit messages. *Wall Street Journal,* p. A13.

Marcus, A., & Goodman, R. (1991). Victims and shareholders: The dilemmas of presenting corporate policy during a crisis. *Academy of Management Journal, 34*(2), 281–305.

Marra, F. (1998). Crisis communication plans: Poor predictors of excellent public relations. *Public Relations Review, 24*(4), 461–474.

Mason, J. (1965, January). The molasses disaster of January 15, 1919. *Yankee Magazine,* pp. 52–53, 109–111.

Myers, K. (1993). *Total contingency planning for disasters: Managing risk . . . minimizing loss . . . ensuring business continuity.* New York: John Wiley.

Millar, D. (2003). *ICM crisis report: News coverage of business crises during 2002.* The Institute for Crisis Management. Retrieved September 3, 2004, from http://www.crisisexperts.com

Mitroff, I., & Anagnos, G. (2001). Crisis in crisis management. *Corporate Counsel, 8*(2), 58–61.

Murphy, P. (1996). Chaos theory as a model for managing issues and crises. *Public Relations Review, 22*(2), 95–113.

Olasky, M. (2006). *The politics of disaster: Katrina, big government, and a new strategy for future crisis.* Nashville, TN: W Publishing Group.

Olshansky, R. (2006). Planning after Hurricane Katrina. *Journal of the American Planning Association, 72*(2), 147–153.

Palmer, J. (2008, May 3). Emergency 2.0 is coming to a Website near you: The Web spells a sea change for crisis management. How should emergency services respond? *New Scientist,* pp. 24–25.

Paraskevas, A. (2006). Crisis management or crisis response system? A complexity science approach to organizational crises. *Management Decision, 44*(7), 892–907.

Park, E. (1983). Without warning, molasses in January surged over Boston. *Smithsonian, 14*(8), 213–230.

Parnell, J. A. (2008). *Strategic management: Theory and practice.* Cincinnati, OH: Atomic Dog Publishing.

Pearson, C., & Clair, J. (1998). Reframing crisis management. *Academy of Management Review, 23*(1), 59–76.

Pearson, C., & Mitroff, I. (1993). From crisis prone to crisis prepared: A framework for crisis management. *Academy of Management Executive, 7*(1), 48–59.

Penrose, J. (2000). The role of perception in crisis planning. *Public Relations Review, 26*(2), 155–171.

Preble, J. (1997). Integrating the crisis management perspective into the strategic management process. *Journal of Management Studies, 34*(5), 769–791.

Puleo, S. (2003). *Dark tide: The great Boston molasses flood of 1919.* Boston: Beacon.

Richardson, B. (1994). Socio-technical disasters: Profile and prevalence. *Disaster Prevention & Management, 3*(4), 41–69.

Sellnow, T., Seeger, M., & Ulmer, R. (2002). Chaos theory, informational needs, and natural disasters. *Journal of Applied Communication Research, 30*(4), 269–292.

Sheaffer, Z., & Mano-Negrin, R. (2003). Executives' orientations as indicators of crisis management policies and practices. *Journal of Management Studies, 40*(2), 573–606.

Sheaffer, Z., Richardson, B., & Rosenblatt, Z. (1998). Early-warning-signals management: A lesson from the Barings crisis. *Journal of Contingencies and Crisis Management, 6*(1), 1–22.

Shrivastava, P. (1993). Crisis theory/practice: Towards a sustainable future. *Industrial & Environmental Crisis Quarterly, 7*(1), 23–42.

Shrivastava, P., Mitroff, I. I., Miller, D., & Miglani, A. (1988). Understanding industrial crises. *Journal of Management Studies, 25*(4), 285–304.

Smith, D. (1990). Beyond contingency planning: Towards a model of crisis management. *Industrial Crisis Quarterly, 4*(4), 263–275.

Smith, D. (2005). Dancing around the mysterious forces of chaos: Exploring complexity, knowledge, and the management of uncertainty. *Clinician in Management, 13,* 115–123.

Vielhaber, M. E., & Waltman, J. L. (2008). Changing uses of technology: Crisis communication responses in a faculty strike. *Journal of Business Communication, 45*(3), 308–330.

Weiss, J. (1998). *Business ethics: A stakeholder and issues management approach.* Fort Worth, TX: Dryden.

Appendix

*Sample Outline of Items
to Include in the Crisis Management Plan*[1]

A. Title Page

   1. Name of organization

   2. Title of document: Crisis Management Plan

   3. Last revision date

B. Table of Contents

C. Purpose of the Crisis Management Team (CMT)

   1. The CMT identifies the crisis threats the organization is facing.

   2. The CMT develops the crisis management plan.

   3. The CMT leads training in the area of crisis management.

   4. The CMT actively manages the crisis when one occurs.

   5. The CMT leads the postcrisis evaluation so that learning can occur.

D. Definition of a Crisis

   A crisis is an event that has a low probability of occurring, but should it occur, can have a vastly negative impact on our organization. The causes of the crisis, as well as the means to resolve it, may not be readily clear; nonetheless, its resolution should be approached as quickly as possible. Finally, the crisis impact may not be initially obvious to all of the relevant stakeholders of our organization.

E. Activating the Crisis Management Team (CMT)

   1. In the event of an emergency or crisis, any member of the CMT can activate the team by notifying one or more of its members.

   2. Upon activation, the remaining team members will be notified of the crisis in the most expedient manner possible.

3. The CMT will meet at the primary command center. If this location is not operational, the secondary location will be utilized.

4. The CMT will meet to discuss strategies for managing the specific crisis at hand. Other meetings will be called as necessary until the crisis is resolved.

F. Command Center Location

1. Primary command center location
   This is where the CMT meets when the primary command center is available. Sometimes, in a crisis, this location is unavailable due to building damage, perhaps from a fire or weather event. When that is the case, a secondary command center location should be used.

2. Secondary command center location
   Keep in mind that this location should not be in the same building as the primary location.

G. Members of the CMT

List the members of the CMT and their contact information. Be sure to include each member's office, home, and cell phone numbers, as well as their e-mail address.

H. Responsibilities of the CMT

1. The members of the CMT are usually selected from the major departmental areas of the organization. During a crisis, it is expected that each member can offer advice and input from his or her departmental area. An alternate for each member should be chosen as well, in the event the main CMT member is not available.

2. In addition, there will need to be a predesignated leader of the CMT, as well as an alternate.

3. There will also need to be a predesignated spokesperson for the organization, as well as an alternate.

4. The remaining responsibilities will vary, depending on the type of organization.

J. Responses to Specific Types of Crises

1. Many crisis management plans have brief outlines for how the organization will respond to a specific type of crisis. For example, school districts will have plans for how students should evacuate a classroom building in the event of a fire. They will also have a specific procedure for how to conduct a "lockdown," an event where students are kept inside a classroom for security reasons.

2. The specific types of crises listed will be organization specific. For example, the following crises might be included in a plan for a college or university:

   Bomb threat

   Building mold

   Death of student or faculty member while on campus

   Earthquake

Flood

Hazardous materials spill

Incident of violence on campus

Inclement weather involving quick notification of the campus community

Lockdown of a building

Loss of an academic building due to fire, weather, or some other event

Loss of electrical power

Residence hall fire

Student protest (peaceful)

Student protest (nonpeaceful)

Widespread outbreak of flu or other illness

K. Appendix

1. Contact information for key stakeholders:

   Even though information technology (IT) systems house this information, it is advisable to have hard copies in the event the IT system should go offline.

   a. Client/Customer contact list
   b. Supply contact list
   c. Emergency provider contact list
   d. Employee contact list
   e. Media contact list
   f. Other lists as deemed necessary by the organization

2. Forms: Many organizations will include a set of forms that can be used in the crisis management process. The types of forms will vary according to the organization. Some potential forms that might be used for a college or university are as follows:

   a. Incident report: used to document important data about the crisis.
   b. Media response form: used to document which media outlets have been contacted and what was communicated to each outlet.
   c. List of hazardous chemicals: this list is necessary since the science labs typically house a variety of dangerous chemicals.
   d. Debriefing form: used during the debriefing meetings. These forms offer a useful way of identifying key items that can be learned from the crisis.
   e. Telephone bomb threat checklist: these have been in existence for a number of years. The checklist seeks to identify various clues that might have been transmitted over the phone while the bomb threat was being communicated.

Note

1. The plan should be available both in hardcopy form and on the organization's Web site. This outline reflects what would typically be included in a crisis plan for a college or university.

Index